Blockchain Enabled Applications

Understand the Blockchain Ecosystem and How to Make it Work for You

Second Edition

Vikram Dhillon
David Metcalf
Max Hooper

Apress®

Blockchain Enabled Applications: Understand the Blockchain Ecosystem and How to Make it Work for You

Vikram Dhillon
Orlando, FL, USA

David Metcalf
Orlando, FL, USA

Max Hooper
Orlando, FL, USA

ISBN-13 (pbk): 978-1-4842-6533-8
https://doi.org/10.1007/978-1-4842-6534-5

ISBN-13 (electronic): 978-1-4842-6534-5

Managing Director, Apress Media LLC: Welmoed Spahr
Acquisitions Editor: Spandana Chatterjee
Development Editor: Laura Berendson
Coordinating Editor: Shrikant Vishwakarma

Cover designed by eStudioCalamar

Cover image designed by Pexels

Distributed to the book trade worldwide by Springer Science+Business Media LLC, 1 New York Plaza, Suite 4600, New York, NY 10004. Phone 1-800-SPRINGER, fax (201) 348-4505, email orders-ny@springer-sbm.com, or visit www.springeronline.com. Apress Media, LLC is a California LLC and the sole member (owner) is Springer Science+Business Media Finance Inc (SSBM Finance Inc). SSBM Finance Inc is a **Delaware** corporation.

For information on translations, please e-mail booktranslations@springernature.com; for reprint, paperback, or audio rights, please e-mail bookpermissions@springernature.com.

Apress titles may be purchased in bulk for academic, corporate, or promotional use. eBook versions and licenses are also available for most titles. For more information, reference our Print and eBook Bulk Sales web page at http://www.apress.com/bulk-sales.

Any source code or other supplementary material referenced by the author in this book is available to readers on GitHub via the book's product page, located at www.apress.com/978-1-4842-6533-8. For more detailed information, please visit http://www.apress.com/source-code.

Printed on acid-free paper

Vikram Dhillon would like to dedicate this work to Aaron Hillel Swartz and his legacy.

David Metcalf would like to thank Katy, Adam, and Andrew for their patience during the extended hours and effort required while putting the book together, and the colleagues and students at UCF and through the NSF I-Corps program who identified the power of Bitcoin and blockchain technology years ago and shared their knowledge and future strategies that inspired us early on to pursue this area of research. Thank you to my co-authors and our outside collaborators and contributors, and of course to God for the wisdom, ability, and grit needed to bring this effort to life.

Max Hooper would like to thank his co-authors and colleagues at UCF/METIL Lab, along with special thanks to Mindy Hooper for her help and support. Additionally, he thanks God for his inspiration, guidance, direction, and wisdom. He would like to acknowledge His leadership.

Table of Contents

TABLE OF CONTENTS

About the Authors

Vikram Dhillon is an internal medicine resident physician at Wayne State University, Detroit Medical Center, as well as a research fellow at the Institute of Simulation and Training, University of Central Florida (UCF). A graduate of the University of Central Florida, he holds a Bachelor of Science degree in molecular biology with a focus in bioinformatics, as well as a Doctor of Osteopathic Medicine doctoral degree from Nova Southeastern University. He has authored four textbooks on blockchain design and published several scientific papers in the fields of computational genomics and public health. In the past, he worked as a software and business development coach at the Blackstone Launchpad to mentor young entrepreneurs and startups through the process of building technology products. He was previously funded by the National Science Foundation through the Innovation Corps program to study customer discovery and apply it to commercializing high-risk startup ideas. Currently a member of the Linux Foundation, he has been involved in open-source projects and initiatives for the past several years. He often speaks at local conferences on the topics of blockchain design, security, and entrepreneurship. He can be reached on Twitter @opsbug.

David Metcalf is a serial entrepreneur who has launched multiple successful ventures and spinoff companies. He has reviewed thousands of emerging technology companies as an advisor and investor. He is the director of the Mixed Emerging Technology Integration Lab at UCF's Institute for Simulation and Training. His past projects involving XR and IoT span across education, health, space, cyber, and transportation. Current efforts include smart cities, blockchain, and enterprise learning transformation for government and industry. He is the co-editor/author of

Voice Technology in Healthcare (2020) and *Blockchain in Healthcare* (2019) as part of the HIMSS Emerging Technology Series, *Blockchain Enabled Applications* (2018), *Connected Health* (2017), *HIMSS mHealth Innovation* (2014), and the HIMSS best-seller *mHealth: From Smartphones to Smart Systems* (2012).

Max Hooper is the chief executive officer of Merging Traffic. He is responsible for the company's management and growth strategy, serving as the corporate liaison to the financial services industry and various capital formation groups. Prior to starting the company, he was co-founder of Equity Broadcasting Corporation (EBC), a media company that owned and operated more than 100 television stations across the United States. He was responsible for activities in the cable, satellite, investment banking, and technology industries, and during his tenure, EBC grew to become one of the top ten largest broadcasting companies in the country. He is a lifelong learner and has earned five doctorate degrees—PhD, DMin, PhD, ThD, and DMin—from a variety of institutions. Hooper studied financial technology with cohorts at MIT, and cryptocurrency and business disruption with cohorts at the London School of Economics. As an avid runner, he has completed more than 100 marathons and an additional twenty ultra-marathons, which are 50- or 100-mile runs. He has completed the Grand Slam of Ultra Running. He is committed to his family and is a husband, father to five children, and grandfather to seven grandsons. He is active in many organizations and serves on various boards of directors. He works globally with several ministries and nonprofit aid groups and was honored to speak at the United Nations in New York in 2015.

About the Technical Reviewer

 **Prasanth Sahoo** is a thought leader, an adjunct professor, a technical speaker, and a full-time practitioner in blockchain, cloud, and scrum working for Tata Consultancy Services. He has worked on various cloud platforms, including Azure and Google Cloud, and also led cross-functional teams to achieve goals using agile methodologies. He is passionate about driving digital technology initiatives by handling various community initiatives through coaching, mentoring, and grooming techniques.

He is a Certified Blockchain Expert and Certified Admin from Microsoft and is a working group member in the Blockchain Council, CryptoCurrency Certification Consortium, Scrum Alliance, Scrum Organization, and International Institute of Business Analysis. He has also received accolades for his presentation at the China International Industry Big Data Expo 2018, run by the Chinese government.

Acknowledgments

The authors would like to acknowledge our editors, Shrikant Vishwakarma and Spandana Chatterjee, for their help and guidance throughout the writing process.

The figures throughout this book were made with the help of Lucidchart. All figures from external sources were used with permission.

In addition, we wish to acknowledge the authorship and stellar contributions from the following authors toward this book:

Chapter 6: Colin Forward

Chapter 13: John Bass

Chapter 15: Katherine Kuzmeskas

Chapter 16: Heather Flannery, Jonathon Passerat-Palmbah, and Sean T. Manion

Chapter 17: Tory Ceraj

Without their resilience and tireless hard work, our book would be less complete.

Introduction

Blockchain technology is poised to fundamentally change our online world. Bitcoin was the first implementation of the blockchain; however, it has ushered in a fundamental shift for the offline world by allowing the transfer of value across the World Wide Web without the need for a centralized authority. Digitization and democratization of trust via the blockchain is enabling a new class of applications and companies to grow. Marc Andreessen famously authored a piece in the *Wall Street Journal* describing the theme of "software eating the world," where numerous industries are undergoing a rapid transformation after being consumed by software. To that end, we hope that our book provides an outlook to the world as blockchain actively transforms enterprises and creates entirely new verticals.

The fundamental shift that blockchain technology represents is a method for moving away from having a central trusted authority in a massively distributed network. Instead, it allows for having multiple sources of trust that must all agree, based on an algorithm, that this transaction can be trusted as valid. Furthermore, most blockchain solutions offer an immutable and enduring record of a transaction that is hard for any source, trusted or not, to change or modify. This presents a completely new level of security, privacy, and trust to our online world. As you will see throughout this book, a variety of uses, protocols, and standards make up the current blockchain ecosystem.

We also strive to strike the perfect balance between being a technical reference and a how-to handbook that shows practical examples of both current- and future-state use cases. While not comprehensive, we do select several high-promise areas where blockchain technology is beginning to enable applications for entirely new industry segments. We hope this book will inform you and provide a roadmap to your success in leveraging blockchain technology to enable new applications for your business.

Throughout the book, you will see many examples of applications to reinforce key points. Early examples extend beyond financial transactions to cover other aspects of FinTech, RegTech (regulation), InsuranceTech, GovTech (eVoting, licensing, records, and certification), HealthTech, and many others.

In order to understand these early examples, it is necessary to explore blockchain's history; fundamentals of distributed trust; consensus; hardware; software; and encryption in the early chapters. Next, you'll learn about the network transactions and simplified payments in blockchain fundamentals. We'll compare this with the extended capabilities of Ethereum and specific characteristics like how gas works and DApps, along with examples of Blockchain-as-a-Service. To further extend these capabilities, two chapters are devoted to DAO/Decentralized Organizations and the details and examples in these areas. In Chapter 7, Ethereum tokens are highlighted for value creation, with various technology and business-sector examples that highlight the power of smart contracts to allow multiple sources of value and rules to be directly embedded in the transactions. The next three chapters—8, 9, and 10—provide updates on blockchain in science and blockchain in healthcare, and details on the structure of the Hyperledger Project, respectively. Chapter 11 focuses on many recent developments, such as the EOS blockchain, Enterprise Ethereum Alliance, Quorum, R3, and Corda. Chapter 12 focuses particularly on ICOs and their effect on financial markets and processes. The next chapter is a conversation between the authors and John Bass from Hashed Health on building a healthcare consortium. Chapter 14 highlights the new cloud-blockchain computing landscape with an emphasis on Blockchain-as-a-Service. The following four chapters—15, 16, 17, and 18—are interviews with prominent figures from the blockchain world discussing the transforming roles of blockchain in education, artificial intelligence, machine learning, and quantum simulations.

Presently, during the COVID-19 pandemic, blockchain-based applications are being repurposed to help with contract tracing, developing "health passports" for the general public, and tracking physician burnout. In the near future, supply-chain applications built on the blockchain could assist in maintaining personal protective equipment (PPE) inventory and even therapeutics such as vaccines. We hope you find the information in this book useful as well as enjoyable as you explore the fundamentals, current best practices, and future potential of blockchain-enabled applications. We welcome your feedback at info@metil.org.

CHAPTER 1

Behold the Dreamers

Anxiety is perhaps the best way to describe the attitude that dominated the minds of investors and the general public concerning the financial markets toward the end of 2008. The 2008 financial crisis is considered by numerous economists to have been the worst financial crisis since the Great Depression. The years leading up to the crisis saw a flood of irresponsible mortgage lending and a massive systemic failure of financial regulation and supervision. The fallout was so immense that it threatened the collapse of large financial institutions, and national governments had to intercede to bail out the major banks. In this chapter, we will begin our discussion with an overview of the 2008 financial crisis and its aftermath: an environment where a new banking system and an alternative currency such as Bitcoin could thrive. Then, we will dive into the technology stack that powers Bitcoin. Remarkably, the components of this stack are not completely new, but have been integrated in a very intricate design to build a new system. Finally, we will end the discussion by talking about the heightened interest in blockchain, a major technical breakthrough that has the potential to revolutionize several industries. Imbolo Mbue wrote a book (Random House, 2017), which has the same name as this chapter, and tells the story of "dreamers" in New York City going through the financial crisis, and how their lives had changed as a result. This book chronicles the dreamers who envisioned building a more resilient financial system.

© Vikram Dhillon, David Metcalf, and Max Hooper 2021
V. Dhillon et al., *Blockchain Enabled Applications*, https://doi.org/10.1007/978-1-4842-6534-5_1

Paradigm Shift

Revolutions often look chaotic, but this one was brewing quietly, headed by an unknown individual(s) under the name Satoshi Nakamoto who dreamt of changing the financial world. Any number of parties can be blamed for the financial crisis; however, the common denominator was that fundamental financial and accounting instruments used to maintain the integrity of the entire system became too complex to be used efficiently. Trust, the ultimate adhesive of all financial systems, began to disappear in 2008. The regulations have since changed to not allow similar circumstances to arise; however, it was clear that there was a dire need for auto-regulation of trust between counterparties and transparency into their ability to enter into any type of sales contract. A **counterparty** is essentially the other party in a financial transaction. In other words, it's the buyer matched to a seller. In financial transactions, one of the many risks involved is called **counterparty risk**—the risk that the *other* party involved in a contract may not be able to fulfill its side of the agreement. The systemic failure referenced earlier can now be understood in terms of counterparty risk: both parties in the transaction were accumulating massive counterparty risk, and in the end, both parties collapsed under the terms of the contract. Imagine a similar transaction scenario involving multiple parties, and now imagine that every single player in this scenario is a major financial institution, a bank or an insurance company that further holds millions of customers. This is what happened during the 2008 crisis.

The next issue we need to discuss is that of **double spending**. We will revisit this topic again strictly in the context of Bitcoin, but let's get a basic understanding of the concept by applying it to the financial crisis. The principle behind double spending is that resources committed to one transaction cannot be simultaneously allocated to a second disparate transaction. This concept has obvious implications for digital currencies; however, it can also summarize the central set of problems during the 2008 crisis.

Here's how it started: Loans (in the form of mortgages) were given out to borrowers with poor credit histories, who struggled to repay them. These high-risk mortgages were sold to financial experts at the big banks, who packaged them into low-risk public stocks by putting large numbers of them together in pools. This type of pooling would work when the risks associated with each loan (mortgage) are not correlated. The experts at big banks hypothesized that property values in different cities across the country would change independently, and therefore pooling was not risky. This proved to be a massive mistake. The pooled mortgage packages were then used to purchase a type of stock called collateralized debt obligations (CDOs). The CDOs were divided into tiers and sold to investors. The tiers were ranked and rated by financial standards agencies, and investors bought the safest tiers based on those ratings. Once the housing market in the United States turned, it set off a domino effect, destroying everything in the way. The CDOs turned out to be worthless, despite the ratings. The pooled mortgages collapsed in value, and all the packages being sold around instantly vaporized. Throughout this complex string of transactions, every sale increased the risk and incurred double spending at multiple levels. Eventually, the system equilibrated, only to find massive gaps, and collapsed under the weight. Following is a brief history of 2008. This timeline was made following a presentation by Micah Winkelspech at Distributed Health, 2016:

- January 11: Bank of America buys the struggling Countrywide

- March 16: Fed forces the sale of Bear Stearns

- September 15: Lehman Brothers files for Chapter 11 bankruptcy

- September 16: Fed bails out American International Group (AIG) for $85B

- September 25: Washington Mutual fails

- September 29: Financial markets crash, Dow Jones Industrial Average falls 777.68 points, and the whole system on the brink of collapse

- October 3: US government authorizes $700B for bank bailouts

The bailout had massive economic consequences, but more important, it created the type of environment that would allow Bitcoin to flourish. In November 2008, a whitepaper (https://bitcoin.org/bitcoin.pdf) was posted on the Cryptography and Cryptography Policy Mailing List titled "Bitcoin: A Peer-to-Peer Electronic Cash System," with a single author named Satoshi Nakamoto. This whitepaper detailed the Bitcoin protocol, and along with it came the original code for early versions of Bitcoin. In some manner, this whitepaper was a response to the economic crash that had just happened, but it would be some time before this technological revolution caught on. Some developers were concerned with this electronic cash system failing before it could ever take hold, and their concern was scalability, as we can see pointed out in Figure 1-1.

So, who is Nakamoto? And what is his background? The short and simple answer is that we don't know. In fact, it is presumptuous to assume that he is actually a "he." The name Satoshi Nakamoto was largely used as a pseudonym, and "he" could have been a "she" or even a large group. Several reporters and news outlets have dedicated time and energy in digital forensics to narrow down candidates and find out the real Satoshi, but all the efforts so far have been wild-goose chases (https://www.technologyreview.com/s/527051/the-man-who-really-built-bitcoin/). In this case, the community is starting to realize that maybe it doesn't matter who Satoshi is, as the nature of open source almost makes it irrelevant. Jeff Garzik, one of the most respected developers in the Bitcoin community, described it as follows, "Satoshi published an open-source system for the purpose that you didn't have to know who he was, and trust who he was, or care about his knowledge." The true spirit of open source makes it so that the code speaks for itself, without any intervention from the creator/developer.

Re: Bitcoin P2P e-cash paper

James A. Donald | Sun, 02 Nov 2008 17:55:45 -0800

```
Satoshi Nakamoto wrote:
  I've been working on a new electronic cash system that's fully
  peer-to-peer, with no trusted third party.

  The paper is available at:
  http://www.bitcoin.org/bitcoin.pdf

We very, very much need such a system, but the way I understand your proposal,
it does not seem to scale to the required size.

For transferable proof of work tokens to have value, they must have monetary
value. To have monetary value, they must be transferred within a very large
network - for example a file trading network akin to bittorrent.
```

Figure 1-1. *Initial reception of the Bitcoin protocol. Concerns about scalibility and realistic prospects of Bitcoin*

Technology Stack

Satoshi's real genius in creating the Bitcoin protocol was solving the Byzantine Generals Problem. The solution was generalized to financial transactions with components and ideas borrowed from the cyberpunk community. We will briefly talk about three of those ideas, how the components work, and how they help the Bitcoin protocol: Hashcash for proof-of-work, Byzantine fault tolerance for the decentralized network, and the blockchain for removing the need for centralized trust or a central authority. Let's dive into each one, starting with Hashcash.

Hashcash was devised by Adam Black in the late nineties to limit email spam with the first of its kind proof-of-work (PoW) algorithm. The rationale behind Hashcash was to attach some computational cost to sending emails. Spammers have a business model that relies on sending large numbers of emails with very little cost associated with each message. However, if there is even a small cost for each spam email sent, that cost multiplies over thousands of emails, and their business becomes unprofitable. Hashcash relies on the idea of cryptographic hash functions—a type of hash function (in the case of Bitcoin, it's SHA1) that takes an input and converts it into a string and generates a message digest, as shown in Figure 1-2. The hash functions are designed to have a property called one-way functions, which implies that a potential input can be verified very easily through the hash function to match the digest, but reproducing the input from the digest is infeasible. The only possible method of recreating the input is by using brute force to find the appropriate string of input. In practice, this is the computationally intensive element of Hashcash and has been imported into Bitcoin. This principle has become the foundation behind the proof-of-work (PoW) algorithms powering Bitcoin today, and most cryptocurrencies. The PoW for Bitcoin is more complex and involves new components that we will talk about at length in a later chapter.

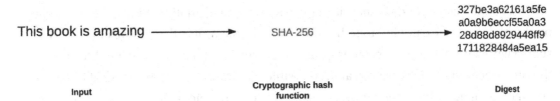

Figure 1-2. *Mechanism of a cryptographic hash function. It takes an input and consistently converts it to a string of an output digest*

The next idea we need to discuss is the Byzantine Generals Problem. It is an agreement problem between a group of generals, with each one commanding a portion of the Byzantine army, ready to attack a city. These generals need to formulate a strategy for attacking the city and communicate it to each other adequately. The important task is that every general must work toward the same action, as a tepid attack by a few generals would be worse than a coordinated attack or a coordinated retreat. The crux of the problem is that some of the generals are traitorous. They may cast a vote to deceive the other generals and ultimately lead to a suboptimal strategy. Let's take a look at an example: In a case of odd-numbered generals, say seven, three support attacking and three support retreat. The seventh general might communicate an agreement to the generals in favor of retreat, and an agreement to attack to the other generals, causing the whole arrangement to fall apart. The attacking forces would fail to capture the city because no intrinsic central authority could verify the presence of trust among all seven generals.

In this scenario, Byzantine fault tolerance can be achieved if all the loyal generals can communicate effectively to have an indisputable agreement on their strategy. If so, the misleading (faulty) vote by the traitorous general would be revealed and would fail to perturb the system as a whole. In the Bitcoin protocol, Satoshi's key innovation in enabling Byzantine fault tolerance was to create a peer-to-peer network with a ledger that could record and verify a majority approval, thereby revealing any false (traitorous) transactions. This ledger provides a consistent means of communication and further allows for the removal of trust from the whole system. The ledger is also known as the blockchain. With blockchain attached, Bitcoin became the first digital currency to solve the double-spending problem network-wide. In the remainder of this chapter, we will present a broad overview of the technology, and of the concept of a blockchain-enabled application.

A blockchain is primarily a recording ledger that provides all involved parties with a secure and synchronized record of transactions from start to end. A blockchain can record hundreds of transactions very rapidly, and has several cryptographic measures intrinsic to its design for data security, consistency, and validation. Similar transactions on the blockchain are pooled together into a functional unit called a **block** and then sealed with a timestamp (a cryptographic fingerprint) that links the current block to the one preceding it. This creates an irreversible and tamper-evident string of blocks connected together by timestamps, conveniently called a blockchain. The architecture of blockchain is such that every transaction is very rapidly verified by all members of the network. Members also contain an up-to-date copy of the blockchain locally, which allows for consensus to be reached within the decentralized network. Features such as immutable record-keeping and network-wide consensus can be integrated into a stack to develop new types of applications called decentralized apps (DApps). Let's look at a prototype of a DApp in Figure 1-3, in the context of the Model-View-Controller (MVC) framework. The Model-View-Controller framework is a software design concept that separates an application into three components: The model (that contains the data-related logic), the view (UI component that customers often interface with), and the controller (an interface that interacts between the model and the view). This framework is frequently used to design traditional web applications that are extensible and scalable. Here, we want to extend an industry standard and use it to explain a DApp.

Note   The first block of the blockchain is called the Genesis block. This block is unique in that it does not link to any blocks preceding it. Satoshi added a bit of historical information to this block as context for the current financial environment in the United Kingdom, "*The Times 03/Jan/2009 Chancellor on brink of second bailout for banks.*" This block not only proves that no Bitcoins existed before January 3, 2009, but also gives a little insight into the mind of the creators.

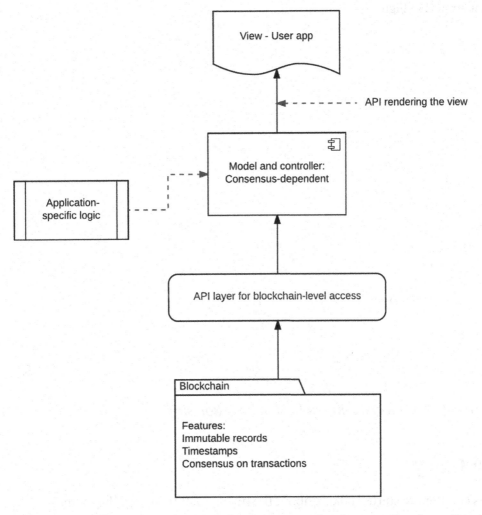

Figure 1-3. *This figure presents a simple prototype of a decentralized application that interacts with the end user at the final steps*

The model and controller here rely on the blockchain for data (data integrity and security) and accordingly update the view for the end user. The secret sauce in this prototype is the API, which works to pull information from the blockchain and provides it to the model and controller. This API provides opportunities to extend business logic and add it to the blockchain, along with basic operations that take blocks as input and provide answers to binary questions. The blockchain may eventually have more features such as oracles that can verify external data and timestamp it on the blockchain itself. To better understand the concept of blockchain-enabled applications, we have to appreciate the full stack of services that could power an end-user application; this is demonstrated in Figure 1-4.

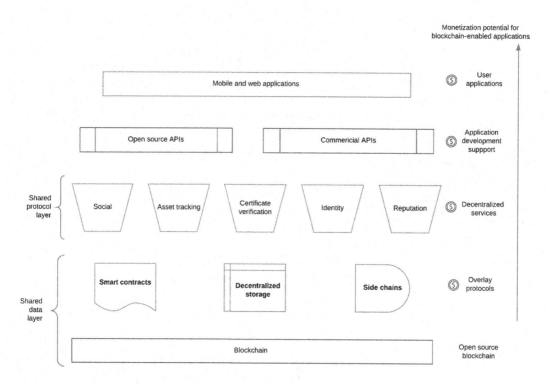

Figure 1-4. *The blockchain-enabled application stack*

Summary

In this chapter, we started talking about the history of Bitcoin and the financial environment around the time it came to exist. We will continue our discussion of blockchain and specific features of the peer-to-peer network, such as miners and more, in the upcoming chapters.

CHAPTER 2

The Gold Rush: Mining Bitcoin

Mining is a key operational concept in understanding how the Bitcoin protocol functions. It refers to a decentralized review process performed on every block of the blockchain to reach consensus, without the need for a central authority to provide trust. In other words, mining is the computational equivalent of peer review in a decentralized environment where neither party involved trusts the other. We will continue our discussion of the hash function here in more depth, as it refers to mining and solving proof-of-work functions. Then, we will integrate the concepts of block target values and network difficulty with mining and how mining has evolved to keep up with the increasing network difficulty. This will lead us further into talking about the different types of hardware mining that have been developed recently. We will end the chapter with an analysis of startups that began selling dedicated hardware for mining, leading to the Bitcoin mining arms race and the startups' eventual failure.

Reaching Consensus

Mining is central to the Bitcoin protocol and has two primary motivations: add new Bitcoins to the overall economy and verify transactions. In this chapter, we will look at the mechanisms behind these two processes. Essentially, mining is the appropriate solution to the double-spending problem that we discussed previously. To remove the need for a central authority, individuals running the Bitcoin client on their own machines (called miners) participate in the network and verify that transactions taking place between two parties are not fraudulent. Mining is actually a computationally intensive activity, but what incentive does anyone have to help mine for new Bitcoins? The key incentive for miners is getting a reward in the form of Bitcoins for their participation. Let's look at a simplified view of the mining process in Figure 2-1.

© Vikram Dhillon, David Metcalf, and Max Hooper 2021
V. Dhillon et al., *Blockchain Enabled Applications*, https://doi.org/10.1007/978-1-4842-6534-5_2

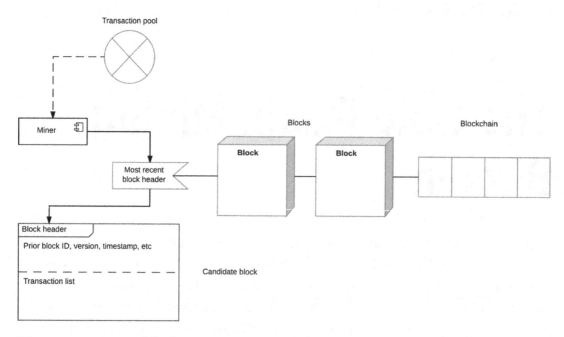

Figure 2-1. *A simplified overview of the mining process*

Unpackaged transactions that have occurred recently on the Bitcoin network remain in the transaction pool (also known as the mempool, where all valid transactions wait to be confirmed by the Bitcoin network) until they are picked up by a miner to be packaged into a block. A miner selects transactions from the transaction pool and packages them in a block. After the block has been created, it needs a header before it can be accepted by the blockchain. Think of *this* as shipping a package: once the package has been created, it needs to be stamped so that it can be shipped. A miner uses the header of the most recent block in the blockchain to construct a new header for *this* current block. The block header also contains other elements such as a timestamp, version of the Bitcoin client, and an ID corresponding to the previous block in the chain. The resulting block is called a candidate block, and it can now be added to the blockchain if a few other conditions are satisfied.

The process of mining is very involved, and Figure 2-1 only served to paint a broad picture regarding the participation of miners in the protocol. Next, we will explore the technical aspects of the stamp (in the analogy just referenced) and the mechanism of stamping a package. Keep in mind that mining is a competitive process. Figure 2-1 only describes this process for one miner, but in reality, a very large number of miners from the network participate simultaneously. The miners compete with each other to find a stamp for the package (block) that they created, and the first miner to discover the stamp wins. The race between miners to find a stamp is concluded within ten minutes, and a new race begins in the next ten minutes. Once the stamp is discovered, the miner can complete the block and announce it to the network. Now the block can be added to the blockchain. Let's take a look at the process behind searching for the stamp, better known as a block header, in Figure 2-2.

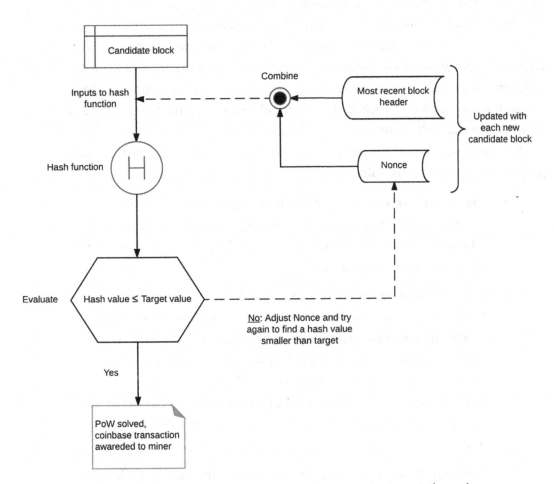

Figure 2-2. *Generating a block header by solving proof-of-work (PoW)*

The package created by a miner is almost a block, but it is missing a header. It's called a candidate block and can only be added to the blockchain after the stamp, or the header, is added. The header from the most recent block in the blockchain is retrieved and combined with a 32-bit value called nonce. This combination is directed to the hash function (SHA-256) as an input. The hash function computes a new resulting hash as an output. This generated hash is then compared to the target value of the network (at the given time).

If the hash value is larger than the target value, then the nonce is readjusted and a new input is sent to the hash function to obtain a new potential output. The problem of finding the appropriate hash value that is smaller than the target value is at the heart of PoW, and it can only be solved using brute force. Once a hash value smaller than the target value is discovered by a miner, this hash can now be used in the block header for the candidate block. The first miner to discover the hash is considered the winner. The winning miner has shown proof of work that she did to discover the hash; therefore, the transactions contained within the block are now considered valid. This block can now be added to the blockchain. Additionally, the winning miner also wins a reward for solving the PoW problem, which is a certain number of Bitcoins. This whole process from packaging transactions into a block, to finding the hash and announcing the block to the Bitcoin network, repeats itself approximately every ten minutes.

We introduced some new terminology in Figure 2-2; let's describe them here properly for the sake of completion:

- **Candidate block:** An incomplete block, created as a temporary construct by a miner to store transactions from the transaction pool. It becomes a complete block after the header is completed by solving the proof-of-work problem.

- **PoW:** The problem of discovering a new hash that can be used in the block header of the candidate block. A computationally intensive process that involves evaluating a hash taken from the most recent block and appending a nonce to it against the target value of the network. This problem can only be solved using brute force; i.e., multiple trials of using the hash (from most recent block header) and nonce's being adjusted each time are necessary to solve the PoW problem.

- **Nonce:** A 32-bit value that is concatenated to the hash from the most recent block header. This value is continuously updated and adjusted for each trial, till a new hash below target value is discovered.

- **Hash function:** A function used to compute a hash. In the Bitcoin protocol, this function is the SHA-256.

- **Hash value:** The resulting hash output from a hash function.

- **Target value:** A 256-bit number that all Bitcoin clients share. It is determined by the difficulty, which will be discussed shortly.

- **Coinbase transaction:** The first transaction that is packaged into a block. This is a reward for the miner to mine the PoW solution for the candidate block.

- **Block header:** The header of a block, which contains many features such as a timestamp, PoW, and more. We will describe the block header in more detail in the following chapter.

Note   After going over the terms defined, revisit Figures 2-1 and 2-2. Some concepts that were abstracted out will become clear now, and the information will integrate better.

Now that we have a better idea of how mining works, let's take a look at mining difficulty and target values. These two concepts are similar to knobs that are adjusted over the course of time for the network, and all Bitcoin clients get updated to follow the latest values. So, what is mining difficulty? Essentially, it can be defined as the difficulty of finding a hash below the target value as a miner is solving the proof-of-work problem. An increase in difficulty corresponds to a longer time needed to discover the hash and solve the PoW, also known as mining time. The ideal mining time is set by the network to be approximately ten minutes, which implies that a new block is announced on the network every ten minutes. The mining time is dependent on three factors: the target value, number of miners in the network, and mining difficulty. Let's look at how these factors are interconnected:

1. An increase in mining difficulty causes a decrease in the target value to compensate for the mining time

2. An increase in the number of miners joining the network causes an increase in the rate at which PoW is solved, decreasing the mining time. To adjust for this, mining difficulty increases and the block-creation rate returns to normal.

3. The target value is recalculated and adjusted every 2016 blocks created, which happens in approximately two weeks.

As we can see, there is a common theme of self-correction in the Bitcoin network that allows it to be very resilient. Miners are the heartbeat of the Bitcoin network, and they have two main incentives for participation:

- The first transaction to be packaged in a block is called the coinbase transaction. This transaction is the reward that the winning miner receives after mining the block and announcing it on the network.

- The second reward comes in the form a fee charged to the users of the network for sending transactions. The fee is given to the miners for including the transactions in a block. This fee can also be considered a miner's income because as more and more Bitcoins are mined, this fee will become a significant portion of their income.

Now we can put these concepts together in the form of another flowchart in Figure 2-3. This will help solidify the process of mining in the context of difficulty and target values.

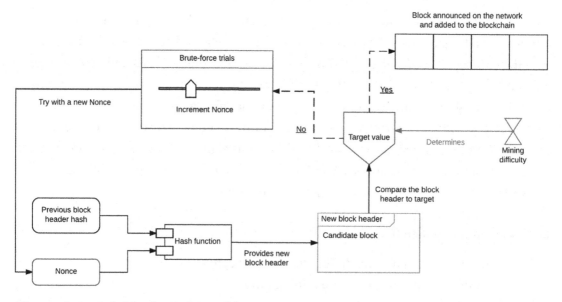

Figure 2-3. *Solving the PoW problem*

Miners across the network compete to solve the problem, and the winning miner announces the block to the network, which then gets incorporated in the blockchain. To solve the PoW, a miner has to keep generating new hash values (through the hash function) using the incremented nonce until a hash below the target value is discovered. In this case, notice that the nonce is the only adjustable value. This is a simplified PoW scheme, and there are small differences in its implementation versus reality.

Note   The term *mining* came about because the process is similar to the mining of rare metals. It is very resource intensive and makes new currency available at a slow rate, just like the miners in the Bitcoin protocol getting rewarded.

We talked about the self-correction properties of the Bitcoin network and how they allow the network to adapt. Next, we will take a look at an unexpected consequence of getting a very large number of miners in the network as Bitcoin gained popularity. This led to an arms race of sorts, and it had far-reaching consequences. But first we need to talk about the new types of mining hardware that emerged.

Mining Hardware

As Bitcoin started to gain more popularity and acceptance with merchants, more miners joined the network in hopes of getting the rewards. Miners began to get more creative with how they approached mining, such as using specialized hardware that can generate more hashes. In this section, we will discuss the evolution of mining hardware as Bitcoin started to spread globally.

- **CPU mining:** The earliest form of mining available through the Bitcoin clients. It became the norm for mining in the early versions of the Bitcoin client but was removed in the later updates due to better options' being accessible.

- **GPU mining:** The next wave of mining advancements. It turns out that mining with a GPU is far more powerful because it can generate hundreds of times more hashes than a CPU. This is now the standard for mining in most cryptocurrencies.

- **FPGAs and ASICs:** FPGA stands for Field-Programmable Gated Array and is an integrated circuit designed for a specific use case. In this case, the FPGAs were designed for mining Bitcoins. The FPGAs are written with very specific hardware language that allows them to perform one task very efficiently in terms of power usage and output efficiency. Shortly after the introduction of FPGAs, a more optimized, mass-producible, and commercial design came out in the form of ASICs (Application-Specific Integrated Circuits). The ASICs

15

have a lower per unit cost, so the units can be mass produced. The ASIC-based devices are also compact in form, therefore more can be integrated in a single device. The ability of ASICs to be combined in arrays at a low price point made a very convincing case for accelerating the rate of mining.

- **Mining pools:** As the mining difficulty went up due to the rise of ASICs, miners realized that individually, it was not financially wise to continue mining. It was just taking too long, and the reward did not match the resources that went into mining. So the miners organized themselves into groups called pools to combine the computational resources of all the members and mine as one unit. Today, joining a pool is very common to get started with mining in almost every crpytocurrency.

- **Mining cloud services:** These are simply contractors who have specialized mining rigs. They rent their services to a miner according to a contract for a given price to mine for a specific time.

It is easy to see how ASICs completely changed the mining game after developers and hardware hobbyists realized that custom arrays of ASICs could be made at a fairly cheap price point. It was the beginning of a kind of arms race in Bitcoin hardware, and developers began designing new chips and buying new equpiment for mining rigs that could allow them to mine the most Bitcoin. This initial push driven by profit accelerated Bitcoin's reach and created a golden era for the alternative currency. More developers and enthusiasts joined in on buying custom hardware to maximize their profits. The network responded by increasing the difficulty as the number of miners increased. Within a short span of time, the bubble could not sustain itself for the miners because of the self-correcting features present in the protocol, and the difficulty kept rising. In some cases, the hardware that miners purchased could no longer mine profitably by the time it arrived from the factory. A significant investment of capital was required up-front to make any appreciable returns. Most of the ASIC hardware is now historic, and even Bitcoin mining pools are not profitable for the average miner. The startups and companies that commercialized ASICs and custom hardware made a decent profit for a short time and then flopped. We will examine a few of those massive failures in the next section.

Startup Stories

In this section, we will highlight a few stories from the "gold rush" era of Bitcoin, which lasted from mid-2013 to late 2014. The startups covered here followed the strategy of selling slightly outdated mining hardware to make profits, but some took it a step further. The first startup we will talk about is Butterfly Labs. This was a company out of Missouri that came about in late 2011 with the promise of selling technology that was capable of mining Bitcoin leaps and bounds ahead of the competition. The Application-Specific Integrated Circuits (ASICs) were supposedly able to mine Bitcoin one thousand times faster than a single computer, and they opened up for pre-orders soon after the initial announcement in 2012. Miners flocked to purchase the hardware, which was promised to be delivered by December of the same year. Butterfly Labs collected somewhere between $20 million and $30 million in pre-orders, as reported by the Federal Trade Commission (FTC). The shipments started to roll out to only a few customers around April of 2013, but most customers did not receive their mining equipment for another year. When the customers did receive their machines, they were obsolete, and some accused Butterfly Labs of using the hardware to mine for themselves before delivering them. Despite being unable to follow through with their initial orders, Butterfly Labs began offering a new and much more powerful miner and opened pre-orders for it. Ultimately, the company became one of the most hated in the Bitcoin community, and the FTC had to step in to shut it down.

The second company we will discuss is CoinTerra. This is a more complicated case because the startup was founded by a team that had deep expertise in the field. The CEO, Ravi Iyengar, had previously been a CPU architect at Samsung, and the company's board had many other leaders in the field. Initially, they were venture backed and well funded, and in 2013 they announced their first product: TerraMiner IV, which was supposed to be shipped in December of the same year. The company could not ship the product in time and eventually pushed the date back. The miner still didn't arrive in 2014, and eventually CoinTerra apologized to the customers, offering them some compensation, which was also largely delayed and frustrated the customers even further. It seems that the company is trying to pivot to cloud-mining services, but they've already lost most of the customer base's trust.

The last of our cases will focus on a startup called HashFast. Similar to the previous two examples, HashFast was offering a miner product called Baby Jet that would be delivered in December 2013. The team at HashFast overpromised the features and under-delivered in a time when the difficulty level skyrocketed. It is likely that the company took the cash from early adopters to fund its own development, and when they encountered difficulties, the customers demanded refunds for their orders. The problem at the time was that the price of Bitcoin was increasing steadily, so the company did not have enough funds to pay back the customers. They were facing multiple lawsuits and running out of cash reserves very fast. Eventually, In May 2014, a judge ruled to allow the auctioning of all assets that the company owned to pay back the creditors and investors.

A common theme across these companies is that they were frequently unable to deliver mining hardware at the promised time and significantly delayed or refused to issue any refunds to their customers. We can construct a general scheme of operations from the cases presented here and other ASIC startups that similarly failed:

- Open for pre-orders at very high prices and falsely advertise a ridiculously high hashing rate with huge return on investment.

- Invest all the funding from pre-orders to begin R&D for ASICs and custom hardware.

- Once the mining hardware has been obtained from overseas manufacturers, use it to mine non-stop for months internally.

- Broadcast to customers through social media that the manufacturing process is taking longer than expected.

- Deliver the hardware only to the customers that threaten to sue as early proof that shipments have begun rolling out.

- Deliver the ASIC hardware to other customers when it is already severely out of date.

- Customers complain and file lawsuits, the company eventually falls apart and faces huge fines.

New Consensus

We will conclude this chapter by talking about the same idea that we started this chapter with: consensus. This chapter's central idea was that in Bitcoin, mining is used to reach consensus to prevent users from double spending and validate all the transactions. However, since the advent of Bitcoin, other consensus algorithms have been developed. We will refer to the proof-of-work algorithm referenced in the original Bitcoin protocol for reaching consensus as Nakamoto Consensus. A new consensus algorithm that has recently become popular is known as proof-of-stake, where the participants essentially play the role of validators. In Bitcoin, bad actors with fraudulent transactions have to face the rigorous approval and validation process from the network of miners. In proof-of-stake (PoS), the participants have a stake in the network (hence the name) in the form of currency. As such, they want to see the network succeed, and trust emerges in blocks that have the largest stake of currency invested by the validators. Additionally, the malicious validators will get their stake slashed for acting in bad faith. We will dive into the technical aspects of PoS, and how it compares to the mechanism of PoW, later in the book. Our journey ends in this chapter with consensus, and we will pick up our discussion on the Bitcoin network and the blockchain in the next chapter.

Summary

In this chapter, we talked about the concept of mining and presented the technical background necessary to understand how miners verify blocks. We discussed in depth the backbone of mining in Bitcoin, called PoW, and throughout the remainder of the book, we will present other consensus mechanisms. Then, we described the arms race in Bitcoin mining over producing the best hardware, which led to the huge rise in difficulty, and the startup failures that resulted from that time period. Finally, we ended the chapter with a mention of PoS, which we will return to in a later chapter.

References

The key references used in preparing this chapter were Michael Nielsen's post (http://www.michaelnielsen.org/ddi/how-the-bitcoin-protocol-actually-works/) on Bitcoin mining, and Aleksandr Bulkin's post (https://keepingstock.net/explaining-blockchain-how-proof-of-work-enables-trustless-consensus-2abed27f0845). The remaining references can be found in Appendix A at the end of the book.

CHAPTER 3

Foundations of a Blockchain

A **blockchain** is a decentralized data structure with internal consistency maintained through consensus reached by all the users on the current state of the network. It is an enabling technology that resolved the Byzantine Generals Problem (described as a problem of establishing trust between three generals such that a coordinated strike can take down an enemy; more in Chapter 1) and opened a new horizon of possibilities for application development with trustless transactions and exchange of information. If the internet democratized the peer-to-peer exchange of information, then the blockchain has democratized the peer-to-peer exchange of value. We will begin this chapter by exploring how transactions work between users on the Bitcoin network. This will entail a technical discussion of the structures of a block and a transaction. Then, we will dive into the role of wallets and user addresses. After talking about wallets, we will shift our focus to Simple Payment Verification (SPV), which is implemented in the Bitcoin network. SPV will allow us to understand why blocks have a peculiar structure and, more important, how the Bitcoin network can retain efficiency despite the network's scaling at a high rate. Finally, we will end our discussion by talking about hard and soft forks in the Blockchain. We will present the implications of forks in the context of forward compatibility for merchants and users involved in running the Bitcoin core code. Even though there are numerous variations of blockchain during this "Cambrian explosion" phase of tech development, the core principles remain the same.

21

© Vikram Dhillon, David Metcalf, and Max Hooper 2021
V. Dhillon et al., *Blockchain Enabled Applications*, https://doi.org/10.1007/978-1-4842-6534-5_3

Transaction Workflow

The central purpose of the Bitcoin protocol is to allow transactions to occur over the network between users in a decentralized manner. Thus far, we have been talking about small fragments of the protocol to build up a background. Now, we can integrate those concepts into a single framework and explore the blockchain. The ultimate result of mining is an increase in the number of blocks as the network evolves over time. To understand how transactions occur between two users (Alice and Bob), we first need to understand the structure of the blocks that hold the transactions. In the simplest terms, the blockchain is a collection of blocks bound by two main principles:

- Internal consistency: There are a few design principles inherent to the functioning of each block that make the blockchain internally consistent. For instance, each block links to the previous one in the chain and has a timestamp of creation. Such mechanisms in the blockchain allow it to be an internally coherent data structure that can keep a stable record of transactions.

- Consensus of transactions: The concept of mining described in the previous chapter is just one implementation for verifying transactions; there are other mechanisms where no brute-force hashing is involved. However, in every one of these implementations, there is a scheme for reaching consensus on the transactions that have transpired during some x interval on the network. We can generalize this verification of transactions in a decentralized system by using either proof-of-work or another protocol that pools transactions that are then checked by participants of a network.

A transaction is essentially carried as a property of the block, a data structure propagated through the network, but how does this happen? To better understand the process, let's look at a more complete structure of a block, shown in Figure 3-1. Each block has at least two unique components: the block header containing a hash (called the Merkle root) that uniquely identifies a block, and the transaction list, which contains new transactions from the pool. Note that each block contains the same amount of transactions in the list, but the precise transactions between users are different. This is because only one block wins the mining race every ten minutes on the blockchain.

In our simplified model, there are only two other components of a block: the block size, which is kept consistent for the entire network, and a counter for the number of transactions in each block. Here, we will be focusing more on the block header and the transaction list.

The block header contains a few standard components, such as difficulty target and the nonce discussed previously. It also contains the version number of the Bitcoin core code that the winning miner is running. The timestamp is also a unique feature of every block; it unequivocally identifies one particular block in the network. The header also contains a hash from the previous block in the chain, and a special hash that identifies this block, called the Merkle root. We will discuss how this special hash is constructed later in this chapter.

Proof-of-life   Recently, there were rumors that Julian Assange, the WikiLeaks founder, had died. Assange recently did an Ask-Me-Anything session on Reddit and responded to the rumors by reading the most recent block hash from the blockchain to prove that he was indeed alive. The block had been created only ten minutes previously, so this could not have been a pre-recording, thus proving beyond any shadow of the doubt that Assange was alive. This was the first time the block hash had found a use in a sense of popular culture, and Assange called it a proof-of-life.

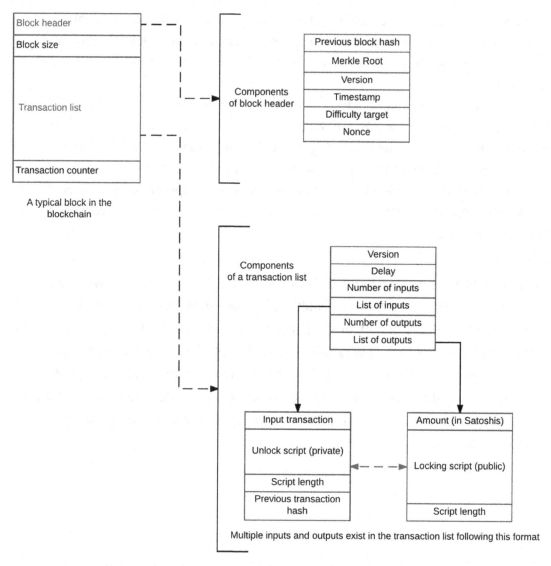

Figure 3-1. *Simplified overview of the structure of a block*

The text in red shows the two components that stay unique to every block. We break down these two components further as follows. The block header is made from several smaller parts, the most peculiar of which is the Merkle root, which is a hash that uniquely identifies a block. The header contains the hash of the previous block, the nonce used to create that particular block, and the difficulty of the network. These are standard mining components that we discussed previously. As mentioned earlier, each block also contains a list of transactions. Aside from the actual transactions, the transaction list also contains a few components that are crucial to how a block will accept the transaction. For instance, the lock time delay dictates when a transaction can be accepted into a block. Finally, the list contains all the transactions accepted into this block as a series of signed inputs and outputs that ensure the transfer of Bitcoins from the senders to the receivers.

Components of Transaction List

There are several new terms and concepts introduced here, and we will go through all of them now. We already talked about the block header and the concepts of the timestamp on a block, the Merkle root, and a hash from the previous block. Now we will focus on the components of the transaction list, and let's begin with the delay. The full technical term is lock time delay, which refers to the time after which a transaction can be accepted into a block. The precise mechanism involves the use of a parameter called *blockheight*, which increases as more blocks are added to the blockchain. A given transaction remains locked and unverified until the blockheight specified for that transaction is exceeded.

Next, we need to talk about the concept of transaction inputs and outputs. These two parameters guide the flow of transactions across the whole network and remain deeply integrated with the concept of spending power. As a currency, the fundamental unit of spending power on the Bitcoin blockchain is called an Unspent Transaction Output (UTXO), which has a value given in satoshis. One Bitcoin can be further broken down into one hundred million satoshis, analogous to a dollar's being broken down into 100 cents. The network records the entire Bitcoin economy as transactions that have been either spent or unspent. During a transactional event, all of the buyer's Bitcoins are applied toward purchasing an item, and this yields two outputs: a spent transaction that is locked for the buyer, and the remaining Bitcoins that are put into an unspent transaction. These unspent transactions are returned to the buyer and grant spending power toward future transactions. For an end user, keeping track of unspent transactions has been automated by the use of wallets. The idea of an account balance is created for a user by the wallet software that searches the blockchain and collects all the UTXO belonging to a particular address. Essentially, the Bitcoins belonging to a user result from UTXOs generated across several transaction events. We will discuss the concepts of wallets and addresses shortly.

To understand UTXO practically, we need to talk about the concept of change and change addresses. The idea is very simple actually—think about the last time you bought groceries and paid with cash. Your transaction had two components: you paid for what you purchased and that payment was designated to the merchant, and you received some change back that was left over from your payment. UTXOs are the change you receive back. This change goes to a Bitcoin address (called change address) that you own; refer to Figure 3-2 for a graphical depiction of this process and follow along. Every transaction is split into two parts: a portion that is spent and locked (or assigned) to the merchant, and a portion that is returned back to the buyer. The returned portion is the unspent transaction output that can be used for future transactions. In a transaction, UTXOs that are consumed by the transaction are called the inputs, and the UTXOs left over or created from a transaction are called the outputs. Only transaction outputs (the UTXOs owned by a user) can be spent in future transactions. The example in Figure 3-2 illustrates a similar scenario, where Bob wants to send 1 BTC to Alice, but in the process, the 10 BTC owned by Bob are split into two parts: the 1 BTC sent to Alice, which is now assigned to her, and the 9 BTC that are returned to Bob in the form of UTXO. Both of these components are recorded on the blockchain because they are a part of a transaction, as shown in Figure 3-2.

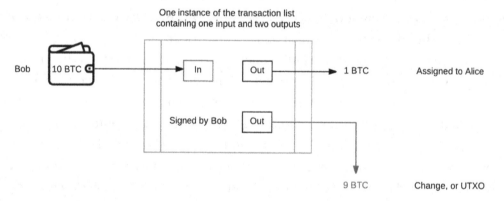

Figure 3-2. *Format of a UTXO in the transaction list*

In this example, Bob wants to send 1 BTC to Alice, and the figure shows how this transaction occurs. The BTC owned by Bob are used as the input of the transaction, and the output is in two parts, one sent to Alice for 1 BTC and the second one returned as change back to Bob. It should be noted here that the initial transaction, newly assigned transaction, and the change are recorded on the blockchain as the input and output.

Now that we have a better grasp of UTXOs, let's talk about how transactions are assigned from one user to the other. This involves the use of private–public keypairs that lock and unlock the transactions. The process works as follows:

- A user, Alice, initiates a transaction that she wants to send to Bob.

- Alice uses her private key to sign the transaction.

- The transaction is broadcasted on the network, and anyone can use Alice's public key to verify that the transaction originated from her.

- Bob receives the transaction after it has been verified on the network and propagated to him.

- Bob unlocks the transaction using his private key. The transaction was signed with a script such that only the recipient could unlock the transaction and assign it to themselves.

We mention that the transaction locking and unlocking mechanisms use a script, so what is this script? The Bitcoin protocol uses a minimal, bare-bones, and Turing-incomplete programming language to manage transactions. Satoshi's intention was to keep the programming logic very simple and largely off the blockchain whenever possible. A script is attached to every transaction and contains instructions on how the user receiving Bitcoins can access them. Essentially, the sender needs to provide a public key that anyone on the network can use to determine that the transaction did indeed originate from the address contained in the script, and a signature to show that the transaction was signed using the sender's private key. Without the private–public keypair authorization, transactions between users would not occur. Let's complete the picture that we started to create with the UTXOs, shown in Figure 3-3.

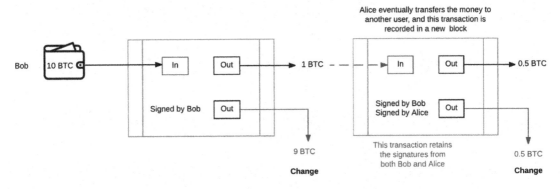

Figure 3-3. *Propogation of transactions on the blockchain*

Conceptually, it might be bizarre to consider spent transactions as locked, and unspent transactions on the network as UTXOs spread across hundreds of blocks, but this process is exactly how transactions are propagated across the network. In our example shown in Figure 3-3, Bob first initiated the transaction that was sent to Alice, and 1 BTC was assigned to Alice. He received 9 BTC in change as the unspent output. Alice further sends 0.5 BTC to another user, and in doing so, she receives 0.5 back in change from her transaction. Notice that the first transaction was signed by Bob, who initiated the transaction, and then Alice signed the second transaction. In a sense, the output from the first transaction became an input for the second, so Bob's signature was retained as proof of the first transaction, and Alice's signature now serves as the unlocking mechanism. This is how transactions can be tracked across the Bitcoin network from the origin to the final owner (final address). By using network addresses, the network retains a level of pseudonymity.

Now that we have talked about UTXOs, signatures, scripts, and how transactions are recorded, let's integrate these concepts and review the workflow of a transaction between Alice and Bob, shown in Figure 3-4.

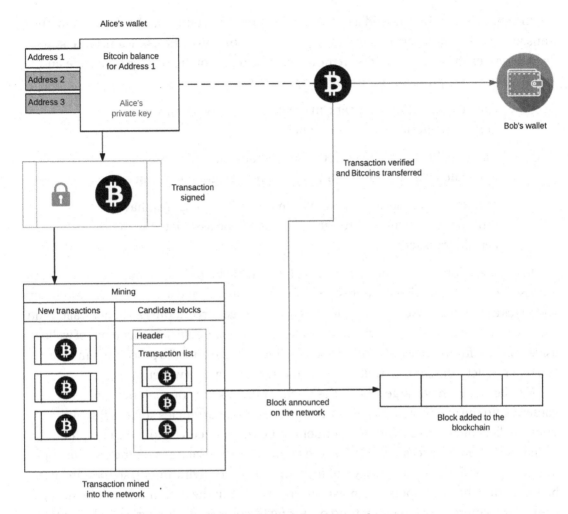

Figure 3-4. *Overview of a transaction on the network*

In Figure 3-4, Alice initiates the transaction from her wallet, which contains multiple addresses. Each address has a certain amount of Bitcoin balance (the sum of all UTXOs associated with that address) that can be used to create new transactions. The transaction is then signed using Alice's private key, and then it enters the mining phase, where it will be packaged into a candidate block. As the mining concludes, the winning miner announces the block on the network, and the block is included in the blockchain. The transaction propagates to Bob, who can now use his private key to unlock the transaction output amount and use it. The ideas of UTXOs, signing, and script lock/unlock provide deeper insight into how the blockchain remains internally consistent as a decentralized ledger.

In Figure 3-4, we introduced a new concept of the wallet that can be used to initiate transactions. In simple terms, a wallet is essentially a **bitcoin address + a private key** used to unlock the wallet. Wallets are now a standard part of the Bitcoin core code and mainly serve three purposes for users:

- Create transactions: A user can create transactions easily using a graphical interface using the wallet.

- Maintain balance: The wallet software tracks all the UTXOs associated with an address and gives a user their final balance.

- Maintain multiple addresses: Within the wallet, a user can have multiple addresses, where each address can be associated with certain transactions.

In a sense, addresses are the only means of ownership in the Bitcoin network. UTXOs are associated with a particular address (as account balances), and a user can create as many addresses as they want. We saw in Figure 3-4 that Alice had three addresses in her wallet, and each of the addresses can work with her private key. There are actually other types of wallets, aside from a software wallet. Figure 3-4 used a software wallet, but the process is similar for two other wallet types: mobile wallets and a cold storage physical wallet.

Mobile wallets have largely been designed for the sake of convenience and as a gateway into the world of mobile payments using cryptocurrencies such as Bitcoin. These wallets often serve as an independent but miniaturized version of a complete wallet, and allow for access to balance and conducting transactions on the go. The apps that work as wallets are often designed in an open source environment, so they are also helping bring the developers and power-users together in the community. Cold-storage wallets are a more permanent method of storing Bitcoins over a longer period of time. There have been instances where wallet software was corrupted, or the users couldn't remember the key to unlocking a wallet, rendering their account balance effectively useless. There is no direct recovery mechanism for a password on a wallet. The idea behind physical storage is to create a new wallet and send a transaction to a new address on that wallet. Now the new wallet can be backed up and saved to physical device such as a flash drive and stored away securely. Once that transaction has been verified on the blockchain, your Bitcoins are safe to be retrieved from the flash drive at any time. This can be done to prevent any accidents from happening and to keep your currency separate from the main wallet that you use to conduct transactions or mine for Bitcoins. Some developers have taken a step further and created paper wallets where the address is encoded in a QR code, and a private key for that particular wallet is also printed on the paper in another QR code.

Note   How can you actually see your transaction taking place on the Bitcoin network without having to write a script or code yourself to do it? In Bitcoin (and most cryptocurrencies), there is a feature called Blockchain Explorer, usually a website where all transactions are visible from the Bitcoin network. You can obtain all sorts of details about transactions such as the origin of the transaction, the amount, the block hash, or how many verifications it received.

Simple Payment Verification (SPV)

So far, we have talked about the structure of blocks, transaction lists, how transactions occur between users, and how they are recorded on the blockchain. Blocks are fundamentally data structures linked on the blockchain, and transactions can be thought of as properties of that data structure. More precisely, in the case of blockchain, transactions are represented as leaves of a Merkle tree. Hashes have been used throughout the Bitcoin protocol as a method for maintaining data consistency because a hash is very easy to verify and nearly impossible to reverse engineer. Building on these properties, we can tackle a very difficult technical challenge on the blockchain: How can we check if a particular transaction belongs to a block? Checking through an N number of items in a list would be very inefficient; therefore, we can't simply check every transaction in a blockchain containing millions of blocks to verify. This is where a Merkle tree provides speed and efficiency.

To visualize a Merkle tree, refer to Figure 3-5. It is constructed from the transactions of a block to allow fast access for verification purposes. Let's follow the example shown in Figure 3-5. In this case, there are eight transactions collected in a block and represented on a Merkle tree. The lowest level is the transactions themselves, and they are abstracted to a higher level by hashing two transactions together and obtaining an output hash. This hash is combined with a second one and hashed again to abstract a higher level. This process repeats itself until only two hashes are left. Notice that each level contains information about the level below, and finally the highest level holds a hash with information from the entire tree. This hash is called the Merkle root. So how would a Merkle root assist in finding a transaction? Let's run through an example in Figure 3-6 and try to find transaction 6 from the Merkle tree. For starters, the Merkle root allows us to skip the other half of the tree, and now our search is limited to transactions 5 through 8.

The hashes guide the search further, allowing us to step into (reach) transaction 6 in just three steps. Compare this to searching through the whole tree, stepping into every level and comparing every transaction to see if it is indeed transaction 6. That process would be more involved in terms of the steps taken and the time needed, and this becomes too exhaustive if the search expands to millions of transactions.

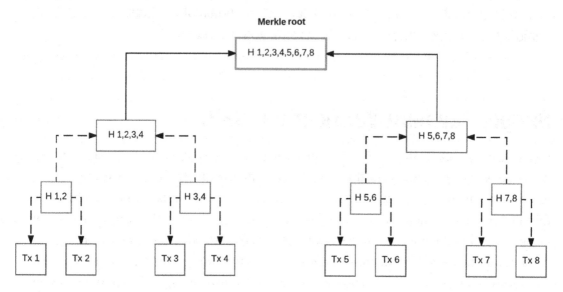

Figure 3-5. *Constructing a Merkle root*

In Figure 3-5, the lowest level is formed from the transactions, and the general idea is to keep hashing two elements together and retain some information about the level below. Ultimately, we are left with only two elements that are hashed together to form the Merkle root. So, when would searching for a transaction be helpful? For new users to get started with the standard Bitcoin wallet-client, every user has to download the entire blockchain. Over time, the blockchain has increased in download size and recently reached a few gigabytes. This can be intimidating to new users, who can't use their wallets until the blockchain download has finished, and it might turn them away. To solve the problem of having to download a bloated blockchain with historic transactions, Satoshi came up with a solution called Simple Payment Verification (SPV). The rationale in SPV is to create a wallet client that only downloads the block headers instead of the entire blockchain. This new lightweight client can use the Merkle root in the block headers to verify if a particular transaction resides in a given block. The precise mechanism requires the wallet to rely on a Merkle branch and reach the specific transaction, much like the example shown in Figure 3-6. Currently, for Bitcoin, there is an alternative wallet client known as Electrum that implements SPV and allows new users to avoid the hassle of downloading the entire blockchain.

Merkle root

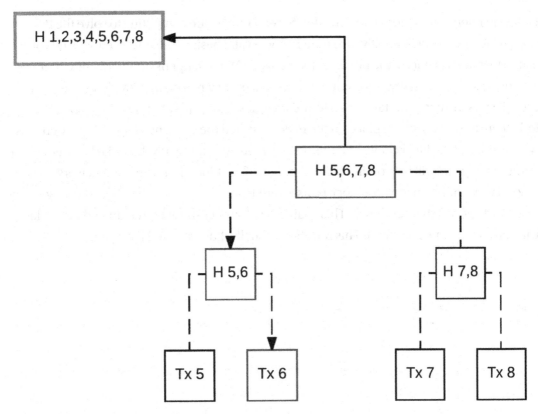

Figure 3-6. *Finding a transaction using the Merkle root*

In Figure 3-6, the root allows us to skip half of the tree during our search, and the next level narrows down the search even further. Using the Merkle root, we can reach the transaction in just three steps, which allows for very high operational efficiency that we need on the current Bitcoin network. The path to reaching transaction 6 is also known as a Merkle branch—connecting the root to a leaf.

Blockchain Forks

Here's an interesting scenario to consider: Several miners are competing to solve the PoW and create a block. Incidentally, two miners find a valid hash within just a few seconds of each other and broadcast the blocks to the network. What happens now? This situation is known as a fork, and this is a completely normal occurrence on the Bitcoin network, especially as the network starts to scale and includes thousands of miners. To resolve the fork, there are a few rules in place on the network called the consensus rules. The tie creates two versions of the blockchain, and this tie is resolved when the next block is discovered. Some of the peers will be working on one version of the blockchain, and others work on the second version. When the next block is discovered, one of the chains will become longer due to the inclusion of this new block. This chain now becomes the active chain and the nodes will converge to the new chain. This process is visually illustrated in Figure 3-7.

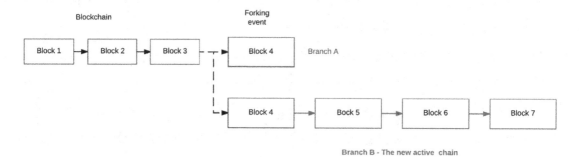

Figure 3-7. *Fork in the chain*

In the example shown in Figure 3-7, block 4 is discovered at the same time by two miners, but the tie is resolved when the next block is discovered on Branch B. This branch now becomes the active chain, and all the nodes converge to using Branch B as the new active chain. Normal forks on the blockchain are not a concerning event, because they are usually resolved within a matter of minutes. But soft and hard forks are an entirely different matter. These can occur in the case of upgrades to the Bitcoin core code, where a permanent split happens between non-upgraded nodes that can't validate any newly created blocks and upgraded nodes that have begun creating blocks following the new consensus rules. Two entirely different types of blocks being to appear on the network, and the network is unable to converge on a single active chain until the nodes are upgraded to the new rules.

In this case, there are two possible outcomes: in one, the majority of the network switches over to the new rules (a soft fork), and the new rules allow for the carryover of some portion of the valid old blocks. Or, the second alternative is that the old blocks remain invalid for the new nodes, and no old blocks are accepted in the network by the new nodes. This is a hard fork, where no forward compatibility exists and the old blocks will no longer be accepted by the new nodes. All the miners and nodes have to upgrade to the new software so that their blocks can be considered valid under the new rules. A hard fork can be chaotic and a problem for users and merchants that have created payment terminals and interfaces relying on the old rules for transactions. They have to upgrade their backend software in order to be compatible with the new rules and ensure the smooth transition of incoming Bitcoins. A hard fork is not upcoming for the Bitcoin network, however, as developers have begun researching just how complex the process might be. We will end our discussion of blockchain forks here, but we will return to it soon. In the next chapters, we will take a look at circumstances where a hard fork may become necessary in the next generation of Bitcoin protocols.

Summary

In this chapter, we integrated the concept of mining into the whole blockchain network. We described what a blockchain is and how it functions at a technical level. Then, we described the workflow of a transaction and tracking unspent transaction outputs. We talked about how transactions are put together and propagated on the blockchain and also mining software such as a wallet and mining client. Then, we put mining in the context of a proper network and showed how a transaction goes from being included in a block to being propagated. After that, we talked about the concept of SPV and the importance of Merkle hashes and roots in Bitcoin. We ended the chapter with a discussion of blockchain forks and how they influence the network, a topic we will revisit later in the book.

References

The main references used to prepare this chapter are the Bitcoin Developer Guide (`https://developer.bitcoin.org/devguide/transactions.html`) for discussions on UTXOs and block headers. Georg Becker's work on Merkle tree signatures was used to prepare the sections on Simple Payment Verification and Merkle roots:

Becker, G. *Merkle signature schemes, Merkle trees and their cryptanalysis.* Ruhr-University Bochum, Tech. Rep. 2008 Jul.

CHAPTER 4

Unpacking Ethereum

Ethereum is an open source, decentralized blockchain platform with computational capabilities that reconstruct an elementary currency exchange into a transfer of value between users via a scripting language. Ethereum is widely recognized as a successor to the Bitcoin protocol, generalizing the original ideas and enabling a more diverse array of applications to be built on top of the blockchain technology. Ethereum has two essential components. First, there is a Turing-complete virtual processor that can calculate the necessary computational resources and execute scripts called the Ethereum Virtual Machine (EVM). The second component is a token of value called ether, which is the currency of the network and is used for user-to-user transactions or compensation to miners of the network. In this chapter, we begin our journey with an overview of Ethereum's architecture in comparison to Bitcoin, focusing on the EVM and Turing-completeness properties. Following the architecture section, there is a short discussion of the accounts model in Ethereum and account representation with Merkle-Patricia Trees. This will lead us to the topics of global state representation in Ethereum, account storage, and gas, which is a spam-prevention mechanism in the network. Then, we deconstruct the notion of a smart contract enabled by EVM, the security concerns revolving around sandboxing executable code, and how the EVM pushes executable code (bytecode) to the blockchain. After that, we provide an introduction to Solidity and Vyper, two programming languages used for writing smart contracts in Ethereum. We explore the syntax of Solidity and Vyper, as well as the popular integrated development environments (IDEs) being used, and provide a brief list of key developer resources. Next, we focus on the World Computer model proposed in Ethereum and introduce supporting decentralized technologies such as IPFS and Whisper. Then, we look at the state of decentralized apps (DApps) along the publishing platform called Mist available in Ethereum. This allows us to transition into talking about the Layer 2 updates to Ethereum—the major technical focus of this chapter and the Ethereum ecosystem in 2020. Finally, we conclude the chapter with a brief discussion of the enterprise side. Here, we introduce a particularly noteworthy development of Blockchain-as-a-Service (BaaS) deployed on the Azure cloud by Microsoft.

© Vikram Dhillon, David Metcalf, and Max Hooper 2021
V. Dhillon et al., *Blockchain Enabled Applications*, https://doi.org/10.1007/978-1-4842-6534-5_4

Overview of Ethereum

It was around mid-2013 when a majority of the Bitcoin community was starting to flirt with idea of applications beyond currency on the blockchain. Fairly soon, there was a flood of new ideas being discussed in online forums. A few popular examples included domain registration, asset insurance, voting, and even Internet of Things (IoT). After the hype started to fade away, a more serious analysis of the Bitcoin protocol revealed severe limitations of potential applications that can be built on top of the blockchain.

A crucial point of debate was whether a full scripting language should be allowed on the blockchain, or whether we should build applications with logic residing outside of the blockchain. There were two key issues that sparked this debate:

- The scripting language and OPCODES in the Bitcoin protocol were designed to be very limited in functionality.

- The Bitcoin protocol itself was not generalizable. There were attempts; for instance, Namecoin was designed for one specific task (domain name registration). The big question at the time was: How can a protocol be generalized such that it becomes forward-compatible with future applications that we know nothing about?

Eventually, two schools of thought emerged regarding scripting. Traditionally, Satoshi's paper proposed to keep the scripting language very limited in functionality. This would avoid the security concerns of having executable code in the blockchain. In a sense, the blockchain's executable code is limited to a handful of necessary primitives that update the distributed states. The second school of thought was championed by Vitalik buterin, who thought of the blockchain as more than just a ledger. He envisioned the blockchain as a computational platform that could execute well-defined functions using contracts and arguments. This is made possible by the Ethereum Virtual Machine (EVM). The EVM allows for complete isolation of the executable code and safe execution of the applications built on the blockchain. We will return to discuss this at greater length later in the chapter. Let's begin with the core design principle behind Ethereum.

Core Idea   Instead of building a blockchain platform to support specific applications, in Ethereum we will build a native programming language with extensibility to implement business logic on the blockchain platform using the language.

We will return shortly to understand the implications of this principle. In the meantime, let's talk about another distinguishing feature in Ethereum: the consensus algorithm. We discussed the concept of consensus in earlier chapters. In Proof-of-Work (PoW)–based cryptocurrencies such as Bitcoin, the network awards miners who solve cryptographic puzzles to validate transactions and mine new blocks. Ethereum proposes a different consensus algorithm called Proof-of-Stake (PoS). In a PoS algorithm, the validator/creator of the next block is chosen in a pseudo-random manner based on the stake that an account has in the network. Therefore, if you have a higher stake in the network, you have a higher chance of being selected as a validator. The validator will then "forge" the next block and get a reward from the network. Here, the validator is truly forging a block (in the blacksmith sense of the term) instead of mining, because in PoS, the idea of hardware-based mining is replaced by a virtual stake. One rationale behind using PoS was to circumvent the high power consumption and energy requirements of PoW-mining algorithms that translated to higher electricity bills and became a frequent complaint. Peercoin was the first cryptocurrency to launch with PoS; however, recently more prominent PoS implementations can be seen in ShadowCash, Nxt, and Qora. The main differences between Bitcoin and Ethereum as protocols are highlighted in Figure 4-1.

Note   The current implementation of Ethereum (also known as Ethereum 1.0) uses Proof-of-Work as the consensus algorithm. However, the Layer 2.0 updates to Ethereum plan for a transition to Proof-of-Stake as the main consensus algorithm. More details regarding this algorithm are provided later in the chapter.

The following is a brief summary of PoS written by Ethereum community developers (https://docs.ethhub.io/ethereum-roadmap/ethereum-2.0/proof-of-stake/):

> *Proof of Stake (PoS) is a category of consensus algorithms for public blockchains that depend on a validator's economic stake in the network. In proof of work (PoW) based public blockchains (e.g. Bitcoin and the current implementation of Ethereum), the algorithm rewards participants who solve cryptographic puzzles in order to validate transactions and create new blocks (i.e. mining). In PoS-based public blockchains (e.g. Ethereum's upcoming Casper implementation), a set of validators take turns proposing and voting on the next block, and the weight of each validator's vote depends on the size of its deposit (i.e. stake). Significant advantages of PoS include **security, reduced risk of centralization, and energy efficiency**.*

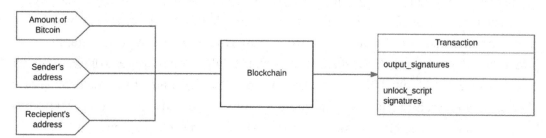

Addresses point to transactions and the blockchain records the transfer function taking place

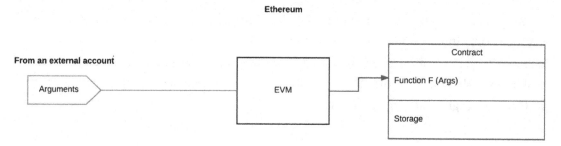

A user passes arguments through the EVM to call a particular function F in a contract

Figure 4-1. *Overview of Bitcoin and Ethereum as computational platforms*

Focusing on Figure 4-1, in the Bitcoin protocol addresses map the transactions from sender to receiver. The only program that runs on the blockchain is the transfer program; given the addresses and the key signature, this program can transfer money from one user to another. Ethereum generalizes this concept by placing an EVM at every node so that verifiable code can be executed on the blockchain. Here, the general scheme is that an external account will pass arguments to a function, and the EVM will direct that call to the appropriate contract and execute the function, granted the appropriate amount of ether and gas are supplied. As a consequence, every transaction in Ethereum can be considered a function call.

Accounts in Ethereum

Accounts are a meta-structure in Ethereum and the fundamental operational unit of the blockchain. All Ethereum transactions require an account. Alternatively, accounts also serve as a model to store and track information on the users in the network. There are two types of accounts available on the network:

- **User accounts:** These are user-controlled accounts, also known as external accounts. These accounts have an ether balance, are controlled by public–private keypairs, and can send transactions, but have no associated code. All actions in the Ethereum network are triggered by transactions initiated by external accounts. In the Bitcoin protocols, we referred to these simply as addresses. The key difference between accounts and addresses is the ability to contain and execute generalized code in Ethereum.

- **Contracts:** This is essentially an account controlled by its own code. A contract account is the functional programmatic unit in Ethereum that resides on the blockchain. This account has an ether balance, has associated code, can execute code when triggered by transactions received from other accounts, and can manipulate its own persistent storage. (Every contract on the blockchain has its own storage only it can write to; this is known as the contract's state). Any member on the network can create an application with some arbitrary rules, defining it as a contract.

If accounts play such a key role, how are they represented on the blockchain? Accounts become an element of the Merkle trees, which in turn are an element of every block header. Ethereum uses a modified form of the binary Merkle trees called Merkle-Patricia trees. A complete explanation of the Merkle-Patricia tree (`http://www.emsec.rub.de/media/crypto/attachments/files/2011/04/becker_1.pdf`)) would be beyond the scope of this text; however, a graphical synopsis is provided in Figure 4-2.

Note   The two-account system explained here may not remain in Ethereum for the long term. Recently, there has been more push toward a one-account model, where user accounts are implemented by using contracts.

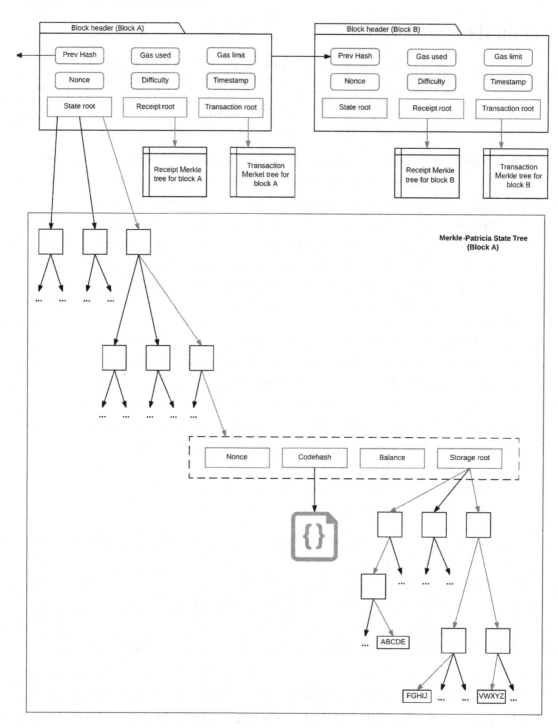

Figure 4-2. *Overview of block headers and Merkle-Patricia trees for Blocks A and B*

In Figure 4-2, the block header contains a few standard definitions that broadcast the status of the network. Additionally, every block header in Ethereum has three Merkle-Patricia trees for three different objects: Transactions (function calls), Receipts (the results of a function call, recording the effect of each transaction), and State objects. Binary trees are useful in managing transaction histories; however, the state has multiple components that need to be updated more frequently. The Merkle-Patricia tree shown contains a state root that further records multiple account objects. One of the deep branches points to a dashed box containing the four parameters that define an account. From these parameters, the balance of an account and the nonce for the network are often updated. Therefore, a more suitable data structure is necessary where we can rapidly calculate a new tree root after an insert, update, edit, or delete operation without needing to recompute the entire tree. This modified Merkle tree allows for rapid queries to questions such as the following: Does this account exist? Has this transaction been included in a particular block? What is the current balance of my account? Of note, the balance is only relevant for an external account, and similarly, the codehash (which holds executable code) is only applicable to contracts. Storage root is the final parameter and contains data uploaded by a user to the blockchain or serves as internal storage available to a contract. This internal storage can be updated by the contract during the execution phase. Let's talk about these account parameters in depth.

State, Storage, and Gas

We briefly mentioned that a contract can manipulate its own storage and update the state, so what is a *state*? Recall that in the Bitcoin protocol, data on users and transactions is framed and stored in the context of UTXOs (Unspent Transaction Outputs). Ethereum employs a different design strategy of using a state object. Essentially, the state stores a list of accounts, where each account has a balance, as well as blockchain-specific information (code and data storage). A transaction is considered valid if the sending account has enough balance to pay for it (avoiding double spending), therefore the sending account is debited, and the receiving account is credited with the value. If the receiving account has code associated with it, the code will run when the transaction is received. The execution of a contract or the code associated with an account can have different effects on the state: internal storage may also be changed, or the code may even create additional transactions to other accounts.

Ethereum makes a distinction between state and history in the network. The state is essentially a snapshot of current information regarding network state and accounts at a given time. On the other hand, history is a compilation of all the events that have taken place on the blockchain such as function calls (transactions) and the changes brought about as a result (receipts). Most nodes in the Ethereum network keep a record of the state. More formally, the state is a data-structure that contains key value maps (KVMs) in order to map addresses onto account objects. Each account object contains four values:

- Current nonce value

- Account balance (in ethers)

- Code hash, which contains code in the case of contracts, but remains empty for external accounts

- Storage tree root, which is the root of the Merkle-Patricia tree that contains code and data stored on the blockchain

Next, let's talk about gas in Ethereum. Gas is the internal unit for keeping track of execution cost in Ethereum. In other words, it is a micro-transaction fee for performing a computation on the blockchain. For a computational platform like Ethereum, this becomes crucial when running code because of the Halting problem: one cannot tell whether a program will run indefinitely, or just has a long run-time. Gas puts a limiter on the run-time as the user has to pay for executing step-by-step instructions of a contract. The nature of microtransactions allows steps to be executed very inexpensively, but even those transactions will add up for very long run-times. Once the gas supplied for a contract exhausts, the user would have to pay for more to continue. Special gas fees are also applied to operations that take up storage.

Operations like storage, memory, and processing all cost gas in the Ethereum network. So, let's talk about storage next. In Ethereum, external accounts can store data on the blockchain using contracts. A contract would manage the upload and storage process; however, the data types that can be stored currently are very limited. Then, a natural question becomes: What are the limits on uploading content and information to the Ethereum blockchain? What would prevent the bloating of the blockchain? As it turns out, there are currently two mechanisms in place preventing a data overload:

- Gas limits per block that dictate how much gas can be spent per block on storage/computational operations

- Amount of money a user would have to spend to purchase the gas needed to store data

The second limitation is usually a deterrent for users to store directly on the blockchain. Instead it becomes much more efficient and economic to use a third-party decentralized service like STORJ or IPFS for the storage and hash the location in Ethereum to include it in a contract. In the future, new distributed storage applications will allow for all sorts of data files to be uploaded and included in contracts on the blockchain.

Let's summarize what we have discussed so far. We started with the differences between Bitcoin and Ethereum regarding using accounts, charging gas for operations, storing data directly on the blockchain, allowing executable code on the blockchain, state objects, and Merkle-Patricia trees. Figure 4-3 provides a simplified functional overview of the processes occurring in Ethereum.

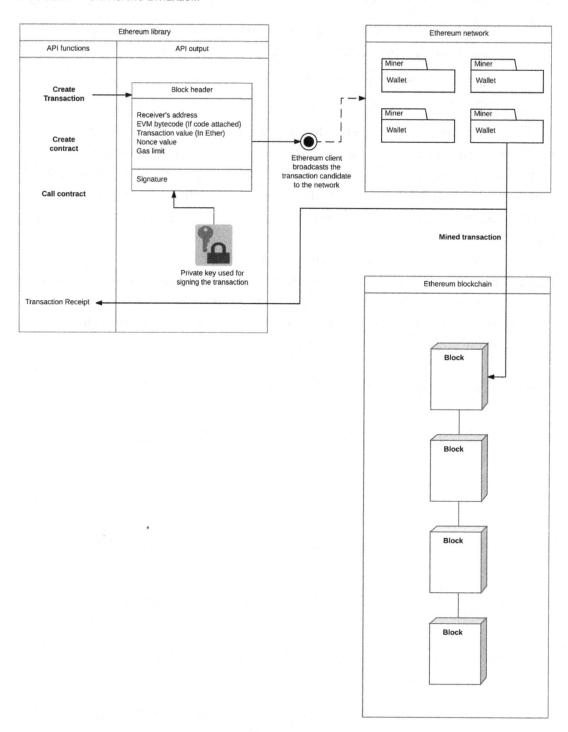

Figure 4-3. *A simplified overview of the Ethereum network*

In Figure 4-3, there are roughly three Ethereum components to discuss: the API, the network, and the blockchain. The Ethereum JavaScript API (also known as web3.js) provides a large feature set for functionality such as constructing transactions and contracts, referring to functions, and storing receipts. An enhanced wallet client for Ethereum such as Mist can take over several of these functions with a GUI. Once a candidate block is constructed, it is broadcasted to the network by the Ethereum client. The validators on the network determine if the transactions are valid, and if any code (in the block) associated with a transaction or a contract is valid. Once the validation is complete, the validators execute the associated code and apply it to the current state. The block is broadcasted to the network, and a miner will "forge" the block; the verified block is then added to the blockchain. This step will also create transaction receipts for every transaction included in the block. The new block also provides updates to the state objects and relational links for the state tree from the current block to a new block.

Note   What will prevent the Ethereum network from being bloated by small, unused contracts? Currently, there are no mechanisms to control the lifespan of a contract; however, there are a few proposals in the air about temporary subscription-based contracts. In the future, there might be two different types of contracts—one that has a permanent lifespan (which is significantly more expensive to create and compute), and the other one that operates till its subscription expires (cheaper and temporary, self-destructs after subscription runs out to prevent cluttering).

Ethereum Virtual Machine

Formally, Ethereum Virtual Machine (EVM) is the run-time environment for smart contracts in Ethereum. Contracts are written in a higher-level language (for instance, Solidity) and then compiled into bytecode using an interpreter in EVM. This bytecode is then uploaded to the blockchain using an Ethereum client. Contracts live on the blockchain in this executable bytecode form. The EVM is designed to be completely isolated from the environment and the rest of the network. The code running inside the EVM has no access to the network or any other processes; only after being compiled to bytecode do contracts have access to the external world and other contracts.

From an operational standpoint, the EVM behaves as a large, decentralized computer with millions of objects (accounts) that have the ability to maintain an internal database, execute code, and talk to each other through message-passing. This model is not yet complete, however. In Ethereum, this concept is often referred to as the idea of a "world computer." Let's return to the topic of code execution on EVM and how it is intimately linked to consensus. EVM allows any user on the network to execute arbitrary code in a trustless environment where the outcome is fully deterministic and the execution can be guaranteed. In a simple contract that executes a read function, no account edits happen, and the state of all the accounts remains the same. However, as we mentioned before, any user can trigger an action by sending a transaction from an external account. We can have two outcomes here: if the receiver is another external account, then the transaction will transfer some ether but nothing else happens. However, if the receiver is a contract, then the contract becomes activated and executes the code within. Executing code within the network takes time, and the process is relatively slow and costly. For every step of executable instructions, the user is charged gas. When a user initiates an execution through a transaction, they commit an upper-limit for the maximum currency that they are willing to pay as gas for that contract or code.

Tip   Ethereum has recently begun the process of migrating over to a Just-In-Time VM, which offers some optimizations in gas usage and performance.

What does it mean for the outcome of EVM to be deterministic? It is essential for every node to reach an identical final state given the same input to a contract code. Otherwise, each node that executes the contract code to validate the transaction would end up with different results and no consensus would be possible. This is the deterministic nature of EVM that allows every node to reach consensus on the execution of a contract and the same final state of accounts. The nodes executing a contract are similar to cogs synchronized to move inside of a clock; they work in a harmonious fashion and reach a matching final state. A contract can also refer to other contracts, but it can't directly access the internal storage of another contract. Every contract runs in a dedicated and private instance of the EVM where it only has access to some input data, its internal storage, the code of other contracts on the blockchain, and various blockchain parameters such as recent block hashes.

Every full node on the network executes the contract code simultaneously for each transaction. When a node is validating a block, transactions are executed sequentially, in the order specified by the block. This is necessary because a block might contain multiple transactions that call upon the same contract, and the current state of a contract might depend on state modified by previous references during the code execution. Executing contract code is relatively expensive, so when nodes receive a block, they only do a basic check on the transactions: Does the sending account have enough ether to pay for gas? Does the transaction have a valid signature? Then, mining nodes perform the relatively expensive task of executing the transaction, include it in a block, and collect the transaction fee as a reward. When a full node receives a block, it executes the transactions in the block to independently verify the security and integrity of the transactions to be included in the blockchain. Let's look at the EVM visually in Figure 4-4.

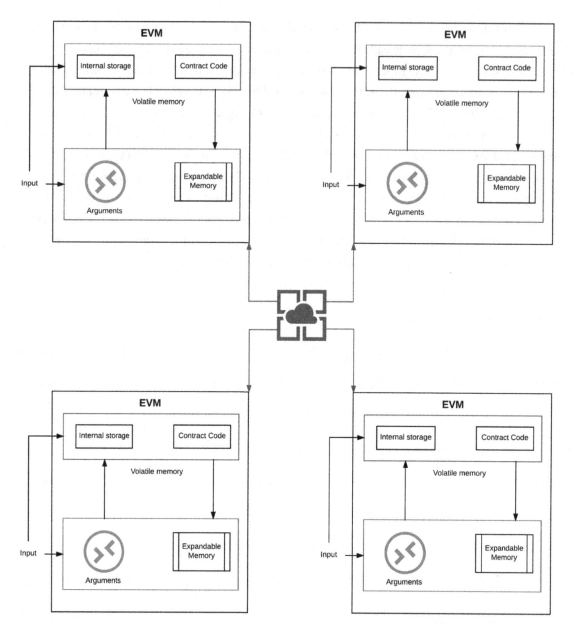

Figure 4-4. *Four instances of Ethereum Virtual Machines running on four different nodes*

In Figure 4-4, the four EVMs are synchronously executing a contract's instructions and will arrive at an identical account state once the execution has been completed. This is due to the deterministic nature of the EVM, which allows the contract to reach consensus across the network at every step of instructions. The EVM has a very straightforward rationale: it has a single run loop that will attempt to execute the instruction one step at a time. Within this loop, the gas is calculated for each instruction and the allocated memory is expanded if necessary. The loop will continue until the VM either receives an exit code indicating successful execution or throws an exception such as out-of-gas.

Solidity and Vyper Programming Languages

Solidity is a higher-level, contract-oriented programming language for writing smart contracts in Ethereum. Any code written in Solidity can be executed on the EVM after being compiled into bytecode, which is an instruction set for the EVM. How does the bytecode encode references to other functions and contracts that are called during execution? This is done by using an Application Binary Interface (ABI). In general, an ABI is the interface between two program modules: machine-level instructions and a human-readable higher-level programming language. Let's break down this answer into three components:

- Contract: A contract is simply higher-level code defined in a formal language such as Solidity.

- Compiled contract: The contract is converted to bytecode to be executed on the Ethereum Virtual Machine (EVM), adhering to the compiler's specifications. Note that function names and input parameters get hashed and obfuscated during compilation. Therefore, for another account to call a function, it must have access to the given function name and arguments, and we need another layer that interfaces encoding into and out of the bytecode.

- Application Binary Interface (ABI): An ABI is a list of the contract's function definition and arguments in JSON format. The function definitions and input arguments are hashed into the ABI. This is included in the data of a transaction and interpreted by the EVM at the target account. An ABI is necessary so that you can specify which function in the contract to invoke, as well as get a guarantee that the function will return data in the format you are expecting.

Solidity has a plugin available for Visual Studio to help write smart contracts in a powerful IDE and deploy them to the Ethereum network. Our discussion of Solidity here will not cover advanced implementations or definitions. Instead, we will be limiting the upcoming discussion to the fundamentals such as storing variables and creating a simple contract. Let's get started:

```
/* defining a contract */
contract ExampleStorage {

    uint storedNumber; //unsigned integer (uint) used to declare a state
                            variable

/* Function set can modify the value of the state variable */
    function set(uint x) {
        storedNumber = x;
    }

/* Function get can retrieve the value of state variable  */
    function get() constant returns (uint retVal) {
        return storedData;
    }
}
```

This storage contract allows a user to store an integer as a state variable storedNumber and then modify or retrieve its value using the get() and set() functions. Solidity also offers several advanced features available in modern programming languages, such as inheritance (for contracts), function overloading, and class interfaces. Next, let's look at a more complex example of a contract. This time we will create a simple bank contract using Solidity:

```
// This bank contract allows deposits, withdrawals, and checking the
balance

// 'contract' is a keyword to declare class, similar to any other OOP
contract SimpleBank {

// 'mapping' is a dictionary that maps address objects to balances
// 'private' means that other contracts can't directly query balances
```

```solidity
    mapping (address => uint) private balances;

// 'public' makes externally readable by users or contracts on the
    blockchain
    address public owner;

// Events trigger messages throughout the Ethereum network
    event LogDepositMade(address accountAddress, uint amount);

// Constructor
    function SimpleBank() {

        // msg provides details about the message that's sent to the
        contract
        // msg.sender is the address of contract creator
        owner = msg.sender;

    }

    // Deposit ether into the bank
    // Returns the balance of the user after a deposit is made
    function deposit() public returns (uint) {
// Add the value being deposited to the account balance
        balances[msg.sender] += msg.value;

// Log the deposit that was just made
        LogDepositMade(msg.sender, msg.value);

// Return the balance after the deposit
        return balances[msg.sender];
    }

// Withdraw ether from bank
// withdrawAmount is the amount you want to withdraw
// Returns the balance remaining for the user
    function withdraw(uint withdrawAmount) public returns
    (uint remainingBal) {

/* If the account balance is greater than amount requested for withdrawal,
subtract it from the balance */
        if(balances[msg.sender] >= withdrawAmount) {
```

```
        balances[msg.sender] -= withdrawAmount;

// Increment the balance back to the original account on fail
        if (!msg.sender.send(withdrawAmount)) {
            balances[msg.sender] += withdrawAmount;
        }
    }

// Return the remaining balance after withdrawl
    return balances[msg.sender];
  }

// Return the balance of the user
// 'constant' prevents function from editing state variables;
  function balance() constant returns (uint) {
      return balances[msg.sender];
  }

}
```

Although this contract has plenty of moving parts, it has a straightforward schematic. We start by declaring state variables, and here we use an advanced data-type called a mapping. Then, we declare an address variable used throughout the contract, and an event logger. The constructor prepares the owner object to be usable, and we attach the owner object to receive messages in the form of return types from functions. There are three functions that follow the constructor, which allow for the basic functions of a bank. The deposit function adds the argument amount to the balance. The withdrawal function checks whether the requested amount is lower than the balance available for an account. If this is the case, the withdrawal is confirmed and the argument amount is subtracted from the balance. If there is not enough balance, the amount that was supposed to be withdrawn is added back to the account and the final balance is returned to the user. Finally, the last function allows us to return the balance of an account at a given time as requested by the contract. Now that we have a better grasp of Solidity, let's shift our focus to Vyper.

Vyper is also a general-purpose, contract-oriented programming language that compiles down to the EVM (Ethereum Virtual Machine) bytecode, much like Solidity. The main design benefit in using Vyper is that it removes numerous barriers in the process of writing smart contracts and presents the contracts in an easy-to-understand manner. As a general principle, any code that needs to run on the EVM must be very efficient to minimize the gas needed for the smart contract to execute. It must be noted that a poorly written contract will cost more ether to execute, and it can become so prohibitively expensive to run that the EVM will terminate the contract. To that end, Vyper follows the same logic as Solidity for writing contracts but removes the need for object-oriented programming paradigms. Vyper focuses on a limited set of definitions that are applied solely to programming micro-transactions on the blockchain. Let's discuss the main features of Vyper:

- Vyper does not contain most of the object-oriented programming constructs that programmers are familiar with: class inheritance, function overloading, and recursion capabilities have been removed. These features are not necessary for Turing-completeness and pose a security threat by increasing code complexity. Code reviews are essential to assess smart contracts; however, the added complexity can further make the audit process more difficult. Simplification leads to more reliable audits.

- Writing code that is easier to follow also reduces the likelihood of errors. In the sense that Vyper offers more security than Solidity, the added security layer is enforced in the coding practices of developers. Even with restricting features such as creating upper limits for gas usage and overflow checks, smart contracts written with Vyper shine in terms of readability, auditability, and simplicity (and therefore security).

- Vyper offers a set of built-in functions to write smart contracts, and although reviewing all of them is beyond the scope of this chapter, we want to highlight the `assert` function. `Assert` throws an error if a certain condition is not met. It is used at the beginning of methods to check if particular criteria are met for the method to process. If not, the transaction is reverted, and the contract terminates. For instance, imagine a crowd-funding scenario where `assert` can be used to revert a contract by checking for a timestamp. If the timestamp of the current block in the Ethereum blockchain is greater than the deadline of the campaign, the contract should be terminated because the campaign has ended. In this way, `assert` is a very clean function with which to apply conditions on contract code.

Developer Resources

As Ethereum has evolved in the past few years, so too has the interest of developers in using the platform for making applications. In this section, we will cover a few developer resources available for rapid prototyping in the Ethereum ecosystem:

- Remix: A web-based IDE for writing and testing smart contracts faster on Ethereum. It has built-in support for writing contracts using Solidity and Vyper, a plugin manager for extending functionality, unit testing, and a blockchain virtual machine.

- Ethereum Studio: Another web-based IDE suited for new developers to learn how to build and deploy smart contracts. Ethereum Studio has project templates, transaction logger, and a built-in Ethereum Virtual Machine for rapid prototyping on the Ethereum platform.

- OpenZeppelin SDK: A smart contract toolkit to help build, compile, and deploy smart contracts and interact with them once deployed.

- Embark: A developer platform for building DApps and smart contracts. Has a command-line interface for deploying contracts, plugin system, transaction explorer, and an active development community.

- ConsenSys Academy: A self-paced, online Ethereum developer course that is open year-round for enrollment. More on educational resources in a later chapter.

- Ethereum Stackexchange: A community to ask any Ethereum-related questions ranging from platform development to getting started.

- Chainshot: An invited bootcamp for blockchain development that focuses on Ethereum smart contracts with a curriculum focused on practical applications.

World Computer Model

The Ethereum project has a grand vision of becoming a shared world computer with millions of accounts powered by the blockchain which becomes a backend for "smart-logging" of communications, contracts that provide the decentralized logic to be executed, and EVMs that act as the execution platform. But computation and processing are not enough; a computer must also be able to store information and allow for a mechanism for applications to communicate amongst each other. This world computer will operate in an Internet 3.0 era, where servers are no longer needed due to the decentralized nature of information flow. In this ambitious endeavor, the Ethereum blockchain is only one-quarter of the World Computer model. Let's introduce the three other components:

- Whisper: A secure message-passing protocol that allows decentralized applications on the blockchain to communicate with each other. This protocol relies on obfuscation and anonymization, similar to the Tor project (which provides anonymous web-browsing), where details regarding the message content, the sender, and the recipient are obscured. Additionally, this information cannot be gathered through packet analysis. The Whisper protocol is implemented on top of the RLPx transport protocol, a TCP-based transport protocol that is used internally by Ethereum nodes to communicate. There are a number of situations in which DApps need to communicate through a message bus; for instance, announcing a flash sale of a virtual asset. Whisper allows for easy broadcasting by using envelopes—encrypted packets that are sent and received by Whisper nodes. To that end, in an effort to avoid spam, a Whisper node must use a proof-of-work function to send a message. The work done is proportional to the size of the broadcast being transmitted. Ultimately, Whisper will provide an automated means of communication between user accounts or apps acting on behalf of the user accounts, as shown in Figure 4-5.

- Swarm: A decentralized storage and distribution service for DApp code, user data, blockchain data, and state data available to the Ethereum blockchain. In the future, Swarm will be able to provide Web 3.0 services such as media streaming, decentralized databases, and state channels. The main problem that Swarm is trying to solve is that currently, storing large amounts of data on the blockchain remains very expensive. This is why any DApps that need storage use an off-chain alternative. The idea behind Swarm is straightforward: a peer-to-peer network of collaborating nodes is used to pool together resources. This P2P network acts as a distributed cloud storage system with ample opportunity for data redundancy. The network is self-sustaining because of the associated blockchain that can incentivize nodes based on trading resources for payment. There are three main components of the Swarm storage protocol: chunks, references, and manifests. Chunks are the fundamental unit of storage and retrieval in Swarm: pieces of data that have a maximum size of 4K, linked to an address. References are unique identifiers of a file that can be used by a frontend client to retrieve the contents. Finally, a manifest is a data structure that describes a file collection along with paths and corresponding hashes to retrieve content. Using Swarm makes it possible to distribute data across the network and to replicate redundancy in a decentralized fashion (using nodes) without having to host a centralized server. Multiple nodes in the network can be incentivized to replicate chunks and use manifests to reference the data, much like a RAID configuration, eliminating the need for hosting centralized servers.

- Smart contracts: The final major pillar of the Ethereum platform. Provide programmatic access to the blockchain and provides the logical framework to power applications that will eventually run on the world computer.

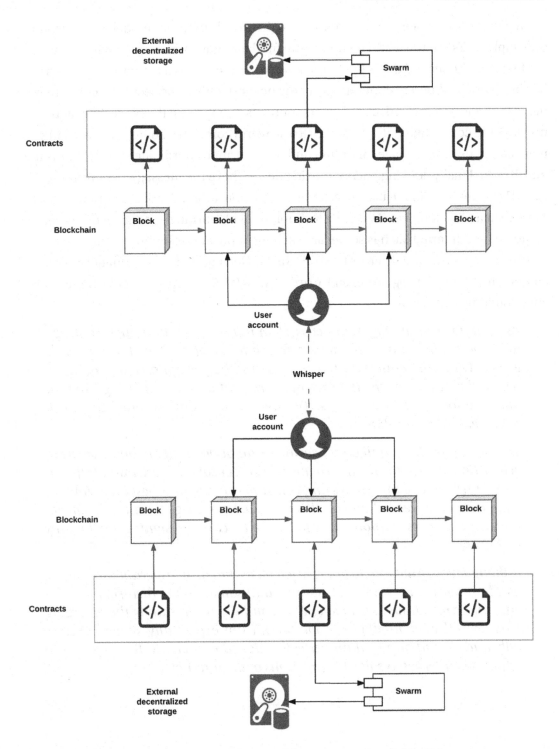

Figure 4-5. *A tiered approach to the world computer model in Ethereum*

In Figure 4-5, we see a tiered approach to the world computer model. User accounts (or simply users) on the world computer are fundamental entities, therefore they are the first tier. The second tier is the blockchain, which serves as a communication serial bus between the different components in the network; this is the second tier. The third tier is the logical framework called smart contracts that lives on the blockchain and provides the computational capabilities to the world computer. Some of these contracts may require external storage for output and use Swarm to coordinate storage; this is the fourth layer. Finally, looking back at the first tier, we have the message-passing protocol called Whisper to facilitate user-to-user or application-to-application communication. More than a philosophical vision or a technological blueprint, the concept of a world computer and Internet 3.0 has some far-reaching implications for how content is controlled and distributed across the Web. Taylor Gerring from Ethereum talks very eloquently (`https://blog.ethereum.org/2014/08/18/building-decentralized-web/`) about building this dream:

> *As economics of the Ethereum ecosystem mature such that open contracts for lowest-rate storage develop, a free market of content hosting could evolve. Given the nature and dynamics of P2P applications, popular content will readily scale as the swarm shares, rather than suffering from the buckling load of siloed servers. The net result is that popular content is delivered faster, not slower.*

> *This metamorphosis will offer developers an opportunity to build the next-generation of decentralized, private, secure, censorship-resistant platforms that return control to creators and consumers of the next best idea. Anyone with a dream is free to build on this new class of next-generation decentralized web services without owning a credit card or signing up for any accounts.*

> *Although we are not told to or expected to, we have an imperative to cherish and improve the very shared resources that some wish to disturb, manipulate, and control. Just as no single person fully understands the emerging internet collective intelligence, we should not expect any single entity to fully understand or maintain perfectly aligned motives. Rather, we should rely on the internet to solve the problems of the internet.*

Layer 2 Upgrades

The classic Ethereum protocol and network described in this chapter so far belongs to Layer 1. To reach the ideal world computer model, scalability and security upgrades are needed so that more applications can interact with blockchain and complex code can be executed. These upgrades are all part of Layer 2, which will begin rolling out in 2020. There are four components of Layer 2 that we discuss here: sharding, beacon chain, state channels, and plasma. The explanation for each component will lead to the next one in order.

Sharding

There are three pillars absolutely necessary for blockchain protocols to operate: decentralization (defined as the lack of a central validating authority), scalability (defined as the ability to process more transactions and have high throughput), and security (broadly defined as all nodes running on the same copy of the network). All blockchain implementations suffer from a phenomenon called the scalability trilemma, which claims that only two out of the three pillars can be successfully deployed. Layer 2.0 updates are necessary to Ethereum in order to enable scalability and overcome the trilemma.

Presently, in all known blockchain protocols, every node has to store the entire network state (data describing account balances and contract code), and every node has to process all of the transactions. This provides a large amount of consistency, but also a bottleneck that limits scalability: a blockchain cannot process more transactions than a single node. This has practical consequences; for instance, Bitcoin is limited to three to seven transactions per second. In an attempt to remove this bottleneck, we are faced with the following question: Can we design mechanisms where only a small subset of nodes verifies transactions and still keep the overall network secure? The idea is to split up transaction processing amongst smaller groups of nodes that can verify each transaction in parallel. Even though each group of nodes validates one transaction at a time, the parallel execution can offer incredible scalability benefits.

Sharding is an attempt to answer this design problem. In this solution, the state and history of Ethereum are split into smaller partitions that we call shards. Essentially, in sharding, a large database (or blockchain in this case) is partitioned into smaller, more efficient shards, making the whole network more scalable. A shard is a self-managing partition and has its own transaction history. In simple forms of sharding, the transactions contained in a shard are limited to that shard only. For instance, one DApp can map a set of addresses to one whole shard, so all transactions related to that DApp will remain on that shard. As a result, a whole set of business verticals and applications can run on one shard.

Beacon Chain

Hsiao-Wei Wang has provided an overall architecture diagram for the Ethereum 2.0 system, which is shown in Figure 4-6.

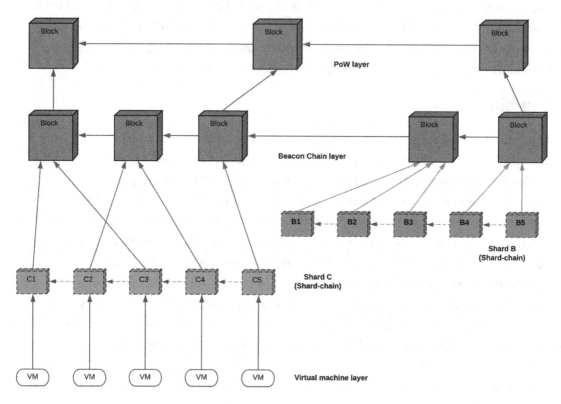

Figure 4-6. *Architectural organization of Ethereum 2.0*

- PoW Chain: This is the part of Ethereum that is currently online and operational. In the Ethereum 2.0 system, this layer will continue to work as-is, and new layers will be added on top.

- Beacon Chain: The proof-of-stake deployment in Ethereum 2.0. Currently under development and will be the first component to be delivered.

- Shards: Shard chain is a composite of the shard along with all transactions belonging to the shard. This enables scalability in the beacon chain. Initially, a limited run-time will begin where the shards will aggregate transactions and reach a consensus on the order of transactions, without executing them.

- Virtual Machines: A VM layer will provide for computation and execution abilities for contracts and transactions on the Ethereum 2.0 platform.

Why do we need a beacon chain? The main function of the beacon chain is to implement and manage the proof-of-stake protocol for the Ethereum blockchain, and for all the shards attached to the blockchain (the shard chains, to be specific). To do this, the beacon chain needs to manage the following aspects: managing validators, nominating block proposer for each shard, organizing validators into committees to vote on proposed blocks, and finally, apply rewards and penalties to validators. The name beacon chain originates from a NIST random beacon generator that provides a source of randomness; we will shortly see why randomness as a property is important to the network.

Managing Validators

In a traditional PoW algorithm, any user can use their hardware to become a miner. However, in Ethereum 2.0, users will stake their ether (ETH) to activate validators. It is important to note that validators are virtual and activated by a staker who puts forth ether. For every 32 ETH staked (put forward), one validator is activated. A major function of the beacon chain is to maintain a set of validators: nodes that have staked the required 32 ETH and are now responsible for running the Ethereum 2.0 protocol.

A node can join the validator set by sending its stake to a contract running on the proof-of-work chain (the current Ethereum blockchain). After an initial check for validity, the stake put forth is frozen and the contract broadcasts an announcement that can be received by all beacon chain clients. At this point, the node is said to have been inducted into the validator set on the beacon chain. Once a node is active, the validator can participate in the Ethereum 2.0 protocol by proposing blocks when chosen by the beacon chain and join committees that vote for the blocks.

Block Proposers

In a proof-of-work protocol, the node that first solves the mining challenge gets to assemble/mine the next block. However, in a proof-of-stake, there is no mining involved. A block proposer is essentially a validator selected pseudo-randomly to build a block. A source of this randomness is necessary to select validators, hence the name beacon chain.

The beacon chain provides a rhythm for the entire Ethereum 2.0 network. It generates blocks every sixteen seconds on the network, as opposed to a proof-of-work protocol that generates a block irregularly, roughly averaging every fifteen seconds. The sixteen-second periods are called slots, and each slot is a chance for a block to be added to the beacon chain. For every slot, a chosen block proposer from the beacon chain gathers all the votes from the validator set for previous blocks, forges the block itself, and publishes it on the blockchain. In the future, each shard will have its own proposer at the beginning of a slot. This shard-block proposer will gather up all the transactions for that shard and form them into a block for voting to commence.

Committees

For this new proof-of-stake protocol in the Ethereum 2.0 blockchain, a crucial source of security is the committees that vote on which blocks will get added to the blockchain and form the true history of the chain. The beacon chain relies on counting the votes (also known as attestations) from its own committee in order to reach consensus over blocks and add them to the blockchain. This committee comprises validators in the system, and their collected attestations create the history of the beacon chain. In the future, there will be provisions for creating smaller subcommittees that only govern one shard at a time. This will allow the sub-committees to confirm the block proposers from the shard and keep a consistent history.

Rewards and Penalties

An important administrative job of the beacon chain is to track and update the deposit that validators stake upon joining the validator set. To that end, validators receive rewards for maintaining network consensus and acting in good faith, which incentivizes them to participate in block committees. If the validators refuse to follow the rules set forth by the validator set, they can be issued a penalty: their initial stake of 32 ETH is slashed, or the validator can be ejected from the system. Additionally, if a validator's balance falls below 16 ETH, the beacon chain will remove it from the validator set.

State Channels

State channelsare a general model to think about interactions that occur on the blockchain, but can be shifted off-chain without compromising the security of the network. A well-studied example of a state channel in Bitcoin is a payment channel: instant, friction-less transaction of payment between two parties, without having to wait for the long confirmation periods on the Bitcoin blockchain. Broadly speaking, the idea of a state channel can be applied to any state-altering interaction happening on a blockchain protocol. Moving a subset of transactions or blockchain interactions off-chain without undermining security can lead to significant improvements in network speed.

There are three basic components of a state channel:

- Locking mechanism: A segment of the blockchain state is locked by a multi-signature smart contract such that a specific set of users must completely agree with the contract in order to update it.

- Off-chain actions: The off-chain users update a local state by signing transactions and constructing blocks that can be submitted to the main blockchain. These transactions are aggregated and updated locally in the payment state channel.

- Unlocking mechanism: The participants submit the aggregate state from the payment channel to the blockchain, and if the contract is satisfied, the state is unlocked on the blockchain from the first step.

Here, the first and third components lock and unlock a partition of the global state and are considered blockchain operations. However, the second component can be done completely off-chain and can involve a large number of transactions/updates. These updates can be made rapidly and retain internal consistency on the payment channel, without needing to involve the blockchain. This step provides scalability and immense performance benefits. In this manner, only the first and the third steps need to be published to the network and confirmed on the blockchain. The transactions in the middle can be carried out at a much faster rate on a state channel.

Plasma

Plasma is a framework for conducting off-chain transactions while using the consensus and security mechanisms from the Ethereum blockchain to sync these transactions. Plasma chains are partially independent sub-chains that are registered with the main Ethereum blockchain. These sub-chains can commit transactions to the main Ethereum blockchain in a batch. In this manner, some of the transactional demand for computational power is relieved from the main blockchain. The nodes can now dedicate this computational power to contracts and other higher-level tasks. Plasma takes the concept of payment channels even further by allowing for the creation of child blockchains attached to the main Ethereum blockchain. These child chains can in turn spawn even more child chains. Essentially, plasma is a framework for many branching blockchains linked to one main blockchain (the Ethereum blockchain in this case).

In terms of security, plasma-based chains rely on the main Ethereum blockchain for consensus and consistency mechanisms. Users can rely on security measures put forth by the Ethereum network in order to redeem any assets decided on the child chain. Plasma chains use MapReduce along with a Merkle tree construct to ensure transactional verification and detect fraud. Additionally, members with a stake in the plasma chain will self-police and monitor the chain. If any disputes arise, they can submit a timestamp or proof of malicious behavior to the main Ethereum blockchain for resolution. Plasma chains include another fraud-prevention mechanism called roll-back. This feature is activated when a double-spending-type activity causes a payment or transaction to fail. When this feature is active, all funds are returned to the state of the network before the attempted fraud. In the proposed implementation, the roll-back process is very cheap computationally for the parent Ethereum blockchain and offers enormous security.

Blockchain-as-a-Service

Microsoft recently announced a partnership with the Ethereum Foundation to launch a blockchain-based service on their cloud platform Azure. This Infrastructure-as-a-Service approach to offering fast and easy implementations of blockchain will allow developers to experiment with new features and deploy DApps at reduced costs. Marley Grey from the Azure Blockchain Engineering team describes how Blockchain-as-a-Service (BaaS) will foster an ecosystem of DApps:

> *Microsoft and ConsenSys are partnering to offer Ethereum Blockchain as a Service (E-BaaS) on Microsoft Azure so Enterprise clients and developers can have a single click cloud based blockchain developer environment. The initial offering contains two tools that allow for rapid development of SmartContract based applications: Ether.Camp—An integrated developer environment, and BlockApps—a private, semi-private Ethereum block-chain environment, can deploy into the public Ethereum environment.*

> *"Ethereum Blockchain as a Service" provided by Microsoft Azure and ConsenSys allows for financial services customers and partners to play, learn, and fail fast at a low cost in a ready-made dev/test/production envi-*

ronment. It will allow them to create private, public and consortium based Blockchain environments using industry leading frameworks very quickly, distributing their Blockchain products with Azure's World Wide distributed (private) platform. That makes Azure a great Dev/Test/Production Environment for Blockchain applications. Surrounding capabilities like Cortana Analytics (machine learning), Power BI, Azure Active Directory, O365 and CRMOL can be integrated into apps launching a new generation of decentralized cross platform applications.

This initial update on BaaS was provided at the end of 2015, and currently a whole ecosystem of Blockchain Labs is flourishing within the Azure DevTest community. The DevTest Labs allow users and developers to explore and test a template designed for a specific use case. In addition, the platform began with Ethereum blockchains, but recently more startups have started to build on Azure, offering new services such as Emercoin, which offered a SSH service, PokiDot, with their healthcare-oriented blockchain called Dokchain. Over time, more startups have begun using Azure as the standard to run a blockchain and build applications on top. With the integration of intelligence services such as Cortana, it may become easier to develop oracles that can sign incoming data from external streams (such as IoT devices) and provide a level of integrity.

Note   Two developments from Microsoft in the BaaS space are noteworthy here. The first is the introduction of Cryptlets, a secure middleware to interface with external events for building enterprise smart contracts. The second development is the Coco framework, an open source system for building a high-throughput network on top of a blockchain, where nodes and actors are explicitly declared and controlled. By design, Coco is compatible with any ledger protocol, and would allow enterprises to build production-ready blockchain networks. More about Microsoft's platform will be presented in a later chapter.

Decentralized Applications

We alluded to decentralized applications (or DApps) in our discussion of Whisper, but we will talk about them in more depth here. A decentralized app is a serverless application that runs on the Ethereum stack and interfaces with the end user via an HTML/JavaScript frontend that can make calls to the backend stack. Classically, a mobile or web app has a backend running on centralized dedicated servers; however, a DApp has its backend code running on a decentralized peer-to-peer network. A simplistic model of how a DApp operates on the blockchain is shown in Figure 4-7.

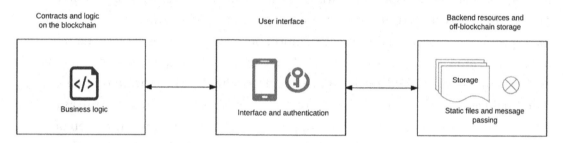

Figure 4-7. *Structure of a DApp*

As seen in Figure 4-7, the user interface is often written in HTML or JavaScript and is the only component loaded on a user device. The interface makes backend calls to the blockchain in order to execute a particular contract and also to the backend resources such as Swarm or Whisper if external storage is needed or when the application needs to communicate with other apps. If a traditional app comprises a frontend and a server running the backend, then a DApp running on the Ethereum stack would be made from a frontend and contracts running on the blockchain. DApps usually have their own set of associated contracts on the blockchain that are used to encode business logic and allow persistent storage of their consensus-critical state. Recall that all code on the Ethereum stack runs within an EVM, which keeps track of step-by-step operations and charges gas to the owner of a contract. This prevents DApp developers from running too many operations on the blockchain or bloating it by storing data directly on the blockchain.

Note   To briefly review, the DApp stack relies on decentralized storage (provided by Swarm-like architecture) for user data or app data, on the blockchain for contract logic and transactional operations, and on the frontend for the end user. The frontend interface makes calls to the blockchain to specific contracts running the decentralized application based on user actions.

How does the backend of a DApp pull static content for the frontend, such as JS from the Ethereum stack to static content and receive the updated global state from the blockchain? Let's look at an example using IPFS as storage to understand these backend calls (Figure 4-8):

- The backend code is essentially a contract that executes on the blockchain given the appropriate amount of resources.

- Some application needs to use a persistent database to host static content used in the app; we can rely on IPFS that stores static files, hosted throughout the network on several nodes.

- Hashes from IPFS are delivered to the DApp, and the contract's execution updates the global state, which is delivered to the DApp from the Ethereum stack.

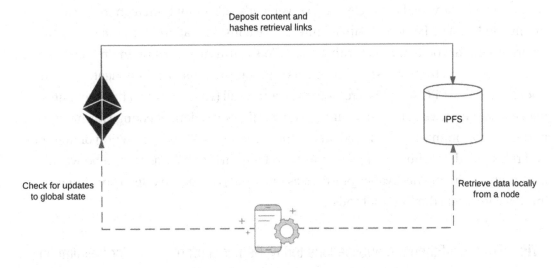

Figure 4-8. *A simple schematic of backend calls made by a DApp*

In Figure 4-8, the blockchain can deposit content to an IPFS-like system on one of the nodes, and the hashes can be made available to the app for retrieval when necessary. The app can request updates from the blockchain on the global state as it affects the app running on a device. Finally, as needed, the app can retrieve and download the full content from the decentralized storage to the user device. Splitting up roles in this manner allows for more-innovative user interfaces as a developer can switch it out without having to change the backend at all.

Geth and Mist

There are two more tools we need to discuss briefly that play a role in DApp development. Geth is the command-line interface (written in Go-lang) for running a full node on the Ethereum network. Using Geth, you can interact with the Ethereum blockchain and perform tasks such as the following:

- Mine ether on the network

- Transfer funds between addresses

- Create contracts and send transactions

- Use the DApps API

Geth comes with two interfaces that are used in development: the JavaScript console with *web3.js* library, and the JSON-RPC server. Let's talk about both technologies briefly. Geth can be launched with an interactive console that provides the JS run-time environment for you to interact with a node. This run-time environment includes the *web3* library, which can construct contracts and transactions to be propagated to the node. The JSON-RPC server is a remote procedure call (RPC) protocol that facilitates data exchange between the node and its clients (JSON is a data-exchange format that nodes use to communicate with clients). More precisely, RPC is a collection of methods and rules that define how data (commands and output) can be transferred between a node and a client. The JavaScript API uses the *web3.js* library to offer a convenient interface for using the RPC methods.

Tip   For most Ethereum applications today, Geth is a prerequisite for installation as a command-line tool. Often, during the installation, Geth is provided as an add-on so that a user doesn't have to download and install it separately.

Mist is the official Ethereum wallet application. In early discussions, Mist was conceptualized to be a standalone app store–type browser for DApps, but that vision has evolved. In order to interact with the Ethereum blockchain, we need a blockchain client like Geth. This client is responsible for broadcasting transactions to the network, mining ether, signing transactions and deploying smart contracts. Most end users are not comfortable with using a command-line interface, so a wrapper such as Mist was made to be the frontend interface. Mist connects to Geth in the background and serves as an interface for the wallet software to the user. Additionally, Mist provides an interface for writing and deploying smart contracts, or DApps. The wallet software integrates payments seamlessly for contract deployment.

Eventually, the most powerful entities on the Ethereum network using Geth and Mist will be decentralized autonomous organizations (DAOs), which are essentially automated companies powered by smart contracts that run on the Ethereum network. We will end our journey of exploring Ethereum here and pick up our discussion of DAOs in the following chapter.

Summary

In this chapter, we introduced Ethereum, one of the biggest alternate currencies competing against Bitcoin. In recent years, it has gained a lot of attention from developers and investors. We began our discussion with a broad overview of what Ethereum is in comparison to Bitcoin. We talked about accounts and function calls as being foundational to Ethereum. We then provided some more depth to the ideas of accounts as entities on the blockchain. After that, we discussed the use of gas on Ethereum for smart contract execution, how internal storage is adapted to work with Merkle-Patricia trees, and the concept of internal state for an account. After that, we talked about EVM and how smart contracts are executed on the blockchain. Then, we discussed a model for writing smart contracts using Solidity and Vyper, along with developer resources to rapidly prototype smart contracts. This led to a discussion about the world computer model as it applies to Ethereum components such as IPFS and Whisper. Finally, the major technical focus of this chapter was the Layer 2 upgrades that are being rolled out for the Ethereum network. We ended the discussion with a short review of DApps and the Blockchain-as-a-Service model, which we will expand on in a later chapter.

References

The main reference material used to prepare this chapter was Ethereum Homestead developer documentation (`https://ethdocs.org/en/latest/contracts-and-transactions/developer-tools.html`) and Solidity documentation. A detailed list of references is given at the end of the book.

- Mukhopadhyay, M. *Ethereum Smart Contract Development: Build blockchain-based decentralized applications using solidity*. Packt Publishing Ltd; 2018 Feb 23.

- Antonopoulos, A. M., and G. Wood. *Mastering ethereum: building smart contracts and dapps*. O'Reilly Media; 2018 Nov 13.

- Nizamuddin, N., K. Salah, M. A. Azad, J. Arshad, and M. H. Rehman. "Decentralized document version control using ethereum blockchain and IPFS." *Computers & Electrical Engineering*. 2019 Jun 1; 76: 183–197.

- Wohrer, M., and U. Zdun. "Smart contracts: security patterns in the ethereum ecosystem and solidity." In *2018 International Workshop on Blockchain Oriented Software Engineering* (IWBOSE) 2018 Mar 20 (pp. 2–8). IEEE.

- Mavridou, A., and A. Laszka. "Designing secure Ethereum smart contracts: A finite state machine based approach." In *International Conference on Financial Cryptography and Data Security*, 2018 Feb 26 (pp. 523–540). Springer, Berlin, Heidelberg.

CHAPTER 5

Decentralized Organizations

Bitcoin can be thought of as the first prototypical Decentralized Autonomous Organization (DAO). It created a network-based ecosystem of participants who contribute computational power toward a singular goal. In Bitcoin, the underlying protocol created a financial service that rewards miners for providing verification services, and this setup became a rudimentary decentralized organization. In this chapter, we will focus on more-complex organizations created on the blockchain with Aragon. Aragon is a decentralized application (DApp) that lets anyone create and manage different kinds of organizations (NGOs, non-profits, foundations) on the Ethereum blockchain. In the early days of Ethereum, creating a DAO and implementing even the most basic functions required complicated smart contracts and Solidity code. Aragon has simplified this process. It implements the basic features of an organization in a base template that gets deployed whenever a user instantiates a company. Most of the traditional features such as a cap table, voting abilities, fundraising, and accounting are offered in the Aragon template as a decentralized counterpart running on the blockchain. In addition, an Aragon company can be customized in a very granular fashion and extended with new modules that can be added to a company's existing smart contracts. Aragon enables different organizations to control the level of trust built into them.

© Vikram Dhillon, David Metcalf, and Max Hooper 2021
V. Dhillon et al., *Blockchain Enabled Applications*, https://doi.org/10.1007/978-1-4842-6534-5_5

We begin this chapter by introducing the concept of a decentralized organization. We rely on Ralph Merkle's framework to describe what a DAO requires to operate and how Aragon implements all the theoretical constructs as apps. Then, we introduce the technology stack that powers Aragon and the derivative frameworks under development. After obtaining a better understanding of Aragon, we present a special case of fundraising and social venture development with Aragon. This brings us to the heart of this chapter: a thorough walkthrough of how to create, set up, deploy, and manage a DAO on Aragon. In this tutorial, we have three topics. The first topic shows the reader how to set up MetaMask, a wallet for connecting to Aragon. The second topic introduces templates for organizations and how you can create and deploy a DAO. The final topic provides a run-through of how to perform day-to-day operations in a DAO, as well as advanced features. This chapter follows the structure of a conceptual background leading to practical implementation advice. We hope that by the end of the walkthrough you feel comfortable setting up a wallet and experimenting on the Ethereum test net with your own DAO.

Aragon Stack and Aragon Network Token (ANT)

Aragon is an ecosystem for building a governance system for Ethereum-based decentralized organizations. From a technical perspective, Aragon is a full-service stack for building and managing decentralized organizations, and it treats them as multiple processes running concurrently on an operating system. Even though Aragon has thousands of decentralized autonomous organizations (DAOs) running at a time, here, we will keep our focus limited to just one DAO. Before we delve deeper into Aragon, let's describe the concept of a DAO in simpler terms. **A DAO is a blockchain entity built on a consensus of decisions by its members.** A DAO widens the concept of consensus inherent to the blockchain to include decisions and choices made by members of a DAO that have a stake in it (usually in the form of DAO tokens). As such, a DAO is built with automation at its core and members at the periphery that rely on a majority-vote-based consensus to make decisions for the organization. Although this approach to understanding a DAO is a general descriptor, it is incomplete. Perhaps a better approach to defining a DAO would be through the functions it performs. The concept for a DAO was originally derived from Bitcoin, which might be viewed as the first prototype for a DAO.

Note   The simplest functional unit on the Aragon network is a DAO, and therefore the majority of our discussion is focused around a minimal use case. Aragon provides a base template that can be used to set up a DAO, and you can modify this template to set up a custom set of rules. Other types of organizations (such as NGOs or non-profits) are built on the base template with significant modifications that allow new modus operandi. Additionally, throughout the remainder of this chapter, the terms *DAO*, *Company*, or *Organization* may be used interchangeably to represent the same concept.

Ralph Merkle talks about a DAO as an entity that owns internal property that has value, can update its internal state, is responsive to the members, and runs smart contracts. These are some of the most basic functions that any DAO should be able to perform; however, currently there are no compliance standards (like the ERC20 for tokens) for DAOs. Aragon implements Merkle's ideas through a system of *organs* that have specific functions in the day-to-day operation of a DAO. At the core of every DAO model is a *kernel*. The kernel then uses a set of organs to carry out most of the daily activities. Let us review the organs implemented by Aragon:

- **Kernel:** Coordinator of all other components in the DAO. To that end, the kernel only provides two features, upgradeability and authorization.

  - Taking a long-term view, organizations on Aragon need to be secure and modular so that they can be extended with new features. It is essential to provide a mechanism for any organization on Aragon to upgrade itself, including the kernel. As such, the kernel has the ability to upgrade itself and any other apps that rely on it.

  - The kernel needs to keep track of all the addresses involved in the DAO, the permissions assigned to them and, in turn, the actions that can be performed by those addresses. This authorization system is also called an Access Control List (ACL), and it protects the users of a DAO against privilege escalation attacks.

- **Meta organ:** A self-aware (in terms of internal state) and self-actionable organ that is responsible for updating the DAO internally in response to actions by the members, or externally. This organ also maintains a global registry of organs operating within the kernel.

- **Vault organ:** The vault organ serves as a collective wallet for the DAO. It stores the funds owned by the DAO as tokens and approves any spending requests.

- **Token organ:** The token organ specifically deals with governance tokens allocated to the members of the DAO. This organ also contains the operational logic for adding new types of tokens or replacing/removing older tokens.

- **Dispatch organ:** A validator organ that determines whether a requested action or a transaction can be carried out on behalf of the requestor. This can be done through an oracle, or programmed logic that filters requests based on specific criteria. The outcome of the dispatch organ is a simple pass or fail. If an action fails, it will not be carried out. However, if an action or transaction passes, it will be dispatched to a more apt organ for processing or execution. The dispatch organ also maintains a list of priorities for each request to be triaged and directed appropriately.

- **Applications organ:** The smart contract collective that operates at the core of a DAO. The applications running in this organ are sandboxed from the remainder of the organization, but most of the business logic resides in this organ. Aragon provides a basic set of Ethereum contracts responsible for default actions, but this organ is extensible. New applications or modules can be added to the organization to increase functionality to satisfy specific use cases.

Note   The organs described are essentially theoretical constructs that should be implemented by a DAO that is modular and extensible. The formal implementation of these organs as apps will be better demonstrated during the DAO tutorial section.

The walkthrough of a DAO presented later in this chapter will demonstrate how these organs are applied in practice. In the remainder of this section, we will provide an overview of the Aragon technology stack. The following are all components of the ecosystem that have enabled rapid development and prototyping of DAOs:

- **aragonCLI:** Command-line interface to Aragon. Provides all the functionality needed to set up and deploy a DAO with more granular control over the global parameters of the template. In addition, more-advanced features such as deploying custom tokens, integration with IPFS, and accessing the package manager are available.

- **Aragon client:** The web client that brings Aragon to the user for creating and deploying DAOs to the Ethereum blockchain. All the day-to-day management and operations occur within this client. Additionally, all the apps, permissions, and voting are accessible through the Aragon client. This client is essentially all of Aragon's services offered to the end user.

- **aragonPM:** A package manager for Aragon that connects to community-built repositories, enables upgradability, and distributes the latest versions of packages that form the Aragon client. In the near future, updates through aragonPM will allow for the core components and smart contract code to be updated on the fly, without any disruptions in service for the DAO. It also connects with the aragonCLI and allows for a traditional CLI-based approach to installing packages, similar to package managers in Linux distributions.

- **aragonUI:** The design language standardized for all apps running on Aragon. Developers and designers can adopt this UI scheme and design language to make their apps appear native to Aragon. The theming engine and the UI components are detailed in the aragonUI guide (`https://ui.aragon.org/`).

- **App Center:** A marketplace for developers to publish apps that can be used by any DAO. These are usually open source; however, being tied to the blockchain and having a token economy, novel payment mechanisms can be implemented by DAOs for access.

- **Access Control List:** A master list of all permissions and actions assigned to every address in a DAO. Contained within the kernel.

- **Aragon Court:** An arbitration layer that deals with subjective disputes and conflicts occurring on the Aragon platform. The court handles cases with higher complexity that require human intervention in the form of jurors. The jurors stake a special token called ANJ (Aragon Network Jurors), which allows them to join a jury. Successfully adjudicating a conflict results in a reward in the form of network fees proportional to ANJ staked.

- **Meta-DAO:** The Aragon project itself is run as a DAO, with the token ANT on the Ethereum blockchain. Users can purchase a stake in ANT and influence the direction of Aragon itself. All the features afforded by Aragon to the DAOs running on it also apply to the Meta-DAO itself, only at a much larger scale.

Aragon for Social Good: Fundraising App

Aragon has made it easier to create a DAO, and the addition of a fundraising app enables social entrepreneurship use cases to be built. In this section, we briefly describe how fundraising campaigns work in Aragon and the new potential for blockchain-based social ventures.

Raising a round of funding on the Aragon blockchain is very different from traditional fundraising. Currently, there are two options for fundraising implemented in Aragon. The first one involves raising a round from a specific investor in return for a stake in your company. The second option is to do a crowdsale where any participant of the network can buy stock in your company. The core idea is simple: once your DAO is operational, you can issue shares, and then you can offer a class of those shares to an investor in return for ether. These shares can be offered either to an individual investor or more broadly to any participant in the network during a crowdsale. There are significant differences between traditional fundraising and the fundraising done through a DAO. Let's take a look at a few of these differences.

Fundraising on a DAO requires more structure so as to remain decentralized in decision-making. The project team leading the fundraiser is represented as the council in a DAO. The council members have a separate token and enforce their decisions through voting that resembles a multisig account (multiple signatures needed to perform an action). It is important to note that the privileges of council members are limited by design to reduce their influence over the DAO members, and over the fundraiser. The council has four main responsibilities: deciding who should be included in the council, opening up the pre-sale campaign, transferring assets owned by the DAO into the vault, and opening votes for DAO members to pass resolutions that affect the organization.

Note   There is a distinction between council members and *regular* DAO members. This concept is confusing to describe in abstract terms, so let us work with this example: the Council members will be represented by a token called High Table (HTBL), and HTBL will be used in transactions to designate all council responsibilities. DAO members use tokens that are purchased during the pre-sale (opening event for the fundraiser). These members, also known as token holders, will be represented by a separate token, Continental (CTL), and CTL will be used to influence the DAO and its daily activities.

DAO members are defined as non-council token holders that provide input toward the overall direction and decision-making of the DAO; enjoy a variety of privileges, including redeeming tokens bought in pre-sale and exchanging them for ETH; deciding which apps are installed and what permissions are updated; deciding how much of the funds gets transferred by the council into the vault; and deciding how the fundraising fees and collateralization setting should be updated.

Pre-sale marks the beginning of a fundraiser and is a crucial event with a goal of selling a pre-specified number of tokens (following our example, we would sell CTL tokens). During pre-sale, anyone on the Ethereum network can purchase CTL tokens by first buying DAI. DAI is a Stablecoin on Ethereum that attempts to maintain a value of $1.00 USD. In pre-sale setup, an organization can set a price for their new tokens in DAI, and buyers will convert their DAI to purchase this new token. If the pre-sale event reaches the pre-specified goal, it is considered successful, and now the trading period can begin for the new token. Otherwise, the fundraiser is considered to have failed and all invested capital is returned to involved parties. More advanced options on token trading, such as cliff vesting, are available in the Fundraising app; however, this is beyond the scope of this chapter.

Identity Management Use Case

The identity management use case in Aragon is no longer under active development, which was explained by Aragon devs as having been a bridge until they could extend and generalize more existing features:

> *Although Aragon previously integrated with Keybase, the existence of ENS now allows us to build an identity system that avoids relying on a centralized 3rd party. In doing so, we lost a number of features that were previously provided by Keybase, such as off-chain storage (e.g., profile photos or other service identifiers). In the future, we plan to integrate Aragon ID with decentralized off-chain storage services, such as Swarm or IPFS, to provide such functionality.*

> *In light of this, Aragon ID is a simple identity system to bridge the gap until such projects are ready. It leverages the existing ENS infrastructure to securely provide two-way, first-in-first-served mappings of addresses to* `<name>.aragonid.eth` *identifiers. Afterwards, users will be able to resolve and reverse-resolve any* `<name>.aragonid.eth` *to an address and trust that their name registrations are safely in their own control.*

Editor Note   We decided to keep this use case because it provides value in highlighting the thinking behind an approach toward identity and building a hybrid organization where users are identified, yet the organization is powered by smart contracts.

The concept of identity is a conundrum for crypto-technologies because it requires a certain level of trust to be inherent in the network architecture. Most generalized approaches toward integrating identity in a consensus-based system usually involve some variation of cryptographic proofs and signatures. In Aragon, an external service called Keybase along with a registry contract were used to establish a "trustless" two-way verification scheme. The logic behind this scheme is very straightforward: establish that a particular address belongs to you, and then verify that your username owns the address. How do these two statements reconcile in a functional setting?

Let's introduce the two components that made a two-way bridge possible. In simple terms, Keybase is a public–private keypair management service with OAuth integrations that allow a user to authenticate and verify accounts. Keybase can serve as a centralized hub for a user to link and verify external accounts. For instance, after creating an account on Keybase, the public profile of a user can display all their linked social media accounts, establishing their legitimacy and connection. The second component is a registry contract that provides an account-to-address association mechanism from within the Aragon network. The two-way bridge is formed from using the address (linked to an account on the network) to cryptographically sign a file that can then be hosted on Keybase (linked to user identity through various social media integrations).

Note   It is crucial to keep in mind that in Aragon, identity is an opt-in feature. The breadth of use cases developed for Aragon range from providing complete anonymity, such as in the case of a DAO, to full usernames integrating Keybase for a next-generation blockchain company.

So, how would a user make their identity available to the two-way verification scheme? The workflow in Keybase Registry 2.0 was simplified to one simple step: upload the signed proof to KBFS. This introduces a few new components, as follows:

- **Keybase filesystem (KBFS):** A cryptographically secure local and cloud storage directory. KBFS only allows the owner of the directory to add new files, and these files are made available publicly. In KBFS, every file added to the directory is automatically signed by the owner's private key, and the signature can be verified by anyone through Keybase.

- **Signed proof:** Aragon uses a standard proof of identity signed by the user and uploaded to the KBFS public directory. There are four components of this proof: the username on Keybase, the Ethereum account address owned by the user, a string or comment by the user, and finally the public key of the signature. Anyone who wishes to verify an identity can obtain this proof file and use a function such as getUsername(args) to perform a username reverse lookup given the account address in the proof.

- **Oraclize:** The reverse lookup is an on-chain verification process performed through the registry contract within the Aragon network. For Keybase lookup, a data carrier service called Oraclize is utilized. Oraclize requests the signature for a given Keybase username and creates a mapping of the username to an Ethereum account address. The signature on this proof file should validate with the user's public key on the network. Oraclize performs an on-chain check to verify the proof signature and ensure that the mapping is legitimate. The party initiating this verification on behalf of another user also has to pay for the steps, including Oraclize reference calls.

- **Keybase Resolver:** The Ethereum Name Service (ENS) allows us to resolve human-readable links into Ethereum addresses. Recently, Aragon has begun testing a Keybase resolver that will map callbacks to usernames into addresses such that `john.keybase.eth ->` `0x99...cx88`. This simplifies the reverse lookups and username references throughout the network.

Now that we have a basic understanding of Aragon, the components that make a DAO, and how fundraising works, the remainder of this chapter will focus on a walkthrough of how to create and manage a DAO on Aragon.

DAO/Company Walkthrough

In this section, we will go through the process of creating a DAO and becoming familiar with the main DAO-focused operations in Aragon. For the sake of simplicity, we will only have two entities (accounts) participating in this DAO. This walkthrough is split into three topics:

- **Setting up the DAO environment:** We will introduce the participants of this DAO, see how to create a wallet with MetaMask, and get familiar with the interface.

- **Setting up the DAO:** After MetaMask is set up, we will connect the account to the Ethereum test net and use it to set up a DAO.

- **Daily operations:** Once the DAO is set up, we will walk through basic operations such as minting new tokens, voting, and making withdrawals. Then, we will dive into more advanced features, such as DAO finances and adding new app permissions that offer a whole new level of fine-tuning for governance of your company.

Topic 1: Setting Up the DAO Environment

Aragon can be used to create DAOs completely online (without downloading a client) through the website (`https://aragon.org/`). Currently, there are two components to Aragon: a DAO-maker (Aragon Core) and a wallet (MetaMask). The DAO-maker component of Aragon turns into a full-fledged dashboard for managing the DAO, and all operations related to the DAO can be carried out on the apps available through the dashboard. The second component is MetaMask: a digital wallet designed as a plug-in for Chrome or Firefox browsers to interface with the Ethereum blockchain and make it accessible to pragmatic daily users. MetaMask is one of the four wallet options available that can integrate with the Aragon UI, and we will be using it throughout this chapter as it requires minimal setup time. Let's begin with setting up MetaMask, followed by connecting Aragon to MetaMask and then connecting to the faucet (that can disperse test coins). The first steps involve adding the MetaMask extension to Chrome. Once installed, the opening screen should look like Figure 5-1.

Note   Ad blockers and pop-up blockers will interfere with MetaMask. For the reader to follow along with this tutorial, you may need to disable them for the Aragon website and the faucet.

Welcome to MetaMask

Connecting you to Ethereum and the Decentralized Web.
We're happy to see you.

1. Get Started

Figure 5-1. *The MetaMask opening screen*

MetaMask will ask you to set up a wallet before using the add-on. Click on (1) to begin; this will bring you to the setup screen shown in Figure 5-2. There are two options available: create a new wallet (the option we will choose) or import a wallet (used in the instance where you already have a MetaMask wallet, or if you want to import the wallet from a different browser). Click on (2) as shown in Figure 5-2, and this will bring you to creating a password for the wallet. The password comes with a backup phrase that you can use to recover your wallet in case you lose your password.

Note   This secret phrase is also required if you want to import your wallet into MetaMask.

New to MetaMask?

Figure 5-2. *Setup screen. Select (2) to set up a password for your MetaMask wallet*

After creating a wallet password, you'll be taken to the secret phrase screen. This phrase is used for wallet recovery in case you lose your password. Click on (3) to reveal the secret phrase as shown in Figure 5-3, and then write this down. On the next screen, you will be required to re-enter your secret phrase, and then you will get a confirmation that your wallet has been set up. After setup, you can click on the MetaMask icon to see the full wallet view, as shown in Figure 5-4.

Note   As previously mentioned, there are ways to connect with Aragon and Ethereum blockchain through hardware wallets that offer superior-grade security and do not require a secret phrase. A more comprehensive review is provided elsewhere in the references.

Secret Backup Phrase

Your secret backup phrase makes it easy to back up and restore your account.

WARNING: Never disclose your backup phrase. Anyone with this phrase can take your Ether forever.

Tips:

Store this phrase in a password manager like 1Password.

Write this phrase on a piece of paper and store in a secure location. If you want even more security, write it down on multiple pieces of paper and store each in 2 - 3 different locations.

Memorize this phrase.

Download this Secret Backup Phrase and keep it stored safely on an external encrypted hard drive or storage medium.

CLICK HERE TO REVEAL SECRET WORDS

3.

Remind me later   Next   **4.**

Figure 5-3. *Secret phrase for password recovery. Click on (3) to reveal the phrase and write it down. Click on (4) to continue*

The wallet view is presented in Figure 5-4. Let's quickly review the information presented here. Note that the first change we made was switching to the Ethereum test net, specifically Rinkeby (5). This test net is compatible with Aragon, and we will be doing all our transactions here, instead of on the Ethereum main net. Once you feel comfortable with using Aragon, you can switch over to the main net. (6) shows you the account that you are currently using. MetaMask allows a user to hold multiple accounts (addresses) in the same wallet. As such, the current account address is given by (7), and this is the account in use. Next is the current balance for this current account, given by (8). The wallet software offers two basic functions (9), including sending ETH to another address and depositing ETH into the wallet through a direct deposit from an exchange or from a test faucet that we will be using. Finally, a history of all transactions made through the wallet is presented in (10).

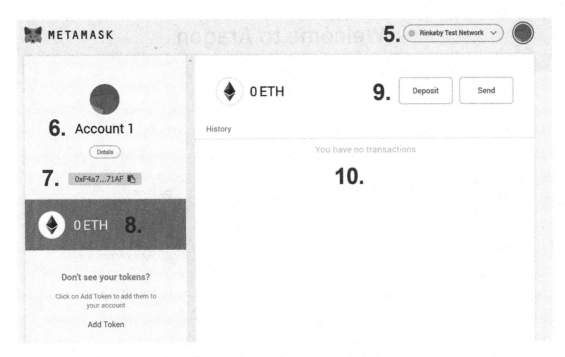

Figure 5-4. *MetaMask wallet main screen*

Now that we have MetaMask set up, let's talk about interfacing it with Aragon on the Ethereum test net. You can access the Rinkeby test net at `https://rinkeby.aragon.org/`; this will be our interface for building a DAO. The interface is shown in Figure 5-5, where (11) confirms that we are on the test net and allows us to switch to the Ethereum main net. (12) starts the process of creating your DAO, but before we do that, let's link our account.

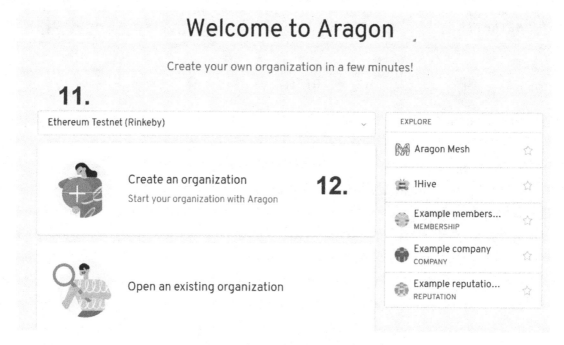

Figure 5-5. *Interfacing with Ethereum test net*

On the right upper-corner of the screen, you will see a *Connect account* button; clicking on it will reveal four options, as shown in Figure 5-6. Frame is a desktop-native Ethereum provider that allows for multiple different wallets to interact with the DAO (including hardware wallets). Fortmatic and Portis are services providing electronic Ethereum wallets with direct exchange (to buy Ethereum with Fiat) options available.

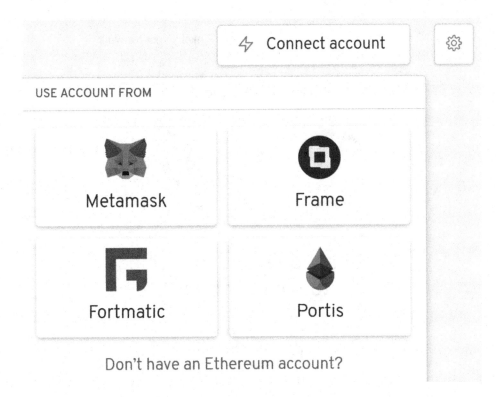

Figure 5-6. *Connecting MetaMask account to Aragon*

Once you click on MetaMask, you will be asked for permission to connect the wallet to Aragon, as shown in Figure 5-7. After accepting the permission, the right-hand side of the screen should show the wallet address and green text reading *Connected to Rinkeby*.

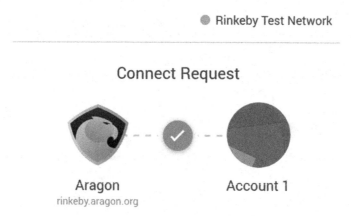

Connect Request

Aragon
rinkeby.aragon.org

Account 1

Aragon would like to connect to your account

This site is requesting access to view your
current account address. Always make sure you
trust the sites you interact with.
Learn more.

Figure 5-7. *Connecting Aragon and MetaMask wallet*

Once the wallet is connected to Aragon, we need to obtain some test ETH for setting
up a DAO. Even on a test net, actions such as signing contracts at every step of setting up
a DAO will cost gas to carry out. As a result, we can use a faucet to send some test ETH
that have no real value but can be used for our purposes. The faucet we will be using can
only send ETH every 24 hours and sends a maximum of 0.2 ETH per use,

linked here: `https://testnet.help/en/ethfaucet/rinkeby`. There are more official faucets available, but this one does not require extensive social media verification. The faucet screen is shown in Figure 5-8. The address for your MetaMask wallet goes in (13), and the amount is optional (14) because the faucet will only dispense a maximum of 0.2 ETH. You can add a message to your transaction, which will be visible on the test net blockchain explorer. You do need to pick a reason for using the faucet; select any of the presented reasons in (15) and accept the conditions (16). Once done, solve the captcha (17) and hit the *Claim* button to have 0.2 ETH dispensed to your MetaMask wallet.

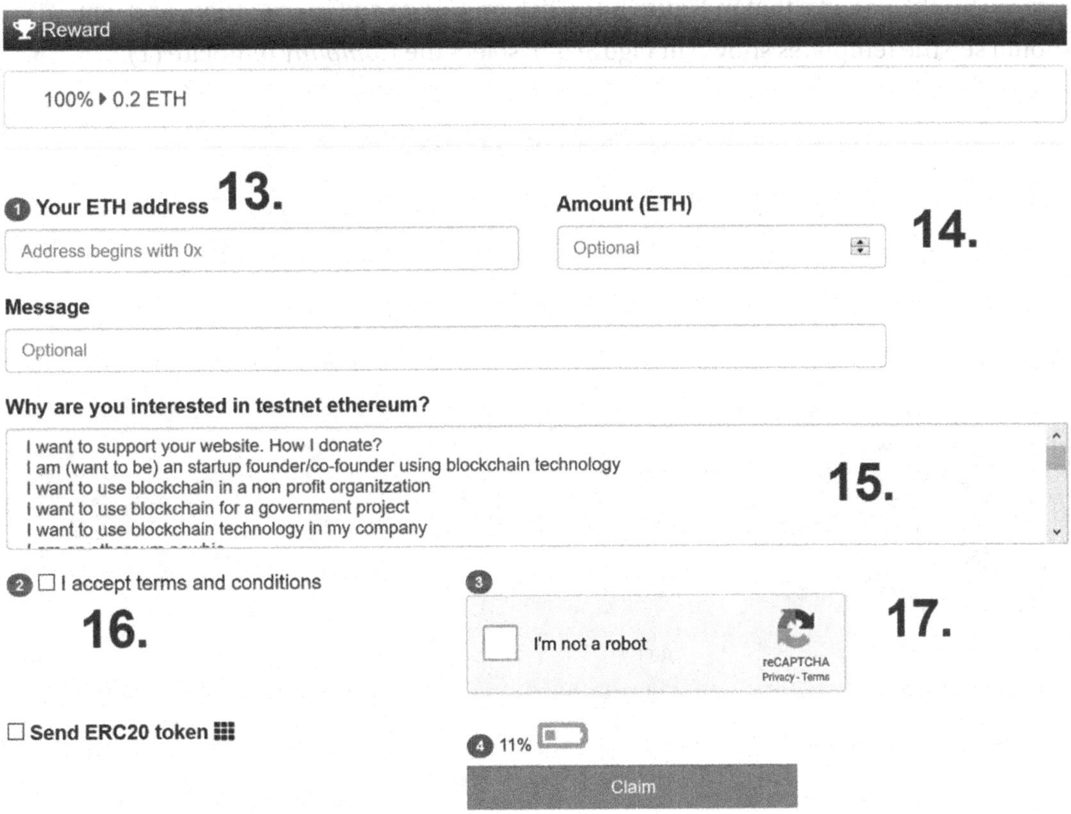

Figure 5-8. *Rinkeby test net faucet*

Now that the faucet is connected to the wallet, and you have some initial funds, you can start with the DAO. You may want to visit the faucet another day to get enough ETH to explore other DAO features/templates.

Topic 2: Setting Up the DAO

Aragon provides a few starter templates to make DAOs for specific use cases; the two we will be focusing on in this chapter are the Company template and the Fundraiser template. These templates are open source and available on GitHub. Any developer can extend the templates with new parameters and create new templates better suited for a job.

Once your wallet is connected to Aragon and the faucet has dispersed 0.2 ETH to your wallet, you can move ahead with creating a DAO. The Aragon DAO-maker for the Ethereum test net is available at `https://rinkeby.aragon.org/`, and your starting screen should look like that in Figure 5-5. Click on *Create an Organization*, and you should see the templates shown in Figure 5-9; select the *Company* template (1).

Select template

Create your organization with our pre-configured templates

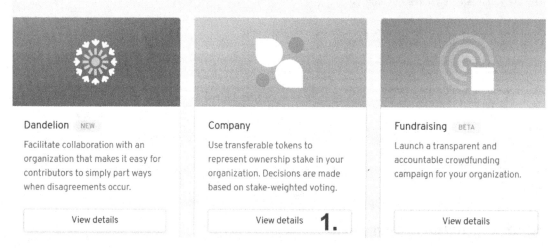

Dandelion NEW

Facilitate collaboration with an organization that makes it easy for contributors to simply part ways when disagreements occur.

View details

Company

Use transferable tokens to represent ownership stake in your organization. Decisions are made based on stake-weighted voting.

View details **1.**

Fundraising BETA

Launch a transparent and accountable crowdfunding campaign for your organization.

View details

Figure 5-9. *Open source DAO templates available in Aragon*

Selecting the Company template brings you to the overview of the template shown in Figure 5-10. The template comes with a set of apps installed as shown in (2), which we will review shortly. Click on (3) to begin the setup.

Company

Use transferable tokens to represent ownership stake in your organization. Decisions are made based on stake-weighted voting.

USER GUIDE
help.aragon.org/article/30-create-a-new-company-organization

SOURCE CODE
GitHub

REGISTRY
aragonpm.eth

Use this template

Template configuration

INCLUDED APPS

  Voting   ✓ Included
  Tokens   ✓ Included
  Finance   ✓ Included

OPTIONAL APPS

  Agent

2.

3.

Figure 5-10. *DAO Company template overview*

Clicking on (3) moves you forward to claim an organizational name. Aragon uses the Ethereum Name Service, analogous to the DNS system that refers a web address to your DAO. We will use the following name for our organization, as shown in Figure 5-11.

Claim a name

ORGANIZATION'S NAME

bestorganization   .aragonid.eth

Aragon uses the Ethereum Name Service (ENS) to assign names to organizations. The name you choose will be mapped to your organization's Ethereum address and cannot be changed after you launch your organization.

← Back   Next: Configure template

Figure 5-11. *Naming our DAO. Click on Configure template to move forward*

The next step is setting up the voting preferences for the DAO. These preferences will dictate how most decisions within the DAO are made. Let us discuss the voting configuration, shown in Figure 5-12. (4) declares the percentage of votes that are needed within the organization for a given resolution to pass. We will stick to the default 50 percent. (5) sets the minimum percentage of votes needed for a resolution to be considered valid, in case a majority vote is not established. For instance, we have this parameter set to 15 percent. If 8 percent of the votes cast disapprove of a resolution, and 5 percent of the votes cast approve the resolution, this vote will fail because it has not reached the minimum approval number of 15 percent (in number of votes needed) for a resolution to be considered valid. (6) determines the duration of the voting period. Longer voting periods may be necessary for issues that require considerable deliberation.

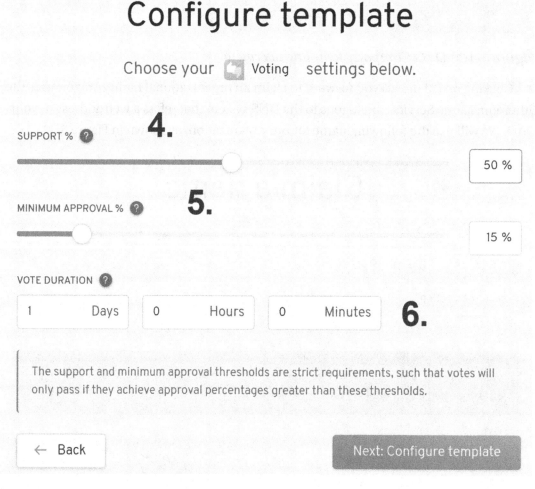

Figure 5-12. *Voting preferences for our DAO*

Now that we have voting preferences set up, next is setting up a token that will be treated within our DAO as equivalent to voting power, shown in Figure 5-13. The voting power of a user increases if the user has a higher stake of tokens in the organization. We will call our token Best (7) and use the symbol BST to represent it (8). Initially, all the tokens will be assigned to the wallet address (9) from MetaMask; this assignment also makes that address the default account in our DAO. We will begin with minting 100 tokens for the DAO. This implies once the DAO is online, it will have 100 of the BST tokens. Any further minting of tokens will be done through a voting process (10). You can always add more token holders to the DAO in this initial process; other addresses can be accounts that you manage on the MetaMask wallet.

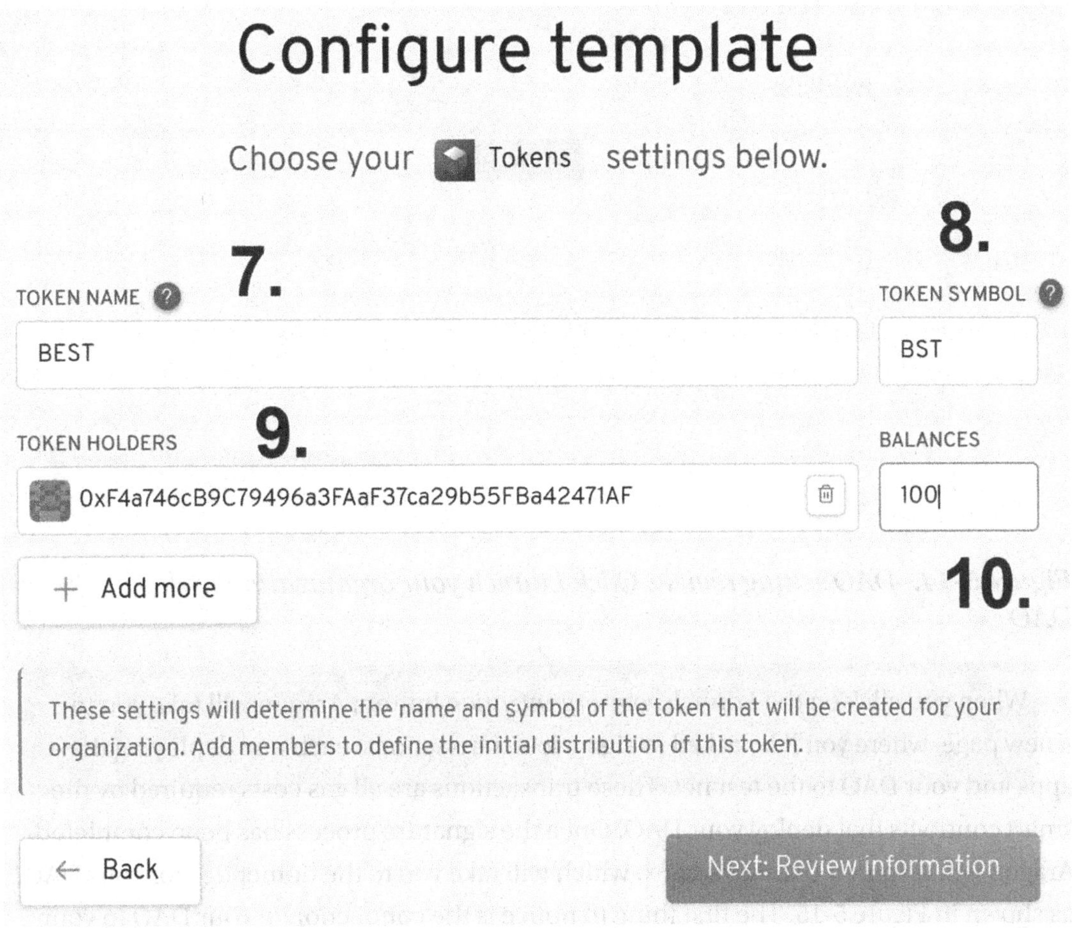

Configure template

Choose your 🔷 Tokens settings below.

7.   **8.**

TOKEN NAME ❓   TOKEN SYMBOL ❓

BEST   BST

TOKEN HOLDERS **9.**   BALANCES

🔲 0xF4a746cB9C79496a3FAaF37ca29b55FBa42471AF   🗑   100|

➕ Add more   **10.**

These settings will determine the name and symbol of the token that will be created for your organization. Add members to define the initial distribution of this token.

← Back   Next: Review information

Figure 5-13. Token settings for our DAO

This was all the setup required to deploy a DAO. Review the settings as shown in Figure 5-14, and then we can start interacting with our DAO.

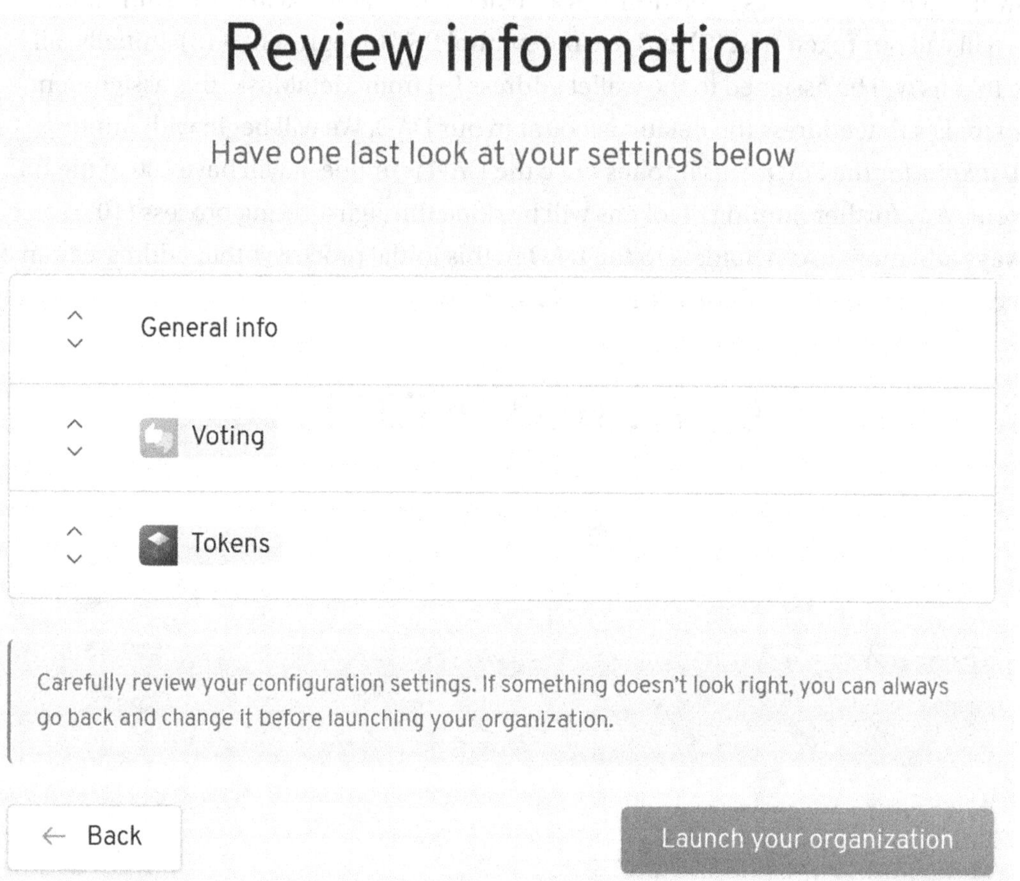

Review information

Have one last look at your settings below

⌃⌄	General info
⌃⌄	▢ Voting
⌃⌄	◈ Tokens

Carefully review your configuration settings. If something doesn't look right, you can always go back and change it before launching your organization.

← Back		Launch your organization

Figure 5-14. DAO setting review. Click Launch your organization to deploy the DAO

When you click on the *Launch your organization* button, Aragon will take you to a new page, where you'll be asked to sign a few transactions, each one deploying the apps and your DAO to the test net. These transactions are all gas costs required by the smart contracts that deploy your DAO. Once the signature process has been completed, Aragon will display a *Get started* box, which will take you to the homepage for your DAO, as shown in Figure 5-15. The first thing to notice is the connection of your DAO to your MetaMask wallet, shown in (11). You can perform all the daily operations of the DAO only if you're connected to the wallet. Notice that on the left-hand side of (11) is the address of our DAO, as captured in Figure 5-11. There are two applications installed with this DAO that we will review in the next topic (12), and, finally, the DAO permissions that we will review later in the chapter (14). To that end, the common functions of a DAO are presented as shortcuts (13).

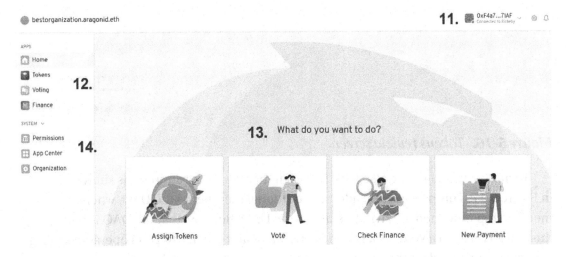

Figure 5-15. *Homepage of the DAO*

Topic 3: DAO Apps and Permissions

In this topic, we will review the DAO app, including tokens, voting, and finance. Then, we will dive into the system permissions and show how to add permissions to apps for your DAO. Let's start with the Tokens app.

Tokens App

To begin, click on the Tokens app in the left sidebar; you should see the Token review screen, as shown in Figure 5-16. Here, the tokens we minted during the DAO setup process are represented as the balance (1) assigned to the wallet address we provided. On the right-hand side is basic information about our tokens, including the total supply of tokens (the amount of tokens minted thus far), whether the tokens can be transferred, and the token name (2). We can create tokens that are not transferrable, and this can be used to designate a rare asset. Currently, this DAO only has one member, so by default, that member has 100 percent of the token ownership (3). We can mint new tokens, and to begin that process, click (4), *Add tokens.*

Figure 5-16. *Tokens review screen*

To mint new tokens, we also have to assign them to a new address, as shown in Figure 5-17. This process also adds an additional member to the DAO, where membership is defined as having a stake in the DAO. But now that the DAO is online, this will go through a vote. As a general rule, any major change to DAO operations will go through a vote based on the voting parameters we set in the previous section.

Note   Newly minted tokens can be assigned to any address; here, adding a new address concomitantly allows us to add a new member with a stake in the DAO.

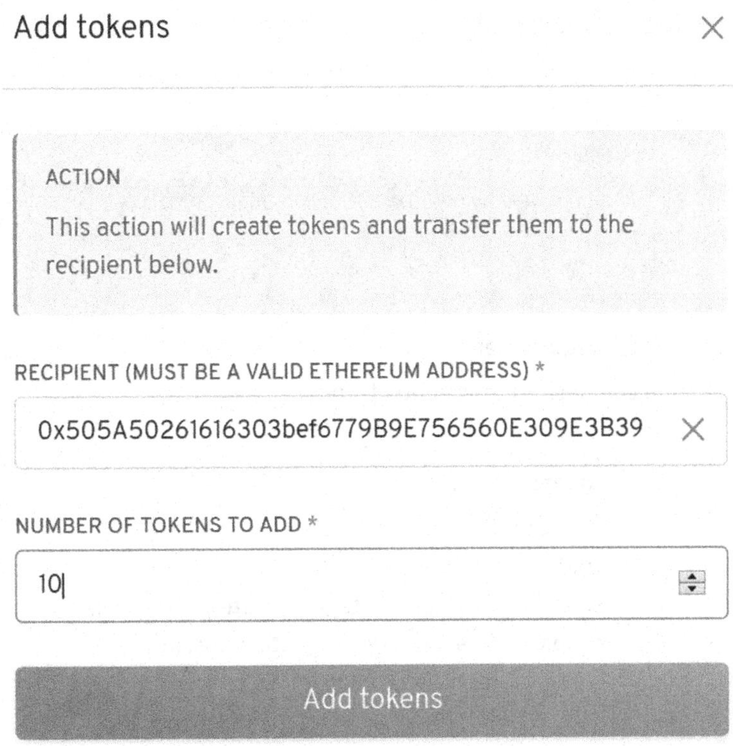

Add tokens   ✕

ACTION

This action will create tokens and transfer them to the
recipient below.

RECIPIENT (MUST BE A VALID ETHEREUM ADDRESS) *

0x505A50261616303bef6779B9E756560E309E3B39   ✕

NUMBER OF TOKENS TO ADD *

10|

Add tokens

Figure 5-17. *Minting ten new tokens and assigning them to a new address*

Clicking on *Add tokens* will lead you down a four-step process:

- Create a transaction that implements the minting function.

- Create a vote that will decide whether the minting of new tokens is approved by the DAO.

- Use the DAO smart contract to deploy these two functions to the Ethereum test net.

- Create a transaction that uses the minting function to mint new tokens.

This general process remains the same for most of the actions taken through apps in Aragon; the first step is shown in Figure 5-18. (5) ascertains that you can only mint for new tokens after a vote has taken place. (6) informs us that after a vote is successful, this transaction will mint new tokens. Clicking on *Create transaction* will require MetaMask to pay for gas and sign.

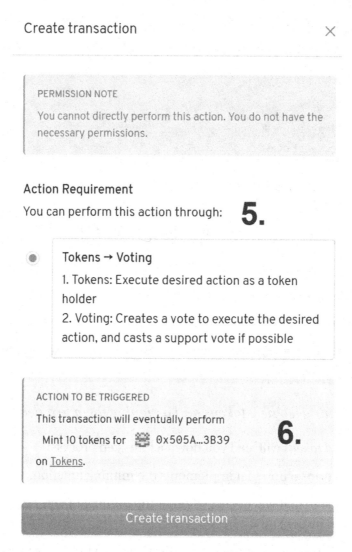

Figure 5-18. *Creating a vote and a transaction to mint new tokens*

Navigate to the Voting tab, and you should see an open vote with the action from (6) in Figure 5-18 listed as the vote title. These votes are created automatically by the DAO. Clicking on the vote will take you to the voting screen. Select *yes* and sign the transaction to vote on your decision. The confirmation is shown in notifications, as seen in Figure 5-19.

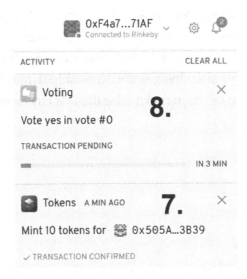

Figure 5-19. *Notifications for voting: (7) refers to the transaction that will mint ten new tokens, and (8) refers to the vote being carried out*

The vote summary page is shown in Figure 5-20. This represents the voting outcome. (9) is the description of this vote; as this was the first vote of our DAO, it was assigned to be Vote #0. Additionally, the description and vote creator are mentioned. For now, our DAO only has one member, so the voting outcome was decided by one voter who has the majority stake of 100 BST tokens (10). On the right-hand side is the resolution of the vote (which passed), along with some information about support needed and the minimum approval (11).

Figure 5-20. *Vote summary page*

Now that the vote has passed, let's look at the changes it brought to our DAO, shown in Figure 5-21. (12) is the first major change; the ten new tokens that we minted are now assigned to a new wallet (account) on the DAO. The total supply of tokens has increased from 100 to 110 (13), and this also changes the ownership dynamics. The new account now has a 9 percent stake in decision making for the DAO by owning 10 tokens (14).

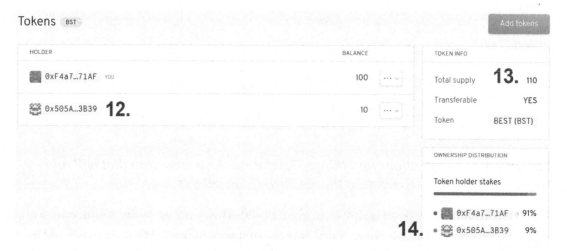

Figure 5-21. *Minted tokens appear in our DAO*

Voting App

Voting is an integral part of every major DAO operation. As such, we used the Voting app to authorize minting ten new tokens. In a similar manner, we can use it to propose questions, going through the same process. Let's share a brief example. Navigate to the Voting tab, and click on *New vote* to get started. Enter the question you would like to propose to the DAO, as shown in Figure 5-22. For instance, prior to minting new tokens, the issue can be discussed as a simple vote. Once a question is entered, the voting begins for the DAO based on pre-set rules.

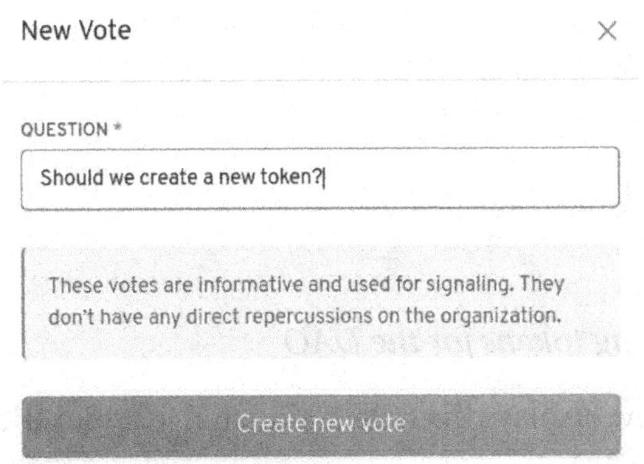

New Vote   ×

QUESTION *

Should we create a new token?|

These votes are informative and used for signaling. They
don't have any direct repercussions on the organization.

Create new vote

Figure 5-22. *Creating a voting question*

The Voting view is shown in Figure 5-23. This shows the current resolutions that are being actively voted on, and the closed resolutions that have passed or failed. Our new vote on creating tokens is shown as open, and it will be available to the DAO members for the next twenty-four hours.

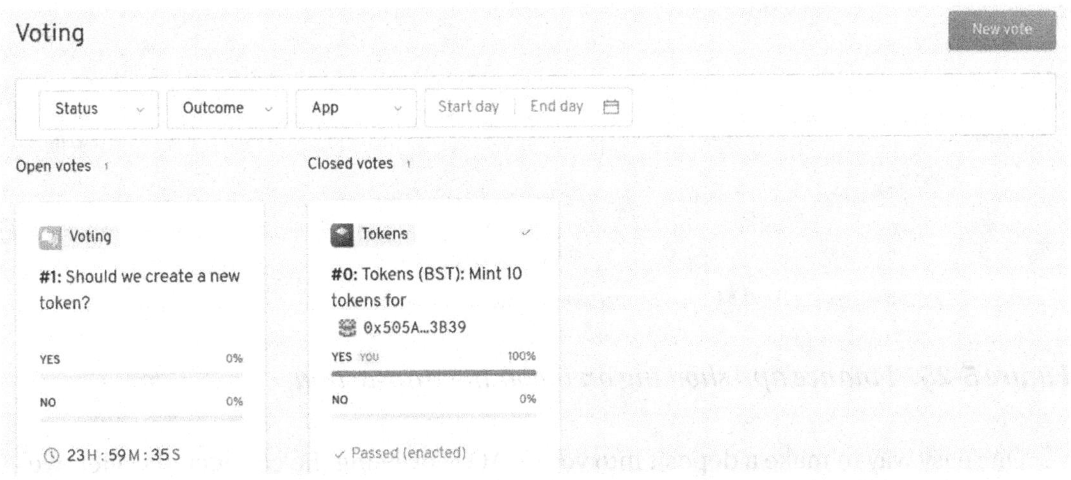

Voting   New vote

Status   ∨   Outcome   ∨   App   ∨   Start day | End day 📅

Open votes ↑   Closed votes ↑

Voting	Tokens ✓
#1: Should we create a new token?	#0: Tokens (BST): Mint 10 tokens for 🏦 0x505A...3B39
YES 0%	YES YOU 100%
NO 0%	NO 0%
🕐 23H:59M:35S	✓ Passed (enacted)

Figure 5-23. *Voting view*

Finance App

The Finance app acts as an internal bank recording all financial activities taking place within the DAO. In this topic, we will go over how to make deposits and withdrawals using the Finance app. To start with banking operations, let's request some test tokens. Navigate to Permissions under the System tab and scroll down to see the *Request test tokens* section. This will allow us to get some test currency, as shown in Figure 5-24.

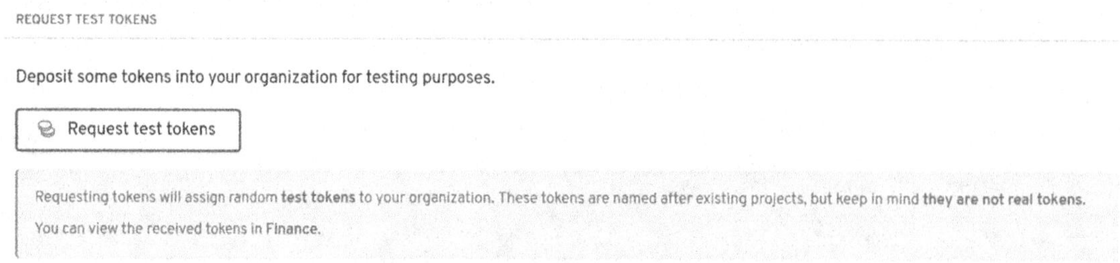

REQUEST TEST TOKENS

Deposit some tokens into your organization for testing purposes.

> ⊜ Request test tokens

Requesting tokens will assign random **test tokens** to your organization. These tokens are named after existing projects, but keep in mind **they are not real tokens.** You can view the received tokens in Finance.

Figure 5-24. *Requesting tokens for the DAO*

The Finance app now displays the transaction that just took place; the updated view is shown in Figure 5-25. (15) shows the twenty Aragon tokens (ANT) that we received upon requesting test tokens. (16) lists the transaction that transferred into our DAO.

Finance   New transfer

TOKEN BALANCES

⊜ ANT

20   **15.**

–

Transfers   ⬀ Export

| Type ⌄ | Token ⌄ | Start day | End day 📅 |

DATE	SOURCE/RECIPIENT	REFERENCE	AMOUNT
02/06/20	▦ 0x39a4...2ff9 **16.**	Requested airdrop (test tokens)	+20 ANT ··· ⌄

Figure 5-25. *Finance app showing an incoming transaction*

One easy way to make a deposit into your DAO is by using the connected wallet. We can deposit by initiating a new transfer in the Finance app. The settings are shown in Figure 5-26. We first need to select the currency that we're transferring. Our MetaMask wallet only contains ETH, so that's what we will bring into the DAO (17). Next, we need to enter the deposit amount of 0.02 ETH (18). Finally, we can add an optional message to the incoming transaction (19).

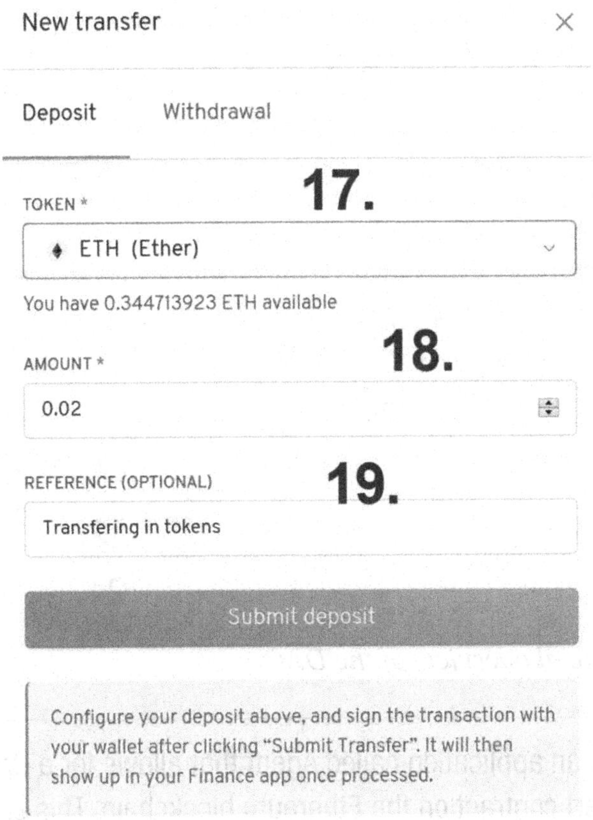

New transfer   ×

Deposit   Withdrawal

TOKEN *   **17.**

  ♦ ETH (Ether)   ⌄

You have 0.344713923 ETH available

AMOUNT *   **18.**

  0.02   ⬍

REFERENCE (OPTIONAL)   **19.**

  Transfering in tokens

                    Submit deposit

  Configure your deposit above, and sign the transaction with
  your wallet after clicking "Submit Transfer". It will then
  show up in your Finance app once processed.

Figure 5-26. *Transferring currency into our DAO from the MetaMask wallet*

Withdrawal of funds from the DAO follows a very similar sequence of steps. Select withdrawal as shown in Figure 5-26 and enter the Ethereum address that will receive the withdrawn funds. Then, enter the amount and currency to withdraw. As an exercise, try to withdraw 0.01 ETH to a MetaMask wallet address. This process should result in the Finance tab's showing what is seen in Figure 5-27. (20) shows the balance remaining in the DAO at any given time. (21) is the test tokens we requested from the faucet. (22) is the 0.02 ETH deposit we made from the MetaMask wallet, and, finally, (23) should show the 0.01 ETH withdrawn. As more transactions happen, the Finance app becomes an in-house tracker for the DAO.

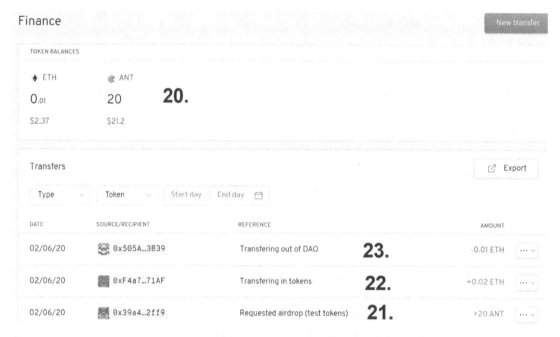

Figure 5-27. Financial overview of the DAO

Note   Aragon has an application called Agent that allows for a DAO to interact with any other smart contract on the Ethereum blockchain. This enables an organization to use the Agent app as an intermediary for sending funds externally or importing them. The resulting transfers will be recorded on the financial overview page with references to Agent.

App Permissions

The DAO comes with a set of standard app permissions that allow for specific functionality. To extend the functionality of an app, or to add new general features to the DAO, new permissions must be voted on and added. Navigate to the sidebar, under System ➤ Permissions. This opens the default Permissions view, as shown in Figure 5-28. The DAO allows you to change permissions for the apps, and at the system level for the DAO. We will only be focusing on the app permissions (24). The apps currently installed are available right below in (25). These apps were available with the template and pre-installed. (26) lists out the actions that are available to the apps on our DAO (27). These actions are assigned to an app, as shown in (28), which denotes the flow of actions from the action being requested on the app to the approval from the assigned app. In the majority of cases, the Voting app will oversee any new actions, as we have discussed. (29) is the manager that can reassign actions to apps that are installed on our DAO.

Figure 5-28. *Permissions overview for our DAO*

On the right-hand side in Figure 5-28, click on *New permission* to begin adding new permissions. Our goal here will be to add a permission allowing any account in the DAO to burn tokens. This replaces the default limiting the action of burn tokens to only the Voting app. The Add Permissions view is shown in Figure 5-29. First, select the app to which you want to add a new permission and then assign a new entity. Here, we will be assigning any accounts to the action that will follow, which is burning tokens. Once you click on *Add permission*, you will be taken to a vote. As with any major changes to the DAO, once the resolution is approved by the DAO, the functionality will become available.

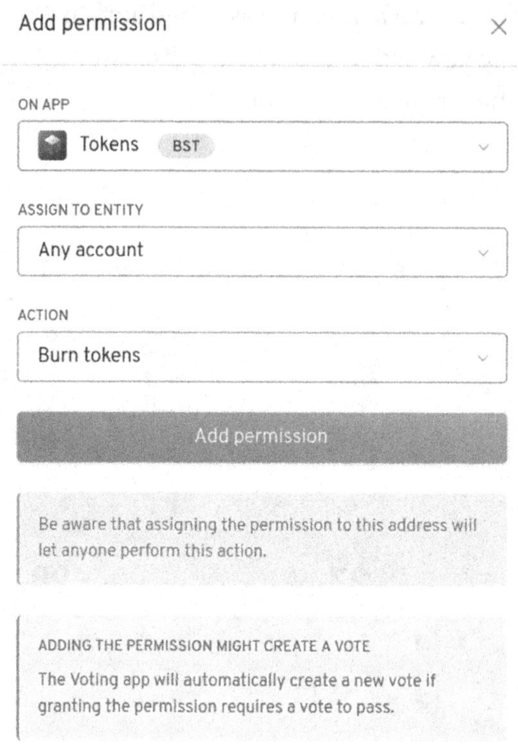

Figure 5-29. *Adding a new permission*

As noted previously, we will need to vote on this resolution prior to adding the permission. Clicking on *Add permission* in Figure 5-29 will take you to the voting screen, shown in Figure 5-30.

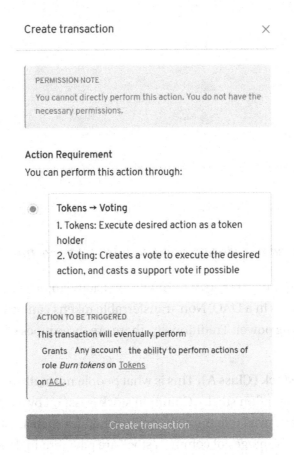

Figure 5-30. *Voting confirmation for adding new permission*

Once the voting is successful, the permission is applied to the DAO and is now visible under the Permissions tab. This is shown in Figure 5-31. This concludes our tutorial, providing a basic overview of how to set up a DAO on Aragon.

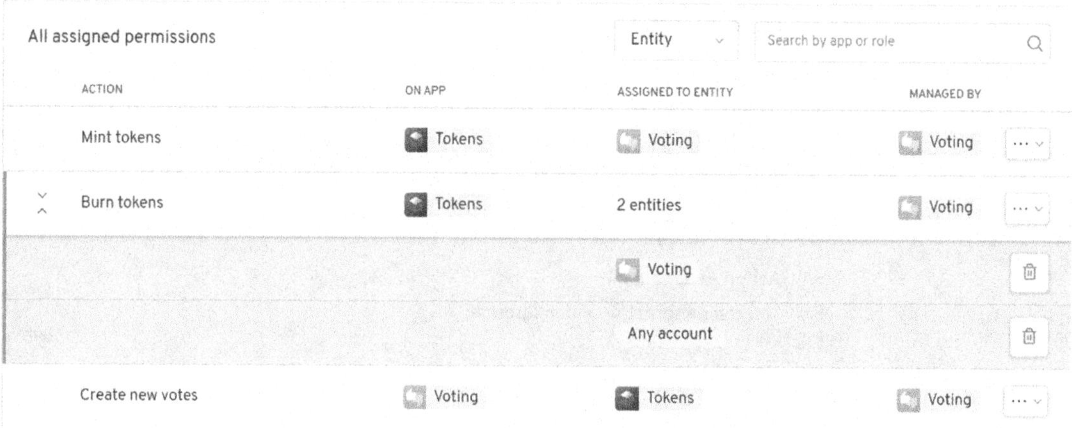

All assigned permissions			Entity ∨	Search by app or role	Q
ACTION	ON APP	ASSIGNED TO ENTITY	MANAGED BY		
Mint tokens	Tokens	Voting	Voting	··· ∨	
Burn tokens	Tokens	2 entities	Voting	··· ∨	
		Voting		🗑	
		Any account		🗑	
Create new votes	Voting	Tokens	Voting	··· ∨	

Figure 5-31. *Updated permissions view for burn tokens action*

Before we finish our discussion, let's briefly look at the topic of codifying stocks as protected/limited assets in a DAO. Non-transferrable tokens can be used as rare assets and have greater voting power. Traditionally, there are three types of stocks issued by a public company:

- **Common stock (Class A):** This is what people normally refer to when they mention stocks. Common stock is issued by a company and is usually available through stock exchanges such as Nasdaq. The main advantages of common stock are payment in dividends and trade in an exchange. A dividend is typically a sum of money paid to the shareholders of a company at the end of a quarter out of the profits generated in that quarter. Common stock can also be traded or sold at any time on an accredited exchange. These can be codified as newly minted tokens issued to members of a DAO once the organization has been set up.

- **Preferred stock (Class B):** Preferred stock is a special kind of stock issued to investors that have a significant stake in the company. This stock has a few financial advantages over common stock, making it a safer investment. In terms of dividends, preferred stock is cashed before common and as a result receives a larger share of a company's profits. Moreover, common stock can vary in terms of dividends paid out, but preferred stock has fixed returns to the shareholders. The process of codifying this type of an asset into a DAO requires `aragon-cli` (command-line interface). Essentially, we use the `aragon-cli` to create a clone of the generic ERC20 token called MiniMeToken for our DAO and import it using Agent. This allows for a novel asset to be imported and used in our DAO.

- **Founder stock (Class F):** Class F shares are an exclusive kind of preferred stock issued to founders of a company. These shares come with greater voting rights; for instance, one founder stock can count for ten votes. In comparison, one common stock would only count for one vote. Founder stock grants super voting rights and is normally used to retain control of a company's decision-making process when a large number of entities are involved.

Note   Using aragon-cli is beyond the scope of this chapter; however, it allows for very powerful integrations. For instance, a novel imported token can be voted on by the DAO as a payment collection asset, letting the holders collect yearly payments in return for investing in the DAO.

Summary

In this chapter, we discussed the concept of decentralized organizations. We started with a presentation of Aragon in the context of decentralized organizations built on the blockchain. We talked about the definition of a DAO and the organs that Aragon implements. Then, we had an in-depth discussion about the Aragon token, and the emergence of a social campaign use case with a DAO. Finally, the heart of this chapter was the walkthrough of how to set up, manage, and operate a DAO, including all its basic functions. This chapter has provided the foundation for creating your own DAO.

References

The main references used to compile this chapter were the Aragon whitepaper (`https://github.com/aragon/whitepaper`) and the aragon-core GitHub docs (`https://github.com/aragon/aragonOS`).

CHAPTER 6

The DAO Hacked

In Chapter 5, we discussed the concept of decentralized organizations and the modus operandi of a DAO. Here, we want to highlight a historic moment leading to the creation of the first DAO, and how it eventually got hacked. Our discussion begins with a fresh perspective on decentralized organizations from Buterin, and leads into the story of Slock. it, the company at the heart of the DAO revolution. Then, we present some code that made The DAO dysfunctional: pieces of the smart contract relevant to the vulnerability, the conditions that allowed repetitive withdrawals from The DAO, and the exploit itself. We conclude the chapter by talking about the consequences of this hack: the debate about hard versus soft forks, and the creation of Ethereum Classic.

Introduction

Discourse in the global blockchain community has been characterized by idealism going back to Satoshi Nakamoto's early writings on Bitcoin as a response to central banking. The line of reasoning is that systems that are vulnerable to corruption, or in any case cater to the wishes of a select few, could be made more accountable if they were governed by code. If that code lives on the blockchain, then it is impervious to biased intervention by minority parties. Following that tradition, in a September 2013 blog post for *Bitcoin Magazine*, Vitalik Buterin explored the notion of the DAO. The article began as follows:

> *Corporations, US presidential candidate Mitt Romney reminds us, are people. Whether or not you agree with the conclusions that his partisans draw from that claim, the statement certainly carries a large amount of truth. What is a corporation, after all, but a certain group of people working together under a set of specific rules? When a corporation owns property, what that really means is that there is a legal contract stating that the property can only be used for certain purposes under the control of those people who are currently its board of directors—a designation itself modifiable by*

113

© Vikram Dhillon, David Metcalf, and Max Hooper 2021
V. Dhillon et al., *Blockchain Enabled Applications*, https://doi.org/10.1007/978-1-4842-6534-5_6

a particular set of shareholders. If a corporation does something, it's because its board of directors has agreed that it should be done. If a corporation hires employees, it means that the employees are agreeing to provide services to the corporation's customers under a particular set of rules, particularly involving payment. When a corporation has limited liability, it means that specific people have been granted extra privileges to act with reduced fear of legal prosecution by the government—a group of people with more rights than ordinary people acting alone, but ultimately people nonetheless. In any case, it's nothing more than people and contracts all the way down.

However, here a very interesting question arises: do we really need the people? [1]

Three years after Buterin's article was first published, The DAO came into existence as a smart contract written in Solidity, perhaps the purest manifestation of this idealism. Despite its canonical label, The DAO was not the first—or the last—decentralized autonomous organization. In fact, by May 2016 when the leadership at Slock.it kicked off The DAO's record-breaking initial coin offering (ICO), DAOs were well established as the third wave of the increasingly mainstream blockchain phenomenon. [2]

To better understand the DAO terminology, please refer to the Ethereum developer blog (https://blog.ethereum.org/2014/05/06/daos-dacs-das-and-more-an-incomplete-terminology-guide/) describing this at great length. Although many people consider Bitcoin to be the very first DAO, there were drastic differences in the natures of the two services. Although it is true that Bitcoin was governed by code shared by every miner in the network, Bitcoin doesn't have an internal balance sheet, only functions by which its users can exchange value. Although other DAOs at the time did have a concept of asset ownership, what made The DAO unique was that central to its code were the radically democratic processes that defined how The DAO would deploy its resources. It was a realization of Buterin's concept of a corporation that could conduct business without having a single employee, let alone a CEO.

From the DAO white paper:

This paper illustrates a method that for the first time allows the creation of organizations in which (1) participants maintain direct real-time control

---

[1] See https://bitcoinmagazine.com/articles/bootstrapping-a-decentralized-autonomous-corporation-part-i-1379644274/

[2] To put this in perspective, fifteen days into The DAO's crowdsale, members of the MakerDAO subreddit were discussing proposals that would trigger an investment in MakerDao by The DAO.

of contributed funds and (2) governance rules are formalized, automated and enforced using software. Specifically, standard smart contract code has been written that can be used to form a Decentralized Autonomous Organization (DAO) on the Ethereum blockchain.

Buterin talked about the balance between automation and capital in the context of what sets decentralized organizations apart from traditional companies. Paul Kohlhaas from ConsenSys presented Figure 6-1 to illustrate where DAOs fall on the spectrum of autonomous organizations. Note in this figure that different types of autonomous organizations fall on the spectrum between automation and human controlled, such as simple decentralized organizations (DOs) and traditional decentralized corporations (DCs).

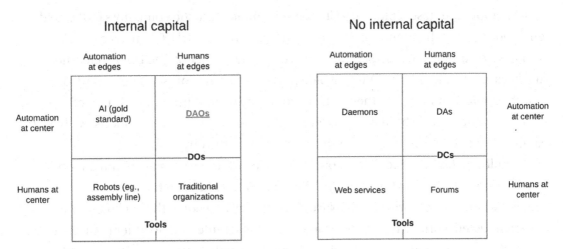

Figure 6-1. *DAOs as automation-powered decision-making entities with human participants*

In essence, DAOs are a paradigm shift from automated entities that previously contained no capital. Using a blockchain allows us to infuse capital and build hybrid business models where we can fine-tune the degree of automation for specific use cases. The following is a brief glossary that explains three new terms used in Figure 6-1:

- DAs: Decentralized agents, essentially bots that were programmed for specific tasks by developers. The main difference between DAs and DAOs is that the latter has internal capital.

- DCs: Decentralized corporations, essentially a medium between forums that run without any internal capital and decentralized agents that are completely automated.

- DOs: Decentralized organizations, essentially a medium between traditional companies and fully autonomous DAOs

The Team

As often is the case in the blockchain world, much confusion surrounds the nature of the relationship between the employeeless DAO and the humans who wrote and maintained The DAO's code. Those humans, in the case of The DAO, were led by the top brass at Slock.it, a German company set on disrupting the sharing economy by way of a technology they called the Universal Sharing Network (USN).

Christopher Jentzsch, Slock.it's CEO, and Stephan Tual, the company's COO, held senior positions at the Ethereum Foundation (Lead Tester and CCO, respectively) prior to starting Slock.it. Jentzsch was the primary developer of The DAO code, and Tual became the face of The DAO via blog posts, conference presentations, and forum contributions. So how would their current company benefit from the creation of a leaderless venture fund built on Ethereum? To understand their motivations, we have to examine Slock.it's vision to connect the blockchain to the physical world.

In building the USN, Slock.it set out to play a central role in mainstream adoption of IoT technology. By providing a way to interact with devices on the network from anywhere in the world, the USN would, hopefully, become the backbone of a hyperconnected world, where your property could be rented out to other people without the need for centralized companies like Uber and Airbnb. Instead, the USN would provide an interface to the Ethereum blockchain, where decentralized applications can govern the transactions that make up the sharing economy.

The company intended to build a specialized modem, called the Ethereum Computer, for connecting IoT devices to the USN. Slock.it's vision for The DAO was to create a decentralized venture fund that would invest in promising proposals to build blockchain-supported products and services.

At the time of writing (a few years after the original DAO's ICO), Slock.it has raised $2 million in seed funding to continue developing the USN and the Ethereum Computer. According to Tual's blog posts on the company website, Slock.it will now make the Ethereum Computer available as a free and open source image for popular system-on-a-chip (SoC) systems such as Raspberry Pi. The company also built and supports Share&Charge, a service that lets owners of electric vehicle charging stations sell their power to electric vehicle owners via a blockchain-powered mobile app.

Jeremiah Owyang, in a presentation titled "How Technology Improves Hosting of the Future" (given on 11.19.2016) from Crowd Companies, summarized one of the main use cases of Slock.it in a slide shown in Figure 6-2.

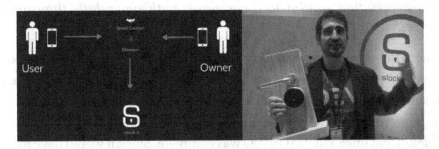

When someone purchases a Slock, it's connected to the Slock smart contract in the Ethereum blockchain and controlled by it. The owner of a Slock can set a deposit amount and a price for renting his property, and the user will pay that deposit through a transaction to the Ethereum blockchain, thereby getting permission to open and close that smart lock through their smart phone.

Figure 6-2. *Slock.it can act as a decentalized Airbnb by linking the purchase of a physical device (a smart lock) to a smart contract*

Ultimately, the idea expressed in Figure 6-2 was expanded to become a decentralized IoT platform, where any device could be connected to the blockchain.

The DAO

The original conception of The DAO was not the radical experiment in democratic business processes that was eventually released at its ICO. Jentzsch described the process on the Slock.it blog:

> *In the beginning, we created a slock.it-specific smart contract and gave token holders voting power about what we—slock.it—should do with the funds received.*

After further consideration, we gave token holders even more power, by giving them full control over the funds, which would be released only after a successful vote on detailed proposals backed by smart contracts. This was already a few steps beyond the Kickstarter model, but we would have been the only recipient of funds in this narrow slock.it-specific DAO.

We wanted to go even further and create a "true" DAO, one that would be the only and direct recipient of the funds, and would represent the creation of an organization similar to a company, with potentially thousands of Founders.[3]

To achieve this decoupling of Slock.it and The DAO, Jentzsch designed a Solidity contract that would allow any DAO token holder to make proposals for how The DAO's resources should be handled. All token holders could vote on active proposals, which had a minimum voting period of fourteen days.

That meant that once The DAO's ICO was complete, Slock.it would have to submit a proposal to The DAO just like anyone else. Other users could use the Mist browser to evaluate the proposal. This is how proposals were structured:

```
struct Proposal {
address recipient;
uint amount;
string description;
uint votingDeadline;
bool open;
bool proposalPassed;
bytes32 proposalHash;
uint proposalDeposit;
bool newCurator;
SplitData[] splitData;
uint yea;
uint nay;
mapping (address => bool) votedYes;
mapping (address => bool) votedNo;
address creator;
}
```

---

[3]See https://blog.slock.it/the-history-of-the-dao-and-lessons-learned-d06740f8cfa5

As you can see, proposals—the core of this automaton code base that would quickly raise $150 million—were relatively simple requests for The DAO's resources (uint amount).

Any DAO token holder could vote on proposals by calling the vote function:

```
function vote(
uint _proposalID,
bool _supportsProposal
) onlyTokenholders returns (uint _voteID);
```

The votes from any one address would be weighted proportional to the amount of DAO tokens held at that address. If token holders wanted to vote for two separate positions, they could transfer the amount of tokens they wanted to vote with to another address, and vote again from there.[4] Any tokens voting on an open proposal were locked (could not be transferred) until the end of the voting period.

The uint proposalDeposit was the deposit (in wei) that creators of a proposal had to stake on the proposal until the voting period closed. If the proposal never reached quorum, the deposit would remain with The DAO.

There were two special types of proposal that did not require deposits that would play a key role in the fate of The DAO. The first type was a proposal to split The DAO, effectively withdrawing the funds of the recipient of the proposal into a new "child" DAO, which was a clone of the original, but at a new contract address. Split proposals had a voting period of seven days, instead of fourteen, and anyone who voted yes on a split proposal would follow the recipient, withdrawing their tokens from the original DAO and moving them into the resultant child DAO.

The second special type of proposal was to replace the curator of The DAO. DAO curators were addresses set at the creation of The DAO and the creation of any child DAO that could whitelist recipient addresses, effectively serving as gatekeepers.[5] If the majority vote no on a proposal to replace a curator, the yes votes can elect to stand by their decision, creating a new DAO with their chosen curator.

---

[4]This could be the case, because proposals required a quorum of 20 percent of votes to have weighed in on a proposal for the vote to be valid.

[5]Curators weren't necessarily human gatekeepers. Gavin Wood "resigned" as a curator of The DAO to make a point that curation was merely a technical role and that the curator had no proactive control over The DAO.

The ICO Highlights

The ICO for the initial The DAO concept was an overnight success:

- It raised 12 million ETH (~$150 million).

- Both Jentzsch and Tual admitted that they never expected their idea to be so successful.

The Hack

The idea that The DAO was vulnerable to attack had been floating around in the developer community. Vlad Zamfir and Emin Gün Sirer first raised the issue in a blog post calling for a moratorium on The DAO until the vulnerabilities could be addressed.[6] Just days before the attack, MakerDAO cautioned the community that their code was vulnerable to an attack, and Peter Vessenes demonstrated that this vulnerability was shared by The DAO.[7]

These warnings prompted a now infamous blog post published on June 12, 2016, by Tual on the Slock.it website titled, "No DAO funds at risk following the Ethereum smart contract 'recursive call' bug discovery." Within a couple of days, fixes had been proposed to correct many of the known vulnerabilities of The DAO, but it was already too late. On June 17, an attacker began draining funds from The DAO.

The DAO attacker exploited a well-intentioned although poorly implemented feature of The DAO that was intended to prevent tyranny of the majority over dissenting DAO token holders. From The DAO white paper:

> A problem every DAO has to mitigate is the ability for the majority to rob the minority by changing governance and ownership rules after DAO formation. For example, an attacker with 51% of the tokens, acquired either during the fueling period or created afterwards, could make a proposal to send all the funds to themselves. Since they would hold the majority of the tokens, they would always be able to pass their proposals.
>
> To prevent this, the minority must always have the ability to retrieve their portion of the funds. Our solution is to allow a DAO to split into two. If an individual, or a group of token holders, disagrees with a proposal and

---

[6]http://hackingdistributed.com/2016/05/27/dao-call-for-moratorium/
[7]http://vessenes.com/more-ethereum-attacks-race-to-empty-is-the-real-deal/

wants to retrieve their portion of the Ether before the proposal is executed, they can submit and approve a special type of proposal to form a new DAO. The token holders who voted for this proposal can then split the DAO, moving their portion of the Ether to this new DAO, leaving the rest alone only able to spend their own Ether.

Unfortunately, the way that this "split" feature was implemented made the DAO vulnerable due a catastrophic reentrancy bug.[8] In other words, someone could recursively split from the DAO, withdrawing amounts equal to their original ETH investment indefinitely, before the record of their withdrawal was ever recorded in the original DAO contract.

Here is the vulnerability, as found in the Solidity contract file *DAO.sol*:

```
function splitDAO(
uint _proposalID,
address _newCurator
) noEther onlyTokenholders returns (bool _success) {
...
// [Added for explanation] The first step moves Ether and assigns new
tokens
uint fundsToBeMoved =
(balances[msg.sender] * p.splitData[0].splitBalance) /
p.splitData[0].totalSupply;
if (p.splitData[0].newDAO.createTokenProxy.value(fundsToBeMoved)(msg.
sender) == false) //
[Added for explanation] This is the line that splits the DAO before
updating the funds in
the account calling for the split

...
// Burn DAO Tokens
Transfer(msg.sender, 0, balances[msg.sender]);
withdrawRewardFor(msg.sender); // be nice, and get his rewards
```

---

[8]Reentrancy is a characteristic of software in which a routine can be interrupted in the middle of its execution, and then be intiated (reentered) from its beginning, while the remaining portion of the original instance of the routine remains queued for execution.

```
// [Added for explanation] The previous line is key in that it is called
before
totalSupply and balances[msg.sender] are updated to reflect the new
balances after the split
has been performed
totalSupply -= balances[msg.sender]; // [Added for explanation] This
happens after the
split
balances[msg.sender] = 0; // [Added for explanation] This also happens
after the split
paidOut[msg.sender] = 0;
return true;
}
```

As shown here, The DAO referenced the balances array to determine how many DAO tokens were available to be moved. The value of p.splitData[0] is a property of the proposal being submitted to the DAO, not any property of the DAO. That, in combination with the fact that withdrawRewardFor is called before balances[] is updated, made it possible for the attacker to call fundsToBeMoved indefinitely, because their balance will still return its original value.

Looking more closely at withdrawRewardFor() shows us the conditions that made this possible:

```
function withdrawRewardFor(address _account) noEther internal returns (bool
_success) {
if ((balanceOf(_account) * rewardAccount.accumulatedInput()) / totalSupply
< paidOut[_
account])
throw;
uint reward =
(balanceOf(_account) * rewardAccount.accumulatedInput()) / totalSupply -
paidOut[_
account];
if (!rewardAccount.payOut(_account, reward)) // [Added for explanation]
this is the
statement that is vulnerable to the recursion attack. We must go deeper.
```

```
throw;
paidOut[_account] += reward;
return true;
}
```

Assuming the first statement evaluates as false, the statement marked as vulnerable will run. There's one more step to examine to understand how the attacker was able to make that the case. The first time the `withdrawRewardFor` is called (when the attacker had legitimate funds to withdraw), the first statement would correctly evaluate as false, causing the following code to run:

```
function payOut(address _recipient, uint _amount) returns (bool) {
if (msg.sender != owner || msg.value > 0 || (payOwnerOnly && _recipient !=
owner))
throw;
if (_recipient.call.value(_amount)()) { // [Added for explanation] this is
the coup de
grace
PayOut(_recipient, _amount);
return true;
} else {
return false;
}
```

PayOut() as written in the second `if` statement references "_recipient"–the person proposing the split. That address contains a function that calls `splitDAO` again from within `withdrawRewardFor()`, before the token balance at that address is updated. That created a call stack that looked like this:

```
splitDao
      withdrawRewardFor
         payOut
            recipient.call.value()()
               splitDao
                withdrawRewardFor
                   payOut
                      recipient.call.value()()
```

The attacker was therefore able to withdraw funds from The DAO into a child DAO indefinitely. To recap, the attacker accomplished the following:

1. Split the DAO.

2. Withdrew their funds into the new DAO.

3. Recursively called the split DAO function before the code checked to determine if the funds were available.

This process is visually represented in Figure 6-3.

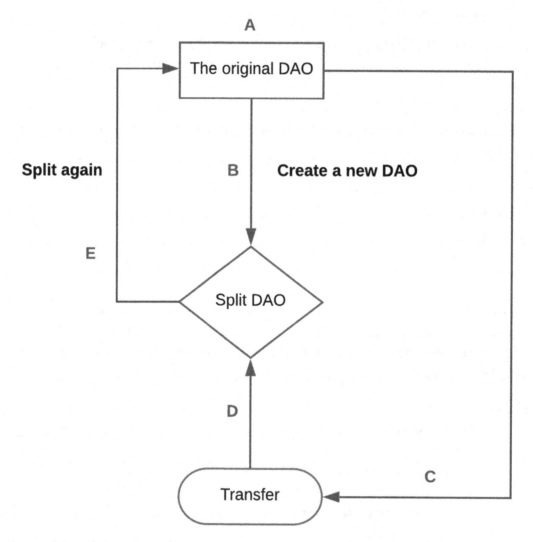

Figure 6-3. *The process of iterative withdrawal*

In Figure 6-3, we can see the iterative process visually. The original DAO is represented by A, and a sub-DAO is created in B. Then, a transfer function requests some funds be withdrawn from the original DAO in C. Finally, the funds are transferred to the new DAO created. This process is repeated again as new DAOs are created with each loop.

The Debate

However, The DAO investors weren't the only ones with an interest in the outcome of this turn of events. The hype surrounding The DAO had reached the religious proportions predicted by Buterin back in 2014. Almost 5 percent of ETH in circulation at the time was invested in The DAO. That had a number of implications for the entire Ethereum ecosystem, and led to one of the most contentious debates in the short history of blockchains.

On one side of the debate were those looking to protect the fledgling Ethereum ecosystem from a malicious actor in possession of a nontrivial portion of the total ETH in circulation. They were not necessarily concerned with whether or not The DAO would survive, but ultimately wanted to ensure that Ethereum would survive as a reputable blockchain platform on which other DAOs could be built in the future. This was the disposition of Buterin and many of the core members of the Ethereum development team.

On the other side were those committed to the ideals of decentralization and immutability. In the eyes of many in this camp (we'll call them the justice camp), the blockchain is an inherently just system in that it is deterministic, and anyone choosing to use it is implicitly agreeing to that fact. In this sense, the DAO attacker had not broken any laws. To the contrary, the reentrancy attack used the software code that made up The DAO's bylaws and turned it against itself.

The decentralization camp believed that rewriting the blockchain to roll back the attacker's sequestration of ETH in child DAOs would compromise the integrity of the blockchain. The blockchain, according to this line of thought, was supposed to be immutable and without any central authority, including the Ethereum Foundation. They were concerned the moral hazard of a small group of people rewriting the blockchain could open the door to other interventions, such as selective censorship.

The two sides debated their positions passionately over social media and in news outlets. The process made famous the concepts of soft forks and hard forks. Forking blockchains—or any software code for that matter—was not new to Ethereum or The DAO, but it became the focus of the debate between the justice camp and the immutability camp.

Meanwhile, a group of white hat hackers was working around the clock to try to hack the hacker. The white hat group consisted of people both for and against the hard fork, but they worked together, nonetheless, to perform some of the same attacks that had been identified before June 17 to move the stolen ETH into new contracts in hopes of returning it to its rightful owners.[9]

The white hat team reached out to people who had made significant investments in The DAO to raise money for stalking attacks, in which they could follow the attacker into new DAOs with greater funds than the attacker was able to withdraw, giving them majority voting rights in the resulting DAO.

The Split: ETH and ETC

On July 30, over 90 percent of the hashrate signaled its support for the fork. The DAO funds were returned to investors as though the organization had never existed. Sort of.

Opposition to the hard fork led to the emergence of Ethereum Classic (ETC), as a small portion of the community continued to mine the original Ethereum blockchain. These immutability fundamentalists were committed to the idea that blockchains represented a new, disruptive governance model. The most visible member of the movement was Arvicco, a Russian developer using a pseudonym. In a July 2016 interview with *Bitcoin Magazine*, he characterized the disagreement in this way:

> By bailing out the DAO, the Ethereum Foundation is attempting to reach a shortsighted goal of "making investors whole" and "boosting confidence in Ethereum platform." But they're doing quite the opposite. Bailing out the DAO undermines two of the three key longterm value propositions of the Ethereum platform.[10]

---

[9]https://www.reddit.com/r/ethereum/comments/4p7mhc/update_on_the_white_hat_attack/
[10]https://bitcoinmagazine.com/articles/rejecting-today-s-hard-fork-the-ethereum-classic-projectcontinues-on-the-original-chain-here-s-why-1469038808/

Despite the tenacity of this vocal minority in the Ethereum community, many people did not expect both versions of the blockchain to survive long term. Major exchanges and cryptoservices added support for ETC, but many were skeptical of the long-term prospects of a platform that essentially duplicated Ethereum's capabilities.

Erik Vorhees, founder and CEO of Shapeshift.io, expressed skepticism about ETC's ability to remain relevant, but explained that, ultimately, he believed that the split was good for the blockchain ecosystem. In November 2016 he told *Decentralize Today*:

> *While this caused quite a bit of turmoil (still ongoing), it's hard for me to say it was a failure. A division within the community has now been resolved, and since both camps were significant enough in size, we now have two Ethereums, for a while at least. It has actually made the community more peaceful, because instead of the two camps arguing over who is right, both of them can be "right" in their own way, and the market will decide whose product is actually better. I expect ETH to win out over ETC, but I have to admit ETC has survived longer than I thought.*

At the time of this writing, ETC continues to grow as a platform and as a community. Despite ETC appreciating less rapidly than ETH, BTCC and Huobi recently announced that they would be adding the token to their exchanges. ETC developers have also accelerated their departure from Ethereum as a platform, with the release of Mantis, the first client built from scratch for ETC (as opposed to Ethereum's Mist, Parity, and other clients).

The Future

When a technology fails after being hyped in a massive spotlight, it is incredibly difficult to recover the credibility of the ideas powering that technology. What does the future of DAOs look like? Any user investing in a DAO token should be cautious, but there have been massive security advances to a DAO's structure and governance. Interestingly, Paul Kohlhaas also presented a new outlook of DAOs as the next generation of automated VCs called Decentralized Fund Managers. According to Kohlhaas, DAOs represent a new class of financial asset management tools where a software can manage a fund that would normally be entrusted to traditional venture capitalists. By implementing software-based management at its core, any profits made by a DAO are distributed directly to the token holders. The members of this new DAO are essentially investors, and they would be issued a new class of tokens that represent their holdings (or stake) and earnings. Ultimately, in a DAO, the members can guide how the funds are being allocated and what benefits are offered in return for investment. It would stand to reason that a DAO managing funds would operate in traditional VC cycles:

- The transition first cycle involves investing using the ETH funds.

- The second cycle involves the management of a DAO into a next-generation automated VC. The governance model can provide for new decision-making abilities for early investors such as angel syndicates.

We discuss the idea of artificial intelligence (AI) leading financial investments in Chapter 12 of the book.

Summary

The future of Ethereum is bright despite the DAO hack. With the emergence of Ethereum Classic and the incredible rate of new developments, the platform is pushing closer to maturity. It must be noted that Ethereum as a platform was not the cause of the vulnerability. In its nascent state, smart-contract code is bound to cause bugs such as this hack, which will result in better code-checking mechanisms and secure code-writing practices that can avoid such pitfalls. In the future, as a result of forks, we might end up with a consolidated single-currency platform just like before.

CHAPTER 7

High-Performance Computing

In the Ethereum ecosystem, the transfer of value between users is often realized by the use of tokens that represent digital assets. Ether is the default token and the de facto currency used for transactions and for initializing smart contracts on the network. Ethereum also supports the creation of new kinds of tokens that can represent any commonly traded commodities as digital assets. All tokens (for instance ANT or GLM, explained later in the chapter) are implemented using the standard protocol, so the tokens are compatible with any Ethereum wallet on the network. The tokens are distributed to users interested in the given specific use case through an Initial Coin Offering (ICO). In this chapter, we will focus our attention on tokens created for a very specific use case: high-performance computing (HPC). More precisely, we will discuss a model of distributed HPC where miners offer computational resources for a task and get rewarded in some form of Ethereum token.

We will begin our discussion with an overview of the lifecycle of a token in the network. Then, we will dive into the first token, Ethereum Computation Market (ECM), which is the most generalized and comprehensive distributed processing system. ECM will be our standard model for HPCs that use tokens, and we will introduce concepts such as dispute resolution (firm and soft) and verifiability of off-chain processing with on-chain rewards. The second token we will cover is Golem, which posits itself as the Airbnb for unused CPU cycles. At the time of writing, the latest version, called Clay Golem, will allow distributed rendering of 3D objects using Blender. Future releases will enable more advanced functionality such as processing big-data analytics. The third token we will present is Supercomputing Organized by Network Mining (SONM), which extends the idea of fog computing (a decentralizing computational processing model) to create an Ethereum-powered machine economy and marketplace. SONM has published a technically oriented roadmap focused on neural networks and artificial intelligence. The initial use case will be to provide decentralized hosting to run a *Quake* server.

© Vikram Dhillon, David Metcalf, and Max Hooper 2021
V. Dhillon et al., *Blockchain Enabled Applications*, https://doi.org/10.1007/978-1-4842-6534-5_7

The final token we will talk about in this chapter is iEx.ec, which leverages well-developed desktop grid computing software along with a proof-of-computation protocol that allows for off-chain consensus and monetization of resources offered. We will end the chapter by examining the implications of tokens in a post-blockchain economy and the nimble development of sidechains.

Tokens and Value Creation

To understand the concept of tokens, we first need to understand the context in which they operate—"fat" protocols (`https://avc.com/2017/08/how-to-value-crypto-assets/`). At Consensus 2017, Naval Ravikant talked about the idea of "fat" protocols and the fundamental differences between internet companies and the next generation of startups building on the blockchain. Currently, the internet stack is composed of two slices, a "thin" slice of protocols that power the World Wide Web and a "fat" slice of applications that are built on top of the protocols. Some of the largest internet companies, such as Google and Facebook, captured value in the application layer, but then had to invent new protocols and an infrastructure layer to actually scale. When internet companies reach that size, they have validated their core business model and have enough resources to allocate toward the creation of new protocols.

Blockchain-based companies operate on a different stack with a "thin" slice of application layer and a "fat" slice of protocol layer. The value concentrates in the protocol layer, and only a fraction spills over to the application layer. Joel Monégro and Balaji S. Srinivasan (`https://www.usv.com/writing/2016/08/fat-protocols/`) propose two probable reasons for the large interest and investment in the protocol layer:

- **Shared data layer:** In a blockchain stack, the nature of underlying architecture is such that key data is publicly accessible through a blockchain explorer. Furthermore, every member of the network has a complete copy of the blockchain with which to reach consensus on the network. A pertinent example of this shared data layer in practical usage is the ease with which a user can switch between exchanges such as Poloniex and Kraken, or vice-versa. The exchanges all have equal and free access to the underlying data or the blockchain transactions.

- **Access tokens:** Tokens can be thought of as analogous to paid API keys that provide access to a service. In the blockchain stack, the protocol token is used to access the service provided by the network, such as file storage in the case of Storj. Historically, the only method of monetizing a protocol was to build software that implemented the new protocol, which was superior to the competition. This was possible for research divisions in well-funded companies; however, in academia, the pace of research was slower in the early days because the researchers creating those protocols had little financial gain. With tokens, the creators of a protocol can monetize it directly through an Initial Coin Offering (ICO) and benefit more as the token is widely adopted and others build services on top of the new protocol.

Due to proper incentives, a readily available data-sharing layer, and application of tokens beyond the utility of a currency, developers are spending considerable time on the underlying protocols to solve difficult technical problems. As a result, startups building on the blockchain stack will inevitably spend more time on the "fat" protocol layer and solve technical challenges to capture value and differentiate themselves from a sea of Ethereum tokens.

Recently, with more tokens up and coming in the Ethereum ecosystem, cross-compatibility has become a concern, and to address this issue a new specification called ERC20 has been developed by Fabian Vogelsteller. ERC20 is a set of standards for how tokens can be implemented on the Ethereum network. It describes six standard functions that every access token should implement to be compatible with DApps across the network. ERC20-based tokens can seamlessly interact with other smart contracts and decentralized applications on the Ethereum blockchain. Tokens that only implement a few of the standard functions are considered partially ERC20-compliant. Even partially compliant tokens can easily interface with third parties depending upon which functions are missing.

Note   Setting up a new token on the Ethereum blockchain requires a smart contract. The initial parameters and functions for the token are supplied to the smart contract that governs the execution of the token on the blockchain.

In order to be fully ERC20-compliant (`https://eips.ethereum.org/EIPS/eip-20`), a developer needs to incorporate a specific set of functions into their smart contract that will allow the following actions to be performed on the token:

- Get the total token supply: `totalSupply()`

- Get an account balance: `balanceOf()`

- Transfer the token: `transfer()`, `transferFrom()`

- Approve spending of the token: `approve()`, `allowance()`

When a new token is created, it is often pre-mined and then sold in a crowdsale also known as an Initial Coin Offering. Here, a *pre-mine* refers to allocating a portion of the tokens for the token creators and any parties that will offer services for the network (such as running full nodes). Tokens have a fixed sale price. They can be issued and sold publicly during an ICO at the inception of a new protocol to fund its development, similar to the way startups have used Kickstarter to fund product development. As the popularity of ERC20 tokens has risen, more challenges have become apparent. In a previous implementation, the transfer function only worked one way: if a user accidentally sent tokens to a smart contract, there was no way to recover the tokens, even if the contract owner wanted to return the tokens. As a result, technical errors have resulted in the loss of millions of dollars during pre-sale events. Ethereum developers have since fixed the transfer function by introducing the `transferFrom()` function. In addition, new specifications have been proposed as potential candidates to replace ERC20 or introduce new token types. Let's review three of these specs:

- **ERC223:** A specification (`https://github.com/ethereum/eips/issues/223`) fixing the transfer function error from a previous ERC20 implementation. More specifically, this implementation combines the `transfer` and `transferFrom` functions into a single `transfer` function that can cancel transactions.

- **ERC721:** A specification (`https://eips.ethereum.org/EIPS/eip-721`) that introduces the concept of tokens as assets and collectibles. The original ERC20 specification creates interchangeable tokens such that all tokens have the same value. However, ERC721 allows for the creation of unique tokens that may have a higher value. This idea was picked up by a blockchain gaming app called Cryptokitties, where attributes such as age, color, and breed make the token very rare and a valuable asset.

- **ERC948:** A specification (`https://github.com/ethereum/EIPs/issues/948`) describing a subscription model for businesses that have a physical presence and want to extend to the blockchain by issuing tokens as digital subscriptions.

The next question we should ask regarding tokens is: Given that tokens are digital, what do token buyers actually buy? Essentially, what a user buys is a private key. This is the analogy we made to paid API keys—your private key is just a string of a characters that grants you access. A private key can be understood to be similar to a password. Just as your password grants you access to the email stored on a centralized database like Gmail, a private key grants you access to the digital tokens stored on a decentralized blockchain stack like Ethereum.

Tip   The key difference between a private key and a password stored on a centralized database is that if you lost your private key, you would not be able to recover it. Recently, there have been some attempts to restore access to an account through a recovery service using a co-signer who can verify the identity of the user requesting recovery.

Ultimately, tokens appear to be a better funding and monetization model for technology compared to traditional subscription-based services. Currently, even though base cryptocurrencies such as Ethereum have a larger market share, tokens will eventually amount to 100 times the market share. Figure 7-1 provides a summary of the differences between value creation for traditional internet companies and that for companies building on the blockchain stack using Ethereum tokens. Let's begin with our first token, which will serve as a model for all the tokens that follow. Michael Oved at ConsenSys suggests (`https://media.consensys.net/the-blockchain-killer-app-ethereum-tokens-c3f5e6f4ce7f`) that tokens will be the killer app that everyone has been waiting for:

> If killer apps prove the core value of larger technologies, Ethereum tokens surely prove the core value of blockchain, made evident by the runaway success that tokens have brought to these new business models.

> We are now seeing a wave of launches that break tokens through as the first killer app of blockchain technology. Bitcoin, in many ways, is a "proof of concept" for a blockchain-based asset. The Ethereum platform is proving that concept at scale.

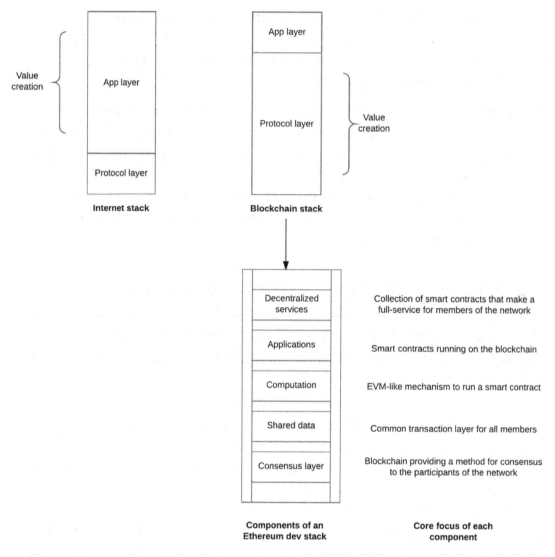

Figure 7-1. *An overview of a blockchain stack used by tokens*

This model is based on Joyce J. Shen's description of distributed ledger technology. Traditional internet companies such as Google and Facebook created and captured value in the application layer by harvesting data that users generated. Blockchain companies have a different dynamic in terms of ownership and the technology available. The blockchain itself provides a mechanism for consensus and a shared data layer that is publicly accessible. Ethereum further provides a Turing-complete programming language and node-to-node compatibility through an EVM that can run the instructions contained in a smart contract. Using smart contracts, a full application can be constructed to run on the blockchain, and a collection of applications can become a full decentralized service such as Storj.

Ethereum Computational Market (ECM)

ECM is a very simplistic and functional token for off-chain computations and is the first token we will consider in this chapter. It will serve as a teaching tool and general model covering all the necessary features that an HPC-token would need. ECM is designed to facilitate the execution of computations off-chain that would be too costly to perform within the Ethereum Virtual Machine (EVM). In essence, ECM is a decentralized version of Amazon's EC2, a web service that provides centralized computational capacity in the cloud. The key technical advance in ECM is the computation marketplace, which allows one user (the customer) to pay another (the host) to execute an algorithm off-chain and report the results back to the customer. Additionally, to preserve the integrity of the computation being done off-chain, each algorithm also has an on-chain implementation. This on-chain component can be used to verify whether the submitted end result is indeed correct. It also plays a role in resolving disputes. Let's take a look at the lifecycle of a request through ECM in Figure 7-2. ECM uses some terminology specific to the project for describing the lifecycle of a request from when it's initially received to the final resolution. We employ some of this terminology in Figure 7-2, along with a few additional terms that we discuss here:

- **Pending:** Indicates when a request is received. Every request begins in the pending status.

- **Waiting for Resolution:** A request for computation has been submitted to the network, and a host has computed the algorithm and is now reporting the result. This is a decision point for the customer; either the answer will be accepted and the request will move to soft resolution status, or the answer will be challenged, in which case the request will move to the needs resolution state.

- **Needs Resolution:** When an answer is challenged, this path is taken from the decision tree. The request is changed to needs resolution status, and the on-chain verification component of the algorithm is required.

- **Resolving:** The interim period as on-chain computation is being performed for a request. The request will remain in this status until the computation has been completed.

135

- **Firm versus Soft Resolution:** Once the on-chain computation has been completed, the request is set to the firm resolution status. If no challenges are made within a certain window of time after the answer has been submitted to the customer, the request is set to soft resolution.

- **Finalized:** Once an answer is obtained through either soft or hard resolution, the original request can be set to finalized status. This unlocks the payment from the customer's end and allows the host to receive payment for off-chain computation.

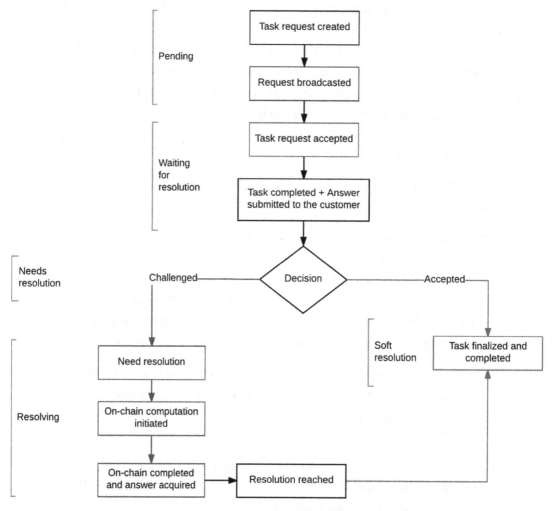

Figure 7-2. *Lifecycle of a request as it goes through ECM*

In Figure 7-2, each request-state described is broken down further into a workflow. Once a task request is processed off-chain, there is a decision point concerning the final answer. If the customer challenges the answer provided by the host, the on-chain component of the algorithm will execute and the request will go through a few states of needing resolution. On the other hand, if no challenges are made, the request will move to soft resolution and be considered finalized. The host receives payment after the request has reached the finalized state.

Now that we have an understanding of how a request gets processed in ECM, let's talk about the marketplace and individual markets within that marketplace. The concept that we have referred to as an *algorithm* being computed off-chain is made from three separate contracts: a broker contract, a factory contract, and an execution contract:

- **Broker:** A contract that facilitates the transfer of a request from the customer to the host who will carry out the computation.

- **Execution:** A contract used for on-chain verification of a computation. This contract can carry out one cycle of on-chain execution in the event that the submitted answer is challenged.

- **Factory:** A contract that handles the deployment of the execution contract on-chain in the case of dispute resolution. This contract supplies relevant metadata such as compiler version required to recompile the bytecode and verify it.

The marketplace itself has verticals (markets within a marketplace) that execute specialized types of contracts and algorithms, creating use case–specific HPC-economics on the Ethereum blockchain using tokens. Figure 7-3 provides a visual summary of the three contracts that are components of each market. So, what's required to make a computation request on ECM? There are primarily two functions that create a request and provide all the necessary details. Here, the requestExecution function is used to create a request for computation, and this function takes two arguments. First is a set of inputs to the function itself, and second is the time window during which a submitted answer can be challenged before the request turns to soft resolved status. This time window is given in number of blocks because blocks are created at a definitive time interval in Ethereum. Lastly, this function also specifies the payment being offered for this computation. The getRequest function returns all the metadata regarding the request. The following are some of the relevant parameters returned from the metadata:

- **address requester:** The address of the customer that requested the computation

- **bytes32 resultHash:** The SHA-3 hash of the result from a given computation

- **address executable:** The address of the executable contract that was deployed on-chain to settle a challenged answer

- **uint status:** The status of a request at a given time in the lifecycle. It is an unsigned integer corresponding to the status of a request given by numbers 0–7.

- **uint payment:** The amount in wei that this request will pay (to the host) in exchange for completion of a computation. Wei are the smallest unit of ether that can be transferred between users, similar to satoshis in Bitcoin.

- **uint softResolutionBlocks:** A time window given by the number of blocks within which a challenge to an answer must be submitted. If no challenges are submitted to an answer in that interval, the request changes to soft resolution.

- **uint requiredDeposit:** Amount in wei that must be provided when submitting an answer to a request, or by a challenger objecting to a submitted answer. This deposit is locked until the request moves to the finalized state and is then released back to the host.

It is important to note that in our discussion a few tasks such as answer verification, conflict resolution, and challenges have required deposits. The deposits are used as a countermeasure to reduce the potential for **Sybil attacks** on the network. In a sybil attack, an attacker creates multiple fake or Sybil identities in order to take over the network. More precisely, in our case, an attacker would create multiple fake nodes on the network. This allows an attacker to vote on the network, refuse block approval, and halt the transmission of blocks on the network. Large-scale Sybil attacks require an attacker to control the majority of computing power or hash-rate on the network. By taking over the majority of computing power, an attacker can theoretically reverse transactions and surpass double-spending. This is also known as "51% attack". However, practically speaking, as the network size grows larger, accomplishing a 51% attack becomes more and more unfeasible.

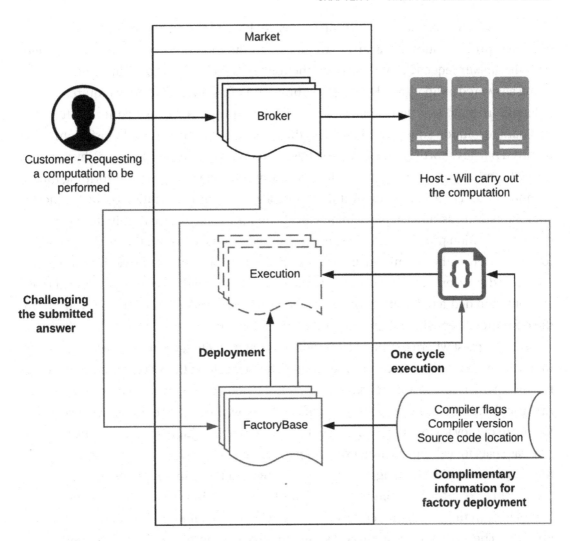

Figure 7-3. *Overview of a market in the marketplace*

In Figure 7-3, we see the three components necessary in a market for responding to a request by a user (customer): a broker contract, an execution contract, and a factory contract. The broker contract facilitates a customer–host interaction, and the other two contracts play a role in dispute resolution. In the case of challenges to a submitted answer, the broker will initiate the deployment of the execution contract through its factory contract (also called FactorBase, shown with the red workflow), which consolidates the information and prepares for a one-cycle execution of the algorithm. The gas necessary for execution will be taken from a deposit that the challenger is required to submit. We will discuss the submission and challenge process next.

Next, we will talk about submitting an answer back to the customer and the challenge process. Submitting an answer for a computation done off-chain is performed with the `answerRequest` function. This function takes the unique ID of the request being answered as an input. The actual submission of a potential answer requires a deposit in ether. This deposit is locked until the request has reached either a soft or a hard resolution state. We will discuss the importance of holding a deposit from involved parties shortly. Once a request has been finalized, the deposit made by the host who submitted an answer is reclaimed, along with the reward for performing the computation. If a submitted answer does not fall within the expectations of the request submitted by a customer, a participant can challenge the answer. This initiates an on-chain verification process that will execute one cycle of the computation within the EVM to verify whether the submitted answer is correct. If the submitted answer is found to be incorrect during on-chain computation, the host's deposit will have the gas costs of that computation deducted from it. The challenger will get a large portion of the reward from the customer's deposit, and the dispute will be resolved.

For a request where a submitted answer has been challenged, the request moves to the needs resolution state. This is accomplished by calling the `initializeDispute` function, which serves as a transition between the point at which a challenge is made and the beginning of on-chain verification. Now the broker contract will use a factory to deploy an executable contract initialized with the inputs for this request. The gas costs for calling this function and performing one-cycle execution are reimbursed from the challenger's deposit. Throughout the resolving state on a request, the `executeExecutable` function is called until the on-chain verification has been completed. At this point, the request is moved to a hard resolution state and eventually finalized. The gas-charge and reward system may seem complicated, but it follows a simple principle: the correct answer receives payment for the computation, and incorrect submitters must pay for gas during on-chain verification. Let's recap:

- In the case of soft resolution, a host reclaims their initial deposit and a reward given by the customer for executing the computation.

- If there were no correct submitted answers, the gas costs for verification are split evenly among the users that submitted answers. The reward payment returns to the customer who originally requested the computation.

- In the case of hard resolution, the incorrect host reclaims their remaining deposit after gas costs have been deducted (for on-chain verification). This host does not receive a reward for the computation.

- If a challenger wins hard resolution, they reclaim their deposit along with the reward payment. The gas costs are debited from the incorrect host's deposit.

On-chain verification of a computation is by nature an expensive task due to gas costs. ECM is designed such that off-chain computation would be cheaper than running a task in EVM. From a technical standpoint, there are two types of on-chain execution implementations: stateless and stateful computations. Figure 7-4 shows a contrast between the two implementations.

An executable contract is stateless if the computation is self-sufficient in that it does not require any external sources of data. Essentially, the return value from a previous step is used as the input for the next step. Piper Merriam (the creator of ECM) proposes that stateless executable contracts are superior to stateful implementations for two main reasons: lower overhead while writing the algorithm and reduced complexity because the computation cycles are self-sustaining. An example highlighted by Piper is the Fibonacci sequence written as a stateless implementation with the algorithm returning the latest Fibonacci numbers as the input for the next cycle of execution. The overhead of writing this in a stateless form is very minor, and there is no additional complexity of introducing local storage.

Tip   For stateless contracts, the execution contract is identical to the algorithm sent as a request to the marketplace for computation. Here, on-chain verification would run the execution contract for one cycle, and hosts would run it for as many cycles necessary to obtain the final answer.

An executable contract is stateful if the computation is not self-sufficient in that it requires an additional data source and the return values from the previous step. This additional data source is often in the form of a data structure holding local storage. Let's go back to our example of the Fibonacci sequence, and now let's make it stateful. To do this, the algorithm would store each computed number in the contract storage and only return the latest number to the algorithm for the next cycle of execution. Every step of execution would require the algorithm to search for the last number stored in order to compute the next number. By including storage, the algorithm must now search through saved results and print out any desired Fibonacci sequence that has been computed. This reliance on local state is what makes this instance of the contract stateful. Stateful contracts enable new and complex features such as using lookup tables and search, but also cause an increase in the complexity of the written algorithm.

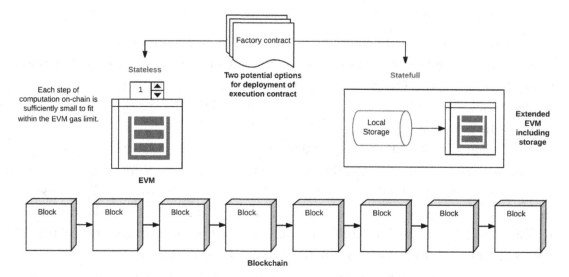

Figure 7-4. *Two models for factory execution contracts in Ethereum Comptuational Markets*

During on-chain verification in Figure 7-4, a single cycle of the execution contract will be executed. However, a self-contained contract in stateless form will be executed efficiently and without any additional complexity. In stateless contracts, each step executed inside an EVM is elementary, so it falls within the gas limits of that virtual machine. On the other hand, some contracts require additional storage due to the complexity of execution. In such cases, a stateful contract is executed where local storage is bound to the EVM during the on-chain verification. This storage is temporary and only exists through the duration of the on-chain processing.

Golem Network

Golem is a decentralized general-purpose supercomputing network. In addition to being a marketplace for renting computational resources, Golem aims to power microservices and allow asynchronous task execution. As a technology stack, Golem offers both Infrastructure-as-a-Service (IaaS) and Platform-as-a-Service (PaaS) through a decentralized blockchain stack for developers. In Golem, there are three components that function as the backbone of a decentralized market:

- **Decentralized farm:** A mechanism to send, organize, and execute computation tasks from individual users known as requesters and hosts known as providers (of computational resources). This provides the users competitive prices for tasks such as CGI rendering and machine learning on network access.

- **Transaction framework:** Golem has a custom payment framework for developers to monetize services and software developed to run on the decentralized network. This framework can be customized to capture value in new and innovative methods, such as escrows, insurance, and audit proofs, on the Ethereum blockchain.

- **Application registry:** Developers can create applications (for particular tasks) that take advantage of Golem as a distribution channel and a marketplace with new and unique monetization schemes. These applications can be published to the application registry, which essentially functions as an app store for the network.

Golem's premise in building the marketplace is that not all members will request additional resources for extensive computation at all times. As such, the requesters can become providers and rent their own hardware to earn extra fees. Figure 7-5 provides an overview of how the three components in Golem work in sync. Currently, Golem inherits the integrity (Byzantine fault tolerance) and consensus mechanisms from Ethereum for the deployment, execution, and validation of tasks. However, eventually Golem will use fully functional micropayment channels for running microservices built on Layer 2.0 upgrades. This will allow users to run services like a note-taking app or hosting websites and even large-scale streaming applications in a completely decentralized manner.

Several more optimizations are needed before Golem reaches that level of maturity; currently, the most pressing developments concern the execution of tasks. Before Golem can execute general-purpose tasks, we need to ensure that the computation takes place in an isolated environment without privileges, similar to an EVM but expanded with more features. We also need whitelist and blacklist mechanisms along with digital signatures recognized in the application registry, which allow providers to build a trust network and allow users to run applications cryptographically signed by trusted developers. Additionally, a network-wide reputation system is necessary to reward the providers that have participated the most during computation tasks and also to detect a malicious node and mitigate tasks efficiently.

Note   The first release, dubbed Brass Golem, only allows one type of task to be executed on the network—CGI rendering. The main goals of this release are to validate the task registry and to have a basic task definition scheme. The developers want to integrate IPFS for decentralized storage, a basic reputation system for the providers involved, and Docker integration in the network. Future releases have added new features discussed later in this section.

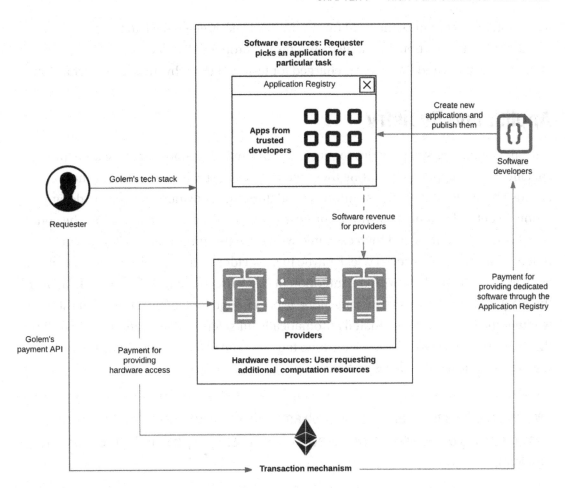

Figure 7-5. *The Golem technology stack*

Three main components of the Golem stack are shown in Figure 7-5. Software developers create applications that automate routine tasks and publish them on the application registry. For instance, a time-limited rendering application can eliminate the need for any complicated transactions or task-tracking. The buyer will simply make a single-use deposit and use the application until the time is up. When buyers use applications from the registry, the revenue generated is used to compensate the developers for their app. The registry contains two types of applications in it: verified apps from trusted developers and new applications from unconfirmed developers. Eventually, verifiers pool in the newly uploaded applications and track them closely for any suspicious activity. After a few uses, the new applications also get a verified status. The developers also receive minor compensation from the execution of these applications on the provider nodes. Providers requisition the hardware for apps, and a lion's share of revenue generated from running a task is given back to the providers (miners). The transaction mechanism assures the proper delivery of funds to the appropriate party, and the buyer is charged for task execution by the same mechanism.

Application Registry

The application registry provides requesters with a massive repository to search for specific tools or applications fitting their needs. The registry is an Ethereum smart contract between three entities: authors, validators, and providers. What's the design rationale behind adding these three entities? For general-purpose computing, the code is isolated in a sandbox and then executed with the bare-minimum privileges. But potential software bugs could wreak havoc in a provider's sandbox, executing malicious code in a virtual machine with the intention of escalating privileges, or even taking over the machine. That's why sandboxing alone is not enough for Golem. One could ask whether the code can be evaluated automatically for safety and security. Theoretically, this is not plausible. We cannot determine the outcome of a complex algorithm before executing it due to the halting problem.

Note   The halting problem is the problem of determining whether a program will finish running or continue to run forever given an arbitrary computer program and an input.

To enable secure and trusted code execution on host machines, the application registry is split between three parties that are responsible for maintaining the integrity of the network. Authors publish decentralized applications to the registry, validators review and certify DApps as safe by creating a whitelist, and providers maintain blacklists of problematic DApps. Validators also maintain blacklists by marking applications as malicious or spam, and providers often end up using a blacklist from validators. Similarly, providers can pre-approve certain Golem-specific applications (certified by validators) to execute on their nodes.

Providers can also elect to curate their own whitelists or blacklists. The default option for Golem is to run using a whitelist of trusted applications. The first set of apps will be verified by the developers to kickstart Golem; however, after the initial distribution, the network will rely on validators. On the other hand, providers can also take the approach of relying only on blacklists. This approach has the advantage of maximizing the reach of a provider (to the marketplace) and offering a wide range of applications that can be executed on a node. Eventually, providers will become specialized and fine-tune their nodes to be incredibly efficient at running one kind of task. This allows the providers more control over what runs on their nodes and custom hardware options for a computing farm. Ultimately, this option is available to developers who want to maximize their profits and are willing to run dedicated machines with bleeding-edge software.

In a decentralized network like Golem, we will see a divide between traditional and vanguard validators. Traditional validators will maintain a set of stable applications that perform very routine tasks. For instance, a request for a complex 3D rendering can launch a preemptible rendering instance on a provider's nodes. Once the job is complete, the instance will terminate to free up memory and send the output to the requester. On the other hand, vanguard validators will include and approve software that pushes the boundaries of what is possible with Golem. Running new and experimental software on a provider's node will require better sandboxing and hardening of the virtual machine. But these features can be a premium add-on running on special nodes offered by a provider. Monetizing the premium add-ons will also disincentivize scammers and malicious entities. Overall, this design approach makes the network more inclusive, costly for scammers, and innovative for developers.

Transaction Framework

The transaction framework can be considered analogous to Stripe: an API for monetizing applications running on Golem. After the crowdsale, the network will use GNT (Golem Network Token) for all transactions between users, to compensate software developers and computation resource providers. The transaction framework is built on top of Ethereum; therefore, it inherits the underlying payment architecture and extends it to implement advanced payment schemes such as nanopayment mechanisms and transaction batching. Both innovations mentioned here are unique to Golem, so let's talk about why they are necessary to the network. To power microservices, Golem will have to process a very high volume of small transactions. The value of a single payment is very low; these payments are also known as nanopayments. However, there is one caveat while using nanopayments: the transaction fees cannot be larger than the nanopayment itself. To solve this problem, Golem uses transaction batching. This solution aggregates nanopayments and sends them at once as a single Ethereum transaction to reduce the applied transaction fees. For instance, Golem developers note that the cost of ten payments processed in a single transaction is approximately half of the value of ten payments processed in ten transactions. By batching multiple transactions, a significantly lower transaction fee will be passed on to a user paying for per-unit usage (per-node or per-hour) of a microservice.

Note For providers, another model to power microservices is credit-based payment for per-unit hosting. Here, the requester makes a deposit of timelocked GNT, and at the end of the day the provider automatically deducts the charges for usage. The remaining credits are released back to the requester.

In Golem, nanopayments work in the context of one-to-many micropayments from a requester to many providers that assist in completing the computational tasks. The payments carried out for microservices are on the scale of $0.01, and for such small sums, the transaction fees are relatively large even on Ethereum. The idea here is that instead of making individual transactions of $0.01, the requester (payer) issues a lottery ticket for a lottery for a $1 prize with 1/100 chance of winning. The value of such ticket is $0.01 for the requester and the advantage is that on average only one ticket in 100 will lead to an actual transaction. This is a probabilistic mechanism to allow nano-transactions, but it does not guarantee that one given Golem node will be compensated adequately if the number of tasks computed is small. Bylica et al. provide the mathematical background to assuring fair distribution of income from this lottery system as the network expands, adding more requesters and providers. Essentially, as the number of tasks offered by requesters increases, the income a node generates from probabilistic lottery rewards will approach the amount it would receive being paid with individual transactions.

The lottery system to be implemented in Golem is much more predictable for the providers than a completely probabilistic scheme. The provider is assured that among the tickets issued to reward the providers of a single task, there are no hash collisions and only one ticket is a winning one. Moreover, if there are 100 providers participating in the lottery payment, then the nanopayment protocol guarantees that the task will only have to be paid out once. Bylica and collaborators discuss a few counterclaim mechanisms in place to prevent malicious entities from claiming to be lottery winners and cashing out. A brief sketch of the lottery process is provided in Figure 7-6. After a task has been completed, the payer initiates a new lottery to pay out the participating providers. The payer creates a lottery description L, which contains a unique lottery identifier, and calculates its hash h(L). The hash is written to the Ethereum contract storage. The payer also announces the lottery description L to the Golem network, so that every participating node can verify that the payment has the correct value and check that h(L) is indeed written to the Ethereum storage. The winner of a lottery payout can be uniquely determined by cross-referencing a given description L and a random value R that is unknown to all parties except the lottery smart contract. After a certain amount of time, if the reward has not been claimed, the smart contract computes the winning provider's address (given the L and R) and transfers the reward from the contract's associated storage to the winner. The hash of the lottery h(L) is also removed from the contract storage, and a new lottery payout cycle can now begin.

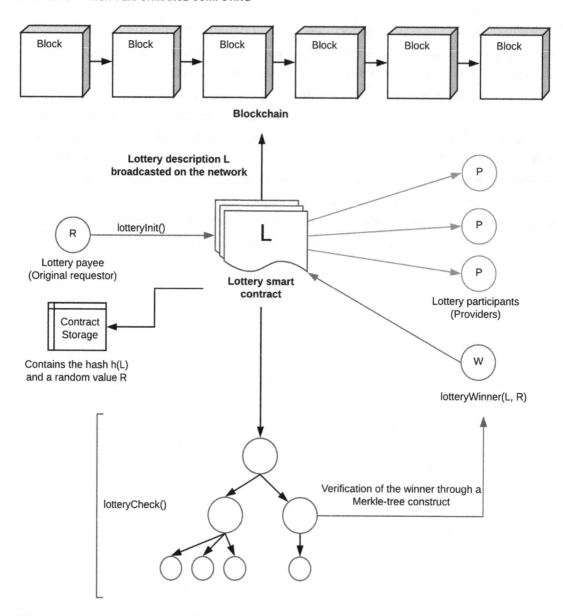

Figure 7-6. *Nanopayment-based lottery payout system*

On a macro scale, Andrzej Regulski wrote a post describing some of the economic principles behind GNT and the long-term appreciation in value of the token enabled by this transaction framework (https://blog.golemproject.net/the-economics-of-the-golem-network-token/). The most pertinent items from his post are quoted here:

GNT will be necessary to interact with the Golem network. At first, its sole role is to enable the transfer of value from requestors to providers, and to software developers. Later on, the Transaction Framework will make it possible to assign additional attributes to the token, so that, for example, it is required to store deposits in GNT.

The number of GNT (i.e., the supply) is going to be indefinitely fixed at the level created during the Golem crowdfunding. No GNT is going to be created afterwards.

A depreciation or appreciation of the token is neutral to the operations of the network, because users are free to set any ask/bid prices for compute resources in Golem, thus accommodating any fluctuations in GNT value.

The constant amount of tokens will have to accommodate a growing number of transactions, hence increasing the demand for GNT. With a reasonable assumption that the velocity of the token (i.e., the number of transactions per unit of the token in a specific period) is constant over time, this conclusion can be drawn from the quantity theory of money. This, in turn, means that the overall success and growth of the Golem network implies a long-run appreciation of the GNT.

This payment framework can also be used as a fallback mechanism for conflict resolution. If a task challenge remains open after going through the traditional Golem mechanics, we would need a method for hard resolution (as we saw in the Ethereum Computation Markets section). Here, we can use a TrueBit-style "trial" for final resolution. TrueBit is a smart contract–based dispute-resolution layer built for Ethereum. It integrates as an add-on on top of the existing architecture for Ethereum projects such as Golem. The design principle for TrueBit is to rely on the only trusted resource in the network to resolve a dispute: the miners. A hard resolution using TrueBit relies on a verification subroutine involving limited-resource verifiers known as judges.

In TrueBit's verification game, there are three main players: a solver, a challenge, and judges. The solver presents a solution for a task, a challenger contests the presented answer, and the judge decides whether the challenger or the solver is correct. The purpose of using the verification subroutine is to reduce the complexity of on-chain computation. This is done as the game proceeds in rounds, where each round narrows down the scope of computation until only a trivial step remains. This last step is executed on-chain by a smart contract (judge), which makes the final verdict on which party is correct. Note that the judges in this scheme are constrained in terms of computational power. Therefore, only very simplistic computations are ultimately carried out on-chain for the judge to make a ruling. A visual guide to the verification game is provided in Figure 7-7.

Note   The verification game works iteratively, with a reward structure benefiting the verifiers (challengers) who diligently search for errors. Accurate detection and eventual verification of errors results in challengers' being rewarded with a substantial jackpot.

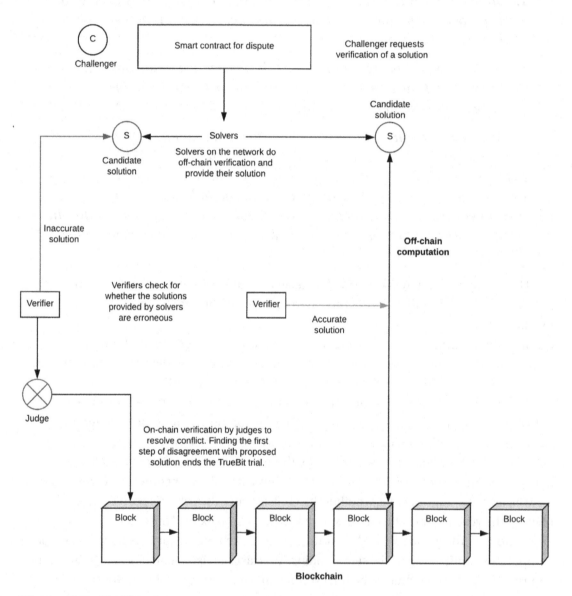

Figure 7-7. *Verification game*

To begin the first round of this game, the solver must commit to a segment of steps (computations) performed over a specific time window. The solver selects computation steps equally spaced in time across the provided window and creates a Merkle-tree mapping to the full internal state of the network. The Merkle roots of these trees are broadcasted to the blockchain. The challenger now performs a binary search through the Merkle trees until she discovers the first instance that mismatches with her own expectations. That is to say, she finds a step i where the Merkle root is not updated as the state transitions from step i to $i+1$. Given step i, the challenger can request a Merkle proof for memory access before and after this step. In this context, a Merkle proof is a path from the step i to the Merkle root together with all the siblings (capturing the state of the network at step i). Note that the siblings are identical before and after (siblings at steps i and $i+1$); only the data for step i will change. At this point, the judge can run step i and check whether updating the state to $i+1$ also updates the Merkle root correctly. The judge can provably discover which party is wrong in this step and broadcast the verdict. In the end, either the cheating solver will be punished, or the challenger will pay for the resources consumed by the false alarm.

TrueBit is an advanced on-chain execution mechanism compared to the on-chain verification implemented in ECM. It offers the ability to verify computations at a lower cost than running the full instruction because only one step is executed on-chain. By using TrueBit as a dispute-resolution layer for off-chain computations, smart contracts can enable third-party programs to execute well-documented routines in a trustless manner. Even for advanced machine learning applications such as deep learning that require terabytes of data, as long as the root hash of the training data is encoded in the smart contract, it can be used to verify the integrity of off-chain computations. The reason TrueBit works for large datasets is simply due to the Merkle roots' mapping the state of the network at a given time t, and a challenger's ability to perform a binary search. For a project like Golem aiming to achieve HPC toward a variety of use cases, TrueBit can enable large datasets to be used off-chain with an on-chain guarantee of accurate outputs.

Note   Off-chain task execution raises concerns about network integrity. Layer 2.0 upgrades to Ethereum are raising overall network security and enabling trustless off-chain task execution. To that end, TrueBit is being considered as a candidate for Layer 2.0 upgrades.

There are three new use cases being considered with the release of Clay Golem:

- **gWasm:** Webassembly (Wasm) is an operating-system-agnostic format for distributing binary files that execute with near-native performance on various platforms. gWasm is a wrapper for integrating new applications into the Golem network. The premise of gWasm is that if an app can be compiled to Wasm, it can be distributed to the Golem network. In early development.

- **gLAMBDA:** An upcoming scientific use case for Golem. Applying parallelization to perform RASPA simulations on the Golem network (in a decentralized fashion). RASPA is a general-purpose simulation package that can be used in simulations of molecules in gases, fluids, and carbon nanotubes.

- **Video transcoding:** Another upcoming use case for Golem. Focuses on digital conversion of large video files from one format to another.

SONM (Supercomputer Organized by Network Mining)

SONM is a decentralized implementation of the fog computing concept using a blockchain. To understand how SONM works within the framework of fog computing, we first need to define two networking concepts: IoT and IoE. The European Commission defines the Internet of Things (IoT) architecture as a pervasive network of objects that have IP addresses and can transfer data over the network. IoT lends itself to the broader concept of Internet of Everything (IoE), which provides a seamless communication bus and contextual services between objects in both the real world and the virtual world. IoE is defined by Cisco as follows:

The networked connection of people, process, data, and things. The benefit of IoE is derived from the compound impact of connecting people, process, data, and things, and the value this increased connectedness creates as "everything" comes online.

While IoT traditionally refers to devices connected to each other or cloud services, IoE is an umbrella term for a heavier focus on "people" as an essential component attached to the business logic for generating revenue. From an engineering standpoint, IoT is the messaging layer focusing on device-to-device communication and IoE is the monetization layer allowing startups to capitalize on the interaction between people and their devices. A staggering amount of data is generated from devices connected in an IoT network. Transferring this data to the cloud for processing requires enormous network bandwidth, and there are delays between when the data is generated, processing this data, and receiving the results (from hours to days). A major limitation of IoT technology is that transfer delay period. Recently, a growing concern has been the loss of value of actionable data due to the transfer and processing stages. By the time we receive those processed results, it is too late to act on that data.

One solution presented by Ginny Nichols from Cisco is called fog computing. Fog computing reduces the transfer delay by shifting the processing stage to lower levels of the network. Instead of processing a task by off-loading it to a centralized cloud, fog computing pushes high-priority tasks to be processed by a node closest to the device actually generating the data. For a device to participate in the fog, it must be capable of processing tasks, have local storage, and have some network connectivity. The concept of fog computing is a metaphor for the fact that fog forms close to the ground. Therefore, fog computing extends the cloud closer to the devices (ground) that produce IoT data to enable faster action. In fog computing, data processing is said to be concentrated at the edge (closer to the devices generating data) rather than existing centrally in the cloud. This allows us to minimize latency and enable faster response to time-sensitive tasks or reduce the time within which an action can be taken on data. SONM makes this layer of fog computing available to a decentralized network of participants for processing computationally intensive tasks.

Note   The need for faster response time to data (or business analytics) collected by large enterprises stimulated the development of real-time computational processing tools such as Apache Spark, Storm, and Hadoop. These tools allow for pre-processing of data as it is being collected and transferred. In a similar manner, fog computing seems to be an extension of IoT developed in response to the need for rapid data triage/processing.

SONM is built on top of Yandex.Cocaine (Configurable Omnipotent Custom Applications Integrated Network Engine). Cocaine is an open source PaaS stack for creating custom cloud hosting engines for applications, similar to Heroku. SONM has a complex architecture designed to resemble the World Computer model of Ethereum. The SONM team designed this world computer with components that are parallel to a traditional personal computer, with one major difference—the components are connected to a decentralized network.

- **CPU/Processor (Load Balancer):** In SONM's architecture, the processor (Hub) serves as a load balancer and task scheduler. The entire network can be represented as a chain of Hub nodes (or Hubs) that distribute tasks, gather results from a computing fog, pay miners for services, and provide status updates on the overall health of the network. Each hub node is analogous to a processor's core, and the number of cores (or Hub nodes) can be extended or reduced on the network as necessary. In a personal computer, the cores are locally accessible to the processor; however, in SONM, the cores are decentralized by nature. The hubs provide support to the whole network for coordinating the execution of tasks. More specifically, hubs provide the ability to process and parallelize high-load computations on the fog computing cloud.

- **BIOS (Blockchain):** For SONM, the BIOS is the Ethereum blockchain. Ethereum offers a reliable backbone for network consensus and payment mechanisms, which SONM can inherit. However, the base Ethereum implementation lacks a load balancer, and high gas costs have inspired alternatives on top of the blockchain, such as SONM.

- **Graphics Processing Unit:** The GPU for SONM is the fog computing cloud. More specifically, this fog comprises the miners in the SONM network that are making computational resources available to buyers.

- **Connected peripherals:** The buyers in SONM are equivalent to peripheral devices. The buyers connect to the network and pay for any resources they use. The requests are broadcasted on the blockchain, and miners select what they want to execute on their machines. Then, the load balancer dictates the execution of tasks.

- **Hard disk:** Storage in SONM will be implemented using well-established decentralized storage solutions such as IPFS or Storj.

- **Serial bus:** A communication module used for message passing and data transfer within the network between the sender (a node) and working machines. This serial bus is based on Ethereum Whisper and enables broadcast and listen functions for messages on the network.

- **Plug-ins circuit board:** A plug-ins board can be thought of as an expansion pack for the network. It allows SONM to expand its processing capabilities by seamlessly integrating compatible networks and computation farms.

Figure 7-8 provides a visual representation of the World Computer's components.

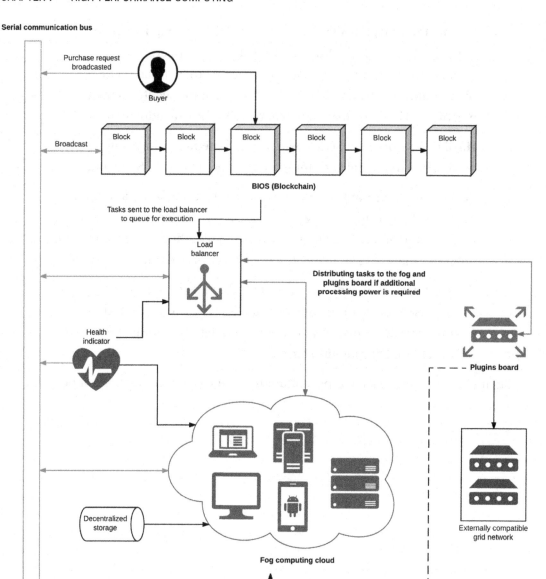

Figure 7-8. *World Computer implemented in SONM*

In Figure 7-8, you can see that the communication bus forms the backbone of this architecture, connecting at every level to the components of the World Computer. The workflow of a request through SONM begins with a buyer requesting computational resources. This request is broadcasted on the blockchain and the serial bus so that other components can verify if a particular request is legitimate. The miners accept the task, and the load balancer distributes the task to be executed in the fog computing cloud. If necessary, the load balancer can also assign a task to run on an application-specific grid network compatible with SONM through the plug-ins board. The fog cloud also has a local storage in the form of a decentralized service such as Storj or IPFS that is used as necessary. Finally, the load balancer also has two more important roles: to follow up with the task results and with the overall network health. The load balancer (Hub) collects the results of a task after it has been completed and sends it back to the buyer. A health indicator reports on the status of every component in the World Computer to the load balancer and the network in order to make better decisions regarding task assignment/execution.

The smart contract system in SONM is a set of protocols (smart contracts) for blockchain governance and management of decentralized applications implemented on the network. This system of smart contracts maintains the integrity of the network and provides several countermeasures against malicious entities, which we will discuss later. Furthermore, SONM uses formal definitions and rigorous proofs to demonstrate the security of communication (cryptographically secure message passing) between buyers and providers. The interactions between various parties on the network are modeled using a high-level mathematical framework called pi-calculus. This framework is a formal language for describing secure and concurrent interactions within a multi-party system over well-defined channels. The governance prototype in SONM includes a Decentralized Autonomous Organization (DAO), a court contract, a network-wide registry of hubs, and a factory contract to deploy new applications to the SONM network (for instance the whitelist, hub factory, and hub wallet). This model is extended to include some new elements (deployed by the factory) necessary for the management of DApps that run on the network. Currently, the process of buying computational resources appears very fragmented on the network. However, in future releases, buyers will complete a pre-purchase computing form to indicate their hardware selection, the DApps they want to use, and any special execution parameters. Let's look at the complete set of smart contracts used in the current SONM "blockchain government" in more depth:

- **SONM Token:** Default currency of the network. The token is used to reward miners for providing computational resources and for user transactions within the network.

- **DAO:** The regulatory body of SONM that grants users voting rights and administrative actions to manage decentralized applications. DApps on the network are required to pay *taxes* to be included in the DAO and gain access to the court. The DAO also has executive privileges to perform actions such as blacklisting a hub, releasing and locking funds to ensure proper payout for miners, and suspending or banning a hub.

Note   The court will be implemented as a dispute-resolution smart contract accessible through the DAO. It will offer protection against unfair buyers or providers in the market, along with result verification in case of challenges toward a solution.

- **Hub factory:** A hub has two extensions in the smart contract system, a factory and a wallet. The wallet can only be created by a hub wallet factory. The factory creates a new wallet contract and then registers this contract in the whitelist.

- **Hub wallet:** The hub wallet is a contract that receives payments from buyers and facilitates the payout of tokens to miners for services. The wallet is created by a factory and can exist in one of four possible states: created, registered, idle, suspected/punished. Initially, all wallets exist in the created state and have a fixed amount of frozen funds. In the created state, a contract can be registered on the whitelist. This contact now switches to the registered state, and has access to advanced functions such as transfer and payday. Now this wallet can begin to pay out miners (but not itself) within a specified amount of time called the payout period. After the end of payout period, the wallet can transfer the remaining money to the owner's wallet using the payday function. If a connected hub is caught performing malicious behavior, the DAO can blacklist the hub and seize the frozen funds. The DAO can further decide to change the state of the wallet to suspected or punished depending on the case.

- **Whitelist:** The whitelist is a registry-type contract that contains detailed information about hubs across the network, including their status. All wallets created by the factory are registered in this whitelist contract. Initially, this whitelist serves as a registry for trusted hubs verified by SONM developers to be safe and secure. Eventually, this functionality will be expanded to open ratings for new and emerging hubs.

- **RegApp:** A simple web app made with React.js used for hub-node registration. This application adds a node to the whitelist contract. It should be noted that the RegApp is language agnostic and only needs a web interface to register the node. In this instance, React.js was used; however, other web programming languages can work just as well.

- **PayOut app:** A payment application that runs on the SONM network to pay and process the tokens given to miners for their services. This application is an example of the types of DApps that a factory contract would deploy.

Figure 7-9 provides a visual companion to the smart contract system just discussed. Anthony Akentiev from Chain Cloud reviewed the SONM whitepaper and provided some comments regarding the crowdfunding efforts using the SONM token to fund the development of this smart contracts architecture in future releases (`https://medium.com/chain-cloud-company-blog/sonm-whitepaper-review-353ca2713ba9`):

> *The crowdfunding is divided into 2 stages—the presale and the ICO. 19% and 20% of all funds are sent to the team as a reward. Development and marketing will require equal amounts of money: 34% for the development and 32% for marketing after the presale; 30% for the development and 33% for marketing after the ICO. It looks good and fair.*

> *Conclusion—45/60*

> *One of the best Whitepapers that I have read. Big project. Big goals. The presale and ICO are gonna be big.*

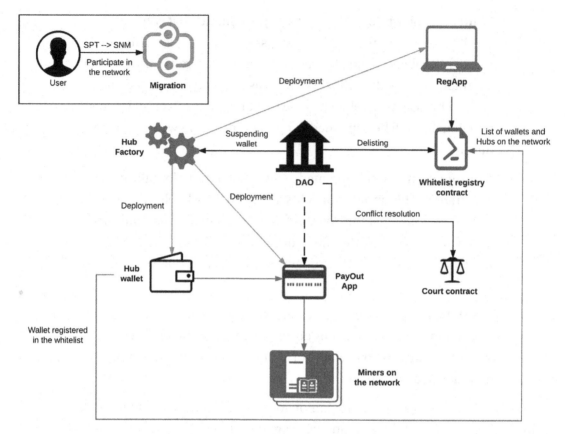

Figure 7-9. *Overview of the smart contract system in SONM*

Recall that the smart contract system in SONM is further made from several contracts working together. The first of these contracts is a migration function that allows users who purchased the SONM Presale Token (SPT, during the presale that Anthony mentioned) to exchange their token for SNM (SONM Token) and participate in the network. Next is the hub factory contract used in SONM for deployment of applications. In the current implementation, the hub factory creates the hub wallet used to compensate miners for their computational resources. The factory also deploys a network-wide whitelist contract that serves as a registry of hubs active on the network and wallets created in each hub. Lastly, the factory deploys a payout application that releases SNM tokens to miners for the provided services. The last smart contract we will consider here is the DAO, which provisions several administrative functions to stop malicious entities. These functions include delisting a hub (from the whitelist contract) if caught in fraud, freezing funds by suspending a hub wallet, or conflict resolution in case of challenges using the court.

Buyer–Hub–Miner Interactions

Posting a task on the SONM network requesting computational resources requires a fair amount of communication between the buyer and the miner who will execute the task. For instance, before processing can begin, there are several verification interactions that occur between a miner, the assigning hub, and the buyer. Once the buyer is verified, a hub will assign the task to a miner's fog computing cloud and ensure the miner is paid for their services. This collective set of interactions is defined here as Buyer–Hub–Miner communication. This interchange can be best demonstrated visually in the two parts of Figure 7-10. The first part, Figure 7-10 (A), explains the miner–hub interactions when a computation begins, and Figure 7-10 (B) provides the full picture by introducing the buyer and miner payout.

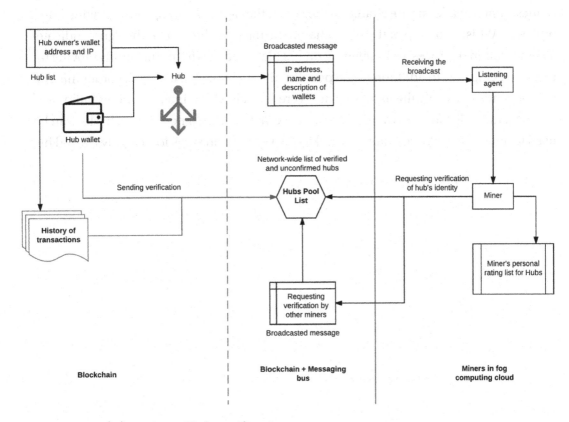

Figure 7-10 (A). *Miner–Hub verification*

In Figure 7-10 (A), we see a hub broadcasting information about an active hub wallet and the hub owner's IP address to the blockchain. This information is gathered by a listening agent and then dispatched to a miner. Before executing any tasks, a miner will go through a series of steps to validate the assigning hub. This process ensures that the hub can be trusted and that there are sufficient funds to pay for the computation in the hub wallet. A miner requests more information on the assigning hub through a global list called the Hubs Pool List. This network-wide list contains all the verified and unconfirmed hubs. To verify itself, a hub wallet sends its address on the blockchain, as well as a history of past transactions, as proof of authentication. The miner accepts the proof and can now begin the computation. It must be noted that all components of this validation process, including hub broadcasts, verification requests, wallet information, and Hubs Pool List, use the same infrastructure: the blockchain. The requests and broadcasts are shared to the rest of the network using the messaging bus built with Whisper on top of the blockchain. The dashed blue line in the figure indicates a continuation of processes happening on the blockchain, with notifications moving to the messaging bus. In addition to the pool list, the miner can also request other miners to independently verify the assigning hub's credentials. Over time, the miner builds a personal rating list for hubs across the network that have assigned tasks. This list can be used to automate task acceptance and skip the verification steps for a highly trusted hub.

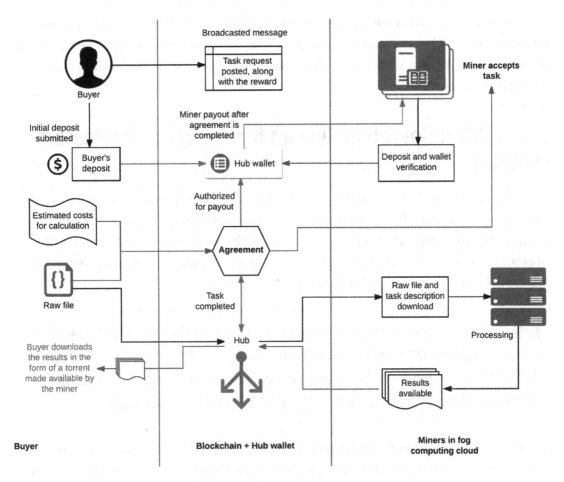

Figure 7-10 (B). *Buyer–Hub–Miner interactions*

In Figure 7-10 (B), we see that after the initial verification of the assigning hub has been completed, the buyer puts forth an initial deposit. This deposit is a rough estimate of the computation costs, and is stored in the hub wallet. The miner verifies this deposit, and the buyer signs an agreement on the blockchain with the estimated costs along with a hash of the raw file. This agreement is sent to the miner as the computational task is assigned by a hub. The raw file is made available to the miner for download through a torrent. After the file has been downloaded, the task description along with any special parameters are applied and the processing begins. Once the task is completed, the results are made available from the fog computing cloud, and the hub collects these results. This hub will now make the results available for the buyer to download through a separate torrent. At this point, the agreement has been completed and funds from the hub wallet are released to the miner for offering their computational resources. In future releases, there will be proper locking mechanisms to account for over/under-estimation of the costs. Until the buyer adjusts for any errors in the estimates, the results will not be released by the hub.

Superglobal Operation System for Network Architecture (SOSNA)

So, how does a buyer know whether a miner satisfies the required dependencies to compile and run an application that the buyer requested? How does a buyer know what applications are compatible with a miner's setup? These questions are handled by the operating system for SONM. A World Computer is not complete without an operating system to power it, and the OS for SONM is called SOSNA.

Note   In this chapter, we have discussed SONM only in the context of buyers and providers for HPC services; however, the first use cases for early versions of SONM will focus on running a *Quake* server in a completely decentralized manner. The roadmap includes the message-passing protocols and the payout app.

The problem of dependency management and compatibility for compilers will be handled by using containers on host machines. A container is simply a minimal virtual machine that can load any specified configuration, from new libraries to standard tools such as the GNU compiler toolchain. The container runs in a minimal isolated environment on the host system. This is done in order to prevent any escalation-of-privilege attacks by malicious programs running within the container. SOSNA can be divided into three main components: the blockchain layer comprising the smart contract system, a grid core, and a layer of consumer-facing applications. We already discussed the blockchain layer and API (enabled by the smart contracts) in detail. Let's shift our focus to the grid core. In SONM, any grid-compatible PaaS stack can be plugged in to work with the network, such as BOINC (Berkeley Open Infrastructure for Network Computing) or Yandex.Cocaine.

A simplified implementation of grid architecture involves two units: multiple worker/slave modules and a master module. These two units form a computing cloud, and a fog computing cloud extends this idea to hundreds of instances deployed across all types of machines. What defines a grid network as such is that a master machine manages workers distributed across a distance to different geographic locations. The master essentially behaves like a hub, managing the execution of applications on miners' machines, balancing load, scheduling tasks, and collecting the results. More generally, we can suggest that a master module works like a traditional miner pool.

Any application executing inside a container is referred to as a service. Technically, all services in SONM are RPC-based and accept a specific set of messages to execute directives. Each service has a list of functions that can be referenced by sending messages to that service after a connection has been established. This set of functions is called a service protocol. A protocol can be dynamically obtained from a service once it becomes active by resolving the service name using a locator. The use of a locator can be thought of as similar to host-name resolution using DNS. We'll return to the locator service shortly. On startup, a node loads the settings specified in a configuration file, including all the services that are to start on this particular node. The services lack the ability to communicate code over the network; they can only receive messages in this state. To allow access to the network and RPC-compatible communication, the node will start a special service called the locator. Every other service running in the container becomes attached to the locator for receiving and sending messages. Once the locator service is activated, it binds to a public endpoint in the network and broadcasts the connection to the blockchain. So, what steps does a buyer need to perform to access a particular service for their task? Using the locator service, a buyer needs to go through the following five steps:

- Connect to locator endpoint on a public port.

- Send a resolve request with the name of a service to the locator.

- Receive a message back from the locator with information about the endpoint container, the protocol description, and function calls.

- Receive a confirmation message indicating that the request for information was completed.

- Request a specific miner with the endpoint information that matches the locator message and call the required service for task execution/ processing.

A visual companion to the components of SOSNA is provided in Figure 7-11.

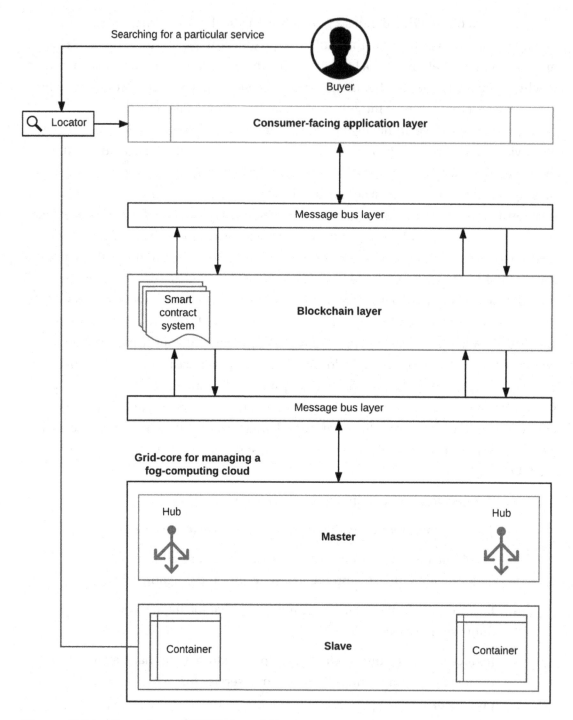

Figure 7-11. Overview of SOSNA architecture

In Figure 7-11, we start at the blockchain layer, which provides the consensus framework to the network, along with the smart contract system for governance. Next is the messaging bus layer, which serves as a two-way communication channel between the various components of the World Computer and users in the network. This layer also exists on both sides, allowing the blockchain to communicate to the consumer-facing applications and the grid-core to coordinate task execution. On the very top, we have a consumer application layer, which is where buyers can access the network and post requests for services. The RegApp is an early example of consumer applications that buyers would interact with in the future. Eventually, the consumer layer would split into more verticals with features such as trusted-runtime skipping the verification stages for users with a high reputation in the network. On the opposite end, at the very bottom, we have the grid core. This is the heart of SONM, where the fog cloud computing takes place. The grid is essentially a parallel implementation of several hundred master and slave modules. The slave modules run containers where services execute, and these services are connected to a locator. The locator runs on a public port accessible to the buyer through the consumer-apps layer.

Three notable updates to the SONM platform have happened as the project has evolved from an early alpha. The first is an installation image of SONM-OS available for devices so they can connect with the SONM marketplace and start mining right away in an out-of-the-box fashion. The resources accumulated are tracked, and the renter is awarded for lending their computational resources. The second is a use case for a machine learning implementation on devices running SONM to handle TensorFlow, Apache Spark, and Theano applications on a decentralized fog-computing platform. The final update to note is the CDN use case for off-loading images and media onto SONM devices and retrieving them from fog-computing-based CDN, which is significantly cheaper than traditional web services and offers comparable performance. A pricing calculator for SONM services is provided on the website.

iEx.ec

We will conclude this chapter with a short discussion of the iEx.ec platform, which is also a distributed HPC token using a domain-specific blockchain. iEx.ec is built on a mature set of research technologies called XtremWeb, which was developed for desktop grid computing by INRIA. So, what is a desktop grid? The idea behind desktop grid computing is to collect the computation resources of idle machines connected to the network to execute intensive parallel applications, at a very small cost (or free, in the case of a volunteer desktop grid) compared to a traditional supercomputer. XtremWeb-HEP is a decentralized version of its predecessor, designed to execute tasks that require intensive computing resources in a marketplace of miners. This open source desktop grid stack belongs to the "Cycle Stealing" family that uses idle resources on machines connected to the network for executing data-intensive applications. XtremWeb-HEP implements most of the features necessary in a HPC token that we've previously seen: fault-tolerance, hybrid public–private infrastructure, deployment of virtual images (containers), load balancing, and a payment mechanism for the miners. The DApps running on the network will rely on the iEx.ec architecture to automatically search for all the computing resources needed to run the app, provision resources, and release funds to the appropriate parties. Using a well-established and well-tested software stack offers three main advantages:

- **Resilience:** If one computation node fails, the task can be reassigned to other working nodes and continue with minimal downtime.

- **Efficiency:** The base performance of applications across the network is high, despite hardware configuration changes that occur for workers from one node to another.

- **Pluggable nodes:** New nodes can be added to the network without any special configuration, and nodes become integrated after a quick setup.

In iEx.ec, any actions that happen externally or off-chain are referred to as a contribution. For instance, providing a data set, transferring files and performing a computation are all actions that would require token transactions between the relevant parties. How do we know whether the action actually took place correctly? How can a particular transaction or set of transactions be associated with a particular action that was performed off-chain? A new protocol is needed to verify that a contribution took place and which transactions correspond to it. iEx.ec has proposed proof-of-contribution as a new consensus mechanism for off-chain contributions. This new mechanism also plays a role in enabling an enterprise feature in iEx.ec called Service Level Agreement (SLA). Using an SLA allows for resource utilization tracking and trusted computing resource orders from the customer to a provider. The iEx.ec team predicts that content distribution to parties on the network will be a tremendously important function of DApps using the iEx.ec blockchain. The buyers will have access to complex data sets on the blockchain through a smart contract, and to a simple payment structure for running their application. Using proof-of-contribution, iEx.ec can guarantee that the content providers are actually giving access to data sets, and that the file was accessible during processing. For payment purposes, the duration of access can also be recorded to protect the buyer against overcharging. In addition, iEx.ec will have several countermeasures against malicious entities that claim file transfers failed in order to reduce their data charges.

The first few releases of iEx.ec will focus on consolidating the core features as well as on a financial trading use case that requires HPC. This service, called eFast, will employ sophisticated computational prediction methods to allow small investors to make better trading decisions. The objective is to create diverse portfolios using cluster analysis of different stocks, but the computational complexity of such an analysis is so immense that only large financial institutions can afford it. A decentralized service like iEx.ec can reduce the processing cost to a tenth of what it would traditionally cost on a computation farm.

Note   Golem and iEx.ec share similar goals for product development; however, they differ in business approach. Golem aims to build the core infrastructure of the network and attract HPC and cloud customers. iEx.ec first focuses on building DApps that will run on the network to attract regular cloud customers that have a need for those applications at a cheaper rate.

So, how do tasks get assigned and executed on iEx.ec? There are two algorithms that manage this process: a matchmaking algorithm for execution and a scheduler for assignment. Let's briefly talk about both of them. A matchmaking algorithm is used in distributed systems to match pairs of resource providers and potential buyers according to the description of the resource provided by the buyer. Recall that in SONM, this task was taken over by a load balancer; however, in iEx.ec, an algorithm performs resource provisioning. The developers propose to eventually store smart contracts on the blockchain that describe the availability of computational resources and the resources required to run a task. This can include information such as available RAM, processor/CPU, disk space, and the type of GPU. For a host machine, the tasks would be deployed to a virtual machine instance or a hypervisor, and the buyer would specify the runtime instructions. The matchmaking algorithm can implement more-intricate policies beyond a simple one-to-one match, and iEx.ec can monetize the more-complex matches. There are several design choices for the matchmaking algorithm, but iEx.ec will be using a language called ClassAd, which has been well tested in the scientific literature. The second algorithm is the scheduler, which is critical to any distributed computing system. The performance and scalability of a network depends on the effectiveness of its scheduler. The design challenge for iEx.ec is to create a scheduler enabled with multiple-criteria decision analysis (MCDA) that can select optimal computing resources for each task and schedule it appropriately to fit the buyer's criteria. MCDA is a branch of operations research that evaluates how to optimize decisions in the setting of multiple conflicting options. MCDA-based solutions might fit a customer's needs, especially based on the cost-versus-performance benchmarks. A customer might want to minimize the price of computation even if it takes longer, while another might want to minimize the time required—these are the types of scenarios that will be handled by a scheduler in iEx.ec.

A versatile schedule and efficient matchmaking algorithm allow for very interesting upgrades to the core blockchain technology in the context of HPC. One remarkable example is the ability to use domain-specific blockchains (or sidechains). A sidechain is an adaptable blockchain designed to meet specific infrastructure requirements for running applications that would underperform in a generalized environment. The goal of such a blockchain is to maximize performance and minimize any time delays between executions. Normally, an application would go through the standard blockchain; however, in cases where a large amount of tasks are submitted, some of the tasks can be offloaded to a sidechain for tracking. The sidechain will track the amount of time spent on host machines and report the information back to the network, and this offloading can reduce the traffic on the generalized blockchain. An advanced system of smart contracts will need to be developed to enable this switch. Figure 7-12 provides a visual companion to the iEx.ec architecture.

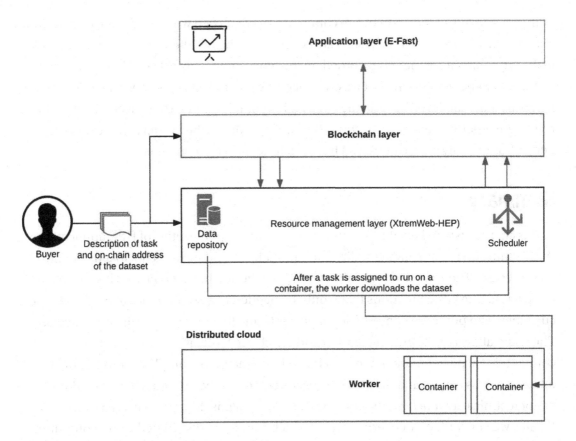

Figure 7-12. *Overview of iEx.ec architecture*

In Figure 7-12, the top-most layer is a consumer-facing application, E-Fast. It is the first use case of iEx.ec that provides the infrastructure to run sophisticated financial prediction algorithms in a massively distributed setting for a fraction of the cost. Underneath is the Ethereum blockchain layer that provides consensus for the network and task-tracking for reimbursement of miners. The blockchain also acts as a platform for the smart-contract system that will eventually run in the network. It is important to note that the blockchain layer does not interact with every level of iEx.ec. The distributed cloud level is managed more directly through a middleware called XtremWeb-HEP. This is the resource management layer comprising a task scheduler and a verified data repository. The scheduler coordinates between the blockchain and assigning tasks to workers on host machines. The repository contains large data sets from various fields such as finance and genomics that are made accessible to applications that buyers want to execute. The buyer connects to the resource management layer and provides a description of the task along with the source of data. This information is also recorded on the blockchain.

Both components of the middleware connect to the deployed workers, use the description, and execute the task. The final results are collected by the middleware and made available to the buyer after a payment is recorded on the blockchain. The last layer is a distributed cloud of miners. Notice here that we don't need a master module, because the middleware performs that function. The tasks are executed in containers or virtual machines, and the results are reported back to the resource layer. This reduces the overall complexity of the network as the only code running on host machines is in the containers.

Summary

In this chapter, we looked at Ethereum tokens from the perspective of HPC applications. We first introduced the market utility and rationale behind introducing tokens as apps on Ethereum. Then, we discussed the prototype HPC token called ECM. This token performs all the basic functions that would be needed in a computational market where customers can purchase computational power from clusters run by dedicated buyers. The token allows for dispute resolution and on-chain verification in a transparent computational power market. We then delved into the more complex computational tokens, such as Golem and SONM. We described both in heavy detail, covering the major technical advancements and how those two tokens differ from each other. Finally, we concluded by covering iEx.ec, which is built on distributed cloud computing software that has been tested for years. The iEx.ec team implemented a decentralized version of Xtreme-Web HPC to perform the same task as Golem and SONM and enable a computational market.

References

The main references used to prepare this chapter were the ECM GitHub documentation (`https://github.com/pipermerriam/ethereum-computation-market`), Golem whitepaper (`https://golem.network/doc/Golemwhitepaper.pdf`), SONM whitepaper (`https://whitepaper.io/document/326/sonm-whitepaper`) and developer docs (`https://docs.sonm.com/`), iEx.ec whitepaper (`https://iex.ec/wp-content/uploads/pdf/iExec-WPv3.0-English.pdf`), and Fred Wilson's blog post on tokens (`https://avc.com/2017/08/how-to-value-crypto-assets/`). Complete references available in Appendix B.

- Somin S., G. Gordon, and Y. Altshuler. "Network analysis of erc20 tokens trading on ethereum blockchain." In *International Conference on Complex Systems* 2018 Jul 22 (pp. 439–450). Springer, Cham.

- Rohr J., and A. Wright. "Blockchain-based token sales, initial coin offerings, and the democratization of public capital markets." *Hastings LJ*. 2018; 70: 463.

- Sun H., S. Hua, E. Zhou, B. Pi, J. Sun, and K. Yamashita." Using ethereum blockchain in Internet of Things: A solution for electric vehicle battery refueling." In *International Conference on Blockchain* 2018 Jun 25 (pp. 3–17). Springer, Cham.

- Xu Q., Z. He, Z. Li, and M. Xiao." Building an Ethereum-Based Decentralized Smart Home System." In *2018 IEEE 24th International Conference on Parallel and Distributed Systems (ICPADS)* 2018 Dec 11 (pp. 1004–1009). IEEE.

CHAPTER 8

Blockchain in Science

Evidence-based clinical sciences are currently suffering from a paralyzing reproducibility crisis. From clinical psychology to cancer biology, recent meta-research indicates a rise in researchers' failing to replicate studies published by their peers. This problem is not just limited to bench-work that happens in a lab; it also plagues translational research where the transformation from bench to bedside happens. Treatments, tests, and technologies are converted from simple lab experiments to FDA-approved devices and assays that affect hundreds of lives. Therefore, replicability is crucial to converting scientific breakthroughs into pragmatic remedies.

The primary role of blockchain technology in the emerging landscape of open-access science is increasing the amount of transparency into these processes. To that end, three use cases and applications are presented in this chapter: the first one involving deposition of data in clinical trials, the second one involving a reputation system that can be developed for researchers and institutes committed to open research, and the third one involving the application of supply-chain management for tracking counterfeit drugs. In these use cases, we provide ample examples of ongoing work that will come to drastically shape the world of blockchain in science. We will begin by discussing the current paradigms of the research method and the importance of negative data; our focus will mostly remain limited to the clinical sciences. Then, we will talk about traditional metrics and altmetrics systems presently implemented to measure the impact of published research. This will allow us to transition into the use cases that supplement traditional metrics and expand them to make open science a fundamental feature. Finally, we will end our discussion by looking at ongoing efforts to incorporate blockchain into the existing research infrastructure.

© Vikram Dhillon, David Metcalf, and Max Hooper 2021
V. Dhillon et al., *Blockchain Enabled Applications*, https://doi.org/10.1007/978-1-4842-6534-5_8

Reproducibility Crisis

Let's begin our discussion with what *reproducibility* means in the context of scientific discourse and investigation. One of the major cornerstones in research is the ability to follow written protocols from a study, using the documented methods to carry out experiments and arrive at the same conclusions as those given by that study. In other words, a published study can be independently verified by other researchers, and replicated to achieve the same results. Recent meta-research in clinical sciences demonstrates that more and more published works are not rigorous experimentally so as to be replicated with ease. Leonard P. Freedman and colleagues estimate that over 50 percent of pre-clinical research cannot be translated from animal models to human clinical trials, thereby placing the approximate annual cost of irreproducibility at $28 billion in the United States alone. Consequently, as pre-clinical findings in animal models are rarely repeated in clinical trials, drug discovery has slowed down its pace, and the costs have risen dramatically. The economic costs are very debilitating, as close to $200 billion is wasted annually because the discovered targets cannot be reproduced. These problems are often inherent to the design of a particular study, or due to very genuine intricacies and complications that arise in experiments on differing cell lines. To understand why, we have to look for answers in meta-research, which is a branch of investigation that statistically evaluates the claims, results, and experiments performed in a study.

A multitude of factors in academia are creating a vicious culture of "bad science," as Dr. Ben Goldacre refers to it: A vanishing funding landscape, a culture of "publish or perish," and an incredible amount of pressure on young researchers to get tenured pushes them to follow erroneous methods that lead to non-reproducible publications. In some cases, the slipshod research methods and manipulations have led to fraud and eventual retractions with serious consequences to the researcher.

Note   Retraction Watch is a blog that recently came about to report on scientific misconduct happening at all levels, from editors working with journals to individual researchers at universities. The blog also tracks papers that have been retracted from journals due to fraudulent data or manipulation of experimental evidence. The interested reader can follow their website, which posts about 500 to 600 retractions per year.

Academic journals are also partly to blame for this mess, though there are signs of real change and improvement in the works. Over the past few years, it has been easier to publish studies with positive findings in journals regarding potential drug targets or effectiveness of a particular drug. But negative findings from experiments, such as a drug target not working even though it was expected to work, have been incredibly difficult to publish. On face value, it seems to make sense: Why would someone want to know if an experiment failed? Negative data usually gets ignored because of similar reasoning, and from a marketing standpoint, a journal claiming that X didn't work as expected isn't a highlight that would sell. Let's take a closer look at positive and negative data in the context of how journals have shaped their use and publication.

Positive data is simply the confirmation of an initial hypothesis, where a researcher predicted a finding and the data validated it. On the other hand, negative data comes from the cases where the expected or wanted effect was not observed. If an experiment showed that no difference existed between the null and alternative hypotheses, the data and results would likely end up buried in the pile of unpublished results of the lab group. Figure 8-1 provides a very simplified overview of an erroneous research method for dealing with positive and negative data, a method that results from the pressures in academia. Replication is sacrificed in pursuit of highly demanding and attractive drug targets, which ultimately do not translate well into clinical trials and lead to more economic waste.

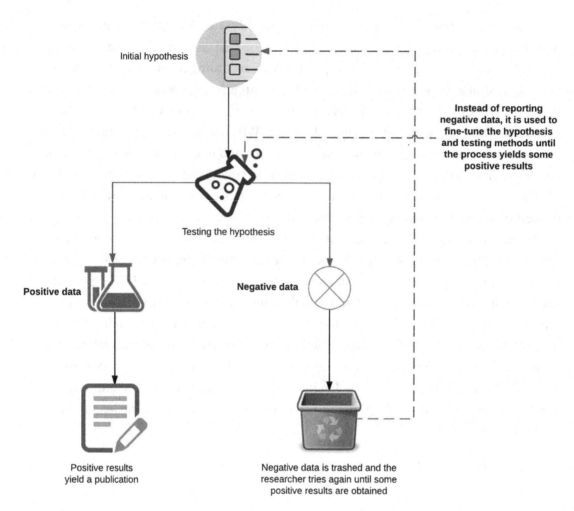

Initial hypothesis

Instead of reporting negative data, it is used to fine-tune the hypothesis and testing methods until the process yields some positive results

Testing the hypothesis

Positive data

Negative data

Positive results yield a publication

Negative data is trashed and the researcher tries again until some positive results are obtained

Figure 8-1. *Overview of positive and negative data in the context of publishing a study*

In Figure 8-1, we see a simple demonstration of hypothesis testing that leads to the publication of "flukes," which are non-replicable in translational research or scaled clinical trials. Due to the nature of publishing in academic journals, positive data usually implies that you're done. Most researchers will stop here and not bother to follow up with any appreciable fraction of all the data that was collected or generated while conducting the experiments. This could include potential negative data regarding an avenue of thought that didn't work, or information that was omitted due to feedback from reviewers. Once a research paper has been accepted, the authors of a publication have no further incentives to release more data or put in more time to clean up and make available other results. This turns out to have some detrimental consequences, which we will discuss later in the chapter.

These trends have been observed by journals internationally, and publishers are beginning to take some action. A plethora of new initiatives are raising the standards for the data that can be included in a publication, as well as the design considerations that must be fulfilled to ensure replication. Let's talk about three of those efforts here:

- **Minimum Publishing Standards:** Print journals have specific requirements for space where only a certain number of pages can be allocated to each section of a research paper. In such scenarios, researchers focus more on making bold claims and showing data that provides evidence for their conjectures. Usually, this comes at the expense of the methods section, which provides instructions for other researchers to follow in order to replicate an experiment. Recently, most journals have moved online and space is a non-issue; however, supplemental materials are still lacking in quality even when they are made available. BioMed Central has released a checklist of minimum standards that must be met before a paper can be published. The purpose of this checklist is to provide a level of standardization so that researchers can write papers with specific criteria in mind that can enhance reproducibility. If all the standards are met, there is a high likelihood that a published study can be replicated to a greater degree.

Note   More prominent journals have added data-sharing disclosures that specify where data sets will be available and what type of data is being shared. For instance, Cell Press created a new journal to publish peer-reviewed, reproducible, and transparent research methods called STAR protocols. Similarly, the EQUATOR network has created structured guidelines for quality standards for data being published in a scientific report.

- **Data Discovery Index:** One of the major problems mentioned earlier was the lack of incentives for researchers to make supplemental data available. The National Institutes of Health (NIH) has sought to create a new measure to credit researchers for uploading additional experimental data, called the Data Discovery Index. This is a citable data repository where researchers can make additional data points available related to their studies. For academic researchers, a huge incentive is to elicit additional citations for their work, which in turn becomes a measure of impact for a published study. By making the database citable, NIH created this new incentive for researchers to dedicate additional time and resources to upload unpublished databases.

- **Reproducibility Project:** The Center for Open Science in collaboration with Science Exchange will be looking at high-impact studies in cancer biology from 2010–2012 and replicating each one with help from members of Science Exchange. Full-length reports on the attempts at replicating experiments, discovering drug targets, and more will be made openly available along with detailed methods. This project is being done in two phases; the first phase culminates in a registered report that documents standardized protocols to carry out certain experiments. The second phase involves one of the member institutes of Science Exchange conducting the experiment using the registered report and documenting the results. Ultimately, both the reports and the data will be peer reviewed by reviewers at the *eLife* journal and made available online.

These three initiatives are examples of a large-scale coordinated effort to enhance reproducibility, and many more are on the horizon. So far, we have discussed the problems in the academic environment leading to differing treatment of negative and positive data, the core of the reproducibility crisis, and the difficulties that arise as a result. Next, we will begin talking about the more serious consequences of data manipulation in the case of drug trials. The data points from clinical trials decide the fate of medications that will affect thousands of lives. Obtaining all relevant data is crucial not only for accurately prescribing medication, but also to avoid pitfalls and avenues already tackled in the past.

Note   Dr. Ben Goldacre gave a TED talk in which he told the story of the drug lorcainide, released in the 1980s. It was meant to be an anti-arrhythmic drug that could prevent abnormal heart rhythms in people who have had heart attacks. A small clinical trial was conducted in under one hundred patients, and unfortunately ten of them died. The drug was regarded as a failure, and commercial development stopped. The data from this failed clinical trial was never published. Over the next few years, other drug companies had similar ideas for anti-arrhythmic drugs, which were brought to market. It is approximated that 100,000 people died because these new drugs also caused an increased instance of death. In 1993, the researchers who conducted the original 1980 study came forth and wrote an apology mentioning that they had attributed the increased death rate to chance in the initial trials, and that had the data from this failed trial been published, it could have provided early warnings and prevented future deaths. This is just one example of the very serious consequences of publication bias. We'll tackle a generalized version of this scenario in the next section.

Clinical Trials

We have already described a few complications that can arise due to flawed data reporting from clinical trials, and here we will begin outlining a potential solution. In this section, we will focus on three specific issues and provide a use case for the integration of blockchain technology in each one:

- **Trial registration:** Registering clinical trials when they begin, providing timely updates, and depositing the relevant results in a public database are crucial for offering clinical trials for new possible medications to patients for whom the standard drugs aren't effective. Even though large-scale clinical trials involving human participants should be registered, more often than not, these trials remain missing in action. The only indications of data coming from the unregistered trial is a publication or perhaps a few papers that contain experiments and results highly tailored toward proving the effectiveness of the drug candidate being proposed. This type of publication bias can mislead clinicians in a dangerous manner; therefore we need to incentivize investigators to send regular updates from registered clinical trials on progress and any relevant clinical protocols.

- **Comparing drug efficacies:** Today, in most clinical settings, multiple drug options are increasingly becoming available to clinicians, but there is often a lack of evidence from head-to-head clinical trials that allows for direct comparison of the efficacy or safety of one drug over another. Computational models allow for parallel processing of large data sets in a type of analysis called Mixed Treatment Comparisons (MTCs). These models use Bayesian statistics to incorporate available data for a drug and generate an exploratory report comparing the drugs. This can become the foundation for automated comparisons as more data is liberated from unpublished or unavailable information silos. Recently, there has been more interest in using umbrella protocols for clinical trials. These protocols test multiple treatment interventions simultaneously for one disease and gather massive amounts of comparative data.

- **Post-processing:** In some cases, when a trial is registered, and it does provide some supplemental data that goes along with a publication, the registry acts more like a data dump than an organized data deposit. Recently, we have seen more carefully prepared and published post-analysis summaries; however, this is often an exception, not the rule. The key here is that once clinical-trial data is linked up to the blockchain, it becomes available to be included in an automation workflow, and now post-analysis summaries/data can be generated by an algorithm rather than a person. A universal backend for the storage of data can foster the development of frontend clients that read the blockchain and, using the appropriate public–private keypair, download the appended data from an external source and locally do the post-processing. After that, the summary reports can be appended back to the blockchain.

Note   Soenke Bartling and some collaborators in Heidelberg, Germany have been working relentlessly on open-science innovation using blockchain technology. Recently, they founded a think tank called Blockchain for Science to accelerate the adoption of blockchain technology in open science. The interested reader can find more on their website: `blockchainforscience.com`.

Let's talk about a prototypical solution that uses the blockchain for making clinical trials more transparent. We will use an implementation of colored coins to make supplemental data available from clinical trials on the blockchain. The scripting language of Bitcoin-core allows for the attachment of small amounts of metadata to the blockchain. A colored coin takes advantage of this feature by attaching static metadata to the blockchain to represent assets with real-world value. In this sense, colored coins leverage the blockchain's capacity to hold virtual assets. We will be using colored coins as a mechanism to introduce scarcity and incentivize users of a network to upload auxiliary clinical data and provide regularly timed updates. For our purposes, there are three components that make colored coins special:

- **Coloring scheme:** The encoding method by which the colored coin data is encoded or decoded on the blockchain

- **Asset metadata:** The actual metadata attached to a colored coin transaction that gets stored in blockchain; we will go over an example of it next. The new colored coins protocol allows for the attachment of a potentially unlimited amount of metadata to a colored coin transaction, by using torrent-keys that provide a decentralized way to share and store data.

- **Rule engine:** In the past, the metadata just contained static information added to colored coins. But recently, a new rules section has been added that encodes an extra layer of logic supported by the rule engine that unlocks smart contracts' functionality to colored coins. Currently, four types of rules are supported that we will discuss.

Here's the generalized syntax for the metadata that can be added to a colored coin transaction:

```
{
  metadata: {...Static data goes here...},
  rules: {...Rule definitions go here...}
}
```

There are two rules from the rule engine that we will be using in our solution: the expiration rule and the minter rule. The expiration rule is used to loan an asset, and it dictates the lifespan of an asset. Upon expiration, the asset returns to the last output (a valid Bitcoin address) that had a valid expiration. The minter rule grants a recipient permission to issue more of the same asset. So, a minter receiving colored coins can further issue more colored coins to others on the network. Both rules play an important role in introducing scarcity in this instance of blockchain economics. What role does scarcity play? To understand this, we need to introduce one more rule: the holder. When an asset is issued, holders are described within the set of asset-issuing rules as the addresses allowed to hold this asset.

Figure 8-2 visually describes the interaction between a researcher and a minter. The researcher registers a clinical trial and provides periodic updates, while the minter acknowledges the updates, issues new colored coins, and requests future cooperation as the next phases of the trial begin. Let's walk through Figure 8-2 step-by-step. The clinical trial begins with our researcher registering the trial, which initiates a genesis colored coin transaction from the minter to the holder (our researcher). This transaction comes with an expiration rule attached, and this in a sense is the deadline for depositing data associated with one of the several phases of a given clinical trial. The researcher must send a colored coin transaction back to the minter, with URLs to metadata containing updates or new data. When the minter receives this transaction, an evaluation is performed on whether the asset was expired, and the result is exported. We will return to this result in the next section. After this return transaction, the minter issues more colored coins to the holder for the next phase, and the cycle repeats. Each phase of the trial results in more data URLs' being appended to the metadata sent by the holder as a sign of continuous updates.

Tip   The rules engine of the colored coin protocol is also a part of the metadata not stored directly on the blockchain; instead, it is stored in plain JSON format using torrents. Torrents provide a decentralized mechanism to share data and make it possible for rules to interact with objects outside of the blockchain. We have abstracted the minter here as an oracle; however, the actual implementation would involve a hybrid of an automated evaluator and a smart contract.

The entire process visualized in Figure 8-2 can be considered analogous to the **SSL-handshake** that forms the foundation of sure server–client interactions and symmetric encryption in our browsers. Perhaps in the future, one can extrapolate, if this type of interaction becomes common, it could become a feature of the colored coin wallet. The evaluation of data received by the minter can be carried out publicly using an add-on that returns the results to the wallet software. In the future, this modular add-on design will enable the integration of new protocols into the wallet client.

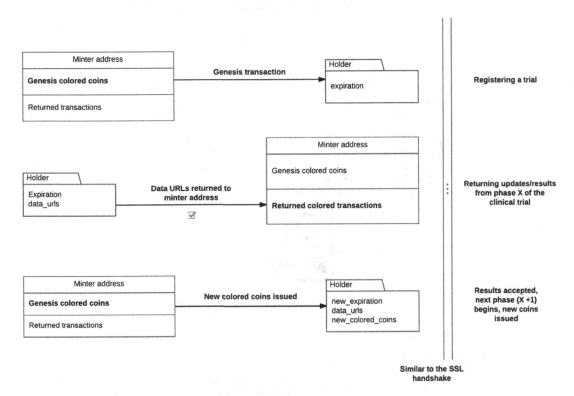

Figure 8-2. *Interactions between a minter and a holder*

The process shown in Figure 8-2 can create artificial scarcity by imposing the expiration rule. The holder (researcher) has to return a colored coin transaction with data URLs corresponding to the update. The minter performs an evaluation of the state of the holder and then acknowledges the receipt of updates. New coins are issued for the next cycle of updates, and the whole cycle begins anew. The evaluator result is exported and will be used to build a reputation system, which we will discuss shortly.

Now that we have discussed the colored coin interactions, let's take a look at the entire clinical trials system in Figure 8-3.

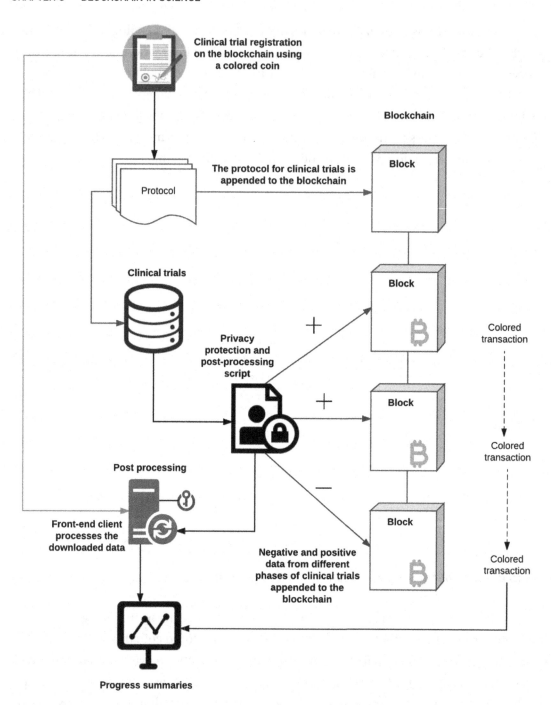

Figure 8-3. *Summary of blockchain integration into clinical trials workflow*

In Figure 8-3, the process begins with registration and a proposed summary of what the clinical trial will entail, the methods being used, and what data/results can be expected. The summary information along with the approved protocol are appended to the blockchain before the trial begins. This completes the registration process.

Colored coins and the rules engine are used to manage updates from researchers. These updates are appended to the blockchain after going through a light privacy-protection check. Once the clinical data is on a common backend, the most important benefit is perhaps the shift of focus from backend clients that hold databases to simply developing frontend clients that can read the blockchain. The management of data will happen automatically within the blockchain—all we need is a mechanism to read the tags or breadcrumbs left over in the metadata to know what to pull from an external location for further processing. An example of this is the post-processing unit shown in Figure 8-3. This unit contains the appropriate public–private keypair and permissions to read the blockchain and access the external locations. The same script that appended data updates to the blockchain also contains a segment for post-processing that tells the post-processing unit how to integrate data from various third-party locations into one local collection.

After that, post-analysis statistical methods are used to determine the quality of the data appended, and an automated report can be generated that summarizes the progress of the trial at given intervals. The intervals at which data updates should be required from researchers, along with instructions on how to process that data once made available, are coded in a script made available to the post-processing unit.

Reputation System

Let's revisit the notion of scarcity. It was crucial for us to build the clinical trials system; however, the introduction of colored coins with the expiration rule also allows us to build another component: the reputation system. The premise of reputation is simply tracking adherence to the expiration rule. Recall that we built an export feature in the evaluator function, and here we can use the export function as a counting mechanism to reward researchers (or holder addresses in the colored coin protocol) who have been proactive in sending periodic updates. In a practical application, this export counter would become added to the metadata by the minter after periodic updates have been established. From here, establishing reputation is a straightforward task: higher export counter corresponds to better reputation.

It is important to note that for our clinical trials system, reputation simply emerged as a property of the design, but it has some far-reaching implications concerning reproducibility. High reputation indicates the commitment of an institution or a research group to quality control. Once a reputation mechanism is implemented network-wide on a blockchain, it can be referenced externally: third-party services can request the reputation score associated with a particular colored wallet. This can be as simple as an API call to return the rep_score of a wallet. Why would this be useful? Earlier in our discussion, we mentioned the Data Discovery Index (DDI), and here we want to expand the notion of DDI from just being a data repository to being a repository with rep_score tags. This can provide another layer of granularity into DDI: a tag of reputation scores (high or low) on data sets linked to clinical trials that are available to the public. Keep in mind that within this design, all the data from clinical trials or updates resides in the DDI repositories; however, the rep_score lives in the blockchain metadata through colored coin transactions. Figure 8-4 describes the sequential evaluation happening with each periodic update and the incremental addition of reputation in rep_score.

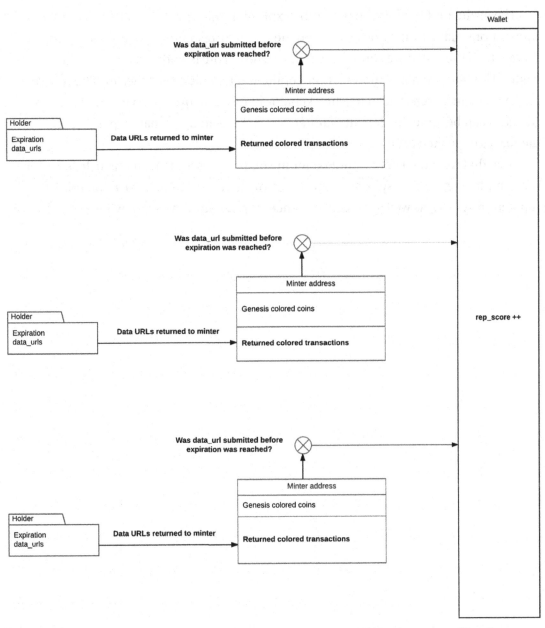

Figure 8-4. *Overview of rep_score increasing with each periodic update*

The evaluator function checks for the expiration rule and if the colored coin transactions made by the holder contain the URLs corresponding to updates in the metadata. If those two conditions are met, the rep_score is updated for the holder's wallet. This slow increase allows for the reputation to build over time, and the rep_score parameter can be referenced in a blockchain-agnostic manner from external services. API calls can become the default manner of attaching an up-to-date rep_score to databases deposited at DDI.

Now that we have a better understanding of the rep_score mechanism, let's look at the complete reputation system. Figure 8-5 provides a comprehensive depiction of a reputation system, as well as its consequences for members network-wide.

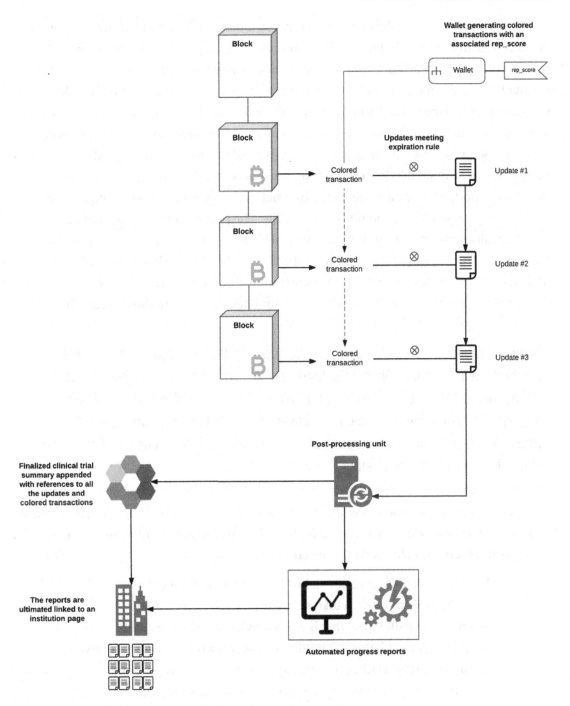

Figure 8-5. *The reputation system*

Figure 8-5 begins with the blockchain recording colored coin transactions happening between the minter and holder roles from the colored coin protocol. These colored coin transactions happen each time the holder provides an update, and the minter evaluates it. After the initial update, the minter sends a rep_score as a part of the returned colored coin transaction to carry on the update process for a clinical trial. The reputation now gets amended to the metadata with each exchange, and the rep_score gets revised each time. This score can eventually become an attribute of the holder's wallet, and in this manner it can be referenced externally from the blockchain. The post-processing unit becomes important after the clinical trial has matured to generate enough updates that can be compiled in one comprehensive overview. The purpose of this unit would be to automatically perform quality control statistical calculations and share the updates by following instructions in a script that was added to the blockchain in the beginning of the trial. In a similar fashion, the post-processing unit will compile a final summary and attach that to the institution's page, along with all the updates shared from the clinical trial.

Note   It must be noted that post-processing and data storage are all functions done off the blockchain. No calculations or data manipulations are performed on the blockchain. We want to limit the blockchain-executable code as much as possible to only the necessary primitives. The only tools that interact with transactions or metadata on the blockchain are in place to update the distributed state of a variable or parameter.

In the last few years, more-significant progress has been made in building reputation systems that are specific for scientific efforts, including open publishing and data deposition. Three such efforts are reviewed here:

- Augur is a prediction platform built on top of the Ethereum blockchain as an ERC-20 token. Augur is powered by a token of reputation called REP that is earned as a reward for accurate reporting on the platform. Members of the network have an incentive to earn reputation (REP) by participating in accurate reporting on outcome of events. Over time, a record of REP building among users leads to the emergence of a reliable set of users that are more likely to make accurate predictions: a group-think model where wisdom of the crowd takes a productive shape in predicting outcomes.

Augur has four components that allow for propagation of reputation on the network: a platform for members from the network to submit predictions toward an outcome, a scoring mechanism to reward points for accurate predictions, a consensus framework to gather the points into a long-term parameter such as reputation, and, finally, a group of overseers who maintain network security and integrity. These characteristics also make Augur suitable for a new generation of scientific hypotheses/predictions in a decentralized market.

- The Academic Endorsement System (AES) is built on the blockchain as a reputation system that uses Academic Endorsement Points (AEP), as compared to Augur, which uses REP. AEP are awarded to scientific works that are worthy of endorsement and public promotion. But compared to Augur, AES is more comprehensively built for scientific publications and endeavors. The amount of AEP awarded to a research item is based on AEP received in the past. This is a premium awarded to researchers who have produced works that received significant endorsements. In this manner, researchers who produce high-quality work receive more AEP and are incentivized to share more quality work. The use of AEP as a global reputation parameter can someday be used by journals along with more traditional citation metrics such as H-index.

- PEvO (Publish and Evaluate Onchain) is a Steem-based decentralized social media platform where content creators can communicate directly with authors of scientific studies. In this platform, authors can share updates, upload new content, reply to comments, and integrate reviews into continuous updates to the research. This creates an extension of a published paper so it becomes a living document, and updates can be tracked on the blockchain powering Steem. In addition, interactions on PEvO result in a payout (in the form of tokens) to the authors. This incentivizes authors to participate in discussions, and meaningful conversations are helpful to the broader scientific community.

Pharmaceutical Drug Tracking

The final use case in this chapter covers tracking pharmaceutical drugs via a supply-chain management framework. Prescription drug monitoring programs are an essential element for controlling drug shopping. The Mayo Clinic defines drug shopping as a patient obtaining controlled substances (most often narcotics) from multiple healthcare practitioners without the clinician's knowledge of the other prescriptions that the patient has. This leads to drug abuse or sales on a large-scale. The Mayo Clinic attributes drug shopping to the following three factors:

- **Poor timeliness of data:** How often does a pharmacy or provider upload prescription data into their existing centralized system? A blockchain-based backend would make drugs associated with all transactions available instantly to all members of the network.

- **Reliability:** Centralized databases have a single point of failure, as compared to the blockchain, which is decentralized by nature, and therefore the data does not rest on a single database, making it more reliable.

- **Complexity of data retrieval:** The current model of data retrieval and compatibility with existing hospital systems is completely broken. Often times, hospitals are not synced up to the databases being used by pharmacies, and updating is an arduous task. Blockchain makes the process universal by providing a common backend to read for external services.

In this system, when a clinician writes a script for a prescription, the provider can check the blockchain to find the patient record for any currently active prescriptions. This can help the clinician determine whether the patient is asking for a prescription from multiple sources or whether another family member is getting the same prescription. An active prescription from a different provider would automatically invalidate the request for a new one, and this can be encoded in the network as a double-spending request. Otherwise, the transaction will go through and the pharmacy will receive a request to provide medication to the patient. The requesting provider and patient can sign the transaction, allowing for better tracking all the way through the care of a particular patient. Although this system seems simple, it fulfills most of the requirements for a Drug Supply Chain Security Act (DSCSA)–compatible system that can be implemented across providers. There are some efforts under way by major blockchain players such as IBM and Deloitte blockchain lab to control the opioid over-prescription epidemic. Recently, some startups have sprung up that are focused solely on pharma drug tracking using the blockchain.

Even though supply-chain management fits the blockchain infrastructure most closely and out-of-box, this field is very new and the technology is immature. The future of drug tracking and open science looks much more promising with new technologies enabling layers of communication that were never possible before. Blockchain, if nothing more, has been an immense catalyst of new innovation in open scientific inquiry and discourse.

At the time of writing, US FDA is partnering with UCLA Health to launch a pilot study called BRUINchain. The results from this pilot were published in *Blockchain for Healthcare Today*, and we want to share some insights written by Ben Taylor from LedgerDomain in a blog post:

As part of a peer-reviewed study commissioned by the US FDA and published in *Blockchain in Healthcare Today (https://doi.org/10.30953/bhty.v3.134), LedgerDomain and UCLA Health joined forces to deploy and test BRUINchain, a last-mile blockchain-driven solution used by real caregivers to help deliver lifesaving medications. The study is among the first of its kind to reveal exactly how blockchain could save pharmacies billions of dollars in labor and safety stock costs alone. In this post I'd like to reflect on the key takeaways from the study and how we can map them onto the new health landscape.*

Background on BRUINchain is available here *(https://www.youtube.com/watch?v=mppc2Qvqrdc).*

Current State of Pharmaceutical Supply Chain

In today's pharmaceutical supply chain, each transacting party typically manages its own database systems. These private databases allow each party to minimize external security threats while maximizing internal data consistency. However, this also means that there's no shared global system of record representing the single source of truth describing the flow of items through the pharmaceutical supply chain. This leaves the supply chain as a whole [lot] more vulnerable to common attack vectors such as man-in-the-middle or spoofing.

Why Blockchain for Pharmaceutical Supply Chain?

In three years, under the Drug Supply Chain Security Act (DSCSA), the US pharmaceutical supply chain will be brought together by an electronic, interoperable system to identify and trace prescription drugs as they're distributed throughout the country. One of the core requirements of the DSCSA is that prescription medications must have a unique product identifier, which takes the form of a 2D barcode.

We realized that these federally mandated barcodes could be the foundational information building block for a common data model. Combined with blockchain, this could enable a system of record that would lessen the need to trade data integrity and privacy for global visibility and interpretability. In this way, blockchain can be a source of universal truth for hundreds of pharmaceutical and biotech enterprises and their vendors to work collaboratively and communicate with hundreds of wholesalers and tens of thousands of dispensers.

The BRUINchain Pilot Application

The keystone of our study was BRUINchain, a blockchain-based mobile solution and notification system designed to track and trace changes in custody of drug within a dispenser organization using FDA-stipulated barcodes. By combining blockchain with commercial off-the-shelf technology, BRUINchain makes it possible to track and verify drugs in a busy hospital or neighborhood pharmacy.

From the receiving bay to patient administration, caregivers scanned unique 2D drug barcodes using the BRUINchain mobile app. During their journey, drugs passed a series of checks until they were administered to the patient. New barcodes were routed to a trading partner for verification, and the drug was held back from being administered. At any time, the prescriber could view the progress of the drug through the pharmacy into the clinic.

BRUINchain Learnings and Outcomes

The BRUINchain pilot provided us with important insights into what a larger implementation of a DSCSA verification system would look like. It also validated the use of commercial off-the-shelf technology in a pharmacy that relies heavily on legacy systems. Barcode scanning was nearly 100% effective with commercial off-the-shelf technology. Drugs could be tracked at a highly granular level. The system was able to track expiration dates, verify barcodes, and make it easier for pharmacists to inspect and report problems.

During the study, we found that the rollout costs for DSCSA compliance could be massively reduced by a real-time blockchain system—a $183 million annual savings to dispensers in the United States, as well as a major bulwark against bad or fraudulent transactions. Real-time verification would also minimize the amount of safety stock that dispensers need to retain in the event of potential quarantine events, freeing up $20 billion in inventory.

Summary

This chapter started with a broad description of the reproducibility problem and its serious economic consequences in evidence-based sciences. Then, we moved into discussing the current solutions and their shortcomings in the science community. After that, we described the idea of building reputation systems using blockchain and covered three use cases: clinical trials, reputation networks, and finally pharmaceutical tracking of drugs from the point of manufacturing. All the use cases highlighted the strengths of blockchain in tracking and accountability, as opposed to traditional methods.

CHAPTER 9

Blockchain in Healthcare

The healthcare sector is a $3 trillion industry, and about $1 trillion of it goes to waste annually. Care coordination is becoming more complex as chronic conditions in the aging population continue to rise. In many instances, the technology available to healthcare providers is not adequate to capture all aspects of the care being provided. The result is a rugged transfer of information between parties that ultimately reduces the quality of care being provided to patients. This is largely due to providers' having legacy systems, lack of integration with non-vendor-specific technologies, paper-based medical records, and a lack of horizontal transfer between allied healthcare professions. Hospitals are investing a considerable amount of resources into duplicating work that can be completed by a sophisticated technology infrastructure and amplifying the inefficiency of using poorly designed systems. In this use case, we discuss the payer–provider–patient model in the context of the incentives and services each provides and how this model is likely to change in the near future. We then introduce how blockchain can integrate into tracking the workflow of a patient from the first visit to the final diagnosis and treatment plan. We introduce two new features that blockchain integration can enable: hot switching of components and medical data curation. Then, we present a use case of physician credentialing using the blockchain. Finally, we conclude by discussing waste management in healthcare and efforts by Capital One + Gem to increase the economic output.

201

Outlook

How should a reader approach this chapter? The following are some learning objectives to keep in mind:

- What is the payer–provider–patient framework? How does it apply to the modern healthcare system? How do claims move within the framework? We will return to claims processing on blockchain later in the chapter.

- Can we design the concept of a patient workflow based on the blockchain that documents the transition of a patient from her primary care physician, to lab work, and finally to a specialist?

- How does the patient workflow demonstrate handling permissions and access controls?

- What is hot switching? Why is it necessary? What implementations of hot switching are available?

- What is physician credentialing and how does it work on the blockchain?

- What are the current economic costs and sources of waste in healthcare claims processing for providers? Can the blockchain reduce these economic inefficiencies and streamline business processes? Can claims be processed on the same blockchain that handles medical records? Can the lessons learned from blockchain-enabled claims processing in healthcare get applied to related verticals?

- How does DeepMind's Verifiable Data Audit compare to the blockchain for auditing and records processing?

Payer–Provider–Patient Model

The payer–provider–patient model is a standard model of interaction between the three major players in healthcare. Figure 9-1 shows these interactions visually, and in this section, we will elaborate on the incentives and benefits for these three players. For the sake of simplicity, let's assume that the payers are largely insurance companies, the providers are hospital systems or private clinics, and patients are a randomized sample served by a given insurance company. Now, we can start to consider the different scenarios involving this model:

- The first scenario is the simplest one: the patient directly pays for procedures and visits to the hospital. This straightforward system involving just two players is still the norm for numerous healthcare systems in different countries. In the United States, the cost of providing healthcare has increased significantly, so a new player emerged within the system.

- The second scenario is the current implementation across the United States. The patients are provided health coverage after buying a premium from an insurance company. This company then gets more negotiating power to set viable prices for procedures, and then pays for them on behalf of the patients. The providers now send the claims for payment to the insurance companies, instead of the patients directly. In this manner, the insurance companies have evolved to become a centralized portal for patients to remove friction out of the system and receive personalized healthcare.

- The third scenario is more about the future of healthcare with the integration of new providers that are specialized entities for administering care through telehealth, off-site monitoring, and remote physicians.

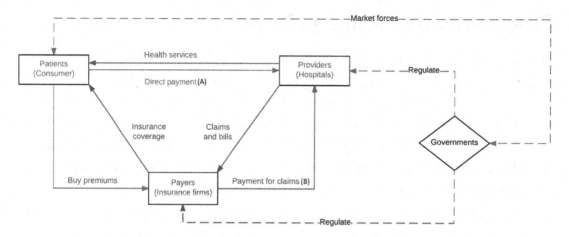

Figure 9-1. *A simplified overview of the payers–providers–patients model*

The simplest case is the patient directly paying for services to the hospital. But more complicated medical procedures and lab tests require some coverage that the patient purchases from an insurance company. Now the insurance company pays on behalf of the patient for any medical bills. The provider also sends claims for payments directly to the insurance, instead of the patient. This model is foundational to understanding the immense complexity present in the healthcare system today, which involves hundreds of other players. For instance, the domain in which insurance companies and hospitals can operate with respect to patients is largely regulated by governmental agencies. These agencies are in turn influenced by economic forces and consumer demand.

Tip   Chris Kay (Humana's CIO) delivered the keynote address at Distributed: Health in 2016 discussing Humana's efforts toward adopting blockchain to reduce processing costs in healthcare and provide personalized care more efficiently to their members. He spoke about a potential path of evolution for the second scenario just mentioned wherein the blockchain can power the flow of payments between providers and payers seamlessly and drive accountability toward outcomes, not just procedures. Shifting the locus of control into the hands of the patient allows them to receive better care and satisfaction, without any increase in friction or overhead costs using the blockchain.

The rationale behind claims processing on the blockchain is to use features such as decentralized consensus, trustless transactions, and network verification to design workflows that reduce overhead costs and time. Let's take a look at a patient visit workflow involving the use of blockchain.

Patient Workflow

Our workflow begins with Jane visiting her primary care physician (PCP) for a checkup following gastric discomfort after eating certain foods. Her physician suspects a viral infection and orders lab work to be performed. She is further referred to a specialist, who makes the final diagnosis and a works with her to develop a treatment plan. Every step of this workflow is recorded on the blockchain as a part of Jane's medical record, with appropriate permissions regarding access rights and ownership. Additionally, Jane's records would also contain a history of every checkout and check-in, including the edits and additions that were made to the medical record. Closely tracking how the ownership changes helps us transition between the different points of care provided to Jane, and she has instant access to her medical records at each step as a more comprehensive picture of her health begins to emerge.

The main objective of this workflow is to demonstrate the concept of how blockchain handles permissions and transfer of ownership between multiple unrelated parties. The use of user signatures using cryptographic keys is leveraged in creating this rudimentary medical record system. We can understand the attributes and permissions within our workflow better using the terminology of version control systems. Just as Git or SVN have commit messages and code commits, every check-in of new data to the medical record will contain commit messages about what changes were made. The blockchain becomes a remote repository of sorts (like GitHub) to which Git can push new changes. There are also locking mechanisms to protect the data: once a document from the medical record is checked out to a user (a doctor or a nurse), it will get locked, and no other user can check-in new changes to the same document until the original user checks in their edits, unlocking the document. Figures 9-2, 9-3, and 9-4 guide us through this workflow.

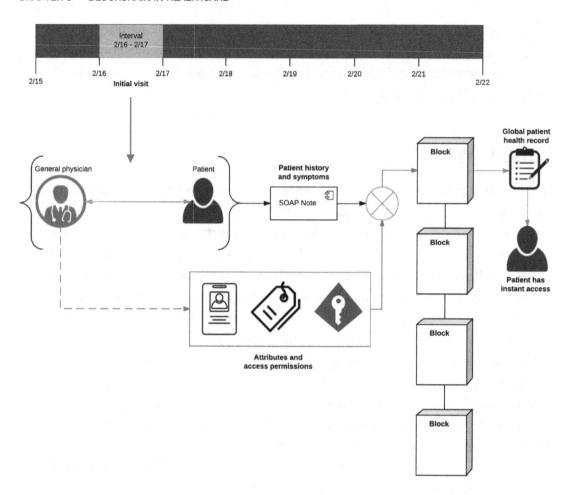

FIgure 9-2. *Initial patient visit*

In Figure 9-2, the workflow begins with Jane visiting her general physician for a regular checkup. The physician takes a history and records any symptoms that stand out from a review of her body systems. He adds this information to a very standard method of documenting patient history called a SOAP note. The note will be added to the blockchain with a unique ID called the hash. Along with the hash, the physician will add permission and user-group roles for accessing the medical record. Initially, only the physician and the patient would have access, but this can be expanded easily. Finally, the note is signed using the physician's key to denote the initial commit of Jane's medical record to the blockchain. Once Jane's records are pushed to the blockchain, she can also instantly access them.

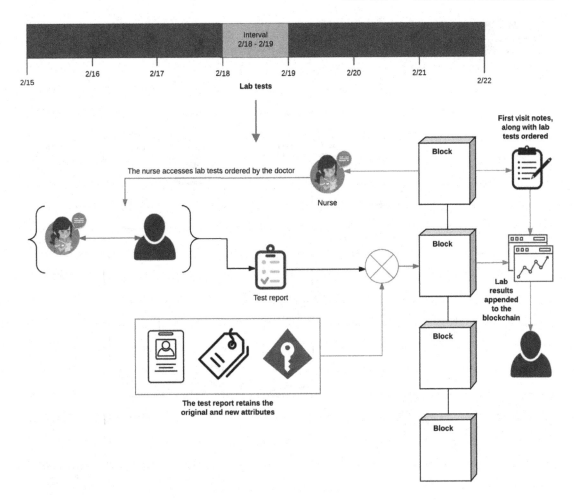

Figure 9-3. *Jane undergoing some lab testing ordered by the physician*

In Figure 9-3, Jane's physician ordered some lab tests to be performed, so two days later, she visits a lab. The tests have been entered into her medical record along with the permissions to let a nurse at the lab access the details. The physician can easily set the access permissions and add new upload privileges for the nurse on the medical record. This workflow begins before Jane's arrival, when the nurse retrieves her record and begins preparing for the tests. As Jane arrives, they have a consult, and the nurse informs her of the tests she will be going through. After performing the tests, a report is generated and appended to Jane's records on the blockchain. We can see this on the right side where Jane's general record now has a new add-on for the lab tests recently performed. All these results are instantly available to Jane as they are uploaded.

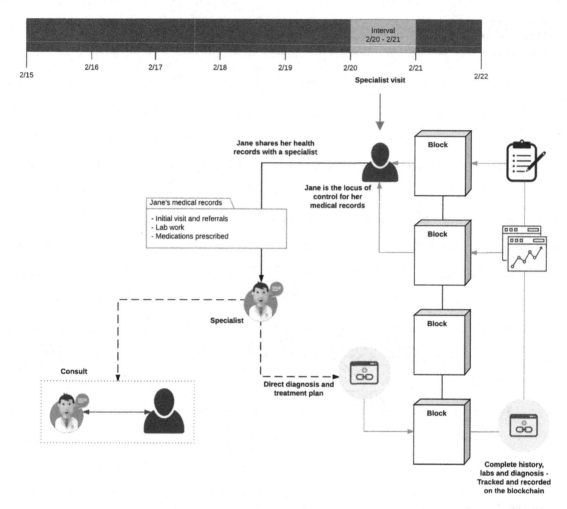

FIgure 9-4. *Jane being referred to a specialist*

In Figure 9-4, a new step is added to the workflow: Jane decides to visit a specialist to better understand the lab results. Two days later, she shares her medical records up to now with a specialist. At this point, the specialist has two choices: she can examine Jane's records and have a diagnosis along with a treatment plan prepared for her without even needing a visit. Or, Jane can go in for a consult and work with the specialist to adopt the treatment plan. The first option may help reduce the cost of visits and services received for Jane, as ultimately the treatment plan and diagnosis will both be made available to her on the blockchain. This completes the workflow from her initial visit to the point that she received a diagnosis. Every step of this workflow from the original notes to the final treatment plan were recorded on the blockchain. However, in the case of a patient with a chronic disease, the records from this point would be transferred to a chronic care facility that can check up on Jane regularly and help her maintain good health.

208

Hot Switching

Hot switching is a design principle enabled by the blockchain to create networks where components can be swapped out, while the system as a whole is running with minimal latency in operations. The purpose of hot switching is to re-route the flow of information, and this concept is only made possible due to the decentralized nature of the blockchain; i.e., there is no single point of failure. Why do we need a new concept such as hot switching at all? Traditional schedulers perform this job fairly well. An operational blockchain-based medical records system will require both live and off-chain components that are synced to the blockchain. IT infrastructure in hospitals should be very stable with minimal downtime, but hot switching can enable isolated system upgrades without disruptions, and gradually transition the legacy systems that are still active to be compatible with the blockchain.

There are two early implementations of hot switching available: the lightning network and pluggable consensus. So, what is this lightning network? The alpha version of lightning offers a mechanism to send transactions over new micropayment channels (sub-channels). This transfer of value occurs off-chain, thereby making transactions instantaneous. These channels ultimately sync upstream with the blockchain and preserve the data integrity of the overall network. In a similar fashion, off-chain channels can replicate and temporarily store the intermittent requests for access and release medical records based on pre-approved access controls. After some defined period, the lightning channel can sync the intermediate changes with the blockchain and become inactive. The second application of hot switching is pluggable consensus, which refers to the idea that you can swap out your consensus algorithm based on the types of transactions being handled on the blockchain. For instance, private transactions carried out on a public–private partitioned blockchain may require a different consensus mechanism than general-purpose transactions. Therefore, multiple consensus algorithms are allowed on a blockchain. We will discuss the implementation of pluggable consensus in more detail in a later chapter.

Note   Payment channels are one implementation of the hot switching concept in Ethereum 2.0. Modularity in designing blockchains offers significant advantages toward building complex applications and interacting with external infrastructure (such as an oracle or a data source).

Physician Credentialing

Credentialing is the process of organizing and verifying a physician's professional records. Any physician who joins an office or a physician network must have their credentials verified. This includes a review of board certifications, education, work history, and more. A shift in mindset that enabled this use case was a realization by entrepreneurs that credentialing can be maintained as a canonical entity, independent from a hospital system. When needed, a physician can simply transfer records under a smart contract to a new hospital, and fulfilling the smart contract would result in validation. This process is frictionless, and using the blockchain can also accelerate payments and validation. Here's an excerpt from a PWC report (`https://www.pwc.com/us/en/industries/health-industries/library/blockchain-could-accelerate-credentialing.html`) that provides insight into the inefficiencies present in the current system:

- *The inefficient credentialing process is costly to providers and payers. The Council for Affordable Quality Healthcare estimates that payers spend more than $2 billion a year maintaining provider databases, 75 percent of which could be eliminated by establishing a single source of truth, such as a blockchain.*

- *Each physician in a practice submits an average of 18 applications for credentialing each year. That requires 80 minutes—including 69 minutes of staff time and 11 of physician time—per physician. Payers then spend time and money verifying these claims.*

- *The National Association of Medical Staff Services (NAMSS) estimates that most physician credentialing takes more than 120 days, while health plan enrollment takes 60 to 180 days.*

- *Those costs don't even take into account another system-wide burden that blockchain could simplify: Credentialing and directory updates to list locations where a physician sees patients and whether a physician is enrolled with a certain insurer or is taking new patients. NAMSS estimates that 12 to 18 percent of provider directories are out of date or incorrectly list a provider as participating in a plan.*

- *A recent CMS audit of Medicare Advantage online provider directories found that 52.2 percent contained inaccuracies. According to CMS' 2019 call letter, it will begin taking enforcement actions against some Medicare Advantage organizations that don't correct serious provider directory deficiencies.*

ProCredEx (`https://hashedhealth.com/blockchain-healthcare-solutions/ professional-credentials-exchange/`) is a Hashed Health partner currently implementing this use case by developing the Professional Credentials Exchange: a blockchain-based information exchange for physician credentialing. More information about the implementation is available on the Hashed Health services page. Here, let's briefly focus on the concept of a generalized credentialing exchange and how it provides value in the context of providers and payers:

- Physicians join an exchange and have their credentials verified. The resulting verification is stored on a blockchain, and the exchange starts to build a repository of credentials. The exchange starts to evolve into a physician directory over time, and payers can make rapid queries about insurance enrollment and other practice-specific details. A micro-transaction cost associated with making queries becomes rewards for maintainers of the blockchain network. This incentivization can be paired with tokens to provide a multiplier, and in a sense, this guarantees an accurate response.

- Providers become partners of the exchange, and request to verify the credentials of a new physician under a smart contract. The exchange automates this process, and the resulting smart contract is fulfilled frictionlessly on the blockchain, resulting in a rapid turnover. A layer of network verifiers is rewarded upon the completion of the smart contract.

- Similarly, payers can partner with an exchange as it grows to have a critical mass of physicians. This allows for more fluid queries into services offered by a physician and contracts with insurers, and could pave the way for frictionless prior authorization.

Waste Management: Capital One, Ark Invest, Gem

A webinar hosted by Gem, Capital One, and Ark Invest outlined the issues of economic costs and overheads plaguing the healthcare system. This economic waste was highlighted in the context of claims processing from the perspective of payers (insurance companies). However, the lessons learned here can be broadly applied to other industries processing claims, such as auto insurance. As an example, Gem announced a partnership with Toyota to port applications it has been developing for the healthcare insurance industry to car insurance. The aspiration is to automate most of the insurance-claim process using a blockchain. Here, we will summarize the key findings outlined by the panelists. In the following discussion, each problem raised by the panelists is represented by a [P], and a proposed solution is represented with a [B]:

- **[P]** For every dollar collected by healthcare providers, 15 cents go toward claims processing, facilitating payments between parties, and manual labor costs. Imagine the 15 cents adding up for a $3 trillion industry.

- **[P]** Providers respond by increasing reimbursement rates, and payers (insurance companies) respond by increasing premiums.

- **[P]** Hospitals are acting as banks by giving loans to patients for out-of-pocket payments and lack the infrastructure to support and absorb inefficient payment frequencies.

- **[P]** Hospitals only have a collection rate of 5 percent on patient out-of-pocket payments that were provided as loans.

- **[P]** These gross inefficiencies are leading to hospitals' charging up to 45 percent more premiums on top of the base rate for services.

- **[S]** On the bright side, reducing the time it takes to process claims from providers can offer $23 billion in savings.

- **[S]** Decreasing the volatility of collections in the billing cycle from out-of-pocket charges can offer $7 billion in savings.

- **[S]** Using the blockchain to track transactions with history can significantly decrease rate of fraud, saving insurance companies approximately $300 billion.

- **[P]** Claims clearing houses have to spend days, and sometimes weeks, to process claims, adding significant overheads.

- **[P]** Providers are using multiple third-party software tools to manage claims. Instead of the technology being assistive, clinics are experiencing more fragmentation and using manual labor to integrate different software.

- **[S]** The blockchain can track the entire continuum of care and the billing cycle to reduce friction between the involved parties.

- **[S]** On a decentralized ledger, transactions and claims can be tracked very efficiently, leading to claims resolution almost instantaneously, if not in a few minutes.

- **[S]** Public ledgers such as the Bitcoin blockchain can't be used, HIPAA laws limit how patient information can be transferred across digital channels. The eventual solution would be to use a permissioned ledger with verified nodes. This will lead to restricted access by permissioned users to medical records being tracked by public and private keys usage.

- **[S]** Smart contracts responsible for coordinating permissions and access roles on the blockchain between various parties requesting medical records. Not every party can see the entire record, as permissioned access allows for only relevant exposure.

- **[P]** Providers are not IT professionals, and don't have enough time to provide training for new systems; therefore, interoperability remains a major issue.

- **[P]** Lack of interoperability spans to:

  - Patient registration in a medical system

  - Authorization of procedures

  - Medical records

  - Co-pay collection

  - Claims submission

  - Patient billing

  - Accounting of claims and bills

213

- **[P]** Functionality and partitioning—Should claims and medical records be on the same blockchain? The panelists talked about a scenario at Aetna, which receives about a million faxes a year from providers regarding claims information. This adds a massive administrative overhead to manage the paperwork. Ideally, both claims and records go hand in hand. A procedure done on a patient uploaded to the blockchain should trigger a claim to be processed. Ultimately, with proper partitioning, having both on the blockchain would be more efficient.

- **[S]** The concept of pegged sidechains may become more relevant for coordinated care involving multiple parties, as shown in Figure 9-5. A domain-specific sidechain could facilitate the transfer of access better, and then sync with the main blockchain. A very basic schematic of a sidechain is presented in Figure 9-6.

In order to improve quality and reduce costs, accountability for a patient's care should be shared among all providers along the health care continuum

FIgure 9-5. *Continuum of care. This image shows the comprehensive array of health services spanning all levels of care providers and community services. This picture was taken from a presentation done by Eccovia on accountable care organizations, with permission*

Blockchain can streamline the flow of information for medical records as it switches hands across multiple parties, and in this section we summarized some of the key findings of economic waste discovered by Ark Invest and Capital One. Even though sidechains are still very early in development, a simple graphic is presented in Figure 9-6.

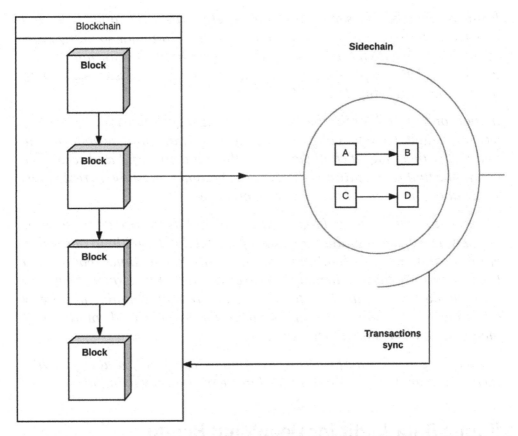

FIgure 9-6. *A simple sidechain performing off-chain transactions. This process can be useful for rapidly granting permissioned access and privileges; eventually these transactions sync with the upstream*

Verifiable Data Audit

Google's DeepMind is working on an interesting blockchain-like service to function as an audit log for hospitals using its health services to assist clinical diagnosis. The hospitals are transferring sensitive patient data over to DeepMind's machine learning and AI services to make clinical predictions, and this project is an effort to ensure the use of data is compliant with patient consent. We reached out to DeepMind inquiring about their efforts, and, with permission, we're reproducing an overview of Verifiable Data Audit.

> *Data can be a powerful force for social progress, helping our most impor-*
> *tant institutions to improve how they serve their communities. As cities,*
> *hospitals, and transport systems find new ways to understand what people*
> *need from them, they're unearthing opportunities to change how they work*
> *today and identifying exciting ideas for the future.*

Data can only benefit society if it has society's trust and confidence, and here we all face a challenge. Now that you can use data for so many more purposes, people aren't just asking about who's holding information and whether it's being kept securely—they also want greater assurances about precisely what is being done with it.

In that context, auditability becomes an increasingly important virtue. Any well-built digital tool will already log how it uses data, and be able to show and justify those logs if challenged. But the more powerful and secure we can make that audit process, the easier it becomes to establish real confidence about how data is being used in practice.

Imagine a service that could give mathematical assurance about what is happening with each individual piece of personal data, without possibility of falsification or omission. Imagine the ability for the inner workings of that system to be checked in real-time, to ensure that data is only being used as it should be. Imagine that the infrastructure powering this was freely available as open source, so any organization in the world could implement their own version if they wanted to.

The working title for this project is "Verifiable Data Audit," and we're really excited to share more details about what we're planning to build!

Verifiable Data Audit for DeepMind Health

Over the course of this year we'll be starting to build out Verifiable Data Audit for DeepMind Health, our effort to provide the health service with technology that can help clinicians predict, diagnose, and prevent serious illnesses—a key part of DeepMind's mission to deploy technology for social benefit.

Given the sensitivity of health data, we've always believed that we should aim to be as innovative with governance as we are with the technology itself. We've already invited additional oversight of DeepMind Health by appointing a panel of unpaid Independent Reviewers who are charged with scrutinizing our healthcare work, commissioning audits, and publishing an annual report with their findings.

We see Verifiable Data Audit as a powerful complement to this scrutiny, giving our partner hospitals an additional real-time and fully proven mechanism to check how we're processing data. We think this approach will be particularly useful in health, given the sensitivity of personal medical data and the need for each interaction with data to be appropriately authorized and consistent with rules around patient consent. For example, an organization holding health data can't simply decide to start carrying out research on patient records being used to provide care, or repurpose a research dataset for some other unapproved use. In other words: it's not just where the data is stored, it's what's being done with it that counts. We want to make that verifiable and auditable, in real-time, for the first time.

So, how will it work? We serve our hospital partners as a data processor, meaning that our role is to provide secure data services under their instructions, with the hospital remaining in full control throughout. Right now, any time our systems receive or touch that data, we create a log of that interaction that can be audited later if needed.

With Verifiable Data Audit, we'll build on this further. Each time there's any interaction with data, we'll begin to add an entry to a special digital ledger. That entry will record the fact that a particular piece of data has been used, and also the reason why - for example, that blood test data was checked against the NHS national algorithm to detect possible acute kidney injury.

The ledger and the entries within it will share some of the properties of blockchain, which is the idea behind Bitcoin and other projects. Like blockchain, the ledger will be append-only, so once a record of data use is added, it can't later be erased. And like blockchain, the ledger will make it possible for third parties to verify that nobody has tampered with any of the entries.

But it'll also differ from blockchain in a few important ways. Blockchain is decentralized, and so the verification of any ledger is decided by consensus amongst a wide set of participants. To prevent abuse, most blockchains require participants to repeatedly carry out complex calculations, with huge associated costs (according to some estimates, the total energy usage of blockchain participants could be as much as the power consumption of Cyprus). This isn't necessary when it comes to the health service, because we already have trusted institutions like hospitals or national bodies who can be relied on to verify the integrity of ledgers, avoiding some of the wastefulness of blockchain.

We can also make this more efficient by replacing the chain part of blockchain, and using a tree-like structure instead (if you'd like to understand more about Merkle trees, a good place to start would be the UK's Government Digital Service's dev blog). The overall effect is much the same. Every time we add an entry to the ledger, we'll generate a value known as a "cryptographic hash." This hash process is special because it summarizes not only the latest entry, but all of the previous values in the ledger too. This makes it effectively impossible for someone to go back and quietly alter one of the entries, since that will not only change the hash value of that entry but also that of the whole tree.

In simple terms, you can think of it as a bit like the last move of a game of Jenga. You might try to gently take or move one of the pieces—but due to the overall structure, that's going to end up making a big noise!

So, now we have an improved version of the humble audit log: a fully trustworthy, efficient ledger that we know captures all interactions with data, and which can be validated by a reputable third party in the healthcare community. What do we do with that?

The short answer is: massively improve the way in which these records can be audited. We'll build a dedicated online interface that authorized staff at our partner hospitals can use to examine the audit trail of DeepMind Health's data use in real-time. It will allow continuous verification that our systems are working as they should, and enable our partners to easily query the ledger to check for particular types of data use. We'd also like to enable our partners to run automated queries, effectively setting alarms that would be triggered if anything unusual took place. And, in time, we could even give our partners the option of allowing others to check our data processing, such as individual patients or patient groups.

The Technical Challenges Ahead

Building this is going to be a major undertaking, but given the importance of the issue we think it's worth it. Right now, three big technical challenges stand out.

No blind spots. For this to be provably trustworthy, it can't be possible for data use to take place without being logged in the ledger—otherwise, the concept falls apart. As well as designing the logs to record the time, nature and purpose of any interaction with data, we'd also like to be able to prove that there's no other software secretly interacting with data in the background. As well as logging every single data interaction in our ledger, we will also need to use formal methods as well as code and data center audits by experts, to prove that every data access by every piece of software in the data center is captured by these logs. We're also interested in efforts to guarantee the trustworthiness of the hardware on which these systems run—an active topic of computer science research!

Different uses for different groups. The core implementation will be an interface to allow our partner hospitals to provably check in real-time that we're only using patient data for approved purposes. If these partners wanted to extend that ability to others, like patients or patient groups, there would be complex design questions to resolve.

A long list of log entries may not be useful to many patients, and some may prefer to read a consolidated view or rely on a trusted intermediary instead. Equally, a patient group may not have the authority to see identified data, which would mean allowing our partners to provide some form of system-wide information - for example, whether machine learning algorithms have been run on particular datasets - without unintentionally revealing patient data.

For technical details on how we could provide verified access to subsets or summaries of the data, see the open source Trillian project, which we will be using, and this paper explaining how it works.

Decentralized data and logs, without gaps. There's no single patient identified information database in the UK, and so the process of care involves data travelling back and forth between healthcare providers, IT systems, and even patient-controlled services like wearable devices. There's a lot of work going into making these systems interoperable (our mobile product, Streams, is built to interoperable standards) so they can work safely together. It would be helpful for these standards to include auditability as well, to avoid gaps where data becomes unauditable as it passes from one system to another.

This doesn't mean that a data processor like DeepMind should see data or audit logs from other systems. Logs should remain decentralized, just like the data itself. Audit interoperability would simply provide additional reassurance that this data can't be tampered with as it travels between systems.

This is a significant technical challenge, but we think it should be possible. Specifically, there's an emerging open standard for interoperability in healthcare called FHIR, which could be extended to include auditability in useful ways.

Building in the Open

We're hoping to be able to implement the first pieces of this later this year, and are planning to blog about our progress and the challenges we encounter as we go. We recognize this is really hard, and the toughest challenges are by no means the technical ones. We hope that by sharing our process and documenting our pitfalls openly, we'll be able to partner with and get feedback from as many people as possible, and increase the chances of this kind of infrastructure being used more widely one day, within healthcare and maybe even beyond.

Summary

This chapter focused on the emerging role of blockchain in payments processing and how that can be applied to healthcare. We began the discussion with a description of the centralized payer–provider–patient model and how that model will change in the near future. Then, we discussed how to build a simplistic electronic health record system using the blockchain. After that, we presented how a patient workflow can be recorded on the blockchain. This led to a brief discussion of a physician credentialing use case. Finally, we talked about the economic wastes in healthcare discussed by Ark Invest and Gem and how the blockchain can alleviate some of those strains in the near future.

References

The main references used to prepare this chapter were Gem's blog posts (`https://enterprise.gem.co/infographic-managing-medical-data-blockchain/`) on blockchain-based EHRs, and the section on physician credentialing was prepared from PwC report on physician credentialing, and Hashed Health ProCredEx overview (`https://hashedhealth.com/blockchain-healthcare-solutions/professional-credentials-exchange/`).

CHAPTER 10

Lean Blockchain

For developers interested in building blockchain products, simply investing time in the
technology is not enough. The blockchain stack comprises business logic integrated deeply
into the technology models. As a result, an introductory level of familiarity with frameworks
that formally describe the components of a startup and how to build a company around a
product is necessary. This chapter begins with lean methodology, a model created by Eric
Ries that relies on three core principles: 1) transform the most basic version of your idea into
a product that a customer can interact with; 2) talk to your potential customers early and
often; and 3) iterate over that basic model with feedback from your customer to achieve a
full product that aligns with customer needs. And we keep in mind this quote from Eric: "As
you consider building your own minimum viable product, let this simple rule suffice: remove
any feature, process, or effort that does not contribute to the learning you seek." Then, we
present the business-model canvas that breaks down lean methodology into nine applicable
components. In addition, we talk about Geoffrey Moore's approach to product-market fit
for high-risk, high-reward technologies. Following this discussion, we present three models
to help determine whether your organization can benefit from using a blockchain. Once a
decision has been reached on using a blockchain, the Hyperledger Project provides multiple
options for enterprise-grade blockchains that can be customized and deployed. Finally, we
end the chapter with a brief overview of Hyperledger Composer and the templates it provides
for capturing business logic.

© Vikram Dhillon, David Metcalf, and Max Hooper 2021
V. Dhillon et al., *Blockchain Enabled Applications*, https://doi.org/10.1007/978-1-4842-6534-5_10

Lean Methodology

Lean methodology is a set of principles for developing products that aims to iteratively question whether a proposed business model solves a problem that the customers actually want, rather than planning for a product without any end-point customer in mind. This is accomplished by shorter product development cycles followed by multiple releases to get customer feedback, business hypothesis experimentation, and validated learning. Eric Ries is the founder of lean methodology. It provides a framework for bringing high-risk, high-reward technologies like the blockchain to market. For any organization trying to incorporate blockchain or experiment with new services that can be offered on blockchain, a rigorous framework is necessary to assess whether the organization will benefit from a blockchain. The practical application of lean methodologies will provide such a toolset, and in this section we want to introduce the fundamentals of lean to the reader:

- **Minimum viable product (MVP):** Arguably the most important aspect of lean methodology. A minimum viable product is the earliest version of a product with a limited number of features designed only to draw in early adopters for the purpose of obtaining data and feedback on the core concept. MVPs must be designed with the least amount of effort directed into assembly and yield the most amount of data about your product and ideas. For instance, a service offering custom stickers does not need to spend months designing intricate stickers. Instead, a simple landing page with a few sticker designs is enough to ask the more important question: Do customers want those stickers? A landing page can test this hypothesis, and our MVP can provide guidance on how to update the product such that it aligns with the needs of our customers. The features packed in MVPs are rudimentary, but the purpose here is not to showcase unique features, but rather to get in front of customers as soon as possible. Carefully defining an MVP to be actionable and mining for customer data is the first step in successfully bringing a high-risk, high-reward product to market.

- **Pivot:** During the iterative development of an MVP, customer interactions will provide valuable guidance on new features and updates to build. However, some customer interactions may point to deficiencies in your product and the need for fundamental changes to your core concept. At this point, you have two choices: either pivot or persevere. A pivot is the idea of changing a very limited set of product attributes and generating a new MVP to prove that your core concept is evolving in sync with the demands of your customer. Having a limited number of changes allows you to examine the direct effect that maximizes your reach to the customer. On the other hand, a persevere approach is a bold risk that further experimentation and tweaking of your product will satisfy the customer. Eric Ries suggests that a metric of bandwidth for a startup is not necessarily capital, but the number of pivots it can make before the product is ready for mass adoption. Decisions to pivot are crucial branch points and therefore pose risks. The use of split-testing can greatly help stratify and reduce the risk.

- **Product-market fit:** This is a stage in your iterative design when the MVP has become feature-rich and the early adopters are convincing more pragmatic users to try your product. Product-market fit places your product just at the cusp of reaching mass adoption. At this stage, you have validated all the hypotheses regarding your product, and the product is in sync with what the market needs. However, your product needs additional support from marketing and sales engines to capture the market and generate revenue. Essentially, the other services in a startup need to be built and deployed.

- **Business hypothesis experimentation:** Assumptions are ingrained in product development (especially when developing a high-risk, high-reward idea), and each assumption carries a risk of failure. Lean reframes the assumptions as hypotheses that need to be proven or disproven before the cycle of product development can progress further. This reduces the cumulative risk by ensuring that our assumptions are internally consistent and validated by the customer. A popular technique for hypothesis testing in lean startup is called split-testing (or A/B testing). In A/B testing, we present two different

223

design decisions to end users wherein half of the early adopters are shown one design feature, and the other half are shown a different feature. Data is collected from both user groups to help determine which design choice was better appreciated by users. In addition, this data collection provides opportunities for direct customer interviews to gain more insight into how the user interacted with the new functionality. There are two major benefits to using this approach. First, you can directly gauge the impact of your work on users. As developers, we may obsess over writing more-sophisticated code or developing interesting features that end users ultimately may not care about. Secondly, A/B testing eliminates conflicts around the priority of feature development—new features can be added to the MVP with each iteration and followed up with A/B testing. We can let data inform us about the features that a user considers relevant. In this manner, if a limited number of changes are made to the MVP, gathering data can reflect whether the changes translate to increased user retention and other parameters.

- **Validated learning:** A/B testing is helpful only if you and your team have the discipline to analyze the experiments rigorously and learn from them. Eric Ries talks about three properties that contribute to validated learning, summarized as the three A's: actionable, accessible, and auditable.

  - Actionable: Well-designed experiments will reveal a causal relationship between changes made to an MVP and new users acquired. These experiments generate data that is actionable as they provide a direction for future development.

  - Accessible: The data collected and metrics used must be simple and accessible to every member on the team. In particular, metrics can become very misleading to anyone collecting the data. As such, what we're trying to measure and the importance of those data points should be stated in the simplest possible terms, and be open to comments from any member of the team.

- Auditable: This is analogous to an independent review of your validated learning and experimental design process. Anyone should be able to go through the raw data and trace the metrics to reach the same recommendations for each iteration of your MVP. This builds rigor in the lean startup model and adds data-based justifications for pivot or persevere decisions.

Note   Lean startup was adopted and transformed by the National Science Foundation into a formal curriculum for university-based researchers who want to commercialize their technology. The Innovation Corps Program (I-Corps) trains teams of researchers and entrepreneurs for twelve weeks and equips them with the customer discovery skills. Every week is an iteration of the MVP based strictly on customer interviews, and the teams receive feedback from a panel of experts at the site hosting the I-Corps program. Each team comprises a technical lead, an entrepreneurship lead, and an I-Corps mentor. The teams are required to log weekly customer interviews and present updates to their business model canvas (which we discuss next). Major decisions such as pivot points are made based on documented data trends from interviews, making the whole customer-interview process very rigorous.

Identifying and building the appropriate MVP can be very challenging. Steve Blank shares a fantastic example on his blog about how difficult and potentially misleading this task can be:

> I ran into a small startup at Stanford who wants to fly Unmanned Aerial Vehicles (drones) with a Hyper-spectral camera over farm fields to collect hyper-spectral images. These images would be able to tell farmers how healthy their plants were, whether there were diseases or bugs, whether there was enough fertilizer, and enough water. (The camera has enough resolution to see individual plants.) Knowing this means farms can make better forecasts of how much their fields will produce, whether they should treat specific areas for pests, and put fertilizer and water only where it was needed.
>
> (Drones were better than satellites because of higher resolution and the potential for making more passes over the fields, and better than airplanes because of lower cost.)

All of this information would help farmers increase yields (making more money) and reduce costs by using less water and fertilizer/chemicals by only applying where it was needed.

Their plan was to be a data service provider in an emerging business called "precision agriculture." They would go out to a farmer's fields on a weekly basis, fly the drones, collect and process the data and then give it to the farmers in an easy understandable form.

Customer Discovery on Farms

I don't know what it is about Stanford, but this was the fourth or fifth startup I've seen in precision agriculture that used drones, robotics, high-tech sensors, etc. This team got my attention when they said, "Let us tell you about our conversations with potential customers." I listened, and as they described their customer interviews, it seemed like they had found that—yes, farmers do understand that not being able to see what was going on in detail on their fields was a problem—and yes—having data like this would be great—in theory.

So the team decided that this felt like a real business they wanted to build. And now they were out raising money to build a prototype minimum viable product (MVP). All good. Smart team, real domain experts in hyper-spectral imaging, drone design, good start on customer discovery, beginning to think about product/market fit, etc.

Lean Is Not an Engineering Process

They showed me their goals and budget for their next step. What they wanted was a happy early customer who recognized the value of their data and was willing to be an evangelist. Great goal.

They concluded that the only way to get a delighted early customer was to build a minimum viable product (MVP). They believed that the MVP needed to 1) demonstrate a drone flight, 2) make sure their software could stitch together all the images of a field, and then 3) present the data to the farmer in a way he could use it.

And they logically concluded that the way to do this was to buy a drone, buy a hyper-spectral camera, buy the software for image processing, spend months of engineering time integrating the camera, platform and software together, etc. They showed me their barebones budget for doing all this. Logical.

And wrong.

Keep Your Eyes on the Prize

The team confused the goal of the MVP (seeing if they could find a delighted farmer who would pay for the data) with the process of getting to the goal. They had the right goal but the wrong MVP to test it. Here's why.

The team's hypothesis was that they could deliver actionable data that farmers would pay for. Period. Since the startup defined itself as a data services company, at the end of the day, the farmer couldn't care less whether the data came from satellites, airplanes, drones, or magic as long as they had timely information.

That meant that all the work about buying a drone, a camera, software and time integrating it all was wasted time and effort—now. They did not need to test any of that yet. (There's plenty of existence proofs that low cost drones can be equipped to carry cameras.) They had defined the wrong MVP to test first. What they needed to spend their time on was first testing whether farmers cared about the data.

So I asked, "Would it be cheaper to rent a camera and plane or helicopter, and fly over the farmer's field, hand process the data and see if that's the information farmers would pay for? Couldn't you do that in a day or two, for a tenth of the money you're looking for?"

Note   This post was taken from Steven Blank's blog and shared here to illustrate the importance of planning the stages necessary to define an MVP. The incorrect MVP will cost more resources and result in tangential data that does not validate your hypothesis directly. On the other hand, a properly constructed MVP will allow you to validate your core hypothesis rapidly without using any significant resources.

The lean principles discussed here capture a market as the product gradually and iteratively matures through multiple stages. Product-market fit is the most important of the stages, and Geoffrey Moore, an organizational theorist, characterizes it as a chasm that products have to cross to be launched into mass adoption phases. Figure 10-1 summarizes the different phases of customer segments that a product can capture. Let us briefly review five of them here:

- **Innovators:** This segment is made of power users—a type of customer with some background and limited domain expertise in the vertical that your product falls under. Financial lucidity is a key property of this segment, as a low risk tolerance allows them to adopt technologies that may ultimately fail, but stable financial resources help absorb the failures. This customer is eager to try new products and will provide valuable technical insights as they have a vested interest in seeing new products succeed.

- **Early adopters:** This segment is very well connected with the innovators and has the highest amount of social capital to influence public opinion. More discrete in adopting new technologies and use this position to signal confidence in emerging trends. Early adopters play a huge role in helping a product appeal to broader audiences and achieve product-market fit.

- **Chasm:** A significant number of startups fail and never cross the chasm. The products developed never achieve product-market fit, and eventually the startup runs out of capital investment. Companies that manage to cross the chasm are now ready for mainstream market.

- **Early majority:** This is the first segment of the mainstream pragmatic consumers. Even though less social capital is invested at this level, word of mouth helps the product spread and reach very broadly.

- **Late majority:** This segment approaches new innovation with significant skepticism. A low financial lucidity plays a major role here, and although late, new product adoption happens long after the average member of society.

Note   There are two sides of applying lean principles. The first is an entrepreneur building out a product from scratch based on lean and customer-discovery methodology, and the second is an entrepreneur within a large organization trying to spin out a smaller company with potential resources and support for innovation. These two scenarios are drastically different in terms of resource allocation; however, the goal for a starting point is building an MVP. This should be done in such a way that minimizes resources used, and therefore not be a cost-prohibitive experiment. Both examples also have varying degrees of flexibility in terms of how an entrepreneur operates and the culture of the larger organization. The core principles involving iterations of MVPs and customer interviews remain the same in both scenarios.

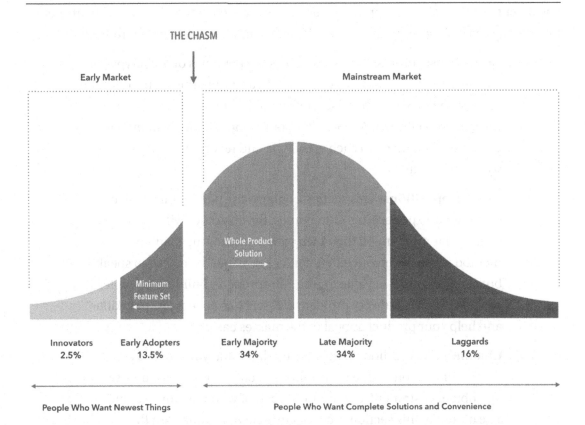

Figure 10-1. *Chasm of product-market fit and customer segments. This figure was originally illustrated by Shah Mohammed from Prototypr*

Business-Model Canvas

Alexander Osterwalder, a Swiss business theorist and entrepreneur, examined the structure of hundreds of companies and discovered that every company could be broken down into a model of nine basic components. To that end, new startups can be built following lean methodologies that take the form of a canvas with these nine components, called a business-model canvas. The idea is to work on a one-page canvas, frequently updating hypotheses about your business/product, and use customer interviews to fill out the nine components. This is opposed to the traditional model of creating lengthy business plans with projections on key metrics and user adoption without any validation from the customer. The canvas has two sides: the left side focuses on your product/business and the right side focuses on the customer. The two sides converge on the value propositions, defined as the key points of value provided to the customer by your business or product. Let us go over each of the nine components here, followed by a visual representation of the business-model canvas in Figure 10-2:

- **Customer segments:** This section lists the personas or archetypes of customers who will buy your product. In addition, this section should address the reasons why customers would want to buy from your company specifically. As such, it is your responsibility to interview customers belonging to each archetype and record how they interact with your products.

- **Value propositions:** This section contains the pain points that your customer is experiencing. Often times, the customer will try to solve a particular problem on their own with a patched-up solution. This method is usually inconvenient for a user, a "headache," so to speak, but a major source of value for the entrepreneur. Building a simpler process to solve that very problem will serve as an instant "painkiller" and help your product appeal to the masses easier.

- **Channels:** This section defines the medium that you can use to communicate your value propositions to customers, make new sales, and obtain customer feedback from each of your customer segments. The output of this section is connecting each persona with the appropriate channel to reach them.

- **Customer relationships:** This section describes how you will interact with your customers and how your customers can reach you. This can be done through social media accounts, dedicated personal service, or forum communities.

- **Key activities:** The section represents the work you must perform to interact with your customers to deliver your value proposition. You need to create a list of key activities linked to your value proposition. It may include product distribution, research and development, strategy, etc.

- **Key resources:** The assets needed to build your value proposition and deliver it to your customers. This includes any equipment, software, and intellectual property in terms of proprietary knowledge, maintaining good relationships with your customers, and defining potential new revenue streams. The key resources should be mapped to your key activities in order to provide a clear roadmap of how to create value for your customers.

- **Key partnerships:** The key external actors that you need to rely on for carrying out all of the key activities. Without these partnerships, you will not be able to deliver on your value propositions. The output from this section is a list of partners and how they tie into your key activities.

- **Revenue streams:** The core financial feature covered by the business-model canvas, answering a simple question of how your business will generate revenue. Traditional startups rely on three key revenue streams, including product sale, subscription fees, or licensing. Most blockchain companies have used the subscription fee model with a free tier, which allows users to try the platform before using it for any serious projects. The output of this section is to link customer segments with a potential revenue stream through value propositions.

- **Cost structure:** This section lists all the costs associated with keeping your startup running. Additionally, with careful planning, this section can help track the key activities or resources that are most expensive.

These nine components are arranged on the business-model canvas, split into a left side and a right side, as shown in Figure 10-1, connected by the value propositions.

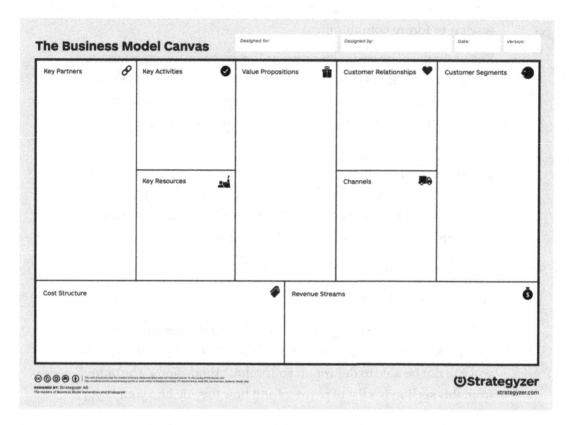

Figure 10-2. *Overview of business-model canvas with nine core components, taken from Strategyzer*

Do You Need a Blockchain?

The hype of blockchain technology has spread like wildfire through the corporate world. All sorts of enterprises and companies have created small blockchain-development teams to investigate how they can benefit from using the blockchain. Beneath the hype, there are signs of very serious technological development in the blockchain world, many of which are cataloged in this book. However, we are still in the nascent stages. The reality of the business advantages of blockchain-enabled applications is they can simplify business processes and reduce friction significantly. In this section, we will present three decision models that can help you critically analyze whether integrating a blockchain into your project/company is indeed the appropriate technical solution:

- **IBM model:** A blockchain model that highlights how the key features of blockchain fit into business processes and applications.

- **Birch-Brown-Parulava model:** A model helping you pick between permissioned and permission-less implementations of a distributed ledger. Designed by developers at Consult Hyperion.

- **Wüst-Gervais model:** A simplified model combining the best from both the previous models. Designed by two researchers from ETH Zurich.

Note Why did we pick these three models? There are several comprehensive decision trees available online to help a business decide which application scenarios would require a blockchain. In this section, we picked the simplest models to illustrate the more important design principles of integrating a blockchain into existing infrastructure.

Before we dive into the specifics of each model, what general principles are shared by all three? You can use the shared designs as criteria to evaluate your business needs, and then create a model specific to your business based on a few simple ideas and questions:

- **Database:** You need to begin by understanding why your business is using a database. Blockchains use a shared database that is visible to all the participants. Are you comfortable with using a shared ledger for your application? The database is constantly updated by transactions that happen over the network; can your application interface with a database that is constantly updated?

- **Writers:** The database is updated by multiple transactions writing to it. Blockchain is designed to have multiple writers; i.e., multiple entities that are generating and verifying the transactions that are published to the ledger.

- **No trust:** Does verifying the identity of writers matter for your application? This could change the ledger implementation that you deploy. The default setting for a blockchain is no trust between parties writing to the ledger. Is that sufficient for your application? Do the parties on your network have competing interests or similar motivations? If they have similar interests, some of the blockchain constructs managing trust can be safely removed.

- **Disintermediation:** Blockchains remove a centralized authority from the network, and the transactions are therefore considered decentralized. These transactions are independently verified and processed by every node on the network. Do you want or need this disintermediation? Given your application-specific use case, are there any significant shortcomings to having a gatekeeper? Good reasons to prefer a blockchain-based database might include lower costs, faster workflows, automatic settlements, or regulatory influences.

- **Transactional interdependence:** A blockchain is best for handling transactions that build on each other as they are published to the blockchain by writers. The interdependence part refers to transaction clearing; for instance, if A sends funds to B, and then B sends funds to C, the second transaction can't be cleared until the first one passes through. Blockchain ensures the orderly and rapid processing of transactions published by writers. In other words, a blockchain truly shines when keeping a log of transactions with a long history involving multiple users.

Let's start looking at decision models; the first one is shown in Figure 10-3.

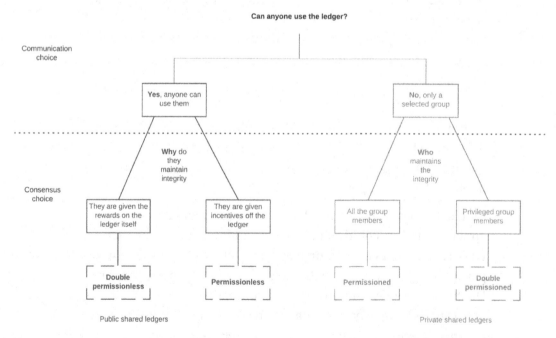

Figure 10-3. *The Birch-Brown-Parulava model showing the consensus algorithm that corrosponds to a ledger type*

This model walks a user through making the decision of whether to deploy a permissioned ledger or a permissionless ledger. This may lead to profound changes for deciding the software base; for instance, between Ethereum and Quorum. The next model is by IBM, shown in Figure 10-4.

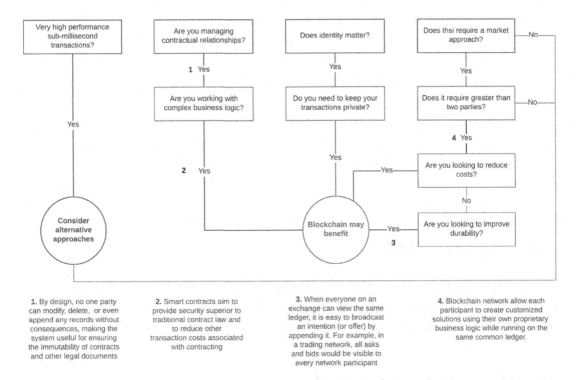

1. By design, no one party can modify, delete, or even append any records without consequences, making the system useful for ensuring the immutability of contracts and other legal documents

2. Smart contracts aim to provide security superior to traditional contract law and to reduce other transaction costs associated with contracting

3. When everyone on an exchange can view the same ledger, it is easy to broadcast an intention (or offer) by appending it. For example, in a trading network, all asks and bids would be visible to every network participant

4. Blockchain network allow each participant to create customized solutions using their own proprietary business logic while running on the same common ledger.

Figure 10-4. *IBM's decision chart for when to use a blockchain*

An important feature to highlight in this flowchart is how certain decisions are associated with features inherent to the blockchain. For instance, contractual relationships can be handled well on the blockchain by using smart contracts. This chart can become a decent preliminary check for blockchain compatibility with your project, and to see the features that are enabled by the blockchain.

The final decision model that we are considering here is shown in Figure 10-5. It was made by Karl Wüst and Arthur Gervais (both blockchain researchers) in a paper titled "Do You Need a Blockchain?" and for us, it sequentially integrates concepts from both the previous models.

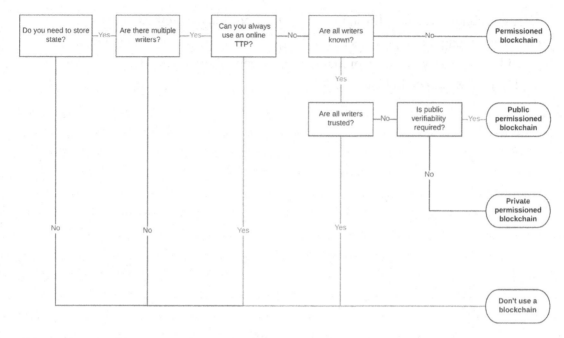

Figure 10-5. *The Wüst-Gervais model*

This model tries to answer for both deployment options and whether you should be considering a blockchain or not. The concepts here are similar to the previous models; however, this flowchart is focused more on properties of the network itself.

The Hyperledger Project

Now that we have provided a framework by which to determine whether an organization needs a blockchain, we will get an introduction to Hyperledger, which is an open source project and set of tools for deploying blockchains. Hyperledger is essentially an umbrella project by the Linux Foundation that offers underlying frameworks, operational standards, best practices or guidelines, and developer tools to set up, deploy, and manage open source blockchains. The open source project is well organized and backed by a community of hundreds of contributors, a governing board, and oversight from a technical steering committee. Presently, Hyperledger frameworks are an active area of study being used to build enterprise-grade blockchains for an organization or for application-specific consortias. In this section, we want to discuss seven Hyperledger frameworks and six developer tools.

> **Note**   This section provides a broad overview of the Hyperledger project. For
> an accurate and up-to-date list of features, please refer to the project website at
> www.hyperledger.org. Additionally, the terms *ledger* and blockchain will be
> used interchangeably in this section.

Hyperledger Fabric

Hyperledger Fabric is a permissioned blockchain infrastructure, and was the first
proposal for a codebase under the Hyperledger umbrella. This project was originally
designed as a foundation for building blockchain apps on top of distributed ledgers.
It featured a collaboration between IBM and Digital Holdings, and was eventually
incubated into Hyperledger. Fabric supplies a unique modular architecture wherein
core components such as consensus mechanism (called configurable consensus) and
membership services are plug-and-play. In addition, there is a clear delineation of user
privileges between nodes in the network, and as a result the execution of smart contracts
occurs differently based on permissions. A notable feature in Fabric is the ability for
members to conduct private transactions that only pass through a subset of verified
nodes, without being broadcasted to the whole network. This is done while maintaining
the integrity of the network, and without needing a centralized authority. Essentially, a
private transaction involves two components: the use of sub-channels and a few nodes
with different properties than the rest of the network. Once broadcasted, only nodes
with higher access privileges can execute and verify the transactions. All the other nodes
simply "skip" the transactions. Briefly, there are two sets of nodes in Fabric: peer nodes
that execute smart contracts (called chain code), endorse (validate) transactions, and
interface the blockchain with applications built on top; and executive or orderer nodes
that are responsible for maintaining the internal consistency of global state across the
network. Orderer nodes ultimately create a block and deliver it to all the members
of the network. Because of this division of labor between nodes, Fabric can support
permissioned deployments, unlike Bitcoin.

Hyperledger Burrow

Burrow is a fully modular blockchain node with a permissioned smart contract execution engine. Essentially, it's a distributed database system that can interpret and execute code. The smart contract execution engine functions as a built-in interpreter with specifications of an Ethereum Virtual Machine. As a result, Burrow can execute EVM smart contract code written in Solidity on a containerized virtual machine. Burrow uses a proof-of-stake consensus algorithm called Tendermint that allows a high transaction throughput and synchronization that scales with increasing network size. Presently, Burrow includes a consensus engine that maintains network integrity and order of transactions, a smart contract application that integrates business logic, an API that interfaces with external applications, and an Application Blockchain Interface that connects the consensus engine to the smart contract app.

Hyperledger Indy

Indy is a distributed ledger designed for building applications with a component of decentralized identity. The ledger comes with a set of libraries, testing tools, and modular components that can be reused to create private digital identities on a blockchain. Ultimately, Indy aims to create identity specifications and standards that are blockchain-agnostic and can work interoperably across any distributed ledger that is compatible with the specs. The private information of a user is not stored on the ledger itself; instead, Indy enables third-party apps to quickly verify that trusted organizations have issued private credentials to a member. This allows users to have more control over their private data and use the blockchain as an authentication gateway to safeguard their information. The use of blockchain architecture increases the overall security profile of an application and provides an effective safeguard against ransomware.

Hyperledger Sawtooth

Sawtooth is an Intel project designed to be a modular blockchain framework for building and deploying distributed enterprise-grade blockchains. The project is designed with a security architecture that isolates the core blockchain network from the smart contracts' execution such that a bad actor is unable to escalate privileges to affect the blockchain. In addition, Sawtooth has hot-swapping enabled for core components such as the consensus algorithm. The nature of dynamic consensus is such that the network can swap consensus algorithms on the fly based on the size of the network. By default, Sawtooth uses Proof-of-Elapsed-Time as the consensus that provides scalability without high energy consumption. As such, Sawtooth allows both permissioned and permissionless deployments. Sawtooth has a parallel scheduler for processing and executing transactions, with a safety mechanism to prevent double-spending. This enables multiple updates to the same global state and delivers better performance in transaction execution compared to traditional models. The first implementation of Sawtooth is an Intel project called Sawtooth Lake. It provides supply-chain management to prove the lineage of various goods, particularly fish, and to track the goods throughout the shipment.

Note   Sawtooth has recently made strides in cross-platform compatibility by adding a transaction processor known as Seth that is based on a Burrow EVM. This allows Seth to execute Ethereum smart contracts written in Solidity on a Sawtooth ledger.

Hyperledger Grid

Grid is a supply-chain implementation by Hyperledger. One of the major enterprise use cases for Hyperledger has been supply-chain management. Some of the contributing organizations identified a strong proof-of-concept for distributed ledgers in this use case, and Grid was designed as a specification to solve supply-chain problems. From an architecture perspective, Grid is not a blockchain framework. Instead, it is a collection of frameworks and libraries that allows developers to select the appropriate components for building business-specific supply-chain applications. The main advantages of having a generalized framework like Grid include having reference models for implementing members with specific roles on the network and nodes, smart contracts that implement common types of business logic, and decentralized data structures that are shared by industry partners.

Hyperledger Iroha

Iroha is designed as a mobile application development framework that can be incorporated into larger blockchain projects to provide a mobile end-point. Iroha provides client libraries for application development in Android and iOS, enabling rapid prototyping. Iroha apps will be cross-compatible with Fabric and Sawtooth ledgers, and the development environment is written in C++ to capture a broader audience of contributors. IoT applications enabled with Iroha will extend blockchain-based data management to peripheral devices and create semi-autonomous networks of connected devices.

Hyperledger Besu

Hyperledger Besu is an open source, Java-based Ethereum client that implements the Enterprise Ethereum Alliance (EEA) specification. Besu can run on the Ethereum main net, test networks such as Rinkeby, and even private permissioned networks that are compatible with the specs. It includes multiple consensus algorithms, including proof-of-work and proof-of-authority. In addition, the permissioning schema is designed to allow Besu in a consortia setting. EEA spec establishes a set of common interfaces for developers building applications that run on the Ethereum blockchain. The standardization of components allows developer teams from both open source and closed projects to not rely on vendor-specific application elements. Besu implements all enterprise-grade features in alignment with the EEA spec. Let's go over three key features of Besu:

- **Ethereum Virtual Machine (EVM):** Besu implements a full EVM through EEA specifications that allows execution of a smart contract through transactions on the Ethereum main net.

- **Consensus:** Besu implements multiple consensus algorithms for different tasks; for instance, block validation is done via a Proof-of-Authority (PoA) algorithm. This is a consensus algorithm where the participants are known to each other and have an established level of trust. IBFT 2.0 is the choice of PoA implemented by Besu where transactions and blocks are verified by a set of trusted accounts called validators. These validators take turns creating the next block, and existing validators can vote to add or remove other validators. In addition, due to the trusted nature of validators, all blocks are added to the main chain; i.e., there are no forks.

- **Privacy and permissioned ledger:** Hyperledger Besu provides the ability to keep transactions private between parties. All other parties cannot access the content of a private transaction, originating address, or list of recipients. This is implemented through a Private Transaction Manager by Besu. In addition, private transactions allow for a permissioned network where only pre-specified accounts can participate in certain transactions or transactional payload. All other nodes without proper access privileges simply pass along the transaction without accessing any details.

For a more comprehensive development environment, the seven Hyperledger frameworks are accompanied by the following six developer tools (with many more in active development):

1. **Hyperledger Explorer:** Explorer is a blockchain module designed for making web applications that interface with a ledger. It can be used for viewing basic network information, newly created blocks, or transaction addresses; or for querying transaction data and other block parameters that are made publicly available.

2. **Hyperledger Caliper:** Caliper is a reporting tool created to compute performance data for blockchain implementations. With Caliper, you can choose predefined use cases and get a report on performance factors, including transaction latency, resource utilization, and transactions per second on your ledger. Caliper can provide help in making business decisions for an organization that is planning to incorporate a distributed ledger.

3. **Hyperledger Composer:** Composer is a UI-based rapid-prototyping tool and a development framework to create blockchain apps and smart contracts. In addition, Composer provides a test network on which to deploy your applications. The development environment is user friendly, relying on widely familiar frameworks such as Node.js and NPM. Composer also comes packaged with sample business abstractions that model common business applications and deployment scripts to make it easier for live-testing in a sandbox. We will return to the rapid-prototyping aspect of Composer later in the next section.

4. **Hyperledger Quilt:** Quilt is a Java implementation of the Interledger Protocol (ILP) that enables payments in a blockchain-agnostic manner across any decentralized network, including fiat. Quilt provides the core libraries and data types necessary for sending and receiving transactions. The libraries are abstracted and provided as payment logic that developers can use for building applications. The apps built with Quilt can request authentication and access other ledgers or any payment system compatible with Interledger.

5. **Hyperledger Cello:** Cello is a blockchain-provisioning dashboard that reduces the administrative workload required for setting up, managing, and using distributed ledgers. For system administrators, Cello can be helpful for maintaining the lifecycle of blockchain networks, supporting customized blockchain parameters, and extending traditional monitoring and logging tools to report on a blockchain network's health. Eventually, Cello will become the frontend for setting up blockchains through Hyperledger. In addition, the advanced deployment features in Cello make it function as a Blockchain-as-a-Service platform for generating and maintaining on-demand blockchains. This chain service is cross-compatible with multiple infrastructures, including virtual machines (VSphere) and container platforms (Docker, Kubernetes).

6. **Hyperledger Ursa:** Ursa is a cryptographic library of shared functions that standardizes security functions for Hyperledger. This allows developers to streamline the code, reducing chances of vulnerabilities and increasing the overall security profile of the network. Notably, Ursa contains a generic library for creating zero-knowledge proofs, and this library will be available to any ledger implementation that is compatible with Ursa.

Rapid Prototyping with Hyperledger Composer

Hyperledger Composer is a suite of high-level application abstractions to model your business. Once you decide that your business might benefit from using a blockchain, you can use Composer to create a blockchain-based prototype of your application. The following is an outline of the process involved in making a prototype:

- Install Hyperledger Composer Tools or try Composer online in the Playground.

- Define business network, assets, and transactions.

- Implement any transaction processors.

- Test the business network within Composer-UI.

- Deploy business network to a live Hyperledger Fabric blockchain instance.

- Create a sample application on top of the low-level abstraction.

- Connect other applications to this deployment through RESTful API or Node.js.

The functional output of Composer is called a business network archive (BNA), which can then be deployed to a test net or a live Fabric blockchain. A business network contains participants that are connected via a role/identity, assets that propagate over the network, transactions that describe asset exchanges, contracts that serve as rules that underpin transactions, and finally the ledger that records all transactions. Aside from modeling components of a business network, the BNA also contains transaction processors, access control lists, and query definitions. A transaction processor (written in JavaScript) implements and enforces business logic on these model elements. The access control lists describe rules that allow fine-tuned control over which participants can have access to what assets in the business network after satisfying certain conditions. The language used to describe these access lists is very sophisticated and can capture complex ownership statements. Keeping access control separate from transaction processor logic allows the developers to maintain and update the two components rapidly, without any fears about compatibility or breaking functionality.

Note   In this section, our focus is on presenting the fundamentals of Hyperledger Composer so that an interested reader can pick up on Composer's modeling language quicker from the reference material. Designing a full business network model would be beyond the scope of this book.

Let's go through the modeling language and discuss the foundations of Composer in depth:

- **Assets:** Represent the resources being exchanged between users on the network. Formally, the description scheme used to define assets is done in the order of `keyword - class - identifier - properties - relationships`. Other optional fields may be added here as well, but this general scheme is followed throughout the modeling language. Assets are defined with the keyword `asset` and have a domain-relevant class name associated with them. For instance, a car can be identified by VIN as: `asset Vehicle identified by vin`. The assets have a set of properties that define them; in the case of a vehicle, it can be a description stored as a `string String description`. Additionally, the assets can have relationships to other resources in the modeling language, such the user that owns the car, denoted by `--> User owner`. All the assets are stored in an asset registry available to the network.

- **Participants:** Represent the users (or counterparties) in the network. Participants are key to all interactions happening on the network, and they are described the same way as an asset. Participants are represented using the `participant` keyword, and they also have a class name relevant to their domain, such as buyer or seller. A full description may be given as `participant Buyer identified by email` and a property of `String firstName`. All the participants are stored in a participant registry, which may not be available to the users of the network.

- **Transactions:** Represent the movement of assets across the network, and the lifecycle of assets as they are exchanged. Transactions are described in the same way as participants or assets, and a sale offer from a participant may be defined as `transaction Offer identified by transactionid` and with a property of `Double saleprice`.

- **Concepts:** Concepts are abstract classes that don't belong to assets, participants, or transactions. Concepts are often used to add specifiers to an asset or transaction and typically are contained by one of the three. For instance, a concept of address can be described as `Concept Address` with properties of `String street` and `String city_default ="Orlando"`. Now an asset can use this concept to specify an address property.

- **Transaction processors:** Represents the business logic to perform state changes and global updates to the blockchain as a result of transactions' being broadcasted to the network. Essentially, these processors provide an implementation for transactions to act on the model. They are written in a separate js file and utilize the definitions from the business network model.

These components are shown graphically in Figure 10-6.

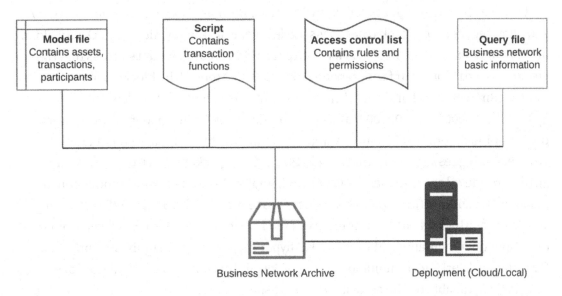

Figure 10-6. *Components of the business network archive*

Summary

In this chapter, we studied three distinct areas relevant to blockchain research and development: using lean startup methodology to develop high-risk research ideas into products that customers want; how to determine if your organization needs a blockchain; and an overview of Hyperledger Project—an open source effort to build enterprise-grade blockchains. The lean methodology was broken down into the business-model canvas by Alexander Osterwalder and the chasm of product-market fit by Geoffrey Moore. These models helped us better understand how products can be designed to capture the market. Then, we presented three models to determine if your project or company can benefit from using a blockchain and how to decide on the type of deployment. Finally, we briefly reviewed the Hyperledger Project, which provides highly customizable blockchain implementations that capture business logic in templates. We hope that our readers can take away practical and applicable tips from this chapter to help bring their own ideas forward.

References

The key resources used to prepare the lean methodologies were *The Lean Startup* (http://theleanstartup.com/book) by Eric Ries, *Business Model Generation* (https://www.strategyzer.com/books/business-model-generation) by Alexander Osterwalder, and *Crossing the Chasm* (https://www.harpercollins.com/products/crossing-the-chasm-3rd-edition-geoffrey-a-moore) by Geoffrey Moore. The blockchain decision models: Birch-Brown-Parulava (https://www.ingentaconnect.com/content/hsp/jpss/2016/00000010/00000002/art00002) model taken from a paper by the authors, the IBM model from blockchain developer documents (https://developer.ibm.com/technologies/blockchain/tutorials/cl-ibm-blockchain-101-quick-start-guide-for-developers-bluemix-trs/), and, finally, the Wüst-Gervais model from a paper by the authors (https://www.researchgate.net/publication/328820555_Do_you_Need_a_Blockchain). The summary of the Hyperledger Project was taken from the developer documentation (https://wiki.hyperledger.org/) of individual projects; for instance, Fabric documentation (https://openblockchain.readthedocs.io/en/latest/) is available on the associated project site.

CHAPTER 11

Blockchain 3.0

The rapid growth of R&D in the blockchain world can be explained by the industry's gaining a deeper understanding of where the value is created and captured for a traditional internet company and a blockchain company. Joel Monegro and Naval Ravikant, both venture capitalists and investors in blockchain technology, talk about the idea of fat protocols, where most of the innovation in the blockchain space will happen at the core technology level. Then a token layer can monetize the use of the underlying architecture and provide access to the application layer. To that end, we have seen three iterations of blockchains in development: the first version was the original protocol by Satoshi that provides a functional blockchain for transactions. The second version was protocols like Ethereum that provide smart contracts and on-chain operations. The next generation of blockchain protocols allow on-chain execution and the integration of services such as machine learning onto a blockchain for advanced tasks.

In this chapter, we will focus on three new technologies that have significantly advanced our understanding of blockchain-enabled applications and opened up several new avenues for research. We begin our discussion with EOS, an Ethereum competitor built with an operating system–inspired architecture and platform-support design philosophy. It uses a new consensus mechanism called Delegated Proof-of-Stake to enable rapid transaction verification and a continuous cycle of voting for delegates that support the network. The message-passing protocols implemented in EOS are very advanced, allowing automated response handlers and action triggers on message delivery, and they make up most of the smart-contract system. There is also support for parallel lockless execution of smart-contract instructions across the network, massively reducing latency in communication and state updates.

© Vikram Dhillon, David Metcalf, and Max Hooper 2021
V. Dhillon et al., *Blockchain Enabled Applications*, https://doi.org/10.1007/978-1-4842-6534-5_11

The second technology we present is a contract-oriented programming language called Chain-core. Chain is no longer in active development; however, we want to illustrate the potential of blockchain-agnostic contract-oriented programming in asset management. On the Chain network, all value is concentrated within assets that can be issued and controlled by users. Chain provides a powerful API (and a graphical user interface) to developers for managing and transferring those assets on the blockchain. We provide a walkthrough of Chain's graphical interface and cover the basics of asset management.

The final technology that we will talk about is enterprise Ethereum. This section will focus on three main contributors: Quorum (an enterprise-grade fork of Ethereum built by JPMorgan), Ethereum Enterprise Alliance (a set of specifications and standards to build enterprise applications), and R3 (a consortium behind the blockchain deployment tool Corda). This technology set is designed to handle the high-volume requirements of businesses and offers some unique upgrades. The most notable features include private transactions and smart contracts, zero-knowledge proofs, and pluggable consensus.

EOS Blockchain

EOS.IO is a new architectural approach to building a blockchain that resembles an operating system. The design considerations allow for core infrastructure that can be scaled with ease for decentralized applications. Here, scalability refers more generally to a set of principles that make blockchain applications analogous to their traditional non-blockchain counterparts. In this section, we will focus on the potential for large-scale adoption made possible due to three major technical innovations behind EOS: an advanced permissions system, a new method for consensus called Delegated Proof-of-Stake, and parallel processing in the EOS blockchain. Let's begin our discussion with a few principles of scalability embodied by EOS:

- **User base:** A disruptive EOS blockchain application should be able to support millions of users and user accounts. The underlying architecture needs to be designed such that a distributed ledger can handle accounts as the fundamental unit (as opposed to transactions). Supporting services can provide synchronous modification of accounts and the blockchain global state.

- **Free access:** The services or applications built on a blockchain should not pass on any execution costs to the users. Large non-blockchain services are essentially free, and the end user is monetized based on data generated from app utilization. To enable widespread adoption, blockchain-based apps would have to eliminate user fees, amortize service costs, and generate revenue from new accounts signing up for the app.

- **Updates and forks:** The integration of new components or features to a service should not require any downtime. Blockchain-based services have to deal with consensus at some level, and disagreements may lead to forks in the chain. These forks create chains with different lengths and are normally resolved very rapidly with the creation of the next block; however, the more serious problems arise with software updates. Bugs in the network should be fixed easily and seamlessly, without the need for a type of hard fork whereby some portion of the network is no longer compatible. The decentralized nature of blockchain services creates a network without a single point of failure and, combined with redundancy, it can provide a unique no-downtime experience.

- **Low latency:** The Bitcoin blockchain currently suffers from high latency and incredibly long verification delays. A pragmatic service used by thousands of users is unsustainable with long wait periods; therefore, services on EOS must provide an incredibly rapid verification and confirmation method where applicable. There are some interesting new features such as parallel processing that may alleviate the pains of slow confirmations on transactions.

Let's start with how EOS handles accounts and user permissions. In EOS, all the accounts can be created with unique human-readable references. Additionally, EOS provides a well-defined message-passing protocol between accounts with handlers and automation rules. Every account on the network can send structured programmatic messages to other accounts and define rules and scripts to handle incoming messages when received. The scripts used to handle messages can also send messages in response to a specific incoming action. Each account also has a private storage that can be accessed by the message handlers to modify the account state. The message-handling scripts along with rules form the smart-contract system deployed by EOS. The design principles behind EOS smart contracts are analogous to well-studied message-passing protocols describing how an operating system communicates with peripherals and other hardware components. The contracts will be executed on a virtual machine similar to an EVM. Existing smart contracts written in Solidity or other contract-oriented languages can be ported and adapted to work with a container on the EOS blockchain. The contracts will also inherit some EOS-specific functions that allow communication with other EOS components.

Note   Another advanced feature in EOS is the ability to communicate between the EOS blockchain and external blockchains compatible with Merkel proofs. This takes place on the client side by using the same fundamental cryptographic principles (proof of message existence and proof of message sequence) to verify messages transferring in/out of the blockchains.

Let's return to understanding how user permissions work. In EOS, the application structure is such that the authentication and permission modules are kept separate from the business logic. This allows developers to design tools specific for permission management and streamline apps to only contain code relevant to app-directed actions. EOS allows the user to define the keys used to sign outgoing messages and the different keys used for each separate service accessed by the user. For instance, a user can have one key to sign messages sent to other users and a different key to access social media accounts. It is possible to provide other accounts with permission to act on a user's behalf, without assigning any keys. This type of limited access can give someone post-only permissions to your social media (with prior permission), but the posts will retain their unique signature. This is accomplished by a concept called permission mapping, which we will discuss next. A key idea in permission mapping is multi-user control of a single account. This is considered a high-level security measure for decentralized apps, and in EOS it is implemented to reduce the risk of password or currency theft.

Note   EOS can be considered a generalized evolution of the blockchain-based social network Steem created by Dan Larimer. Steem was built on the Graphene blockchain, and permission mapping was originally implemented as a feature, but it was very limited. While Steem was designed as a decentralized social platform, EOS is an application development platform with a Turing-complete blockchain analogous to Ethereum.

To understand permission mapping, let's look at an example involving three user roles: the account owner, an active user, and a social media user. The social media permission allows only specific actions by the user, such as voting and posting. On the other hand, active user permission allows almost any action except for removing the owner. The owner can perform all available actions, including withdrawal. In this example, permission mapping refers to an account owner's defining roles and mapping the associated permissions to other accounts. EOS generalizes this example by allowing custom roles and custom actions that can be mapped to different accounts. For instance, an account holder can map the permissions for a social media app to a Friend user group. Now any account added to the permission group (by the account holder) instantly has access to the social media app. They can post, vote, and perform any other actions available to the permission group, but their unique keys will be recorded. Therefore, it is always be possible to identify which user performed an action. The concept of permission mapping is illustrated in Figure 11-1.

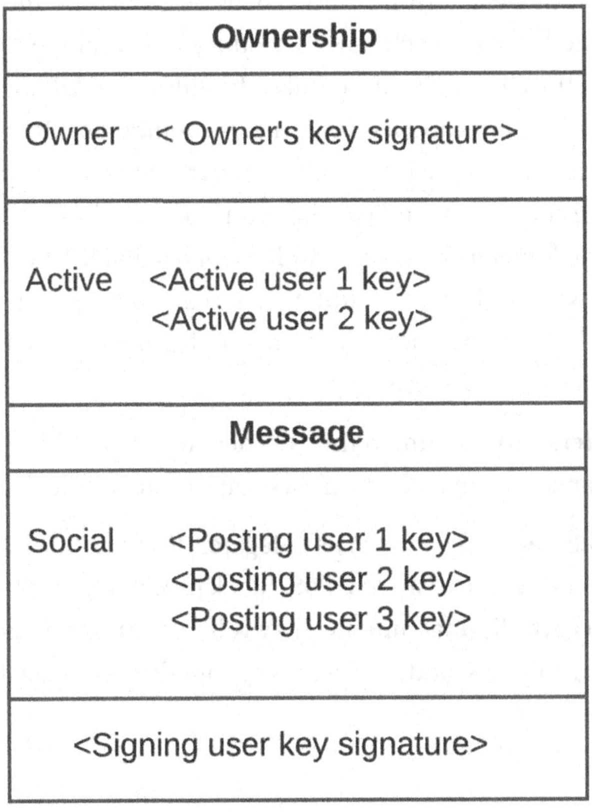

Ownership	
Owner	< Owner's key signature>
Active	<Active user 1 key> <Active user 2 key>
Message	
Social	<Posting user 1 key> <Posting user 2 key> <Posting user 3 key>
<Signing user key signature>	

Figure 11-1. Structure of custom permission mapping

In Figure 11-1, we can divide this representation into two components: the ownership and the message itself. The ownership portion contains keys from the account holder, who can perform all account functions including withdrawal of tokens. It also contains keys from active users that act on behalf of the owner. The second portion of this structure is the message, and here we continue to use an example of social media. There are three social users mapped to this account by the owner, and each user has a unique key. When a message is posted to the social media, the posting user signs the message with their own unique key, so any actions performed by the mapped users can be tracked. The message module here can be replaced by other applications, with the account holder mapping custom permissions to the app, providing limited functionality to the mapped users.

Delegated Proof-of-Stake (DPoS)

EOS uses a new consensus mechanism called Delegated Proof-of-Stake (DPoS). It is a variant of the Proof-of-Stake algorithm with a focus on efficiency and fair access, giving smaller wallets/accounts a candid chance to produce blocks and earn the reward. The difference between a traditional Proof-of-Stake algorithm and DPoS can be compared to the difference between a direct and a representative democracy. In traditional Proof-of-Stake (PoS) algorithms, any user with a wallet can participate in the process of validating transactions, forming consensus, and earning a part of the mining reward. However, it may be unprofitable for users with small wallets, or a smaller "stake." In DPoS, every wallet across the network with any amount of coins can vote for delegates who perform the functions of validation and appending blocks to the blockchain. Ultimately, there are two main players in a DPoS network:

- **Stakeholders:** An account in the EOS network that holds a wallet with a balance. Having tokens allows you to vote for block producers.

- **Block producers:** Also known as delegates, these entities drive the consensus mechanism of DPoS. Block producers are the DPoS equivalent of traditional miners. They validate transactions on the network, sign blocks, and earn a reward for adding a block to the blockchain.

Let's briefly review the mechanism of consensus and the need for global state updates before diving deep into DPoS. Recall that a blockchain can be modeled as a state machine with a consistent history of updates. This state machine is acted upon by transactions, and consensus is the process of network-wide agreement on the order in which transactions will update the global state. The updates occur at specific increments as new transactions are included in blocks, and as the rapid frequency of updates filters out invalid or double-spend transactions. The goal of DPoS is to make block production evenly distributed among the most people and ensure that a democratic, fair process elects the block producers. Regular PoS networks require full consensus to validate, whereas in a DPoS system a limited number of delegated nodes (delegates) can provably validate transactions and reach consensus.

Note   In the current schedule, EOS allows blocks to be produced every three seconds by a singular block producer. By default, the blocks are produced in multiple series, with each series containing twenty-one block producers.

The DPoS algorithm has two major operational roles: electing a group of block producers and scheduling production of blocks. Each account on the network is allowed at least one vote per delegate (miner) in a process known as approval voting. However, accounts with a larger "stake" in the network follow the principle of one vote per delegate per token, and can vote for more than one delegate. The block producers (delegates) are considered a minimally trusted party on the blockchain, being elected through a real-time voting process. The delegates can take turns (in a series) adding transactions to a block and signing blocks to be added to the blockchain. As such, the use of a trusted party prohibits malicious parties' adding invalid transactions to the blockchain. It should be noted that delegates don't have the ability to change transaction or block details; they are only able to either add or not add a transaction to a block. This group of delegates is randomly assigned for block production based on some variation of a weighted fair queueing algorithm. The goal is to efficiently schedule block producers based on two criteria: the number of votes they received and the time a delegate has been waiting to produce a block. Delegates with more votes are more likely to be scheduled next to produce a block. On the other hand, delinquent delegates can be voted out quickly without affecting any significant transaction volume. Let's summarize the main roles of delegates:

- **Block production:** The most important function of delegates is to create blocks at a fixed schedule of every three seconds. This involves validating transactions and signing blocks across multiple series.

- **Network support:** Each time delegates produce a block, they are paid a reward for forging the block. The pay rate is set by the stakeholders; however, some delegates may accept a lower pay rate in order to get more votes from the network. Additionally, instead of taking lower pay rates, delegates may offer additional services such as marketing and legal work to the stakeholders.

Figure 11-2 shows representative block production used in DPoS consensus algorithms.

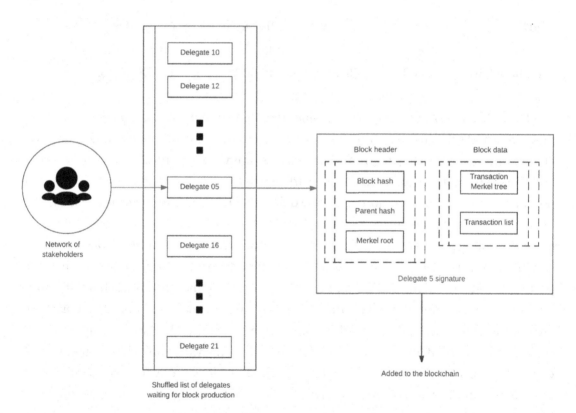

Figure 11-2. *Block production in DPoS*

Stakeholders on the network vote and elect delegates, who in turn validate transactions and produce blocks. This is illustrated in Figure 11-2. From the highest-voted delegates, twenty-one are elected to participate in multiple series and produce blocks. The delegates are assigned to a schedule for producing blocks, and this assignment is made using a round-robin algorithm. A block is considered invalid if a block producer forged outside of their scheduled timeslot. After a block has been signed by the delegate, the final block can be appended to the blockchain, as seen on the right-hand side of the figure. If a block producer fails to be on schedule, the next delegate's block will be larger and include the previous transactions. At the same time, if a block producer fails repeatedly, they will be voted out of the series.

Tip   It is interesting to note that DPoS blockchains do not have a tendency to fork. This is because block producers cooperate to produce blocks, rather than competing as in a PoW system. In the event that a fork does occur, the consensus automatically switches to the longest chain.

Parallel Execution

In Ethereum, the execution of instructions (for instance, from a smart contract) is done in a deterministic and synchronous manner across the network. EOS offers a very interesting upgrade for parallel execution of applications without the use of any locking primitives. In this case, there must be a mechanism inherent to the blockchain ensuring that each account only updates its own database. Incoming instructions update the account state; therefore, they must be applied sequentially such that the $n+1$ instruction updates the account only after nth instruction. There is an exception to this general rule in the case of binary yes/no–type instructions. Some account handlers can process binary instructions as read-only and reply back without any changes to their internal state.

Fundamentally, parallel execution in EOS relies on delivering messages generated from different sources within an account to independent threads so that they can be executed in parallel. Ultimately, the final state of an account only depends on the messages delivered to it. A block producer organizes the delivery of messages to independent threads. Even though a block producer is on schedule for validating blocks, message delivery is done on a more rapid and custom schedule to take advantage of parallelism. Often times, the sources of these messages are scripts running on the blockchain or automatic account handlers sending messages. Due to the parallel nature of EOS, when a message is generated, it does not get delivered immediately. Instead, there is a period of delay between message generation and delivery referred to as latency. The rationale behind introducing latency is because instantaneous delivery could interfere with a receiver already modifying its internal state due to a previous message. Lockless messaging is achieved by scheduling the message to be delivered in the following cycle.

So, what is a cycle? Under normal circumstances, to avoid message collision, an account would have to wait until the next block to send a second message or to receive a reply. A block is created every three seconds; therefore, accounts can expect at least a three-second wait between sending more messages. To remove this wait time between messages, EOS divides a block into multiple cycles and further subdivides those cycles as follows:

- Each cycle is divided into threads.

- Each thread contains a list of transactions.

- Each transaction contains a set of messages that will be delivered.

Figure 11-3 shows the subdivisions and structure of a cycle within a block.

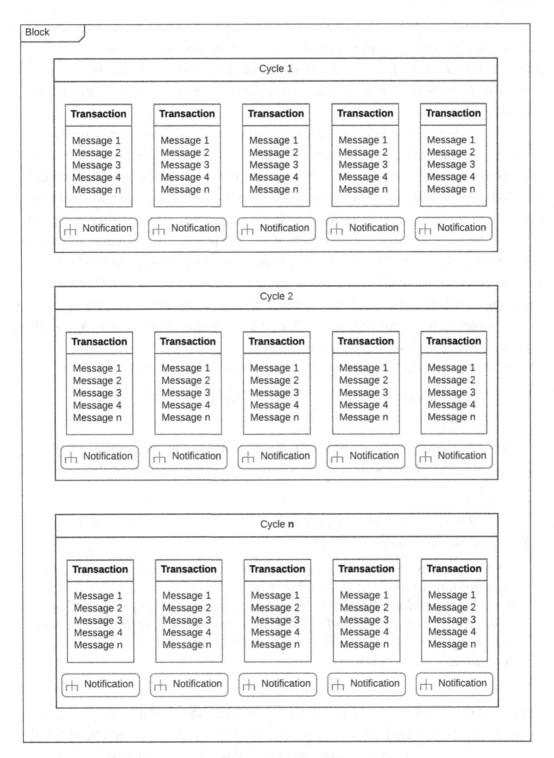

Figure 11-3. *Block structure for messages in EOS*

Each block is divided into a cycle that forms the basis of rapid communication within a single block. If no two transactions within a block modify the same account, all the transactions from one cycle can be executed in parallel. For each transaction that takes place between users, any automated handlers preset by the receiver are notified of incoming instructions.

Block producers. keep adding new cycles to a block until a time limit is reached or no new transactions have been generated. Transactions generated during the time window of one cycle can also be added to a subsequent cycle or the next block. Once a block is finalized, we can ask the following question: Given a block cycle, are there two threads that contain transactions that modify the same account? If not, then any given block can be processed by executing all the threads in parallel. An exchange application developer runs full nodes for the purpose of displaying the exchange state to its users. This exchange application has no need for the state associated with social media applications. EOS.io software allows any full node to pick any subset of applications to run. Messages delivered to other applications are safely ignored because an application's state is derived entirely from the messages that are delivered to it. There are two important take-home points that need to be reiterated from this section:

- An application's internal state is derived from the messages delivered specifically to that app.

- Any changes to an account's internal state happen via messages passed between accounts, and are included in transactions on the blockchain.

Dan Larimer commented on the parallel nature of EOS as a massive advantage for building applications on the blockchain:

Parallel processing capabilities bring continuous scalability and a reliable high performance foundation for your applications. Existing single-threaded capabilities force every application to share the capacity and performance of one single-threaded blockchain, create hard scaling limits, and eventually suffer from network congestion that may result in platform-wide downtime.

Note   EOS.io recently had an ICO to raise funds for development, and CryptoPortfolio reviewed the ICO, making a few points worth considering. The first point is that profit generation comes from the value appreciation of EOS tokens.

The more users and developers, the more valuation. The second point is that there are no transaction fees on EOS, so accounts and DApps need tokens to work. Holding a certain amount of tokens is like having bought a percentage in EOS computational power. The third point is that since there is going to be free usage of the platform, you only need tokens on your balance to operate on this blockchain. Finally, the last point is that users demand a fast response from services they use, so EOS will try to make transaction confirmation happen in less than 1.5 seconds.

Scheduling

The last topic that we want to tackle in this section is that of best-effort scheduling. Recall from our previous discussion of computational marketplaces that a Turing-complete virtual machine (similar to EVM) on the blockchain determined the cost of execution for the instructions contained in a contract. The customer requesting a given task paid for each step of the instruction with gas, and if the number of steps exceeded the EVM gas limit, the task would not execute. In EOS, the delegates take over the role of making global decisions about eligibility to execute, instead of a VM. The block producer (delegates) makes a subjective measurement of the complexity (number of instruction steps) and time required to process the instructions contained within a transaction and deliver a message. This subjective measurement of processing costs is analogous to gas in an Ethereum system. A delegate-based instruction-counting and costs-determining mechanism simplifies the addition of new features and optimizations to the blockchain, without any concern about breaking the cost calculations. It also allows us to categorize the network functionally: blockchain and virtual machines for execution and nodes or block producers for calculating resource allocation and management.

To bill for computational runtime, each block producer calculates resource utilization using its customizations to the EOS algorithms. Across the network, each step has an execution time limit and is charged a fixed bandwidth-usage cost regardless of whether the computation took 1ms or the full time. A crucial point to note is that in EOS all resource usage constraints are subjective and are ultimately enforced by block producers. As a collective, the block producers have agreed on the following criteria on the EOS network:

- For a block producer, there are two options available: include a transaction (a set of instructions) or reject it from being included in a block.

- If a block producer concludes that a given account has consumed an unreasonable amount of the computational bandwidth, they simply reject transactions from that account when producing their own block.

- As long as one block producer considers a transaction valid, and under the resource usage limits, all other block producers will also accept it. However, this transaction will take longer to confirm on the network.

- If a block producer includes transactions that are well beyond the limits of resources, another producer might reject the block and a third producer will be needed as the tie-breaker.

There would be a delay in propagation of the tie-breaker block, giving the stakeholders and other delegates ample time to pin-point the source of resource violation. Over time, if a malicious block producer keeps approving blocks that are over the limits, she will be voted out from the list of delegates. The block producers perform the role of a "best-effort" scheduler in EOS: fair scheduling of tasks for maximum throughput or rejecting tasks from being executed on the network.

Note   EOS.io Core is currently in 2.0.5 release with new stability updates and features. The Quickstart IDE is a web-based development tool for building blockchain applications using EOS.io 2.0. It enables rapid prototyping of smart contracts and setting up of quick deployment within a few minutes. This simplifies the app development process, especially for new developers, without any extensive setup needed.

Chain Core

Chain is a contract-oriented programming language designed to manage assets on a blockchain. Chain is no longer in active development. However, the conceptual framework and design of a programming language for managing assets is immensely valuable for you, the reader, to understand. As a result, we have retained this section in the new edition. The following is an excellent summary of the Chain platform by their team:

> The key characteristic that makes a Chain blockchain a shared ledger, rather than simply a distributed database, is that it is designed to track and control value—i.e., units of one or more assets. Unlike data, value is scarce: once issued, it cannot be copied, only transferred.

> We gain new capabilities when the underlying format of a financial instrument becomes a cryptographically-issued digital asset, one of the most notable of which is the ability to write programs that control the asset. These programs are known as contracts.

> All value on a Chain blockchain is secured by such contracts. Each contract controls, or locks, some specific value—i.e., some number of units of an asset—and enforces the conditions that must be satisfied before that value can be unlocked. From the simplest custodial account to the most complex derivative instrument, contracts define the rules for asset movement on a Chain blockchain network. And Ivy lets you compose those rules.

> When designing Ivy we had a single goal: making it easy to write safe, secure, and simple programs to control the movement of value on a blockchain. Nothing more, nothing less.

At Consensus 2017 (a major blockchain development conference), Chain announced a set of more sophisticated upgrades to the core programming language, making it easier to write contracts that manage assets. Ivy Playground was the result of this effort to make the developer experience as smooth as possible. A core concept that Chain and Ivy have embraced in designing contracts is to limit the amount of information in the blockchain: only state-updating logic and consensus-maintaining variables. This design rationale is explained by the Chain team as follows:

> As much as possible, the business logic of blockchain solutions should be executed off-chain, in the "application layer"—programs written in traditional languages, that interact with Chain Core through its SDK. The only logic that needs to be part of the "smart contract" layer is the set of rules that secure and transfer assets.

261

Some blockchain platforms are marketed as workflow automation tools, as a global database for shared state, or as a platform for building software-as-a-service applications. We believe that these goals make the wrong trad-eoff, by effectively shifting computation and logic from traditional servers, where computation is cheap and information is private, to the blockchain, where every computation must be redundantly executed on every node in the network.

The key to understanding Chain's design is that traditional services can't be transitioned to a blockchain; instead, they need to be redesigned for a new architecture. For starters, additional parameters involving consensus are introduced in an application. The programmatic routines need to distinguish between the business logic that should remain outside of the blockchain and state variables that need to be updated on the blockchain. Therefore, new design decisions are needed. Additionally, traditional services have some inherent redundancies that are normally not a problem for servers in a data center, but become amplified in a decentralized network where each node must update the state of accounts in the same order for every step of computation (replicated state machines). To illustrate how Chain works, we will do a walkthrough of Chain Core with Ivy. The main objectives of this walkthrough are to understand how to create HSM cryptographic keys, how to create accounts, and how to trade assets. The layout will be very similar to Aragon, which we covered in a previous chapter. Pay close attention to how information regarding an asset flows through Chain core (Figure 11-4).

Figure 11-4. Configuring Chain Core

For our walkthrough, we will be joining a test net, which behaves like a blockchain but all the data is reset weekly. The test net helps in understanding how to interact with a blockchain properly and how to manage assets in Chain.

Clicking "Join Network" should take you to the dashboard of Chain Core. Here, you are presented with an option to do a tutorial. We will cover the basics of that tutorial here, adding more information about the main concepts in Chain. To the left of the dashboard is a navigation menu that we will be using heavily throughout the walkthrough. It is shown in Figure 11-5. The nav menu is split into three parts. The top part deals with data related to accounts, assets, and transactions. The middle part deals with private–public keys, which are required to interact with the blockchain. And the bottom part provides some developer services; we will be talking about Ivy Playground later in the chapter. To begin interacting with the test net, we first need to create keys. Chain uses hardware security module (HSM)–backed key management, and this key becomes your gateway to the network. To create a key, go to the nav menu and click on MockHSM under Services.

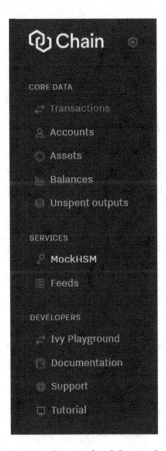

Figure 11-5. *Nav menu layout on Chain dashboard*

The nav menu in Figure 11-5 is split into three pieces: the core data, which comprises accounts, assets, and transactions; the services where we can create HSM keys; and finally a few developer tools. We will be using the MockHSM tab to create a set of keypairs.

So, why do we need an HSM keypair? This keypair will be used to create new classes of assets, issue new assets, and create new accounts. The default view for the Chain dashboard is that of Transactions. Click on MockHSM, and you will see a screen saying, "There are no MockHSM keys," which stands to reason given that we haven't made any keys. So let's start by clicking "New MockHSM keys," and you should see Figure 11-6. Type an alias for the key, and that name will be used throughout Chain.

MockHSM keys › New MockHSM key

KEY INFORMATION

ALIAS

Vik

Submit

Figure 11-6. *Creating a new HSM key*

On the test net, the key data from Figure 11-6 will be erased in a week. After clicking Submit, you should see a confirmation for the key that you just created, shown in Figure 11-7.

Figure 11-7. *Confirmation from key creation with an alias Vik*

Now that we have a keypair, we can use it to create assets. Click on the Assets tab under Core Data, and you should see some default assets (at the time of writing, Chain Core had two defaults), shown in Figure 11-8.

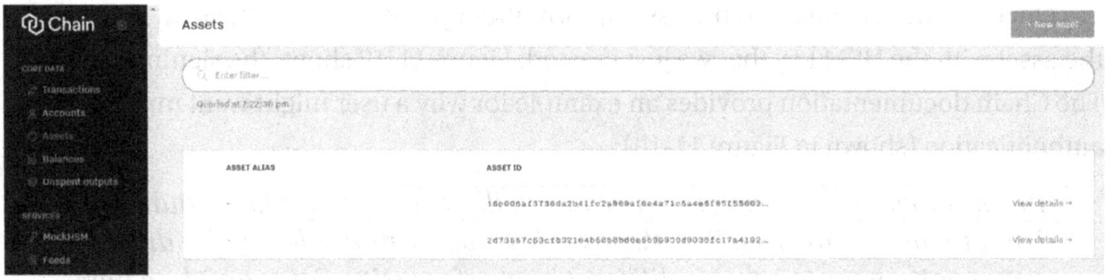

Figure 11-8. *Default assets available in Chain*

We can create new assets by clicking the "New asset" button on the top right-hand corner of the screen. You should see the following asset creation screen, shown in Figure 11-9.

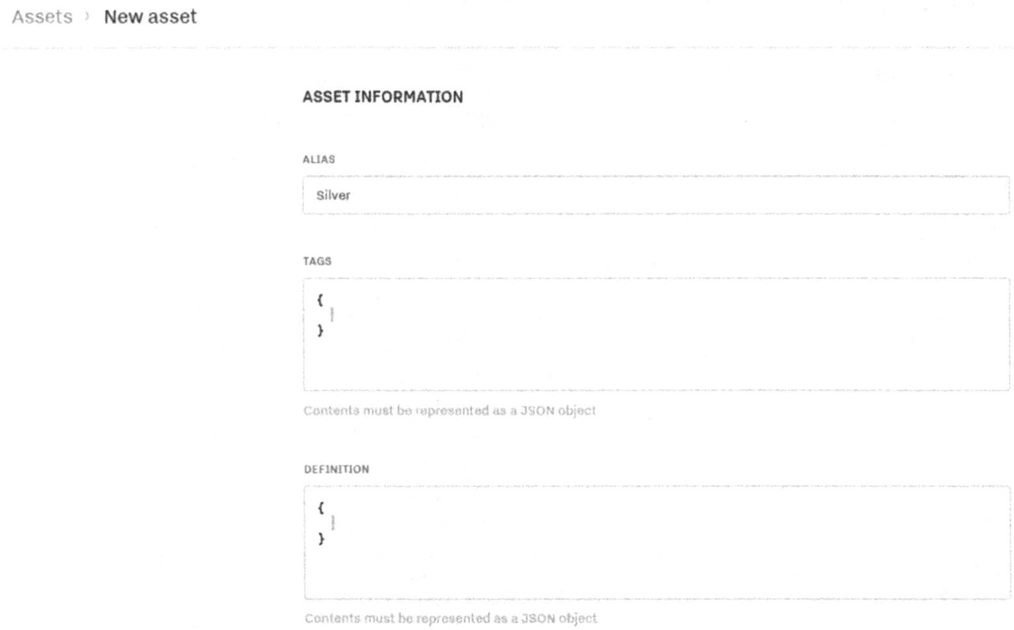

Figure 11-9. *Asset creation and signing*

The process of asset creation in Figure 11-9 requires two steps. First is the asset information, including any identifiers or definitions assigned to an asset in JSON format. The second step is signing the asset with your public key. Here, we are naming the asset *Silver*.

Once you have completed the asset information, you need to scroll down and sign the asset with the HSM key that we just created. Figure 11-10 shows the signing process. The Chain documentation provides an example for why a user might want multi-key authentication (shown in Figure 11-10):

> *In simple cases, an asset or an account will define a single key required for issuance or for transfers. But it's possible to define multiple keys for different usage patterns or to achieve different levels of security. For example, a high-value asset may be defined with two signing keys, requiring two separate parties to sign each issuance transaction. A joint account may also be defined with two signing keys, requiring only one, from either party, to sign each transfer. The threshold number of signatures required is called a quorum.*

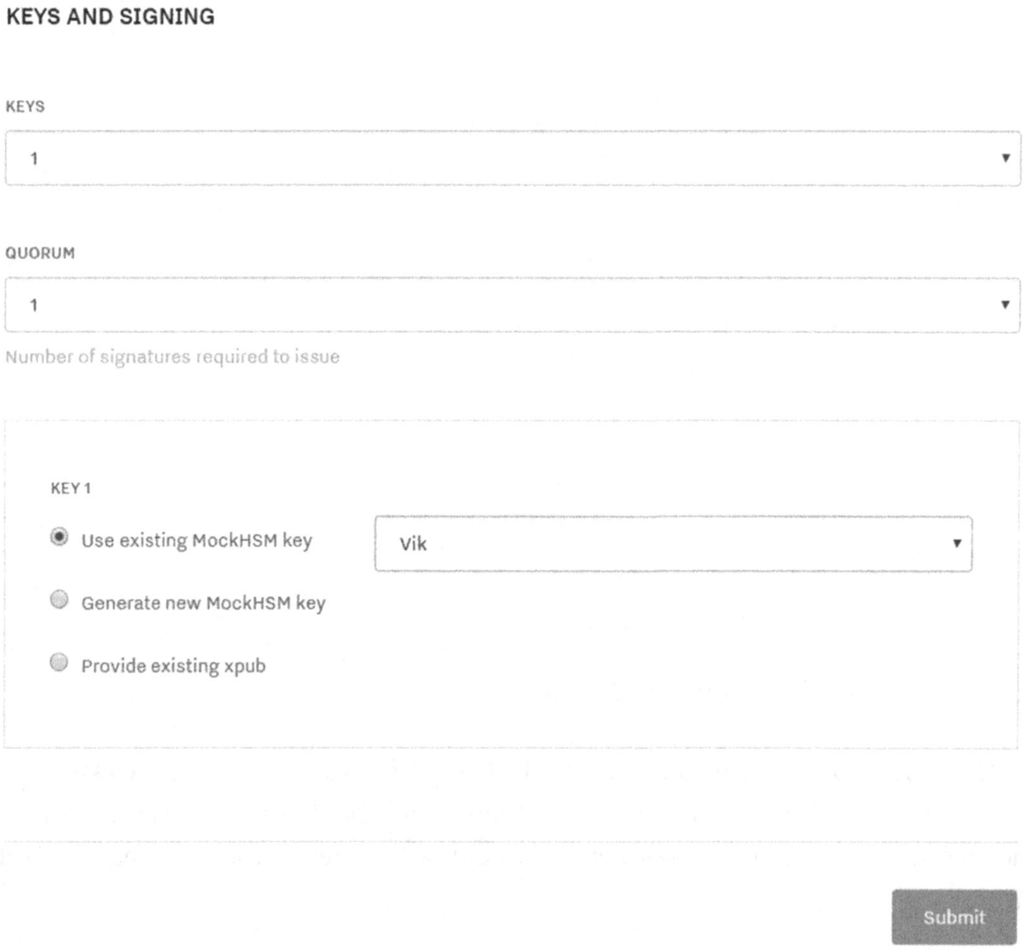

KEYS AND SIGNING

KEYS

| 1 | ▾ |

QUORUM

| 1 | ▾ |

Number of signatures required to issue

KEY 1

◉ Use existing MockHSM key | Vik | ▾ |

◯ Generate new MockHSM key

◯ Provide existing xpub

Submit

Figure 11-10. *Signing an asset*

There are a few parameters to consider in Figure 11-10. By default, a new asset can be created with a signature from one key. The number of signatures required to approve the new asset is referred to as Quorum, and we will use the defaults here. Finally, we have to sign the asset using the key we created. After you click Submit, you should see a confirmation screen with the Silver asset created on the test net.

Now that we have an asset, we need to issue it. In Chain, all assets are managed and controlled by users; therefore, the asset we issue would have to be controlled by an account. We don't yet have any accounts on the network, so let's take care of that by clicking on "Accounts" on the nav menu. This brings us to the Accounts view. There may be some sample accounts on the test net, such as Alice or Bob, but on the right-hand corner of the Accounts screen is the option to create a new account. Click on that, and you will see an interface very similar to that for creating an asset. In fact, most of the steps are exactly the same here, such as filling out the account information and then providing an HSM key to sign it. The New Account view is presented in Figure 11-11.

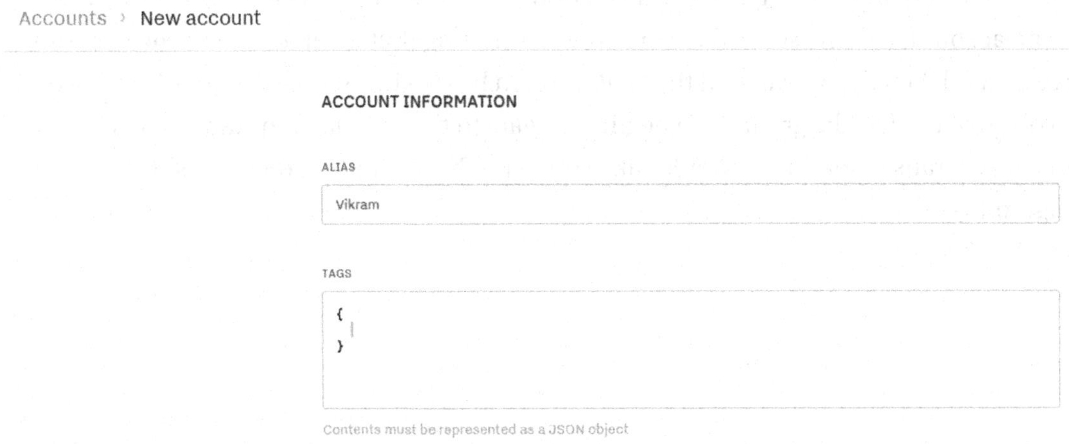

Accounts › **New account**

ACCOUNT INFORMATION

ALIAS

Vikram

TAGS

{
}

Contents must be represented as a JSON object

Figure 11-11. *Creating a new account*

There are two steps for creating an account: providing account information and key signing. The first step is shown in this figure, and the second step is exactly the same as for signing an asset. Once you have provided the account information, sign the account using your HSM key, and you should see a confirmation screen for the account that you just created. Now, to illustrate trading between accounts, we will need two accounts. So, create a second account with the alias "Team Rocket," and the final result should look like Figure 11-12.

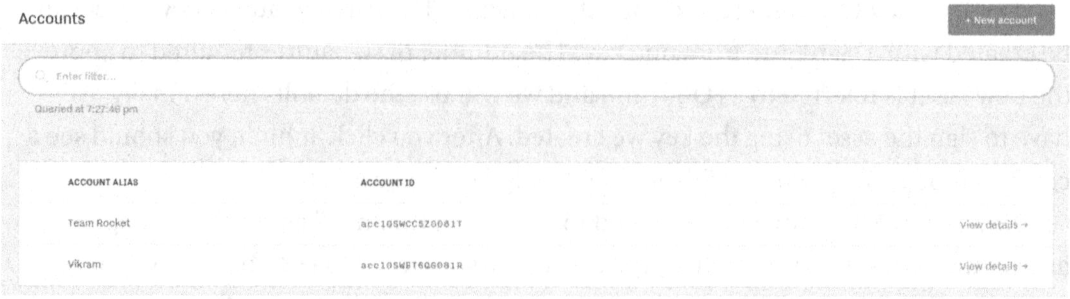

Figure 11-12. *Account summary*

The two accounts on our test net shown in Figure 11-12 will allow us to show trading, locking, and unlocking. Now that we have two accounts, we can start to trade assets between them. It should be noted that in Chain Core, assets can only have four actions performed on them: an asset can be issued, spent, transferred (controlled), or removed (retired). Usually, a combination of these actions allows for transactions between users. We will be looking at two types of transactions here: one is simply issuing a new asset to an account, and the second one will involve trading that asset to the second account we created. Finally, we will end the walkthrough by looking at how these actions have evolved in the Ivy Playground. To begin, navigate to the Transactions tab and click on "New Transaction." This should take you to the New Transaction view, shown in Figure 11-13.

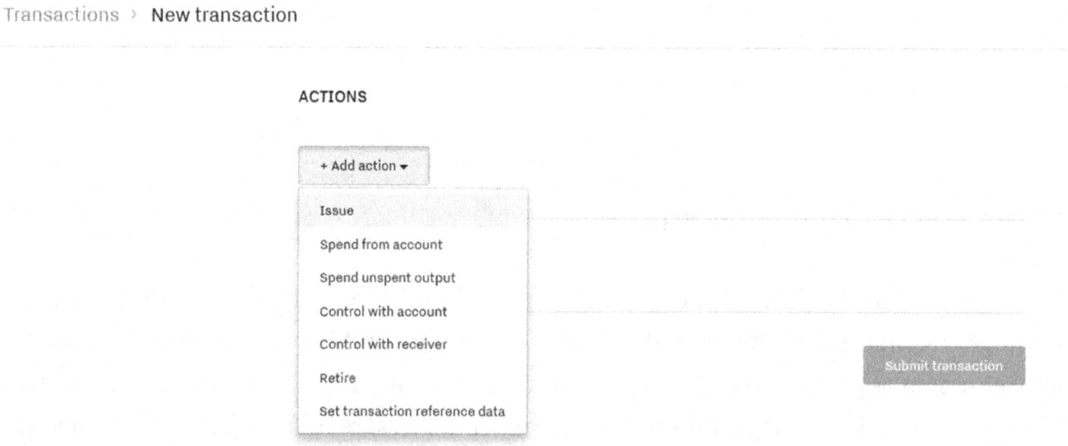

Figure 11-13. *New Transaction view*

A transaction can only be carried out in terms of one of the four actions that we mentioned earlier. Each action has a set of associated parameters that need to be given to complete a transaction. In Figure 11-13, we want to issue a new asset, so we would go with "Issue." Once you click on "Issue," another screen appears, asking you the parameters of the asset that you want to issue, as shown in Figure 11-14.

ACTIONS

Figure 11-14. Creating an asset

The issue action in Figure 11-14 first asks for the name of the asset we want to create and finally the amount that we want to issue. Recall that in Chain, assets can't just be issued in a void; creation of a new asset is coupled with control of the asset by an account. Once an asset has been issued, we will assign it to the first account we created. Figure 11-15 shows the control of the asset being passed to the new account.

Figure 11-15. Assigning an asset to an account

Assigning an asset as shown in Figure 11-15 is also referred to as *control with account* in Chain. The one hundred units of Silver are transferred to the first account that we created. Once the assignment is filled out, you can submit this transaction. It will be added to the test net, and the confirmation is shown in Figure 11-16.

Transactions › Transaction   fe2bad0b4388c4d66b14761e664a3a4bb73

Submitted transaction. Create another?

Summary			Raw JSON
Issue	amount 100	asset Silver	
Control	amount 100	asset Silver	account Vikram

Figure 11-16. Transaction verification

The summary in Figure 11-16 shows one hundred Silver assets being issued and then assigned to Vikram's account. Or, put differently, the assets were issued and then controlled by the first account we created. This was the simplest transaction we can do on Chain; now, let's move to the next transaction involving trade between two users. This time around, we will have to use the *spend* action to make assets available, and *control* action to transfer them. Go back to the Transactions view from the sidebar and click on "New Transaction," but this time instead of using the issue action, we will choose "spend from account," as shown in Figure 11-17.

ACTIONS

+ Add action ▾

Issue

Spend from account

Spend unspent output

Control with account

Control with receiver

Retire

Set transaction reference data

Submit transaction

Figure 11-17. Spend from account action to initiate a trade

Now, we have to specify how much Silver we want to transfer (Figure 11-18). This first step only makes the asset available; it still needs to be claimed.

Spend from account   Remove

ACCOUNT

Alias ▾   Vikram

ASSET

Alias ▾   Silver

AMOUNT

10

Figure 11-18. *Making ten units of Silver available for trade from Vikram's account*

Now that Silver is available, let's switch ownership from the first account to the second (Figure 11-19).

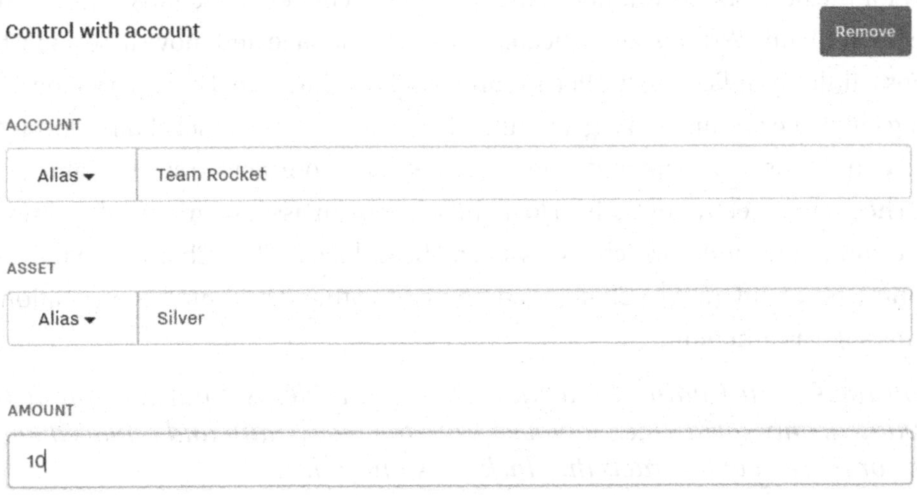

Control with account   Remove

ACCOUNT

Alias ▾   Team Rocket

ASSET

Alias ▾   Silver

AMOUNT

10

Figure 11-19. *Transferring ownership from one account to the second (Team Rocket, in this case)*

Just as with issuing assets, trading assets involves one account making assets available, and the second account taking control of the freed assets. To confirm that the transaction took place, we can go back to the Transactions view and then look at the most recent transaction; clicking on it will expand the transaction (Figure 11-20).

Figure 11-20. *Summary of the most recent transaction*

Notice in Figure 11-20 that ten assets were spent by the first account (Vikram) and ten assets were then controlled by the second account (Team Rocket), completing our trade.

So far, we have discussed two actions of transactions that are key to Chain Core. There are a few more options available, such as retiring assets, which simply means taking a given amount of the asset out of circulation. This has the effect of increasing scarcity for the network. Now that we understand the concept of actions, what more can we do in Chain? Writing sophisticated scripts to manage and move assets in Chain becomes a little complicated. Ivy Playground was introduced to develop a formal scripting language around locking and unlocking assets on the blockchain. Developers can add conditions to a script and write more complex contracts to secure value and assets. The main objective of Ivy is to lock the value of an asset with a set of clauses that describe conditions under which the asset can be unlocked. The Chain team talks about how contracts are different in Chain as compared to other distributed computational platforms such as Ethereum:

> *Contracts on a Chain blockchain are immutable. A contract cannot be updated, only spent—i.e., removed from the blockchain and replaced with one or more new contracts that lock the same value.*

> *This immutable state model distinguishes our approach from that of (for example) Ethereum and Fabric. In Ethereum, contracts can send messages and value to each other and can update their own state in response to these messages.*

*Most current smart contract approaches provide the freedom to write pro-
grams that execute arbitrary logic on a blockchain, but make it essentially
impossible to provide the kind of safety assurances that Ivy is designed to
give. While other platforms have the goal of making it easy to build anything, Ivy's goal is to make it difficult to build anything wrong.*

Note   A programming environment like Ivy would allow developers to write
code that inherits the security and safety of asset management built into the data
structures. This allows developers to code without worrying about introducing new
security vulnerabilities while managing assets in the overall application.

This concludes our walkthrough of Chain Core and Ivy. We focused on how to
create an HSM key, how to create new accounts, and the different modes of transactions
available in Chain. Finally, we talked about managing assets and scripting using Ivy.
Even though Chain Core is not under development, the asset management design and
secure coding around assets will be adopted as a feature of scripting languages by the
Blockchain 3.0 paradigm. Let's continue our journey with the final technology in this
chapter: Enterprise Ethereum.

Enterprise Ethereum

After the recent DAO hack (which we covered in Chapter 6), a few corporations such
as JPMorgan (JPM), Microsoft, and Accenture formed a consortium called Enterprise
Ethereum Alliance (EEA) to make an enterprise-class Ethereum blockchain capable
of handling high-volume transactions and business applications. JPMorgan has
contributed massive development resources in providing the EEA with Quorum: an
enterprise-grade permissioned version of Ethereum. Since the launch of Quorum,
more companies in the same vertical with common enterprise interests have created
new consortiums such as R3 focusing on enterprise blockchain deployments. We will
begin this section with an in-depth discussion of Quorum, a feature-rich enterprise
Ethereum blockchain, and review the whitepaper. Then, we will dive into zk-Snarks,
a zero-knowledge proof technology. Finally, we will talk about R3 and Corda, another
consortium model similar to EEA. Even though EEA started with Quorum, the project
has expanded its scope to encapsulate new goals for the enterprise paradigm. In
2020, the EEA project aims to play a crucial role in creating standards for privacy,
permissioned ledger, pluggable consensus, and usability of modular components in
enterprise. There are four fundamental components of EEA moving forward:

- Create an open-source standard for enterprise Ethereum applications and companies to follow, not a single product.

- Address and model the requirements of enterprise-sized deployments.

- Sync the technology stack with public Ethereum.

- Use existing standards where possible and improve on them.

Note   What is a permissioned ledger? A permissioned blockchain restricts the parties that can be block producers or miners, ultimately limiting who can contribute to consensus of the global state. In the financial world, this kind of verification may become necessary to scale a product for the masses.

Quorum Tech Stack

Quorum's dev page on GitHub lists the following features that are an improvement over Ethereum:

- **Privacy:** A key innovation to make Quorum suitable for enterprise work is the introduction of privacy through private transactions and private contracts. This is accomplished using Constellation, a peer-to-peer messaging daemon that can direct the flow of private information to the appropriate network participants.

- **Alternative consensus:** Quorum does not rely on POW/POS for the permissioned ledger; instead, there are two consensus mechanisms better suited for enterprise-grade blockchains:

  - **QuorumChain:** A new smart-contract-based model that relies on voting by nodes to achieve consensus

  - **Raft-based Consensus:** A consensus model suitable for closed-membership consortium settings, with very fast block-generation times

- **Node Permissioning:** A feature in Quorum that only allows connections to and from nodes that hold the appropriate identification keys and have been registered to participate in the permissioned network

- **Higher Performance:** Quorum has to offer significantly higher performance than Ethereum to be used in a high-volume environment such as the one required to power bank-level transaction volume.

As we dive into the features of Quorum, we will begin by talking about the key concepts behind the two consensus mechanisms available in Quorum. Then, we will cover what modifications have made nodes capable of handling private transactions. Finally, we will talk about Constellation and how it works to facilitate the transfer of data in the permissioned network. A summary of Quorum's features and private transactions from the Quorum whitepaper will follow our technical discussion. Let's begin with the consensus mechanisms:

- **QuorumChain:** A majority-voting consensus mechanism where a smart contract dictates which parties (nodes) can vote toward accepting or rejecting a block. The participating nodes on Quorum can either be maker nodes that actually construct a block or voter nodes that vote on the validity of a block. QuorumChain uses a signature-verification method from Ethereum such as ecrecover to validate the votes received from maker nodes and voter nodes. Once the votes from voter nodes have reached a threshold, the block is accepted into the network.

- **Raft-based consensus:** The fundamental unit of work in a Raft-based system is a log entry. A log is an ordered sequence of events and is considered consistent if all members of the network agree on the entries and their order. In Raft, a node can either be a leader or a follower and all nodes start out as followers. Eventually, through a peer-election process, one node emerges as the leader. Compare that to Ethereum, where any node can mine a new block or become the leader for that particular round. In Raft, only the leader can "forge" a block in the true sense, but the leader doesn't need to present any proof of work. Instead, the leader proposes a block, which the followers vote on, and once it receives a quorum (majority vote) of votes, it is accepted as the next block to extend the blockchain. The followers also send an acknowledgment to the leader, and now the block is committed to the log entry. Once the leader has received the acknowledgment, it notifies every node that this new entry (block) has been committed to the log.

Now that we have talked about consensus, let's look at what makes nodes accept private transactions. In Ethereum, all transactions are public, and by default nodes only accept transactions that are broadcasted publicly. For Quorum to work, the following changes have to be made:

- POW consensus algorithms have been replaced by QuorumChain, which is voting based. The ultimate goal is to have multiple consensus algorithms running on the blockchain in a model called "pluggable consensus."

- A modified connection layer where nodes connected to the permissioned ledgers are identified and registered.

- The state tree has been split into two trees: a public state tree and a private state tree.

- Blocks can be validated with new logic containing private transactions.

- Transactions can be created with some data replaced with encrypted hashes to preserve privacy where required.

What propagates private transactions and contracts through the network and how is the flow of private data handled? For starters, there is a new optional parameter in the Ethereum Transaction Model called privateFor, and it can take multiple addresses. Quorum treats the addresses from this parameter as private in the network. A new transaction type IsPrivate has been introduced to mark certain transactions as private. However, the main tool making the propagation of private transactions possible is Constellation: a peer-to-peer encrypted message exchange. Here's the basics of how Constellation works within Quorum to provide privacy: before a private transaction is propagated to the Quorum network, the message (contained within the transaction) and headers are replaced with the hash of an encrypted payload received from Constellation. Some participants in the network have had their public key included in the payload by

Constellation; when those users receive the payload, they can decrypt it using their own instance of Constellation. Every other participant will only see an encrypted hash, and skip the transaction. The participants who are involved will decrypt the payload and send it to an EVM for execution, updating their internal state as a result.

There are two components in Constellation that play an important role in maintaining privacy: transaction manager and the enclave. The transaction manager stores encrypted transaction data, facilitates the exchange of encrypted payloads between participants, and manages the propagation of private transactions if the satisfying conditions have been met. It also makes function calls to other modules in Quorum, especially the enclave for cryptographic functions. In many ways, the transaction manager behaves like a central hub, controlling the flow of messages from one component of Quorum to another. Enclave is the cryptographic core of Quorum. The transaction manager itself doesn't have access to any sensitive information or the keys, and it delegates cryptographic tasks such as symmetric key generation and data encryption and decryption to the enclave. It also holds the private keys for accounts in the network. Both the transaction manager and enclave are isolated from other components to enhance security.

zk-SNARKs

Zero-knowledge proofs, or Zero Knowledge Succinct Non-interactive Arguments of Knowledge (zk-SNARK), are a new technology native to ZCash where privacy and anonymity are maintained throughout the transactions happening on the blockchain. Recently, the EEA announced that the team behind ZCash would be helping implement a zk-SNARK layer for Quorum to enhance the privacy and security of transactions on the blockchain. How do zero-knowledge proofs work? The use of zk-SNARK technology is usually employed in complex payout situations. Let's look at an example: Say that Alice receives money from a smart contract if either X, Y, or Z happen. Now any of those situations (X, Y, Z) may be sensitive to Alice's health, or perhaps a business decision that she doesn't want to reveal to the public. This is where zk-SNARK can shine, as it can create a proof for the smart contract that one of the three conditions (X, Y, Z) occurred, but not reveal which exact condition occurred. More formally, Christian Lundkvist from ConsenSys describes zero-knowledge proofs as follows:

The goal of zero-knowledge proofs is for a verifier to be able to convince herself that a prover possesses knowledge of a secret parameter, called a witness, satisfying some relation, without revealing the witness to the verifier or anyone else.

In our previous example, the three choices for Alice constituted a witness, and she had to prove that one of those occurred to the smart contract, but didn't need to reveal the specific circumstances. Paige Peterson from ZCash confirmed that zk-SNARK would be coming to Quorum as a settlement layer, proving enhanced privacy and security to transactions. The eventual goal (described at Consensus 2017) is to make zero-knowledge proofs blockchain agnostic, and implement a settlement layer as a service. The future of integration with zero-knowledge proofs can be a paradigm shift for permissioned ledgers to carry out enterprise-level transactions. With some lessons learned, and a better settlement layer, there are some incredible opportunities for applications in healthcare to protect patient data and maintain privacy.

Note   ZoKrates is a higher-level programming toolkit that can be used to write zero-knowledge proofs in a developer-friendly language. These proofs compile to Ethereum-compatible zk-SNARKs and execute on-chain. In addition, ZoKrates can extend verifiable computations to DApps, where, for instance, a proof-of-computation can be performed off-chain for a task and submitted to the Ethereum blockchain for verification.

Review of Quorum Whitepaper

Figures 11-21, 11-22, and 11-23 are taken from the Quorum, whitepaper (with permission) and provide a high-level summary of Quorum graphically, emphasizing the new technical components and private transactions.

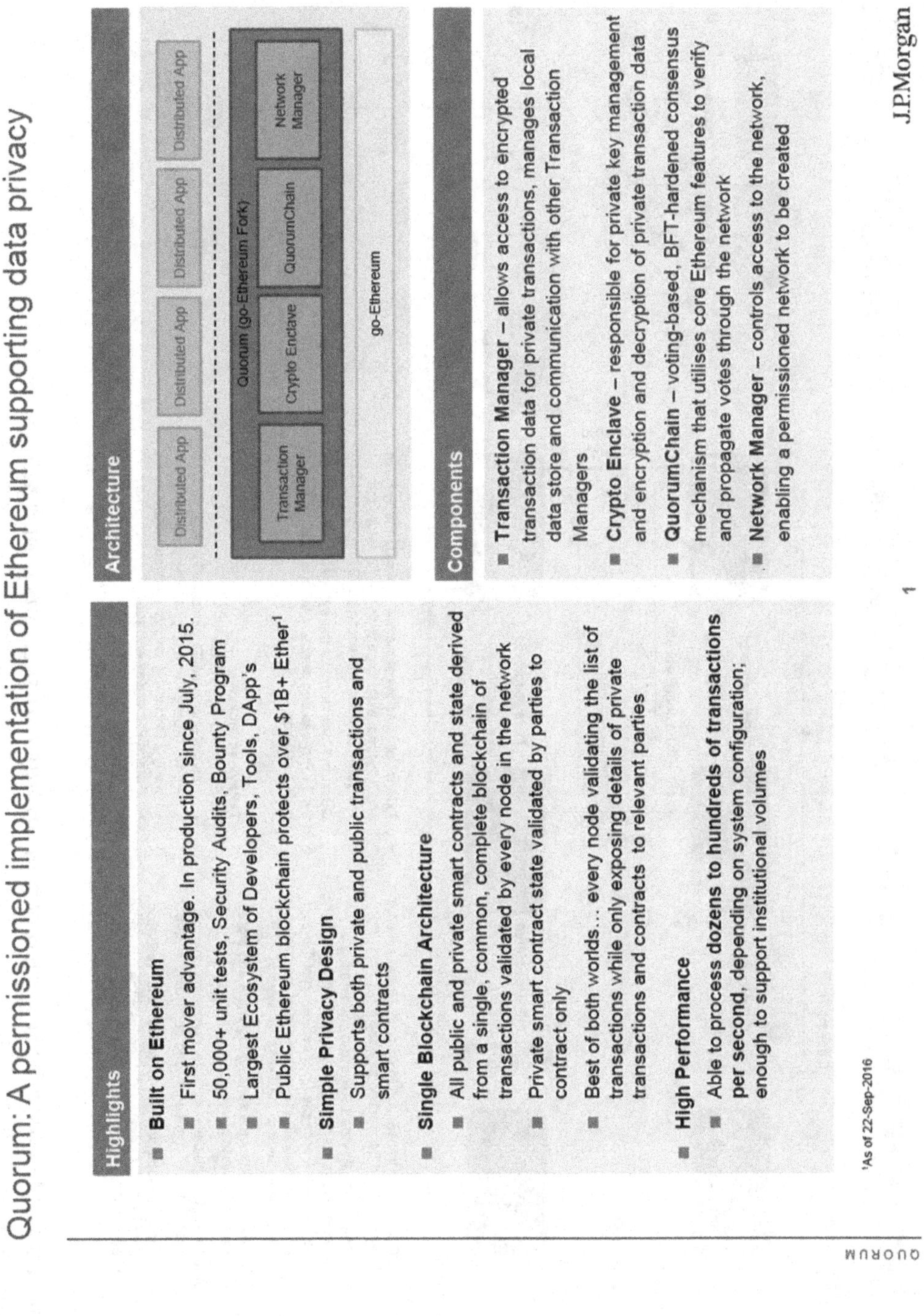

Quorum: A permissioned implementation of Ethereum supporting data privacy

Highlights

- **Built on Ethereum**
  - First mover advantage. In production since July, 2015.
  - 50,000+ unit tests, Security Audits, Bounty Program
  - Largest Ecosystem of Developers, Tools, DApp's
  - Public Ethereum blockchain protects over $1B+ Ether[1]

- **Simple Privacy Design**
  - Supports both private and public transactions and smart contracts

- **Single Blockchain Architecture**
  - All public and private smart contracts and state derived from a single, common, complete blockchain of transactions validated by every node in the network
  - Private smart contract state validated by parties to contract only
  - Best of both worlds…. every node validating the list of transactions while only exposing details of private transactions and contracts to relevant parties

- **High Performance**
  - Able to process dozens to hundreds of transactions per second, depending on system configuration; enough to support institutional volumes

[1]As of 22-Sep-2016

Architecture

Distributed App | Distributed App | Distributed App | Distributed App

Quorum (go-Ethereum Fork)

Transaction Manager | Crypto Enclave | QuorumChain | Network Manager

go-Ethereum

Components

- **Transaction Manager** – allows access to encrypted transaction data for private transactions, manages local data store and communication with other Transaction Managers
- **Crypto Enclave** – responsible for private key management and encryption and decryption of private transaction data
- **QuorumChain** – voting-based, BFT-hardened consensus mechanism that utilises core Ethereum features to verify and propagate votes through the network
- **Network Manager** – controls access to the network, enabling a permissioned network to be created

J.P.Morgan

QUORUM

Figure 11-21. Overview of Quorum and its key innovations

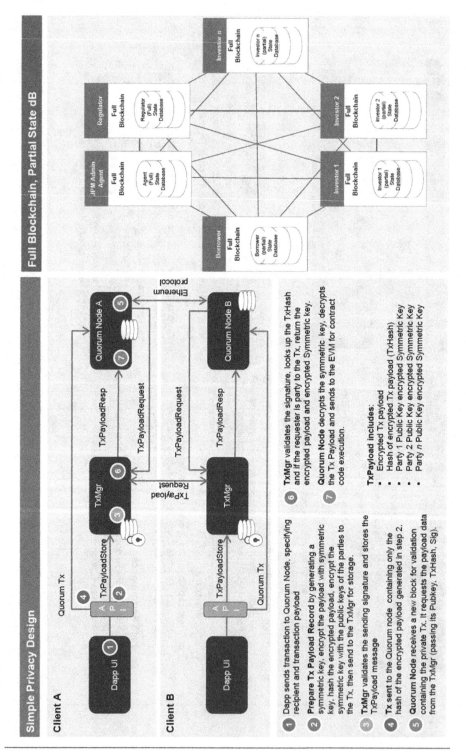

Figure 11-22. Overview of privacy and private transactions propagating the Quorum network

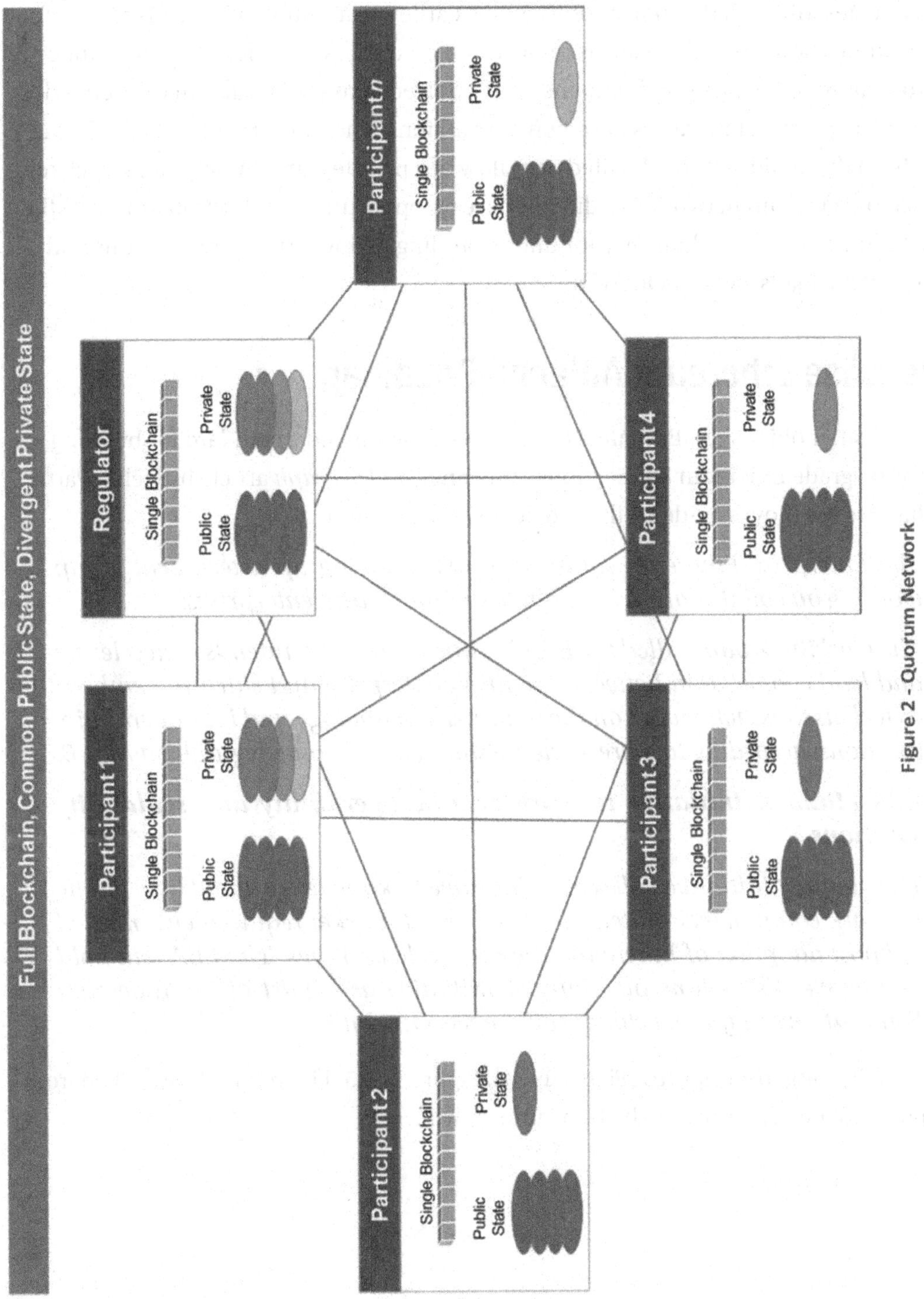

Figure 2 - Quorum Network

Figure 11-23. Segmentation of public and private states

Note the architectural design of Quorum in the top-right corner of Figure 11-21, just as we described all the major components earlier. In addition, Figure 11-23 demonstrates how the global state is maintained on the Quorum network: the public state maintains consensus and remains synchronized across all nodes on the network, whereas the private state varies based on permissions. The most important take-home point from these slides is the detailed workflow of a private transaction as it propagates through the Quorum network. We did not have an opportunity to illustrate this workflow, so including the slides enhances your understanding of how private transactions and encrypted payloads work in Quorum.

Enterprise Ethereum Alliance Roadmap

Above all other objectives, EEA aims to be a specification and a standard for building enterprise-grade Ethereum applications. A recent *Cointelegraph* article by Helen Partz emphasizes the moves made by the project in this direction:

> *The Enterprise Ethereum Alliance (EEA) is setting up a technical group working on collaboration between the mainnet and enterprises.*
>
> *The working group, called the EEA Mainnet Initiative, intends to accelerate and lead cooperation between the EEA's enterprise and startup members, as well as those who work on the mainnet's technology and interoperability solutions, according to a press release shared with Cointelegraph on Aug. 6.*
>
> ***EEA Mainnet Initiative to work on interoperability and scalability solutions***
>
> *The Mainnet Initiative will seek to improve its knowledge about how public network components match the commercial market requirements needed to boost adoption of Ethereum, the press release notes. The EEA will hold interactive discussions on Mainnet Initiative as a part of the Ethereum Foundation's major developer conference, Devcon5.*

The following three figures (Figure 11-24, Figure 11-25, Figure 11-26) are taken from an update to the EEA provided by Bob Summerwill.

ENTERPRISE ETHEREUM ALLIANCE

The Enterprise Ethereum Alliance connects Fortune 500 enterprises, startups, academics, and technology vendors with Ethereum subject matter experts. Together, we will learn from and build upon the only smart contract supporting blockchain currently running in real-world production – Ethereum – to define enterprise-grade software capable of handling the most complex, highly demanding applications at the speed of business.

MISSION & VISION

Enterprise Ethereum Alliance offers:

- A clear roadmap for enterprise features and requirements
- Robust governance model and accountability, clarity around IP and licensing models for open source technology
- Resources for businesses to learn about Ethereum and leverage this groundbreaking technology to address specific industry use cases

Enterprise Ethereum will:

- Be an open source standard, not a product
- Address enterprise deployment requirements
- Evolve in tandem with advances in public Ethereum
- Leverage existing standards (ISO/SWIFT/etc.)

WHY ETHEREUM?

With a global developer community of more than 30,000 contributors, Ethereum is one of the most popular and mature blockchains, and the technology of choice for many Enterprise blockchain developments

- Open source and widely available
- Rapidly growing ecosystem of developers and applications
- Sophisticated, easy to learn native smart contract programming model
- Ability to model complex assets and orchestrate workflows

ENTERPRISES ♥ ETHEREUM

The Enterprise Ethereum Alliance is a community of industry experts developing features and enhancements to Ethereum driven by the needs of Enterprises adopting the technology

- Focus on enterprise needs: permissioned networks, privacy, performance, scalability, integration and interoperability
- Access for vendors to understand enterprise needs and develop solutions in tandem with clients

***Figure 11-24.** Brief overview of the Enterprise Ethereum Alliance*

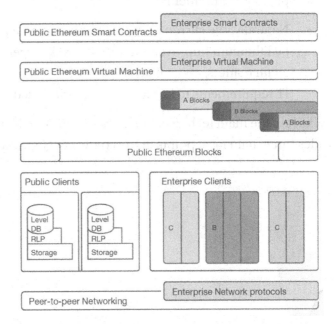

***Figure 11-25.** A new protocol stack for Ethereum modified to handle enterprise-grade transactions*

283

In this example, privacy is important, and most miners (nodes) are known and trusted. Notice that the enterprise protocols sit on top of a shared public–private blockchain with necessary modifications to preserve privacy. The public clients share the same storage and virtual machines, whereas private or enterprise clients would be given isolated storage and VMs that execute encrypted payloads of instructions. More broadly speaking, enterprise Ethereum is a bigger movement than simply Quorum being developed by the EEA. Let's take a step back and talk about why an enterprise version was needed. Jeremy Miller from ConsenSys provides three main reasons:

- Ethereum was developed initially for public chain deployment, where trustless transaction requirements outweigh absolute performance. The current public chain consensus algorithms (notably, proof-of-work) are overkill for networks with trusted actors and high throughput requirements.

- Public chains by definition have limited (at least initially) privacy and permissioning requirements. Although Ethereum does enable permissioning to be implemented within the smart contract and network layers, it is not readily compatible "out of the box" with traditional enterprise security and identity architectures nor data privacy requirements.

- Naturally, the current Ethereum improvement process (dominated by Ethereum Improvement Proposals) is largely dominated by public chain matters, and it has previously been challenging for enterprise IT requirements to be clarified and prioritized within it.

What are the main technical objectives for EEA in the near future? Figure 11-26 provides three main focal points in the context of Quorum development.

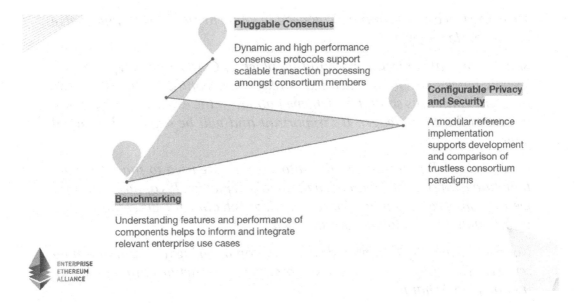

Figure 11-26. *Three areas of focus for EEA in the near future*

The largest focus for EEA is the development of enterprise reference specifications and implementation standards that can be used industry-wide. On the other hand, the major focus for development in Quorum is toward providing a high level of privacy (identified by JPMorgan as a major roadblock) that can be configured for transactions and smart contracts executed by users. A hybrid public–private chain can become the perfect model for consortium-type settings. The next focus is on creating a pluggable consensus model where transactions and complex situations can choose the best consensus mechanism applicable to the use case. Finally, high-volume performance is crucial for Quorum to succeed; therefore, developing better benchmarking tools to measure and improve will become the key to wide adoption.

R3 and Corda

R3 is another consortium similar to Hyperledger or EEA and the driving force behind Corda, a unique permissioned blockchain platform. Corda is different from other DLTs in a number of ways explained in a blogpost by Nick Avramov:

There are three main concepts you need to know to master your knowledge in Corda. Here they are:

State — or, state object. It's a building block of Corda and it represents a specific agreement or contract, like a real-world contract. This is the one thing the consensus should be achieved about — the exact state object, not a state of the entire ledger. It's important and will be described in detail later.

Flow — a small multi-party sub-protocols that are used to share transaction data (state objects) with relevant involved parties. It's opposite to what we can observe in public blockchains like Bitcoin and Ethereum where transaction data is globally broadcasted.

Notary — An entity that provides transaction ordering and timestamping services. The thing is, Corda doesn't organize transactions into blocks, so, it's not a blockchain.

Unlike Bitcoin and Ethereum, Corda is a permission-based network where you have to be granted access. It's specified in flow API — yes, the flow I introduced earlier. It also can be considered as a tribe or something that imposes certain requirements on your identity and you cannot join the specific flow unless you satisfy it. The consensus is achieved on a transaction level (instead of ledger level as in Bitcoin or Ethereum), thus there's no need for all network nodes to verify and approve the transaction.

Indeed, the important thing about Corda is its agility to using different consensus algorithms. As it has no exact one, the notaries can actually use different ones — BFT, Raft, maybe some others. Running ahead it can be said that Corda develops a metanetwork for all these sub-networks or flows. Imagine that there are auditing companies, banks, cleaning companies that serve these banks. All of them have their internal cuisine of bookkeeping, subcontractors, various other financial and non-financial relations. In a way Corda aims to develop a system for all their interactions, both within a single company and with others, using the same protocol.

It's worth mentioning that the developers of Corda from the very beginning claim that they are creating an architecture that will model and automate real-world transactions in a legally enforceable manner. This is a common pitfall of many blockchains that the transactions they store do not have a legal value. Instead, smart contracts in Corda have not only transaction information, but also legal prose.

Unlike other DLTs, where the ledger is shared across every organization, in Corda, the transaction is shared only within the sub-network or flow. In that sense, there's a direct communication instead of a global broadcast, and privacy is preserved.

No entity has an entire history of all the transactions in the network. But there are notaries that know the current states of this particular piece of the network. They serve as validators of the transactions. And the typical transaction looks as follows:

A new transaction A turns ("spend" in Corda terminology) a state X to create a state Y.

You send transaction A to the notary that knows about state X.

The notary checks that state X is still valid and signs transaction A. State X is now invalid, with state Y taking its place.

If state X above were not valid when the transaction was proposed, the notary would respond that state X had already been spent.

Thus, Corda has transmitted the responsibilities of knowing the world state and seeing all transactions from the entire network onto a special notary service. Members of the network don't need to trust everyone, just the organizations that run the notary. There can also be multiple notaries, each trusted for a different purpose.

Summary

In this chapter, we talked about the Blockchain 3.0 paradigm of advanced on-chain execution of applications from three different angles: EOS.io with sophisticated message passing and parallel processing, Chain Core as a model for the future of asset management on a blockchain, and enterprise Ethereum. The enterprise adoption of Ethereum is being guided by consortia formed from companies that want to solve domain-specific problems such as Hyperledger, EEA, and R3. An open source community is behind each of the enterprise efforts, making the codebase more secure, efficient, and practical for large-scale deployments.

References

The key references used to prepare this chapter were the EOS developer guide (`https://developers.eos.io/`) and dev documentation, the Chain developer guide (`https://github.com/chain/chain`) and API docs, Quorum developer docs (`https://consensys.net/quorum/developers/`) and Quorum presentation to Hyperledger, and finally the Ethereum Enterprise Alliance roadmap (`https://entethalliance.github.io/client-spec/implementing.html`) presented by Bob Summerwill.

CHAPTER 12

Technological Revolutions and Financial Capital Markets

Global financial markets are undergoing a drastic change that makes it clear that without innovation most business and financial models could soon become obsolete. A recent overview of the global financial system described the current system as a

> [s]ystem that moves trillions of dollars a day and serves billions of people, but the system is rife with problems, adding cost through fees and delays, creating friction through redundant and onerous paperwork, and opening up opportunities for fraud and crime.

> To the best of our knowledge, 45 percent of financial intermediaries, such as payment networks, stock exchanges, and money transfer services, suffer from economic crime every year; the number is 37 percent for the entire economy and only 20 percent and 27 percent for the professional services and technology sectors respectively. It's no small wonder that regulatory costs continue to climb and remain a top concern for bankers. This all adds cost, with consumers ultimately bearing the burden.[1]

Dan Tapscott, the author of Blockchain Revolution, pointed out that our financial system is inefficient for a multitude of reasons:

---

[1]https://hbr.org/2017/03/how-blockchain-is-changing-finance

© Vikram Dhillon, David Metcalf, and Max Hooper 2021
V. Dhillon et al., *Blockchain Enabled Applications*, https://doi.org/10.1007/978-1-4842-6534-5_12

First, because it's antiquated, a kludge of industrial technologies and paper-based processes dressed up in a digital wrapper. Second, because it's central-ized, which makes it resistant to change and vulnerable to systems failures and attacks. Third, it's exclusionary, denying billions of people access to basic financial tools. Bankers have largely dodged the sort of creative destruction that, while messy, is critical to economic vitality and progress."[2]

We begin this chapter with issues related to the global financial markets and why blockchain can be an innovative solution for efficiencies therein. Then we move to the topics of venture capital, ICOs, cryptocurrencies, tokens, and exchanges. We address the significant ICO market impact, state of regulation, Securities and Exchange Commission (SEC) involvement, unique technologies, business models, RegTech, and related issues. As we review these concepts and issues, there are several questions and thoughts to keep in mind:

- How does crowdfunding scale blockchain applications?
- How can new companies and lending platforms be created?
- Can RegTech answer the need in the market for efficient compliance?
- What is the market impact of FinTech for banking and investment banking?
- What is the state of ICO fundraising and the ICO bubble?
- How can people of all levels of wealth participate in financial markets as technology helps democratize financial opportunities?

We close the chapter with the state of multiple large financial groups and their state of involvement in blockchain, FinTech, and other financial technologies.

State of the Blockchain Industry

The state of the blockchain industry indicated massive growth in the last 3 years, since the second quarter of 2017. According to Smith & Crown, one of the most prominent cryptofinancial research comapnies, this has proven to be a period of immense growth across the blockchain industry. The cryptotokens markets are rising, doubling and tripling in value over the span of a few weeks. The Smith & Crown Index (SCI) has reflected a bull market for cryptotokens, more than doubling in value since 2017. The growth of capitalization in cryptotoken markets was accompanied by a frenzy of activity in the token sale market. By all accounts, the second quarter of 2017 was the beginning of a record-setting period.[3]

---

[2]http://hrb.org/2017/03/how-blockchain-is-changing-finance
[3]https://www.smithandcrown.com/categories/feature/

Blockchain Solution

As we have stated in previous chapters, blockchain is an innovative solution for disrupting the inefficiencies in the financial system. Kastelein, the Chief Marketing Officer of Humaniq, noted that there are five basic principles underlying blockchain technology that allow blockchain to change how financial market transactions are created. It's worth repeating the five basic principles underlying the technology:

- **Distributed database:** Each party on a blockchain has access to the entire database and its complete history. No single party controls the data or the information. Every party can verify the records of its transaction partners directly, without an intermediary.

- **Peer-to-peer transmission:** Communication occurs directly between peers instead of through a central node. Each node stores and forwards information to all other nodes.

- **Transparency with pseudonymity:** Every transaction and its associated value is visible to anyone with access to the system. Each node, or user, on a blockchain has a unique thirty-plus-character alphanumeric address that identifies it. Users can choose to remain anonymous or provide proof of their identity to others. Transactions occur between blockchain addresses.

- **Irreversibility of records:** Once a transaction is entered in the database and the accounts are updated, the records cannot be altered, because they're linked to every transaction record that came before them (hence the term *chain*). Various computational algorithms and approaches are deployed to ensure that the recording on the database is permanent, chronologically ordered, and available to all others on the network.

- **Computational logic:** The digital nature of the ledger means that blockchain transactions can be tied to computational logic and in essence be programmed. Users can therefore set up algorithms and rules that automatically trigger transactions between nodes.[4]

---

[4]https://hrb.org/2017/03/what-initial-coin-offerings-are-and-why-vc-firms-care

Tapscott stated:

> For the first time in human history, two or more parties, be they businesses or individuals who may not even know each other, can forge agreements, make transactions, and build value without relying on intermediaries (such as banks, rating agencies, and government bodies such as the US Department of State) to verify their identities, establish trust or perform the critical business logic—contracting, clearing, settling, and record-keeping tasks, that are foundational to all forms of commerce.[5]

Blockchain applications can reduce transaction costs for all participants in an economy via peer-to-peer transactions and collaboration. Blockchain is truly a game-changing financial-markets solution using new technology and empowered by thought leadership.

Venture Capital and ICOs

The real question is this: Will ICOs supplant traditional venture capital as a fundraising model? Few could ever have imagined that within one year the venture capital industry could be so outpaced and changed by the new innovative methods of fundraising called ICOs. ICOs, also known as token sales, came together as blockchain technology, crowdfunding, innovative wealth ideas, and cryptocurrencies investing developed new models. ICOs are both a threat and an opportunity for the venture capital industry.

The traditional venture capitalist sees opportunities in ICOs for profits from cryptocurrency, blockchain investments, liquidity, and potential for faster financial gains. There might be a disruption in the way traditional venture capitalists operate and in their position in the market. This is a great concern and time of change in the financial markets driven by technological innovation. The SEC recently asserted in a letter that ICOs are subject to security laws. The certainty that the SEC will act on cryptocurrency issues and ICOs clears up one big question. However, it is unclear how individuals, groups, and offerings become SEC compliant. The process will take time to resolve and for rules and precedents to be established.

---

[5]https://hrb.org/2017/03/how-blockchain-is-changing-finance

Initial Coin Offerings

An ICO is a means of crowdfunding the release of a new cryptocurrency. Generally, tokens for the new cryptocurrency are sold to raise money for technical development before the cryptocurrency is released. Unlike an initial public offering (IPO), acquisition of tokens does not grant ownership in the company developing the new cryptocurrency. Unlike an IPO, there is no (comprehensive) government regulation of an ICO.[6]

ICOs and new funding models using distributed ledger methodologies are starting to disrupt both public markets (IPOs) and private investments (venture capital). An article from *Coin Desk* illustrated the blockchain's impact on venture capital formation. *Coin Desk* further noted, "There is proven demand and interest from both the entrepreneurial and investor audiences and limited regulatory guidance. ICOs could continue to gain steam as a funding mechanism."[7]

"Initial Coin Offerings (ICOs) are changing the cryptocurrency markets in rapid and expanding ways. Additionally, the venture capital industry is trying to understand this new financial investment. The bitcoin community created the situation by a convergence of blockchain technology, new wealth, clever entrepreneurs, and crypto-investors who are backed by blockchain-fueled ideas," stated *Harvard Business Review* writer Richard Kastelein.[8]

ICOs are dominating the overall crowdfunding charts in terms of funds raised, with half of the top twenty raises coming from the crypto community. The companies, such as Goldman Sachs, Nasdaq, and Intercontinental Exchange, the US holding company that owns the New York Stock Exchange, that dominate the IPO and listing business have been among the largest investors in blockchain ventures.[9]

An ICO is explained by *Coin Telegraph* as

> *a recently emerged concept of crowdfunding projects in the cryptocurrency and blockchain industries. When a company releases its own cryptocurrency with a purpose of funding, it releases a certain number of cryptotokens and then sells those tokens to its intended audience, most commonly in exchange for Bitcoins, but it can be fiat money as well. As a result the company gets the capital to fund the product development and the audience members get the crypto tokens share, plus, they have complete ownership of these shares.*[10]

---

[6]https://en.wikipedia.org/w/index.php?title=Initial_coin_offering&oldid=784220634
[7]https://www.coindesk.com/ico-investments-pass-vc-funding-in-blockchain-market-first/
[8]http://hrb.org/2017/03/what-initial-coin-offerings-are-and-why-vc-firms-care
[9]http://hrb.org/2017/03/what-initial-coin-offerings-are-and-why-vc-firms-care
[10]https://cointelegraph.com/explained/ico-explained

A specific example of how an ICO is created and the steps for execution are seen in the SONM execution model. First of all, what is SONM? "SONM is a global operating system that is also a decentralized worldwide fog computer. It has the potential to include unlimited computing power (IoE, IoT). Worldwide computations organized using the SONM system can serve to complete numerous tasks from CGI rendering to scientific computations."[11]

The defining feature of SONM is its decentralized open structure, where buyers and workers can interact with no middleman, while building a market profitable for them first, unlike other cloud services (e.g., Amazon, Microsoft, Google).

Unlike widespread centralized cloud services, the SONM project implements a fog computing structure, a decentralized pool of devices, all of which are connected to the internet (IoT/IoE). SONM is implemented using the SOSNA architecture for fog computing. The specific execution steps in the SONM ICO are as follows:

- The SONM platform uses a token of the same name, SONM (ticker SNM).

- Total supply of SNM will be limited to the amount of tokens created during the crowdfunding period.

- SNM tokens will be used by the computing-power buyers to pay for the calculations using the smart-contracts-based system.

- SNM is a token issued on the Ethereum blockchain using standards of implementation and storage and management of tokens, including Ethereum wallet.

- SONM project crowdfunding, ICO, and SNM creation will take place using Ethereum smart contracts.

- Participants willing to support the SONM project development will send ether to a specified ICO Ethereum address, creating SNM tokens by this transaction at the specified SNM/ETH exchange rate.

- ICO participants will be able to send ether to the SONM crowdfunding Ethereum address only after the start of the crowdfunding period (specified as the Ethereum block number).

---

[11]https://sonm.io/Somn-BusinessOverview.pdf

- Crowdfunding will finish when the specified end block is created or when the ICO cap is reached.

- SNM tokens sale ICO.

- SONM presale launched on April 15, 2017, and successfully finished in less than twelve hours, raising 10,000 Ethereum.

- Pre-ICO tokens will be transferred into the main token contract through a special safe migration function.

- Token allocations are completed to all parties.

- Transaction is complete.[12]

This process is demonstrated visually in Figure 12-1.

---

[12]https://sonm.io/Somn-BusinessOverview.pdf

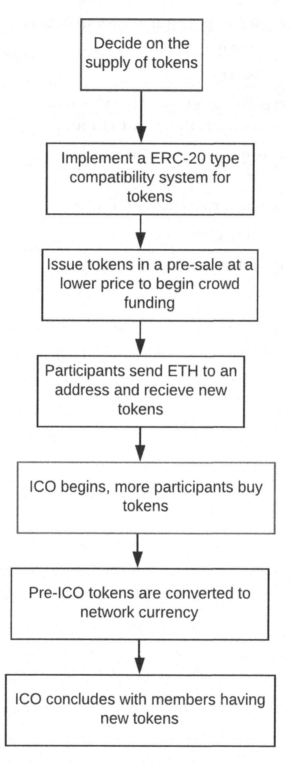

Figure 12-1. *ICO process for the SONM token illustrated visually*

Digital Currency Exchanges

Digital currency exchanges (DCEs) or Bitcoin exchanges are businesses that allow customers to trade digital currencies for other assets, such as conventional fiat money or different digital currencies. They can be market measures that typically take the bid–ask spreads as transaction commissions for their services or simply charge fees as a matching platform.[13]

Typically, DCEs operate outside of Western countries, avoiding regulatory oversight and complicating prosecutions. A US-based global Bitcoin exchange named Kracken is located in San Francisco. The Kracken website says Kracken is the world's largest global Bitcoin exchange in Euro volume and liquidity. Poloniex is described on its website as a US-based digital asset exchange offering maximum security and advanced trading features.

As one works with DCEs, and for all aspects of operating an exchange in the financial world, it is very important to establish identity easily and exactly. The future of identity management looks different with blockchain technology in a decentralized digital world. Digital identity networks built on the blockchain drive trust among businesses as a social enterprise by leveraging shared ledgers, smart contracts, and governance to standardize management, at the same time reducing the cost, risk, time, and complexity of decentralized identity management.

Status of ICO Regulation

Every year in the fall, *Coin Desk* releases a comprehensive report discussing the state of ICO regulation with a focus on legal status in six nations. Several points of interest are quoted by a recent report from Autonomous Next, a FinTech and research firm. The report considers Switzerland and Singapore to be the two most advanced nations for creating welcoming environments for FinTech and cryptocurrencies. In Switzerland, the law is that cryptocurrencies are assets rather than securities. The same is true for Singapore. The Singapore MAS authority does not regulate virtual currency transactions, but does monitor KYC and AML, the report states.

The report singled out the United Kingdom and United States as jurisdictions with high activity, but a lack of legal clarity. The United States, with many regulatory groups and fifty states that implement rules, makes the process of regulation more complex. The state of Delaware has recently passed blockchain-related legislation. In China, tokens are considered a non-monetary digital asset. Russia has been welcoming of cryptocurrencies. Cryptotokens are categorized as legal financial instruments similar to derivatives.[14]

---

[13]https://en.wikipedia.org/wiki/Digital_currency_exchange

[14]http://www.coindesk.com/state-ico-regulation-new-report-outlines-legal-status-6-nations/

In the financial review of second quarter, 2017, Smith & Crown pointed out a significant problem in the legal status of token sales that is still in question. Participants in token sales might not enjoy the same legal status or protections as investors in private- and public-equity sales. Uncapped token sale raises and structures that allow projects to raise large sums of capital while retaining majority control over their token economy could exacerbate this problem by drawing attention from regulatory agencies. A number of countries are actively exploring new regulatory frameworks for token sales, and several groups, including Smith & Crown, are developing guidelines for best practices and self-regulation.[15]

The current regulation status is that the SEC in the United States issued a letter stating that ICOs, cryptocurrencies, and related matters are viewed by the SEC as securities. As stated previously, this brings some clarity to the marketplace on this issue. Although some will read it positively and others negatively, ultimately the SEC statement set in motion an entirely new understanding of the regulatory environment both in the United States and globally.

A Securities Law Framework for Blockchain Tokens describes multiple key thoughts and actions for anyone that is interested in blockchain tokens. "The Framework focuses on US federal securities laws because these laws pose the biggest risk for crowd sales of blockchain tokens. In many jurisdictions, there may also be issues under anti-money laundering laws and general consumer protection laws, as well as specific laws depending on what the token actually does." The Howey Test establishes the criteria for whether an investment contract is a security (*SEC v. Howey*).[16]

The framework illustrates six best practices for token sales:

1. Publish a detailed whitepaper.

2. For a presale, commit to a development roadmap.

3. Use an open, public blockchain and publish all codes.

4. Use clear, logical, and fair pricing in the token sale.

5. Determine the percentage of tokens set aside for the development team.

6. Avoid marketing the token as an investment.

---

[15]https://www.smithandcrowm.com/quarter-two-review
[16]https://www.coinbase.com/legal/securities-law-framework.pdf

Pros and Cons of ICO Investments

The pros and cons of investing in ICOs are illustrated by Jim Reynolds in a recent article titled, a "Invest It In: Investment Ideas." This list of pros and cons is by no means exhaustive, but it does contain many points to consider.

For ICO Founders: Entrepreneurs

- Raise capital efficiently.

- ICOs are much cheaper than IPOs.

- ICOs require much less documentation than IPOs.

- Branding and marketing opportunity to get exposure for an altcoin.

- Community building.

- Create skin in the game with early adopters; this will make them part of the marketing mechanism of the project.

- Entrepreneurs share both the risks and the benefits of their efforts with the investors.

- Founders/developers have a method that can help them finance a project that can make the best use of their skills to the maximum possible extent.

- Well-respected crypto-experts have a channel to cash in on the skills and credibility they built over the years.

- Proof-of-stake altcoins resolve the problem of fair distribution through ICOs, and in PoS the coins come to fruition immediately.

- Venture-capital funding is much more intrusive on the founder's Vision360. An alternative to an ICO is borrowing, but this has many implications on the project cash flow that are not always possible to manage in altcoin/crypto projects.

- Some transparency; for example, an escrow can be used to verify how the funds are being spent after the ICO.

- Early investors will have more liquidity in early-stage companies.

- Early access to a token that has the potential for capital growth.

- Not regulated or registered with any government organization, and there are usually no investor protections other than what is built into the platform itself.

- Investors can be part of a community.

- An innovative way to deploy capital.

- An ICO that uses existing networks, such as Stratis, Ardor, and Ethereum, is tapping into the network capital of an existing ecosystem.

- Divest from main cryptocurrencies into altcoins.

- Investors are usually the first users of the altcoin; thus, unlike holding a stock of a company whose products an investor never used, ironically altcoins can be more tangible than other investments.

- The returns from investing in ICOs can be up to 1,000 percent, and also could be complete losses.

- Diversification into other assets.

- A high-risk, high-reward investment that is (to some extent) disconnected from the stock market and the economy.

- Own an alternative asset not based on fiat currency.

For the Cryptocurrency Community:

- Altcoins will fuel the race to build Web 3.0, a decentralized web. The internet stack becomes fully independent from any central entity.

- Altcoins are the cutting edge of FinTech, even if an altcoin project technology fails. There will be lessons learned regarding the technology and business model being proposed that will benefit the whole community.

- More competition in the crypto space makes the competitors leaner, meaning the "invisible hand" of the market frets much faster in terms of creative destruction and survival of the fittest the more altcoin projects are launched.

- Intra-altcoin competition is healthy, as it prepares the altcoins for the real competition, the crypto-based decentralized projects versus traditional firms.

- There are two schools of thought: Bitcoin maximalists who consider Bitcoin as the one and only true cryptocurrency and altcoins as experiments. Others think the altcoins will eventually replace Bitcoin, just like the video was replaced by the CD, Myspace by Facebook, and old cameras by digital ones.

The following are the risks of investing in ICOs:

- Scammers take advantage of an unregulated industry.

- Amateurs can use ICOs to launch projects that are doomed to fail.

- Longer project delivery timelines increase the risk of competitive products being launched while the ICO to build your own product is not finished.

- Exchanges need to accept the altcoin for there to be a market for the altcoin.

- An ICO can be surrounded by hype and "pumping" to mask the cons of the ICOs and make investors invest emotionally, only to find out later that it was all hot air.

- This is done by piggybacking on the success of Bitcoin, Ethereum, and Dash without offering anything real back in return.

- Regulators can change rules and make coins with certain functionality illegal in the future.

- Altcoin technology is extremely new, and basic issues such as agreement on protocols are not yet resolved. Many altcoins will be born, and others will dissipate, until we eventually see the Google, Facebook, and YouTube of cryptocoins.

- Certain tokens can be copied (forked) and made better. The clone can eventually have more value than the original. This happens when the token is not an intrinsic part of the network[17,18]

---

[17]https://www.investitin.com/crypto-ico-pros-cons/
[18]www.investopedia.com/terms/r/regtech.asp

Regulation Technology: RegChain

Regulation technology (RegTech) is a new innovation area that holds great promise for the regulation industry. RegTech is defined by Investopedia as "a blend word of regulating technology" that was created to address regulatory challenges in the financial services sector through innovative technologies. RegTech consists of a group of companies that use technology to help businesses comply with regulations efficiently and inexpensively.

A summary in Ernst & Young's (a tax advisory organization) publication "Innovating with Reg Tech" illustrates several benefits offering regulation technology:

- Supports innovation.

- Provides analytics.

- Reduces cost of compliance.

There are also some short-term benefits:

- Cost reduction

- Sustainable and scalable solutions

- Advanced data analytics

- Control and risk platforms to be linked seamlessly

Long-term benefits include the following:

- Positive customer experience

- Increased market stability

- Improved governance

- Enhanced regulatory reporting[19]

A current innovation experience of a RegTech model created by Deloitte is RegChain:

Deloitte, in collaboration with Irish Funds and their members, advanced "Project Lighthouse" to assess blockchain technology's ability to service regulatory reporting requirements. The project tested the ability for a platform to provide individual nodes for fund administrators to store and analyze

---

[19]https://www2.deloitte.com/content/dam/Deloitte/lu/Documents/financial-services/performancemagazine/articles/lu_RegChain%20Reaction_Performance23.pdf

*fund data while coding regulatory reporting requirements into smart con-
tracts for execution and data validation. A regulator node was also facili-
tated, allowing the safe and secure exchange of data between firms and the
regulator, as well as to increase overall reporting efficiency and market
transparency. In addition to technical design and development, a comparative business analysis was undertaken to review the cost–benefit analysis
of the proposed blockchain solution.*

*RegChain was developed using Deloitte's rapid prototyping process, which
uses an experiment-driven agile methodology. Key phrases included solution visioning definition of design and test parameters, development sprints,
and ongoing reviews with an industry subcommittee with participants
from across the fund administrator and fund management world.*

*A key consideration and cornerstone for this project was to ensure collabo-
ration among technologists and industry representatives from operations,
regulatory teams, and senior management. This was deemed critical in
order to have a comprehensive PoC design, and moreover, to help define
how a future production solution could be realized.*[20]

Blockchain technology was used because of a number of features and characteristics
that can enhance the overall ability to meet reporting requirements:

- Data integrity

- Reliability

- Storage and speed

- Analytics

- Proof-of-concept (PoC)

The PoC created RegChain, a blockchain-based platform that streamlined the
traditional regulatory reporting processes by acting as a central repository for the safe
storage and review of a large volume of regulatory data. RegChain has been used in the
marketplace successfully in multiple applications and gives hope that the future will see
wider adoption and enjoyment of the benefits of this model.

---

[20]https://www2.deloitte.com/content/dam/Deloitte/lu/Documents/financial-services/
performancemagazine/articles/lu_RegChain%20Reaction_Performance23.pdf

New Blockchain Companies and Ideas

A *Harvard Business Review* article states, "Many businesses have yet to make the leap from the Industrial Age to the Information Age, and the gap between technological and organizational progress is widening."[21]

Goldman Sachs has taken a series of steps that are bold and decisive in the area of digital innovation and blockchain applications. Goldman has been involved in some blockchain technology–based companies like Circle and Digital Assets Holdings. Additionally, in October 2016, Goldman Sachs introduced an online platform offering unsecured personal loans to consumers.

Homechain and SALT

Another new company is Homechain, described as the future of loan origination and regulatory compliance. The business idea is reducing the home loan origination and regulatory compliance process from forty-two days to five days. RegChain allows for compliance to reporting bodies. At this time, blockchain technology is at the stage where the internet was in 1992, and it is opening up a wealth of new possibilities that have the promise to add value to numerous industries, including finance, health, education, music, art, government, and more.[22]

The SALT lending platform allows the holders of blockchain to leverage their holdings as collateral for cash loans. SALT is the first asset-based lending platform to give blockchain asset holders access to liquidity, with their having to sell their tokens. SALT provides investors an innovative and secure opportunity to lend against a high-growth asset class through a fully collateralized debt vehicle. SALT is traditional lending secured by nontraditional collateral.

Each SALT token is representative of a membership to the SALT lending platform. The token is an ERC20 smart contract.

Blockchain technology is making waves in many industries. Companies in various sectors are innovating and using blockchain to create new applications and start up disruptive companies. A report by Accenture shows the cost data of eight of the world's largest investment banks, and states that blockchain technology could help reduce the costs of investment banks by as much as $12 billion per annum by 2025. There are multiple benefits for investment banks using blockchain technology, including safer transmission of data and overhead cost reductions due to a digital medium.[23]

---

[21]https://hbr.org/2017/03/how-blockchain-is-changing-finance

[22]https://hbr.org/2017/03/how-blockchain-is-changing-finance

[23]https://saltlending.zendesk.com/hc/en-us/sections/115002568808-Technology

Ambrosus, Numerai, and SWARM

Another example of a new company is the Swiss blockchain company, Ambrosus. This company was launched to employ smart contracts to track food quality. Innovation using blockchain technology is happening everywhere.

Numerai is a new kind of hedge fund built by a network of data scientists. Numerai is a crowdsourced hedge fund for machine learning experts. In the first year of collection, 7,500 data scientists created algorithms on the Numerai platform, as reported by Tech Crunch. Numerai announced Numeraire, a cryptocurrency token to incentivize data scientists around the world to contribute AI. The Numerai smart contract was deployed to Ethereum, and more than 1.2 million tokens were sent to 19,000 data scientists around the world, as reported by Numerai.[24]

The startup company Swarm advanced several new concepts into the marketplace and was at the leading edge of two emerging concepts, crowdfunding and cryptocurrency, while creating a startup in a market with complex and evolving regulations. The idea was to transform the way entrepreneurs raise money. Swarm created a new idea called crypto-equity, a token that represents the success of your project.

Swarm was built on the following three components:

- Crypto-equity

- Crowdsourced due diligence

- Coins distributed to all Swarm holders. The best description of Swarm is like a crypto-Kickstarter offered via coins.

- Crypto-Kickstarter offered via coins

KICKCO is a new company with a unique model. Their website states:

KICKCO sits at the intersection of two young industries: blockchain and crowdfunding. KICKCO moves crowdfunding from centralized platforms such as Kickstarter, to Ethereum-based smart contracts. This not only allows us to implement the crowdfunding model in a decentralized way— significantly reducing overhead—it also provides a mechanism to protect backers from failed projects—guaranteeing their investment with blockchain-based tokens called KickCoins. KICKCO will provide users with

---

[24]https://medium.com/numerai/an-ai-hedge-fund-goes-live-on-ethereum-a80470c6b681

a powerful, convenient, and up to date platform for both ICO and crowd-funding campaigns. KICKCO is a site for automated and independent ICOs, pre-ICOs, and crowdfunding campaigns built on Ethereum and funded by cryptocurrencies. The purpose of KICKCO is to solve the afore-mentioned problems and create a single platform that will unite the cre-ators and backers of ICO and crowdfunding campaigns to form an active up to date community.[25]

The companies that have been described show some of the innovation and creative thought that works around the blockchain models. The blockchain continues to advance new and exciting ways for financial markets to become more efficient.

Stellar

Stellar is a DLT-based payment protocol that can perform rapid cross-platform transactions between any form of currency by using blockchain anchors. The Stellar blockchain and payment operations are powered by Lumen, the native currency of the network. The network serves as a platform to connect financial institutions to users, offers a high throughput with rapid transaction approval, and provides frictionless conversion between various currencies with micro-transactions.

In Stellar, anchors are entities that can hold a deposit and issue credit to users based on the request and within double-spending parameters. An anchor serves as a bridge between the different currencies on the Stellar network. Besides the network-native currency XLM, all other external transactions happen in the form of credit issued by anchors. The currency exchange mechanism happens through pre-defined offers on the Stellar network. An offer is a trusted commitment to exchange a currency for credit at a fixed rate. In this manner, Stellar acts as a marketplace for buyers to create credit offers, and for sellers to exchange using a credit offer. All the offers for currency exchange are recorded in an orderbook that remains consistent across the network for all currencies. To illustrate the Stellar payment system, let's work through an example transaction between Bob and Alice.

Bob lives in the United States and wants to send $5,000 to Alice, who lives in the United Kingdom. Bob has an account with a bank A in the United States, and Alice has an account with bank B in the United Kingdom. Let's assume that both banks are linked to the Stellar network through anchors. Bob sends his transaction through bank A to the

---

[25]https://www.kickico.com/whitepaper

Stellar network, and after verification of funds, bank B can deduct the amount from Bob's account. The money is transferred to bank A's pool account and moved into the Stellar network in the form of XLM. Once the money is in Stellar, an offer for exchange is used to convert the XLM into Alice's native currency. Once the conversion is done, the amount is transferred into bank B's account and credited to Alice. In this manner, the anchors help move money between banks on Stellar, and offers allow for intranetwork currency exchange at a fraction of the cost compared to traditional mechanisms.

Democratizing Investment Opportunities

Blockchain can help the world's poorest people. A World Economic Forum article described the way that transactions can be recorded in an inexpensive and transparent way, allowing for money to be exchanged without fear, fraud, or theft. Blockchain smart contracts, sending money internationally, reducing costs, insurance services, helping small businesses, humanitarian aid, and blockchain-powered identity systems are just some of the ways blockchain can help many people. For those without passports, birth certificates, phones, or email, blockchain records can speed processing, allowing for a better way of life for many people.

Through crowdfunding smaller investment amounts and many new capital formation ventures, people who have previously not had the opportunity for sharing in the economies of a growing financial market can participate. Blockchain helps to democratize finance and affect lives in new ways.

Regulatory Updates in 2020

The 2020 and beyond regulatory view of financial markets in the United Stats is best illustrated by the SEC's "FINHUB," a "Strategic Hub for Innovation and Financial Technology."[26] The SEC states on their website, "The SEC has joined the Global Financial Innovation Network" and additionally have added tools to "help market participants assess whether the federal securities laws apply to the offer, sale, or resale of a particular digital asset." These proactive actions and efforts illustrate market growth and maturity. The SEC has also sponsored public forums related to distributed ledger technology [DLT] and RegTech. In the last few years, there has been advanced growth in many areas related to regulatory issues around digital assets implementation, education, and guidance.

---

[26]https://www.sec.gov/finhub

The SEC has focused on issues related to the blockchain and distributed ledger technology. Blockchains are often used to issue and transfer ownership of digital assets that may be securities, depending on the facts and circumstances. Additional focus has been involved with the digital marketplace, which generally refers to financing methods that do not use traditional financial institutions as intermediaries, such as crowdfunding, online market lending, and funding portals and platforms.[27]

Major changes and innovations have also taken place in the banking industry in mid-2020. The Office of the Comptroller of the Currency [an independent bureau of the US Department of the Treasury] "has clarified that national banks and federal savings associations can provide cryptocurrency custodial services for customers. The OCC sees banks providing crypto services as a modern form of traditional bank activities related to custody services."[28] This reaffirms the OCC position that "national banks may provide permissible banking services to any lawful business they choose, including cryptocurrency business, so long as they manage the risks and comply with the applicable law."

Blockchain technology is advancing a new era of operational efficiency in the capital markets. There are many innovations that can help financial institutions adopt and capitalize on digital asset processes and innovation. Areas that are innovating with new solutions include asset management, capital markets, decentralized finance, global trade and commerce, and payments and money. Some of the benefits of this capital market innovation are faster access to capital, increased solvency, new financial instruments, transparent and real-time data, reduced counterparty risk, and lower operating costs.

DeFi

A technological revolution in financial capital markets is decentralized finance (DeFi), defined as "open finance." ConsenSys refers to DeFi as "the economic paradigm shift enabled by decentralized technologies, particularly blockchain networks. From peer-to -peer payment systems to automated loans to USD-pegged SFtablecoins, DeFi has emerged as one of the most active sectors in the blockchain space, with a range of use cases for developers, individuals, and institutions." Decentralized finance leverages three key principals of the Ethereum blockchain to unlock liquidity and growth opportunities, increase financial security and transparency, and support an integrated and standardized economic system."[29]

---

[27] http://www.sec.gov/finhub

[28] news.bitcoin.com/us-regulator-banks-cryptocurrency-custody/

[29] consensys.net/solutions/capital-markets/

DeFi's three key principals are as follows:

- **Programmability:** Highly programmable smart contracts automate execution and enable the creation of new financial instruments and digital assets.

- **Immutability:** Tamper-proof data coordination across a blockchain's decentralized architecture increases security and auditability

- **Interoperability:** Ethereum's composable software stack ensures that DeFi protocols and applications are built to integrate and complement one another .

The innovative use cases of decentralized finance as described by ConsenSys are as follows:

- **Know Your Transaction (KYT):** Similar to a process of verifying the identities of customers and counterparties (KYC), blockchain-based DeFi solutions now enable businesses to easily monitor, analyze, and verify transaction details to prevent fraud and meet regulatory requirements.

- **DeFi Data and Analytics:** Track the value locked in DeFi protocols, borrow and supply APRs, exchange volumes, and more with our comprehensive and customizable data platform.

- **Token Utilization:** Programmable "proof of use" standards for token networks align incentives during network launches and minimize speculation, ensuring that tokens end up in the hands of actual users.

- **Eth 2 Staking:** Our staking-as-a-service platform helps qualified validators earn rewards and avoid penalties for attesting blocks on the Eth2 Beacon Chain.[30]

The innovations and possibilities of blockchain innovations are driving rapid change in the US and global financial markets. Many products and solutions are being aligned as never before. Regulations, banking, capital markets, and innovation are creating a new world of finance.

---

[30]consensys.net.blockchain-use-cases/decentralized-finance/

Summary

The future is for creation, innovation, change, and global impact as crowdfunding enables blockchain on a global scale. Reports from both EY and Innovate Finance delve into the capital markets landscape. Chris Skinner, in his blog, "Fintech and the World of Investment Banking," stated that "there is a raft of new technologies that are architecting the landscape of capital markets and hundreds of start-ups leveraging these new technologies to both assist and attack the inefficiencies in the investment banking world. Rather than ignoring these changes the biggest banks are investing in them."[31]

Goldman Sachs, Citicorp, JPMorgan, Morgan Stanley, Wells Fargo, and Bank of America are just some of the large banks and investment bankers investing millions in FinTech, blockchain, and other technology innovations.

Disruption in the capital markets is moving at a rapid pace. A recent *Forbes* article indicated that there are more than 900 cryptocurrencies in existence now, with more being added each day. The ICO market is drawing significant amounts of capital, comparable to venture capital market over the last few years, as of mid-2017. There will be many future market fluctuations, with new regulations coming to the market, and many changes on the way as we experience technological revelations and financial capital changing rapidly.

A special salute goes to the innovators, dreamers, individuals, and groups that are in the marketplace and see the future of a better financial world for everyone. The incredible commitment of incubators, accelerators, universities, and investment firms working toward blockchain efficiencies and innovation will change the way the world views financial capital.

Examples of innovation are everywhere. Goldman Sachs, JPMorgan, Nasdaq, and special alternative investment firms such as Triloma Securities offer unique products, services, innovation, and capital. What is occurring in many local markets is a collaboration of groups working together for common goals in the technology area. One unique group in the Orlando and central Florida area has come together to help startups and advance blockchain research and applications. This group comprises various organizations, including Florida Angel Nexus, Merging Traffic, StartUp Nations Ventures, Institute of Simulation & Training, METIL (Mixed Emerging Technology Integration Lab), the Medical Tourism Association, and many others, all working in a robust public–private partnership ecosystem that drives change for the good of all in the marketplace.

Blockchain will bring about a unique technological revolution in financial capital.

---

[31]https://www.thefinanser.com/2017/08/fintech-world-investment-banking-html/

CHAPTER 13

Building a Healthcare Consortium

John Bass is the founder and CEO of Hashed Health, a blockchain-based health IT consortium with members working to commercialize appropriate use cases in healthcare and deliver a proof-of-concept that can be scaled. In this chapter, we interview John Bass about the following topics:

- His background and previous work in healthcare

- The makings of Hashed Health

- Collaborative and consortium models

- Working groups for high-risk, high-reward model

- Governance in Hashed Health

- Member participation

Vikram: *So, John, can you tell our readers about your background, and what made you interested in building healthcare startups?*

John Bass: Many of us in the healthcare technology industry have spent our professional lives working to build applications and intelligence that help stakeholders (for instance providers, vendors, payers, consumers) understand the opportunities to improve care delivery and curb costs. As a community, we have a hope that we can change the system. That we can make an unfair system fair again. That, using technology, we can go back to a place where healthcare is centered on the individual consumer patient rather than the corporate interest. We all dream of the ever-elusive healthcare platform that captures the hearts and minds of patients, builds the network effects, and makes everything better. We dream of saving our country from run-away health costs, a national security issue of our own making. We dream about delivering

311

© Vikram Dhillon, David Metcalf, and Max Hooper 2021
V. Dhillon et al., *Blockchain Enabled Applications*, https://doi.org/10.1007/978-1-4842-6534-5_13

care to the millions of people who struggle with access. We dream of creating something so viral that it scales globally and helps millions of people around the world get the care they need. We want it so bad we lose sleep. We want it so bad we abandon our families for weeks at a time, hoping to light the fuse.

Vikram: *What got you started thinking about building a blockchain-based healthcare company?*

John: The startups I have been a part of have all focused on web-based products that promoted collaboration, data sharing, shared workflows, and cross-enterprise clinical or financial performance. Our teams have built B2B platforms, patient portals, collaborative workflow solutions, surgical performance solutions, and other trendy IT solutions that I thought would change the industry. These efforts, like most of the solutions you see at the big healthcare technology trade shows, focus on adding applications on top of the existing infrastructure. They essentially support the existing healthcare value chains, with the goal of making them more efficient. Though successful at solving problems, it's clear that these years of work and millions of dollars have had little impact on the macro cost/quality issues facing our country. The killer app and the platform are still out there.

After twenty years I have realized that there is a more fundamental problem that can't be fixed through additive technologies. Step back and you see that, over time, we have built a system that is more and more dependent on middle men, relational databases, and their associated applications. The structural truth is clear to me now. The structural truth is the driver of unstable economic trends, unfair access, failures in preventable illness, suboptimal outcomes, rising out-of-pocket costs, and medical debt. All systems inherit the characteristics of their container, which in the US is a fee-for-service marketplace which lacks any sort of rational, free-market characteristics. Anything built within this container is constrained by those characteristics. I don't believe we can really solve anything building within the existing container.

Vikram: *I think we would both agree that the existing container has worked well for now, but it's not resilient enough to work for the problems that we will be facing in the near future. What are your thoughts on this?*

John: Don't get me wrong . . . the US health system has been remarkably successful. More people die of old age than infectious disease. We have become experts at treating acute care injuries and illnesses. Our pharmaceuticals industry produced a vaccine to Zika in a remarkably short amount of time. I would not say our system is broken or in need of a do-over. It is working exactly as we designed it to work. It is a representation of the user stories and requirements that we drew up for its developers. People from around the world travel to the United States to receive world-class treatment. And we are rapidly exporting our (good and bad) expertise to the rest of the world.

What is clear is that we are no longer getting our money's worth. The US is approaching $5T in spend, and one-third is waste. Medical errors are the third leading cause of mortality behind heart disease and cancer. Significant populations of people in the US and around the world have poor access to care. We all live in environments where unhealthy influences and behaviors have been institutionalized. Yesterday's system we created was not designed to counter-balance the behaviors that have emerged as the leading causes of today's cost and quality concerns. We are realizing that can't be fixed with new applications on top of the as-designed system. We have to re-build, taking advantage of our successes while optimizing for today's social and economic truths.

Vikram: *So, what does the re-build look like? What are the new user stories and requirements? Who are the new developers of this system? Can the current corporate interests be trusted to re-design a platform for the future? How do we get from here to there?*

John: Hashed Health sees the blockchain as the protocol for the next generation of health solutions. By moving trust to the protocol layer, we lay the foundation for more agile care-delivery models, payments systems, value chains, and consumer experiences. It is not THE answer to these questions, but it allows innovators to have a new conversation free of today's limiting factors. When combined with IoT, machine learning, artificial intelligence, cryptocurrency, design thinking, and other tools, blockchain becomes a recipe for true disruption.

The path to real change in healthcare is through the consumer. One reason blockchain is an enabler of disruption in healthcare lies in its potential to change the consumer's relationship with existing systems of health and wellness. It provides an alternative to today's corporate-focused environment that has become a limiting factor for society. The user will interact with this new model through their mobile devices, which will leverage "wallet" software that will become more and more self-sovereign over time. Consumers will become prosumers with controls over their health assets. Patients will no longer be asked to join a series of siloed patient portals as they move through the continuum of care. This provides a more holistic approach across an individual's related health, wellness, social, and socioeconomic events. We have learned that one's health is so much more than the 5 percent fragments that happen during a clinical visit. Patients will be empowered to their information and the ability to donate or monetize their records as they wish. Over time, honeypots of medical records data will be decentralized and distributed, making the user's information less accessible to theft.

Vikram: *By many standards, healthcare IT moves as a slow monolith. This may be due to design, but can you talk a bit more about why we don't have a straightforward consumer-to-provider relationship in health IT, and healthcare more broadly?*

John: The consumer-facing side of health IT is complicated. Consumerization of healthcare has been a buzzword for years now but has proven elusive. There are a few important reasons why this is true. First, on many levels, healthcare is not like other markets. Healthcare is not a traditional commodity or service to be purchased. Even if they were completely free to do so (more on this below), consumers are not in a position to make the best judgments about purchasing healthcare, either because of the complexity of healthcare treatments or due to the emergent need to seek care. Additionally, unlike almost all other products or services, a consumer cannot always predict the results of consuming healthcare. For example, purchasing a car produces predictable results: owning transportation equipment with stated features and in regulatory compliance. By contrast, a given treatment may or may not adequately address the illness or condition.

Beyond these economic basics, consumerization is complicated by the configuration of the healthcare system itself. The drive to "Uber-ize" healthcare runs head-on into the wall of the US payment and delivery systems. The consumer has no knowledge of price for services. Providers themselves often cannot give pricing in advance. Furthermore, the consumer is not a party to the pricing agreement, as the contractual relationship is between the provider and the payor, on behalf of the consumer. These are all well-known, almost hackneyed issues related to US healthcare. By themselves, they do not prevent the creation of potentially useful consumer tools. Instead, to have utility, consumer tools need to "plug in" to the systems that deliver and pay for healthcare services. Given the dizzying array of payors, physician and service providers, as well as their oft-conflicting motivations, consumer tools are often stymied by the unwillingness of enterprises that control the healthcare marketplace. Consumerization of healthcare is elusive—not because of a lack of tools, but rather, due to the lack of an open platform.

As groups of consumers organize or are convened in traditional and innovative ways, these groups will represent new centers of gravity for the future marketplace. The community or group (however you define it—village, employer, values-based group, nursing home, etc.) will also be empowered through the ability to organize, aggregate, and share. Similarly, groups of providers on the sell-side of the marketplace will organize (or be convened) into either traditional or innovative new cohorts for the provision of care in ways that are better, faster, and more economically rational than what can be delivered under today's bloated market structure.

Vikram: *How do you think the large enterprises (provider groups and insurance companies) will evolve to respond to the new opportunities such as blockchain?*

John: Enterprises will, over time, be affected by new opportunities and challenges that result from changing market structures. The effects will be felt throughout today's healthcare value chains, such as supply chain, revenue cycle, claims lifecycle, clinical research, insurance/benefits, and clinical episodes. Audit and compliance activities will fall away to automation. Contracting, rebating, admin fees, and discounting schemes will disappear or be transformed through the use of immutable, transparent shared ledgers. Closed relational databases like EMRs, ERPs, and materials management systems will evolve as the nature of their accounting functions move to the market level. Clinical trials programs will be optimized through sharing of information and streamlined administrative processes. Security will be enhanced, and, over time, data honeypots will fall away to a decentralized structure.

Companies will not throw away their existing databases (at least not at first). First, these legacy systems will transact with the blockchain through APIs and then, over time, we will begin to see new, nimble, ground-up systems emerge. These systems will transform how we currently think about the movement of health, data, clinical, and financial assets across a market.

Machines will also begin to play a larger role in health and wellness. We already see a role for connected health machines, wearables, and a host of web-enabled monitoring devices. Blockchain provides the foundation for a more secure and scalable health IoT environment. Devices can be registered and validated more scalably using the blockchain as a shared ledger. As a result, information from these machines can be trusted. Transfer of ownership can also be tracked more easily, and the operational lifecycle of the device can be recorded. Perhaps most interestingly, the device itself can be given a wallet and a set of smart contracts that allow it to execute commands, transfer assets, and operate in ways that drive clinical and financial value for consumers or for the machines themselves!

This vision of the consumer, the community, the enterprise, and the machine is truly disruptive. It's also a vision with many technical and non-technical challenges.

Vikram: *How do we get to the future that you described? What is the path to the consumer-driven future? How do we create demonstrations that prove the value of the technology? How do we get people on board?*

John: Healthcare is a fast-follower. It is historically resistant to platforms and "uberization" because of regulatory considerations, complexity, and aversion to risk. Blockchain technology is new. Satoshi Nakamoto released the Bitcoin whitepaper in 2009. Ethereum was created in the summer of 2015. Other protocols being considered for healthcare projects, such as Hyperledger Fabric, Tendermint, and other protocols, are even newer. EOS, Tezos, and NEO just arrived on the scene with their record-setting token sales and new ideas around governance, consensus, and scalability. Smart contracts are still not very smart and are even less secure. It's anyone's guess who the winners will be in five to ten years. If given the choice, the chefs in healthcare's institutional kitchen would prefer to sit back and watch the technology marinate for a while.

The real limiting factor may actually be the non-technical concerns. First, for blockchain solutions to be effective you need a collaborative network of participants. This is why you read so much about consortia and blockchain. Without the consortium or the minimally viable network of participants, enterprise blockchain efforts are merely expensive academic exercises. And even if you have the network required, successful governance can be tricky. These collaborative concepts require some getting used to for some, a paradigm shift for most. Secondly, for certain use cases there are serious regulatory concerns that complicate productive use. Many great ideas will be limited by a regulatory framework that never imagined the decentralized marketplace. Third, there is still a significant amount of education and organization of the market required. After a year of operating our consortium, the majority of the market still needs consulting on what blockchain is, how it could affect their market structure, and why networks are key to success. Fourth, we believe that the early efforts to establish blockchain and distributed ledger technologies as a viable solution will require simple demonstrations of value. These early demonstrations will not be designed to change the world. They will solve simple, unsexy problems in today's health system. As a result, there will be early complaints that these products do not deliver the value that blockchain had originally promised.

It will take some time to sort things out. For those of us who are early in the healthcare blockchain space, these are the complicated realities we face. The real question is timing.

Vikram: *So, about the timing, how long do you think it will take for blockchain to become mainstream? How can we accelerate the time it takes to cross the chasm?*

John: I often tell people that starting Hashed Health is the most excited and the most scared I have been in my professional career. From an innovator's perspective, the blockchain healthcare space is a dream. There is no template. Everything is new. The technology is new and immature. The collaborative innovation business model is new. The concept of "fat protocols" is new. We have to not only build products . . . we also have to build a market. We are innovating from every angle. Every day is a 3D chess match. It's high-risk, high-reward research and development. For Hashed, it's the most exciting opportunity imaginable.

We chose the collaborative business model because it is in line with the spirit of the blockchain and it seemed like the only path to success when we started the company in 2016. Unlike previous startups, this was not a "build a product, sell a product" model. Though we had many strong use cases in the queue, we knew we could not place all our bets on one. The market wasn't ready. We knew we needed to do more with less. The collaborative model allows for us to join together with industry thought leaders who can contribute to our ecosystems of shared value. By being a part of several successful projects with the companies who are using the products, we increase our odds that our products will gain productive use. We also lower the risks and increase the rewards for our customers. It was the only way, especially in a new and complex market.

Once we made this decision, we were quickly branded a consortium. We have never been comfortable with this label, though we struggled to come up with anything better. We are more like a mesh network or a product studio. At the end of the day Hashed Health is a products company with many successful solutions in our portfolio. In many ways, any company building blockchain products is a consortium if they want to be successful. The network is often more important than the product itself. It's the relationship between the two where we spend a lot of our energy, because that's where success lies.

Vikram: *So, how do we start building the network? Currently, there is a lack of awareness and understanding in the healthcare space about blockchain technology. How do we bring the providers up to speed and [get them] interested?*

John: To begin, we knew we needed to do a lot of thought-leadership work to educate and organize the industry. We researched the technology heavily and we connected what was happening outside healthcare to our professional and personal healthcare experience. We invested heavily into research. After a time, we began our thought-leadership work. We blogged, wrote newsletters, spoke at conferences. We listened to the feedback we received, and we iterated on our ideas and early products. We used those early products to recruit the initial members. At first, we developed really complicated contracts, and then we simplified them to make getting started as easy as possible. We evolved into a structure that can flex governance, business, and technical requirements as needed based on the workgroup and the product. This allows us to meet a customer where they are, rather than forcing them down a contractual pathway that may be scary or uncomfortable. We started with larger organizations, and we are now opening membership and workgroup activities up to earlier stage companies, universities, entrepreneurs, and thought leaders so that we can bring more contributors into the emerging networks.

Vikram: *Can you talk a bit more about how the Hashed Health model benefits the members? What's the current structure of Hashed Health?*

John: Our goal with our members is to build community and products that make meaningful use of the strengths of blockchain and distributed ledger technologies. We seek out members who will contribute to a project and a conversation, not just look to extract value from the group. We consider ourselves a healthcare company first, so the projects we work on must have the patient's best interest in mind.

Our members usually engage as general members who need some consulting before they are ready to build. The level of business and technical expertise inside healthcare institutions is very weak, so a consultative approach is required. Members usually have a concept or two that they believe they'd like to tackle, but they always require some guidance and some preparation prior to development. By providing healthcare expertise and blockchain expertise, we are able to deliver a unique product that drives productive use-case concepts forward in a more efficient manner. By creating collaborative agreements, we can build incentives that support accomplishing rational milestones on the pathway from concept to productive use.

Each of our networks has its own constituents, cadence, business plan, technical plan, governance structure, and personality. Each is focused on solving a specific business problem, and we choose the protocol that fits the business need. Currently, we have built products and demos on Hyperledger Fabric, Ethereum, a commercial platform called BitSE, and Tendermint and Ethermint. We are currently researching other protocols and various middleware products, including Gem, Bloq, Nuco, Stratumn, Tezos, EOS, and IOTA. The workgroups all share common learnings and best practices that translate across projects. We have experts (either in-house or contracted) who can support any discussion (technical, business, legal, regulatory) required to advance a product.

In order to cross the chasm, we feel it is important to begin with simple demonstrations of value. The simpler the better. We prefer projects that are not highly political, that do not require protected information, and that solve a problem in today's environment while laying the foundation for our vision of the future.

Vikram: *Let's get into the portfolio of operational working groups within Hashed Health and the current target areas. Can you elaborate on some of the use cases for us and how they're using the blockchain?*

John: At the time of writing, Hashed Health has five active enterprise groups:

1.   Provider Identity

2.   Patient Identity

3.   Payments

4.   Supply Chain IoT

5.   Clinical IoT (Wearables)

We are also in the process of forming several new enterprise groups, which we expect to have operational soon, including:

1.   Disease Registries

2.   Clinical Trials

3.   Medical Records

4.   Pharma Revenue Cycle

5.   Enterprise Resource Management Systems

These are areas where the Hashed team has both expertise and customer interest. The general membership dues support the initial business case and technical research. Once there is a decision to build, customers are required to enter a secondary development agreement specific to the project.

Perhaps the most popular example of our work is Decentralized Physician Identity. Provider identity and its related data is foundational to the delivery of care today and in the future. From graduate medical education to stat licensing, medical staff credentialing, and payer contracting, the ready availability and reliability of data about a provider's identity, credentials, and reputation are paramount to ensuring patient safety and high-quality care. Globally, the world is facing a shortage of qualified health workers. That shortage is estimated to be 7.9 million [and] is expected to grow to 12.9

million health workers by 2035. A crucial challenge amidst this shortage is the ability to identify, locate, and communicate with workers in remote locations. The single provider's identity is a complex tangle of data points. There are multiple elements held by multiple disparate stakeholders, such as medical schools, state licensing boards, and more. Some elements remain static over time (such as graduate degree), and others are dynamic over time (such as licensure, affiliation, residence, and contact information).

In this use case, we treat data fields as individual data assets. Providers and credentialing stakeholders jointly manage a distributed provider profile registry. Cryptographic signatures ensure primary source verification of essential credentials and certifications, allowing distributed networks to share real-time updates of crucial data. This process significantly reduces time, expense, and wasteful manual processes that happen today. This use case is attractive because it is fairly straightforward technically, it is not political, the data is not sensitive, and no key stakeholder has a competitive interest. We would argue that it is a good blockchain use case because provider identity is not centralized and there are currently trust and incentive issues that need to be overcome. Although there are current efforts underway to centralize this information, the various data elements are not centrally granted, administered or consumed. An easily auditable market-level data structure will deliver trust and efficiency in a market that currently has neither.

In this example, you can see how Hashed Health has seeded a market with a simple product built upon a simple, yet impactful use case. Blockchain allows us to tackle this problem in a way that was not previously imaginable.

We are equally excited about our other foundational use cases. We are working with providers on patient registration authority products. We are working with a multi-constituent workgroup on an exciting payments model that links payments to benefits and behavior. We are working with government institutions on public health surveillance and clinical trials decentralization. We have begun an exciting journey that continues to pick up momentum, new ideas, and additional expertise in both blockchain and specific healthcare subject matter.

Vikram: *One major problem with blockchain integration into healthcare is concerns about privacy. Blockchain was designed to be anonymized, but for health data, we need this interesting combination of trusted miners, completely private transactions, and yet network consensus on the blockchain. What are your thoughts on the evolution of privacy?*

John: We are the first to admit that healthcare is just getting started and things are not perfect at this early stage. A good example of the immaturity is evident in the conversations we have around public versus private blockchains. The key distinction being that while permissioned blockchains are merely *distributed* solutions, open blockchains offer real *decentralization*. From a technical perspective, we choose the protocol based on the problem we are solving. We are comfortable with the concept of the "blockchain" actually representing a spectrum of trust-based transactional systems ranging from open and decentralized to private and distributed. We believe that the industry will move towards open and public blockchains, but it may take time to get there. Healthcare enterprises, much like financial services and other enterprises, value greater levels of control and, perhaps most importantly, levels of confidentiality that currently are not possible on open, truly decentralized blockchains. It is undisputable that for a range of business use cases, permissioned blockchains are an ideal fit. We believe it will take time for companies to become comfortable with the more traditional blockchain models, even though it's clear those models offer the greatest security.

It is important to critically examine where this preference for control can become a damaging and self-defeating prejudice. Open and decentralized blockchains are continuing to explode onto the scene. The top two cryptocurrencies alone account for $65B in market capitalization. Further, the newer trend of "Initial Coin Offerings" (ICOs) has attracted over $1B via crowdfunding for mostly open source, decentralized blockchain platforms. The overwhelming level of interest and financial backing for these open platforms cannot be ignored, nor should they be. They signal a massive opportunity for both individuals and businesses to think differently about the concepts of ownership, control of the network, and funding for infrastructure that supports the common good. This could be very important in funding platforms that challenge the current corporatocracy. In healthcare, we could fund massive public infrastructure projects that put the power of health and wellness in the hands of the true customers. That's powerful, and it's hard to imagine how that would get funded through traditional means.

Setting aside technical issues of confidential transactions and PHI on blockchains, the prospect of healthcare businesses operating on open networks is truly daunting to many businesses. Centralization, consolidation, and ever-widening control of healthcare networks has been the dominant business strategy for the industry for decades, especially since the introduction of the Affordable Care Act. Business success in healthcare has primarily come from ever greater control of value chains focusing on covered lives, pharmaceuticals, claims, specialty networks, outpatient facilities, and supplies. It is clear that too much value is being extracted by value-chain participants today. An open blockchain solution exposes these relationships and forces re-intermediation with lighter, more nimble value-adding actors. The uncomfortable question that blockchain technology poses for the healthcare industry is the unconventional yet tangible opportunities that open, decentralized networks offer for true value-added healthcare services.

Vikram: *As the blockchain matures, where do you see the main value being created? We spoke earlier about the fat protocols creating and capturing value at the architecture level, but what about the network?*

John: In today's healthcare industry, owning and operating the network is the ultimate business goal. The consumers of healthcare services have very little market power with choices limited by arcane and opaque contractual relationships which define today's healthcare networks. They cannot assemble their own networks of providers and services; they cannot negotiate on price or other value-added services. Instead consumers are "steered." But an open, decentralized market for healthcare services would enable the consumer to be free to make the rational economic decisions. But an open network has to be free of the perverse incentives that constrain choice and drive patient steerage. The essential difference between the status quo and the promise of decentralized networks is this: running a decentralized network is not a business in and of itself.

So far healthcare has resisted the platform movement. In a short period of time we have watched as Uber, Airbnb, and others have disrupted several traditional industries. Healthcare leaders have watched those markets change with some comfort in the reality that their existing healthcare value chains are too complex, too regulated, too sensitive to failure. Resting on these assumptions may be a mistake. The costs are becoming unsustainable, and consumers are demanding another door.

Open blockchain platforms are a new reality that healthcare needs to recognize and embrace. Hashed Health plans to move in this direction and will continue to promote open solutions. These systems, protocols, and tools are maturing rapidly and will not go away. They are proving their economic viability. The platform itself is built upon open source software. Organizations such as non-profit foundations now have the means to raise sufficient funds to launch these platforms. Incentive and fee structures can be implemented to fund ongoing operations, making the platform truly self-sufficient. The core blockchain innovation of decentralized networks supporting common transactional systems can keep the platform the centralized control of any single entity. Open governance models continue to be refined.

Value on open networks is defined purely by economic fundamentals of the services being offered. By contrast, the closed ecosystems of the healthcare industry seem to thrive on distorting true value by constraining choices. Tremendous cost and expensive administrative inefficiencies are in some sense a necessity designed to amass control over the network itself. By giving up control of the basic platform itself, healthcare enterprises can be economically rewarded by providing valued services with much lower burden of overhead and administrative cost.

The most important point is that open, decentralized networks are not fundamentally incompatible with healthcare, despite privacy and regulatory concerns. Technical barriers will soon give way to innovations such as "zero-knowledge proofs" and other means of executing confidential blockchain transactions. The true barrier is an entrenched business mindset that will become obsolete in time. It is not a matter of if, but when open healthcare networks will take root. In the short term, we need private networks to demonstrate value and move the conversation forward. Hashed will be a leader in developing these networks as a step-wise approach to the eventual reality that open blockchains will deliver the most disruptive and effective solutions. It is those enterprises which can give up white-knuckled control of the networks that will reap the greatest opportunity.

Vikram: *Lastly, I have to ask you about the recent ICO craze. Every blockchain company is trying to do an ICO—reminds me of the late nineties environment. Is Hashed Health going to do an ICO? What/how will the tokens be used for?*

John: We have also developed expertise in tokenization, and we believe that one or more of our products will have a meaningful, token-centric architecture. The concept of a token offering is exciting because it has the potential to fund infrastructure concepts for public health. Designed effectively, tokens can also help deliver on the promise of intelligent value exchange in healthcare. Programmable payments are an incredible opportunity to improve how money flows in healthcare today, creating better incentive structures that result in the alignment we have been missing for so long, especially when it comes to physician and patient behavior. Dr. Rasu Shrestha said it well: "At the end of the day, innovation is really about behavior change, whether it's a clinician putting in an order, that radiologist making a specific diagnosis or call on a finding, or the patient making a decision to eat that muffin versus going for that salad. Innovation is about behavior change." [See it at `https://www.healthcare-informatics.com/article/upmc-s-rasu-shrestha-innovation-about-behavior-change-technology-should-be-invisible`.]

We are in no rush to jump into the ICO craze, preferring to take our time and make sure the token mechanism is integral to the product and the token sale is offered in a way that satisfies the interests of our constituents while getting a token into the hands of those who will use it. No one can ignore the power of this innovation. A team of engineers anywhere in the world can make available a secure financial system with clear benefits over what exists today. It's a model that makes it difficult for traditional systems and conventionally funded startups to compete.

We feel confident that several of our use cases and pending partnerships have tokenization opportunities. We see tokens as a new, better container than what we have today. We are extremely interested in and excited by the emerging relationship between companies and tokens in the health industry. We are also interested to see if we can apply our same collaborative principles to the token distribution concept, especially in the areas of governance and coordination models.

The value that Hashed Health delivers is simple and necessary at this stage of market- and product-building. We are a healthcare company first, which means we have the patient as our primary consideration. Our team averages fifteen years in healthcare technology. We know healthcare, and we are able to connect challenges in healthcare with the possibilities of blockchain. This means we are really good at healthcare blockchain use cases. Second, in a world where the technology is changing rapidly, we do not lock customers into a specific technology. Not every protocol or middleware solution is perfect for a specific business problem. At Hashed, the protocol supports the problem. And third, our collaborative approach lowers the risk and increases the likelihood of success for projects. The "build it and they will come" model results in an expensive academic exercise. There's a better path where you can distribute the costs and the rewards across a network of collaborators who are organized around success. We have created a company and a business model that fits the spirit of the decentralized health solutions we build. Together we will innovate, and together we will accelerate the meaningful productive use and realize the potential of blockchain in healthcare.

CHAPTER 14

Blockchain-as-a-Service

In an earlier chapter, we talked about using lean methodologies to discover whether integrating a blockchain is the right choice; we also provided an open source avenue in the form of open source DLTs available through Hyperledger. This chapter extends our prior discussion to Blockchain-as-a-Service: a more immersive environment for testing a blockchain deployment and smart contracts in the cloud.

Blockchain-as-a-Service (BaaS) is a cloud-based blockchain service that provides a development environment for customers to write smart contracts, rapidly prototype blockchain applications, and deploy blockchain-based consortia with ease. It eliminates barriers to entry, particularly the massive up-front costs of hardware and expertise needed to deploy a blockchain network. This allows startups and even large companies trying to experiment with the blockchain to better understand the finances of integrating a blockchain into the existing business model. The role of a BaaS provider is analogous to that of a traditional web host. The provider manages the infrastructure, performs hardware upgrades, and keeps the network operational for customers to build complex business applications that rely on a blockchain. In terms of maintenance, the provider relies on networking tools for proper allocation of resources, manages bandwidth, and provides support for other hosting requirements. Using a BaaS service can help with mass adoption of blockchain technology as customers can focus on their application and core development while avoiding the technical complexities of creating a blockchain network and infrastructure-related support issues.

A very interesting international example of the BaaS phenomenon helping with mass adoption is the Blockchain-based Service Network (BSN): a tailored infrastructure for blockchain development with managed support in the cloud. BSN was the result of a large collaborative effort between local blockchain companies in China with a vested interest in cloud infrastructure. BSN has already integrated with six public chains, including Tezos, NEO, Nervos, EOS, IRISnet, and Ethereum. This project aims to include more than ten public chains in the near future and offer more security features with technical services that allow developers to streamline the development process.

V. Dhillon et al., *Blockchain Enabled Applications*, https://doi.org/10.1007/978-1-4842-6534-5_14

In this chapter, we study the Blockchain-as-a-Service (BaaS) offerings from four providers (three major players in the cloud blockchain world and one ConsenSys-backed startup): Microsoft Azure, Amazon Web Services, Oracle, and Kaleido. Our main focus will be on the unique aspects of BaaS providers and how each provider is supporting the growth of new organizations/startups in the cloud.

Service Providers

At the time of writing, there are ten or so BaaS providers, all offering varying degrees of services and support. While the list of criteria for evaluating a BaaS provider can be endless, each business application will have specific needs. There are two dimensions of evaluation here: the cloud provider hosting your BaaS instance, and the BaaS instance itself. Here, we want to focus on four areas to keep in mind when selecting a BaaS provider:

- Prior experience in setting up blockchain infrastructure: As the BaaS provider market expands, it is crucial to choose providers with an established track record of developing and deploying blockchain infrastructure. The reliability of infrastructure becomes more apparent and crucial as business applications start to scale with more customers. For instance, a cloud provider with experience with blockchain transaction volume can set up load-balancers that can respond appropriately to a scaling BaaS setup.

- Security and data-redundancy standards: It is paramount to get familiar with the security and backup/disaster-recovery policies of the cloud platform hosting your BaaS instance. This comes down to understanding the security of private–public keys being stored and used in the cloud, on-site security team handling cloud provider's BaaS instances, being compliant with security regulations, and redundancy of backups holding your blockchain instance.

- Integrations: Does your BaaS provider have plans for the integration of services that can enable new features and applications to be built on the blockchain? This is crucial for new startups as they pivot to find new avenues, or add new features to their minimum viable product. Additionally, developers must make sure that new features and integrations are easy to adopt into existing workflows. This reduces the additional overhead of becoming familiar with a new cloud system.

- Pricing and tiers of support: Transparent pricing is key in any BaaS provider; this also helps in planning the finances around your BaaS instance. Many providers offer tiers of pricing for using the infrastructure combined with levels of support. Fully managed instances require less in-house management of the instance once it moves online. This option is suitable for startups or companies without domain expertise in setting up BaaS or networking and allows them to focus only on blockchain development. Partially managed options are better suited for startups that are heavily tech-focused and have in-house expertise.

Figure 14-1 provides a graphical summary of the main BaaS providers on the market.

Hosting Platforms	Ethereum	Quorum	Corda	Fabric	MultiChain	Digital Asset
AWS	✓	✓[1]	✓[2]	✓		
Azure	✓	✓	✓	✓	✓[3]	
Google	✓[4]			✓		✓
HPE			✓			
IBM				✓		
Oracle				✓		
SAP				✓	✓	

1. Offered via Kaleido in AWS marketplace
2. Full server offering, not a container module
3. An older template from 2006
4. Full Ethereum version coming out later in the year

Figure 14-1. *BaaS hosting summary*

Microsoft Azure

Azure offers a Blockchain-as-a-Service platform by providing customers with easy-to-deploy enterprise-grade templates for four major distributed ledger protocols, including Ethereum, Quorum, Fabric, and Corda (and many more planned). The Azure BaaS is divided into three main components: a fully managed Azure Blockchain Service, a development and management platform called Azure Blockchain Workbench, and integrations bundled in Azure Blockchain Development Kit. This section was prepared with reference material from the Azure Blockchain Service documentation.

Azure Blockchain Service

This is Microsoft Azure's fully managed BaaS offering. Customers can create and deploy a permissioned Quorum network with a few clicks and manage the network policies along with security options using a GUI in the Azure Portal. In addition, Microsoft is releasing a Visual Studio extension that assists users in 1) writing and compiling Ethereum smart contracts; 2) deploying them to a consortium network through Azure Blockchain service or the public main-net; and 3) managing them through Azure Portal. This service enables organizations and consortia to grow and scale completely in the cloud with Azure without having to worry about underlying provisioning. Granular network governance and simplified infrastructure management allow for simple network deployment, easy-to-manage network operations and security, and the development of smart contracts with developer-friendly tools such as Visual Studio.

Currently, Azure offers Quorum ledger with the Istanbul Byzantine Fault Tolerance consensus mechanism. Using a managed service allows customers to focus on developing their core products and business logic without worrying about the underlying virtual machine infrastructure. As with most cloud services, the use of virtual machines allows for redundant backups of the whole blockchain and the possibility of network restoration from a specific time slot if necessary.

Azure Blockchain Workbench

Azure Blockchain Workbench is a collection of Azure support services that help deploy and manage blockchain applications and share business processes with other organizations on a network. This workbench provides underlying infrastructure to capture business models and codify them into smart contracts that can be deployed to an existing blockchain network. It also provides developers with automation capabilities for redundant tasks. The workbench simplifies setting up a consortium blockchain network by providing a template within Azure Resource Manager; for now, the template only supports Ethereum, but more ledger protocols are under development. The key feature of Workbench is its integrations with existing Azure components; for instance, the REST API as explained by the Azure Blockchain documentation:

You can use the Blockchain Workbench REST APIs and message-based APIs to integrate with existing systems. The APIs provide an interface to allow for replacing or using multiple distributed ledger technologies, storage, and database offerings.

Blockchain Workbench can transform messages sent to its message-based API to build transactions in a format expected by that blockchain's native API. Workbench can sign and route transactions to the appropriate blockchain.

Workbench automatically delivers events to Service Bus and Event Grid to send messages to downstream consumers. Developers can integrate with either of these messaging systems to drive transactions and to look at results.

Azure Blockchain Workbench makes it easier to analyze blockchain events and data by automatically synchronizing data on the blockchain to off-chain storage. Instead of extracting data directly from the blockchain, you can query off-chain database systems such as SQL Server. Blockchain expertise is not required for end users who are doing data analysis tasks.

Azure Blockchain Development Kit

The Blockchain Development Kit is a comprehensive GitHub repository that includes code samples with a particular focus on integrations with Azure intelligent services. The development kit could be extended in the near future to build machine learning apps that run on a blockchain powered by Azure. Here, we will focus on two such examples: IoT Central and Cognitive Search.

Note   Machine learning capabilities are already available in Azure; however, once data from a blockchain system can be imported, it can be accessed by other Azure services. In the future, machine learning services can "scan" the blockchain and have some level of event reporting that allows for network-wide alerts and notifications.

The Cognitive Search sample shows a user how to take ledger data from Ethereum and import that information to Azure Search. Once imported, it becomes available to a wide range of Enterprise applications, and the smart search options allow for the possibility of data-mining and learning from your users. The IoT example demonstrates how to connect physical products to a digital cloud and import data into your blockchain consortium. In IoT Central, you can create simulated devices, provision new devices, manage and troubleshoot physical devices, and define custom rules for incoming data and custom actions for data.

Amazon Web Services

Amazon Managed Blockchain is a fully managed BaaS offering from AWS that makes it easier to build and deploy blockchain networks in the cloud based on open source DLTs, such as Hyperledger Fabric and Ethereum, soon coming to BaaS. Presently, building scalable blockchain networks from scratch and deploying applications is technically challenging. Adding multiple parties to your network extends that challenge as each new network member needs to install software, create new security certificates or private keys, manually provision hardware, and configure networking to support the network. In addition, once a blockchain network is online, the developers have the additional task of monitoring for increased transaction requests, new members joining, and infrastructure health. Amazon Managed Blockchain streamlines this process and reduces the technical overhead. The network can scale, adapting to increased load and transaction volume. In addition, new members can join the cloud with ease without needing any special hardware.

Ease of Setup (taken from Amazon Managed Blockchain documentation)

In the Managed Blockchain offering, launching a new network can be done via templates within minutes, without the need for extensive configuration. After the network is available, new members can join the network with an invite. Once a new member accepts membership, they can configure peer nodes that provide computational storage and memory to execute DApps and maintain a copy of the ledger, all in the cloud. This bypasses the need for any local hardware throughout the process. During periods of heavy transaction load and network traffic, scaling an application simply requires additional peer nodes to be added. New peer nodes can be provisioned within the cloud network with ease. New nodes can be instantiated to support your increased workload via a variety of instance families pre-configured into AWS Cloud Services.

Security (taken from Amazon Managed Blockchain documentation)

Managing private–public keys is crucial for blockchain-based platforms. The keys are needed for accessing your wallet on a blockchain instance, signing contracts, and enrolling in security certificates and identity management. Managed Blockchain relies on AWS Key Management Service to act as the certificate authority for Hyperledger Fabric. To that end, new users signing onto a Managed Blockchain will not have to worry about setting up hardware security modules.

Immutable Ordering Service (taken from Amazon Managed Blockchain docs)

The default ordering service for Hyperledger Fabric to support propagation of transactions across the network is Apache Kafka. Even though Kafka is a messaging service that delivers transactions (and the associated information) sequentially across the network, it is not optimized to create a sequential log of transactional history. Therefore, in case of network failure, Kafka makes it difficult to retrieve historical transactions. Managed Blockchain has a new ordering service built on Quantum Ledger Database (QLDB) that provides an immutable log and maintains a complete network history of all uncommitted transactions in a blockchain network. This QLDB service uses a centralized trusted authority for maintaining histories and supplements the decentralized ledger.

Oracle

Permissioned blockchain networks begin with a few core-member organizations, and network governance is easier; however, as the organization starts to expand with new members, fair allocation of underlying hardware resources becomes more intricate and complex. This is particularly true in the context of ordering responsibilities and selecting members for private channels in Fabric implementations. Recall that a set of ordering nodes bundles current transactions into blocks, finalizes the block, and broadcasts a block to the network. Under an older consensus implementation, a leader is selected at random from the global pool of ordering nodes for creating the next block. The orderers also maintain a list of organizations that are allowed to create private channels.

A channel is created by an ordering node, and it functions as a private subnet on the Fabric blockchain where network members can conduct private and confidential transactions. In the past, a cluster of Kafka and Zookeeper implementations was managing the ordering nodes; however, in the cloud, this setup is more resource intensive. Recently, a new consensus plugin called RAFT was introduced to manage the ordering service and make it ready for enterprise-grade production networks. RAFT is a dynamic leader-based protocol where a set of ordering nodes (called the consenter set) cooperates in an ordering cluster to create blocks. This ensures a more fair and uniform participation of member organizations, even with a large number of members. Additionally, an ordering cluster is configured such that it provides enhanced privacy: any node from the ordering cluster can create a channel with specific member organizations to handle a specific private transaction. This allows more granular control over transaction volume by selecting from specific members, rather than using a global ordering queue. Using RAFT also streamlines computational resource usage by eliminating the need for a resource-intensive cluster in the cloud. Next, we will talk about the main features of Oracle BaaS from three major categories: infrastructure maintenance, identity, and backups.

Maintenance (taken from Oracle Support Documentation)

- Includes Oracle operations monitoring

- Has zero downtime managed patching and updates

- Includes embedded ledger and configuration backups

- Provides a comprehensive, intuitive web user interface and wizards to automate many administration tasks. For example, adding organizations to the network, adding new nodes, creating new channels, deploying and instantiating chaincodes, browsing the ledger, and more.

Identity (taken from Oracle Support Documentation)

- Supports identity federation and third-party client certificate support to enable consortia formation and simplify member onboarding

- Built-in integration with Oracle Identity Cloud Service for user authentication, roles management, and identity federation immediately leverages Oracle Identity Cloud Service accounts and enables easy onboarding of consortium members who prefer using SAML-based federation for authentication against their own identity providers

Backups (taken from Oracle Support Documentation)

- Peer-node containers distributed across multiple VMs to ensure resiliency if one of the VMs is unavailable or is being patched

- Orderers, fabric-ca, console, and REST proxy nodes are replicated in all VMs for transparent takeover to avoid outages.

- Isolated VM environments for customer chaincode execution containers for greater security and stability

- Autonomous monitoring and recovery agents in all components, leveraging dynamic object store backups of all configuration updates and ledger blocks to enable autonomous recovery

Kaleido

Kaleido is a ConsenSys-backed startup that has created two major blockchain offerings: an Ethereum-based software package that can run on Amazon Cloud to simplify development of blockchain applications, and a fully managed Blockchain-as-a-Service cloud called Kaleido Core. There are two main facets to Kaleido that we will discuss in this section.

Network Governance (taken from Kaleido blog on BaaS)

In the managed Kaleido service, a major theme is the creation of templates dedicated to common governance tasks and the provision of them to users through a simple UI. This includes a new-member onboarding workflow that can set up new members and peer-nodes with a few clicks. In addition, once the new members are on-boarded and familiar with the network, they have ownership of their node and key data. This allows for more granular control over node settings and flexibility in opting out of optional network features. Kaleido also provides a network-wide address book that lists all the users and their affiliations (within the consortia) and access permissions. For a more transparent history of transactions and network activity, a standard block explorer and token explorer for the ledger running in BaaS are also included. Finally, a native smart-contract manager is embedded into network governance. This includes common smart-contract tasks such as workflow for security tasks, firewall protection, versioning, and contract deployment to a ledger.

High Availablility and Disaster Recovery (taken from Kaleido blog on BaaS)

A blockchain network hosted in the cloud needs to be adaptive so that spikes in traffic or transaction load can be handled without the network going offline. To that end, high availability is crucial for the consensus algorithms, especially in a decentralized network. This is especially important for provisioning new nodes; for instance, if five new nodes join a network, they should be dynamically added to the consensus algorithm in order to prevent overload on the network. Kaleido's Managed Blockchain also comes with network protections against new/untested consensus algorithms in order to provide some level of disaster recovery support. In the near future, this will allow developers to deploy and hot-switch new consensus algorithms and collect data on how the algorithm behaves during a period of high transaction volume.

Summary

In this chapter, we reviewed the basic concept of a Blockchain-as-a-Service platform and talked about four major platforms. We discussed the main features of each offering, the managed support given by each provider, and opportunities for blockchain companies to grow completely in the cloud.

References

The main references for this chapter were based on developer documentation from Microsoft Azure Blockchain docs (`https://azure.microsoft.com/en-us/solutions/blockchain/`), Blockchain AWS docs (`https://aws.amazon.com/blockchain/`), Oracle Platform docs (`https://www.oracle.com/application-development/cloud-services/blockchain-platform/`), and Kaleido docs (`https://docs.kaleido.io/`).

CHAPTER 15

Rise of Blockchain Consortia

This chapter is transcribed from a conversation between Vikram Dhillon (VD) and Katherine Kuzmeskas (KK) from Tamarin Health on her journey of creating a blockchain company, the challenges faced on the way, the evolving nature of consortia, and the future of her company.

VD: *What were the main customer pain points that you were trying to solve with the company? How did this evolve with time? What roles did the blockchain play in all of this? Can you give us some kind of a timeline?*

KK: When we first started, we were focusing on value-based care. This is an area of healthcare where physicians are being reimbursed for the outcomes they provide as opposed to the volume of services they provide. This has been around since 2008, originally started by Medicare (through Centers for Medicare & Medicaid Services [CMS]), then private payers followed the lead. I learned about value-based care by being a hospital administrator at Yale New Haven Health, and while I was there I needed better tools to manage patients once they physically left the hospital (or, put differently, post-discharge management). This is very challenging because once a patient leaves the hospital, their data is largely inaccessible, and new health data generated from follow-ups sits in silos created by a myriad of clinical applications that are not interoperable. We wanted to be the longitudinal connector of the patient, their care, and their data. As a connector, we have access to data on patient care, regardless of clinical location, that provides information for our provider customers and us to act on, and provides real-time estimates of savings or penalties based on the target price that CMS sets. The target price is basically the total cost of allowable reimbursement by Medicare; as a result, this is the total cost of care [that] providers should stay below.

© Vikram Dhillon, David Metcalf, and Max Hooper 2021
V. Dhillon et al., *Blockchain Enabled Applications*, https://doi.org/10.1007/978-1-4842-6534-5_15

We came out of the gate with this idea when we were incorporated in early 2017. The blockchain connection initially began as a way to create an audit trail of all the longitudinal data in our platform. Ever since we defined how we were going to leverage blockchain in 2016, our focus was to intentionally start with a simple and basic implementation of blockchain: an audit trial for transition-of-care information and insurance reimbursement for value-based care that occurs across different settings. Once this audit trail is created, it cannot be deleted or modified, and this is really important in value-based care because the patient is transitioning between different practices, data sits in different locations, and the only entity up until now that had this complete view was Medicare via its claims data. Looking back to reconcile the care of the patient can be very difficult if you cannot trust or validate the sources of information. We wanted to solve this problem of connecting the patient through[out] their care and providing an immutable audit trail of the data, improving the reliability and trust in the data. Plans were always centered around growing features after proving this core concept. We wanted to test our foundation in the market, and once blockchain technology became more scalable, [and] broadly adopted, and people became more comfortable with it, we could grow, and the opportunities become endless with use in healthcare.

Along with the audit trail, we have always been focused on providing the ability to govern access to data in a meaningful manner through a public–private keypair system. These two concepts, an audit trail and public–private keypair system, have guided our growth through value-based care toward our future, where patients can share their data via simple clicks and benefit from it.

In addition to allowing patients to govern access to their data, another area of interest for us is insurance reimbursement. Many value-based-care programs are presently retroactive, meaning you look back to reimburse, but with blockchain, you can make this system prospective. While there will still be human processes needed, there are exceptional efficiencies we can create for the system, including leveraging smart contracts to distribute funds automatically. With our base foundation Health Nexus (a healthcare safe blockchain protocol), the keypair system that governs access to data, and all the smart contracts that we can build on top of our Health Nexus protocol, more prospective value-based-care programs may be possible in the not-too-distant future.

Editor's Note   Healthcare-specific applications that interface with a blockchain are subject to a rapidly changing regulatory landscape, which makes the discussion very challenging. The authors are sharing their viewpoints here in a purely academic manner.

The evolution in our approach accelerated during the early phase of COVID-19. Once the pandemic started, I became nervous about how value-based patient care would be impacted in regards to hospital admissions due to COVID-related strain on healthcare facilities. Eventually, I made a very difficult decision to withdraw from the Medicare program. My reasoning behind this pivot was rooted in the delay in communication from CMS, and based on how the CMS value-based care systems are set up—specifically bundled payments, which is the main program we support. Presently, a physician provider is responsible for the care of a patient over a ninety-day period after discharge from the hospital regardless of where the patient goes, and largely regardless of what happens to the patient. There are very few exceptions to this ninety-day patient care cost bucket. For example, any readmission during the ninety-day period can result in a penalty if the cost of the readmission pushes the total cost of care over the target price. Meaning, if a patient came to the hospital for a hip replacement, and then had a fall leading to a fracture in the arm within the ninety-day period, the cost of the arm fracture falls into the total cost of care for the *hip fracture*—even though they are unrelated. This is not an ideal situation, and certainly not ideal in a pandemic situation where patients developed severe complications such as pneumonia, cardiac issues, or were put on ventilators.

To give a timeline: The first public health emergency was January 31; by March 13 the White House declared a federal emergency; on March 18, Medicare declared that all elective cases should be postponed so that physicians [could] remain focused on COVID-19 cases and emergency care. In a non-pandemic setting, value-based care roughly operates similar to an insurance program, where the elective cases done by a hospital system can provide reimbursement to balance out high-cost emergent cases. This pandemic shifted the dynamics of reimbursement because of the near sole focus on high-cost critical care, extended hospital stays, and strained healthcare resources. Despite the timeline above and the struggle that all physicians were going through, Medicare provided no guidance until June 28. Earlier guidance was limited to Medicare saying they [were] working on something and would release it "soon."

When I made the decision to pause our Medicare value-based-care focus, I looked at our technology stack more critically. We had an existing platform where we could follow individuals as they transitioned through different modalities of care and tracked their records. So, we began to focus on how we [could] help employers across any industry gather safely during the reopening phases of [the] COVID-19 pandemic. Our platform is able to consolidate external sources of information such as those through health surveys, testing coordination, and general public health awareness/knowledge. Blockchain continues to play a key role with the very simple, intentional audit trail that can be a necessary resource for liability protection and reimbursement. The information we gather on our platform, from symptom surveys to test results, is hashed and becomes a part of the audit trail. In the same way that our platform tracked patients through different modalities of value-based care, an employer can use our new service for data collection to verify that an employee completed a survey and attested to what they put in the survey; as a result, the employees can safely gather in accordance with public health guidelines. Additionally, business owners can document the safety of their workplace from a liability standpoint. Having an audit trail that verifies data reduces the burden of regulatory compliance. That's where we are now.

This shift accelerated our evolution to another significant component of our company vision: user-owned health profiles. Since 2017, we have created a platform where healthcare data flows seamlessly between parties, a network of high-performing, value-based-care-focused physicians, and now a network of user-owned health profiles. Every user owns their healthcare information and carries it, from basic health information to more complex data such as procedures and medications. Over time, the value of the data grows and the user is able to contribute it to our data marketplace, also a key component of the growing ecosystem. With this infrastructure, you will be able to find healthcare providers and services that are dedicated solely to value-based care, you will derive value from your data, and the opportunities are endless in finding ways to create a self-sustaining, value-based-focused ecosystem.

Up next in our user-owned health profiles is adding gamification. For the COVID-19 focus, gamification rewards what will become mundane but required safety protocols such as daily symptom surveys. We will start first with gift cards, but our long-term goal is to tokenize the system, since the base infrastructure is Health Nexus, which requires node runners and validators. The whole idea with tokenization is to incentivize group behavior for providers and patients in this new ecosystem. Because tokens can only be used within the system, this is how the ecosystem will be self-sustaining over time.

However, this gets very tricky due to the current regulatory environment; any discussion of tokenization becomes an expensive and lengthy process with the SEC. Pocketful of Quarters, an organization attempting blockchain gaming with tokens, already experienced this in their more-than-a-year-long discussion with the SEC to obtain a No Action Letter, which allowed them to launch their network. Healthcare is already laden with regulations; introducing blockchain and tokens only adds another layer of complexity, and, while doable, will take time and significant expense.

Note   The tokenization concept is near impossible in the current legal environment. Pocketful of Quarters has demonstrated that launching a network is possible. But not without significant cost and time. Tokenization as globally understood in concept is very different from what is currently possible in the United States.

VD: The core of this chapter is about your consortium model. Tell us more about the proposal for the consortium. Why was it optimal to choose the consortium route? What benefits would members receive in a consortium model?

KK: As you know, we created Health Nexus, which is a public–private healthcare-safe blockchain protocol. *Public* meaning you don't have to be part of the consortium to access the blockchain network. The private side is more involved. There are two requirements in order to run a node on the network: you have to be an approved and authenticated consortium member, and additionally, you have to run a HIPAA-compliant server.

There are very practical reasons that we took this route. Blockchain is a new technology, and you have to educate IT-security teams along with C-suite executives that even though you are offering a blockchain-based tool, your technology is safe. Ultimately, you will have to explain what decentralization means, and your customers must be comfortable with your system. If your customers are not able to understand the benefit of a decentralized protocol or the safety and security of how health data interacts with the infrastructure, there is no way to secure customers. The learning curve to understanding blockchain at a fundamental level is so steep that lack of trust in [the] network becomes a non-starter in many industries, but particularly in healthcare. Teaching the basics of a blockchain leads to questions about the servers. If you mention that a server can be anywhere in the world, you have to be able to explain—in a way that is comprehensible by your customer—why that is not a security risk.

As such, current perceptions of existing decentralized blockchain protocols drove our decision to create Health Nexus. Bitcoin has always had legislative and perception challenges, particularly with a history of Bitcoin exchanges linked to Silk Road activities. Trying to build healthcare applications on a platform linked to historic illegal activity is already a non-starter—it makes conversations with the customer's decision makers impossible. Ethereum is a public model in the truest sense: any user, anywhere in the world, from any country can run a node. We expected that any company that builds on top of our protocol will have to answer questions from healthcare ITS departments about who runs the network. An answer of "I am not sure" or "It looks like folks in other countries"—including those on the Federal Sanctions List—creates a non-starter, which would be the case with Ethereum. In addition, the need to explain this in depth to the ITS department will extend the already long sales cycle for healthcare applications. Again, both of these issues are perception based, but that alone is the issue affecting adoption. Having to explain away Silk Road or servers in countries that are on our OFAC Sanction list adds unnecessary complexity.

Being able to describe a network of known-node runners who are required to maintain a HIPAA-compliant server to run a governance-based blockchain speaks more of the healthcare language than Bitcoin or Ethereum can; thus, the core infrastructure and design of Health Nexus. There are two aspects to the private interface on our network: no one can access your healthcare data without your private key, and secondly, we know who runs the nodes in our network. The servers are all HIPAA-compliant, and your PHI-protected data is not hosted on the blockchain itself. We only use the ledger for propagating metadata links in blocks and [for] transactions that can only be decrypted with a private key. You come to a level ground on this protocol. That's why we call it "healthcare safe."

The reason we took a consortium route is to create this public–private interface. We wanted to create a public network, but it could not be completely permissionless. So, we designed a validation process where anyone who runs the network can validate and verify that potential consortium members are indeed running a HIPAA-compliant server. You can charge a fee for this service, the same way any HIPAA-compliant company pays someone quarterly to test their systems and maintain their HIPAA compliance.

There are technical requirements for becoming a consortium member, and the validation process is two-dimensional: you have to be validated at first by a current consortium member (validator), and then you have to be voted in. New members go through a formal voting process involving the entire consortium and must keep their node available at all times. For the voting process, new members have to describe why they want to join the consortium, their past experiences in blockchain and healthcare, and their interests and commitment to maintaining their role as a consortium member. Then, the consortium votes whether or not to bring new members on board. All members have equal voting privileges, including our company, and the vote is stored on-chain for all member-related actions. To that end, any members can be kicked out for being malicious, and there is a low threshold for tolerating risky actions or inactivity. In the past, through vote, we removed a consortium member due to inactivity. This process ingrains governance into consortia blockchain, and also helps to maintain the protective nature of healthcare entities. This governance process is shown below in Figure 15-1.

VD: *Overall, building a blockchain company is difficult, but you managed to overcome several hurdles. What were the major challenges? How was the fundraising process? Tell us about the NSF grant that you received. Any new features or ideas that you're very excited about?*

KK: It was surprisingly easy to find our early consortium members, as we already had a large network to reach out to. The hardest part has been keeping members engaged (i.e., mining) without a monetary benefit that exists in other, grandfathered blockchain networks such as Ethereum. Even though our technology has been ready since fall 2017, we have only been able to launch our test net due to the expensive and lengthy SEC process that will be necessary for [the] main net launch. We are grateful that, up to now, some members have been running our network out of the goodness of their heart and because of their dedication to blockchain's long-term impact in healthcare. Unfortunately, at this time true blockchain applications in healthcare are very difficult in the US, particularly due to the legislative climate. The necessary shifting in policy will create a more open environment for digital assets across all industries.

Interestingly, in 2020, everyone is excited about DeFi, so it feels like blockchain is "popular" again and we can actually talk about blockchain. From 2018 to 2019, nearly everyone denounced blockchain tech. Innovating in healthcare is very challenging, but innovating with a new technology such as blockchain in healthcare is even harder. We have found success precisely in our strategic focus on keeping the technology as simple as possible (a basic audit trail to start) and building in a way to create a safe adoption for healthcare (focus on a public–private protocol and emphasis on governance).

With regard to fundraising, of course it has been challenging, but particularly due to systemic biases that drive decision making. Right now, women receive only 3 percent of all fundraising dollars. In comparison, WeWork received more investment funds than all the female founders combined in 2019, and we all saw how that turned out. Fundraising can be an uphill battle, and is increasingly more challenging depending on your gender, race, and ethnicity. While we did manage to get the investment we needed in 2017, it was an arduous journey.

However, through grants and loans, the federal government has been much more supportive in funding our company than investors. Specifically, we received a highly competitive Phase I Small Business Technology Transfer (STTR) grant from the National Science Foundation for our research implementation of Graphene on our Health Nexus protocol. Our university partners were Dr. Brian Levine and his postdoc student Dr. George Bissias of the University of Massachusetts–Amherst. Dr. Levine is the director of the Cybersecurity Institute in the `College of Information & Computer Sciences`, where he focuses on security in the context of the internet and mobile systems, including child rescue, privacy, blockchains, cellular networks, and peer-to-peer networking. Drs. Levine and Bissias had successfully implemented Graphene on the Bitcoin blockchain. Our goal, which we achieved, was to similarly leverage this block propagation technology on Health Nexus to compress block size, improving blockchain performance. As the industry continues to wrestle with the complexities of decentralized systems such as speed, energy consumption, and efficiency (including cost), we are proud to have proven that Graphene is an effective tool in making a blockchain more efficient. Using the least amount of bandwidth and latency as possible has numerous advantages for a decentralized blockchain, and we are confident [it] will contribute to necessary innovation and efficiency in healthcare.

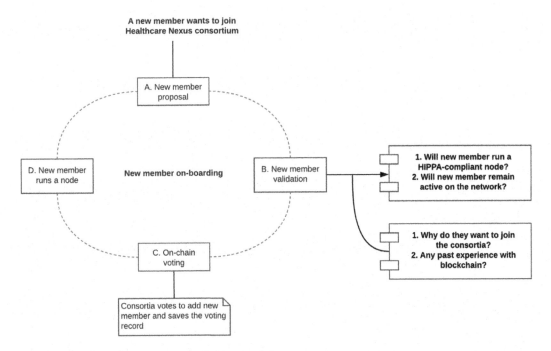

Figure 15-1. *Governance cycle in Health Nexus*

CHAPTER 16

The Art of the Newly Possible: Transforming Health with Emerging Technology and Federated Learning

This chapter is derived from a presentation, "The Art of the Newly Possible: How 5 Emerging Technologies Will Transform Health," delivered by the authors (Heather Flannery, Jonathon Passerat-Palmbah PhD, and Sean T. Manion, and edited by Vikram Dhillon) at the online ConsenSys Health COVID-19 Veterans Health Summit on August 26, 2020.

Introduction

Not since the dawn of the commercial internet have we experienced such a viable convergence of disruptive and transforming technologies as we do now in the world of healthcare. Our earliest attempts to revolutionize healthcare technology, unfortunately, were not fully inclusive, leaving providers, patients, and payers in an increasingly dire situation. We ended up with a massive digital divide with a worsening of disparities, a crisis in physician suicide due to the dehumanization of the art of medicine, and an array of other global problems. For the first time, we have innovations—with extraordinary positive potential for humanity—as significant as the obviously hypothetical,

345

simultaneous debut of the Gutenberg printing press, the steam engine, the integrated circuit, and the internet. Of course, as with any disruptive technology, extraordinary risks and reasons for circumspection and ethically intentional consideration are paramount as we approach these changes that can transform healthcare. The overture to a new era is playing, and the time is now.

This transformation of healthcare is an achievable reality through the implementation of three key areas of technology:

1. **Blockchain** – including optional **tokenization**

2. **Decentralized Artificial Intelligence (AI)** – primarily **machine learning**

3. **Privacy-in-Depth** – including **zero-knowledge cryptography** and **verifiable and confidential computing**

The largest healthcare enterprises in the world have been working on applied R&D, experimentation, planning, and business development regarding new models of blockchain technology in recent years. For example, the Synaptic Health Alliance was announced in April 2018 as a blockchain-focused healthcare industry consortium that includes industry leaders such as United Healthcare, Optum, Quest Diagnostics, Aetna, and other key stakeholders. The Synaptic Health Alliance has led the way not only in technology implementation but also in methods of governance, methods of capital formation, and methods of examining how different aspects of what we do in our industry can be removed from the basis of competition and mutualized.

Blockchain and Tokenization

Blockchain is more than a technology. It is a technology that exists simultaneously at multiple layers of the engineering stack as well as an innovation in the arena of behavioral economics. It has created a new discipline: applied behavioral economics in real time. It is a brand new opportunity to express game-theory principles, form hypotheses, and test the way that different incentive designs inform stakeholder groups in healthcare along with every other industry it touches.

Structurally, it opens the door to new business models that have never been logistically possible before and, therefore, have never been meaningfully considered. And, it introduces radical new levels of personal identity or self-sovereignty, including the potential for credentials or verifications about who you are, your data, and data about you. All of these things are made possible by blockchain. Blockchain exists in the form of networks. Those networks can be public resources, public infrastructures, and neutral platforms like the Ethereum main net or the Bitcoin blockchain. The Ethereum main net can run software that can focus on any kind of application—not only digital money, but any sort of software application.

Compared to public blockchain networks, private blockchain networks have completely different characteristics, though some of the same benefits along with several trade-offs. Looking to the future of blockchain in the healthcare industry, it seems likely that our end state will be an array of hybrid networks—lots of private enterprise networks that are bridged, or tethered, through a single neutral public infrastructure.

Another defining characteristic of blockchain, particularly newer blockchain platforms like Ethereum and others, is the ability to execute and run smart contracts: cryptographically stored and cryptographically verified stored procedures expressed as microservices that run on a blockchain infrastructure. These smart contracts are key because they facilitate secure automation across organizational boundaries. For the last thirty years, most of the focus of enterprise computer engineering work has been looking inward into the four walls of any given enterprise. For the first time, this distributed smart contract infrastructure allows the use of the same kinds of principles for automation and efficiency gains at an ecosystem level, providing technology that can actually deliver the goods for the future of healthcare.

In addition, blockchain provides for digital scarcity from an economics and behavioral economics perspective. In our current legacy data environment, there is no scarcity because data can be infinitely copied. This endless copying continues to expand the disk space required for storage and creates governance difficulties. Through tokenization—either tokenization of single items like something with a serial number or tokenization of units that are replicable like a cryptocurrency, a certificate, or things with a value of any kind—scarcity can be created for actual transactions with established units of value.

One of the most appealing things about blockchain is that a user will not be aware that the technology is "running" in the background to exchange and manage data. Along with a human design–focused and streamlined user experience and interface, frontend Web 3.0 applications, and decentralized apps, a user would never know that the background is any different. Some of the things that a public blockchain delivers, particularly transparency and decentralization, are traded off when implemented as private blockchain networks. What is gained is extreme privacy.

New technologies facilitate off-chain computation and storage to enable aspects of both transparency and privacy in a common infrastructure. When selecting from hundreds of different architectural patterns, dozens of blockchain protocols—public, private, and hybrid—there is always a trade-off between three criteria: 1) scalability of the system; 2) its cybersecurity posture; and 3) the degree to which it is decentralized or centrally controlled. It is possible to correct for any two as architectural patterns are formed.

Blockchain technology is necessary but not sufficient for the healthcare industry. There are additional important areas where the unique requirements of health can be greatly enhanced with this technology, including compliance, the unique cybersecurity environment, the unique privacy environment, and the challenges we have with identity of patients, providers, and devices. All of this also requires a clear eye toward bioethics of health. So, more than blockchain is required for the desired outcome.

Decentralized Artificial Intelligence (AI)

Currently, machine learning, which makes up the bulk of the current artificial intelligence applications in healthcare, is accomplished by 1) putting a lot of data together in a central place to curate it; 2) running analytics on the data sets; and 3) eventually training extremely complicated machine learning models. As an example of when this is a reasonable proposition and scalable, consider data from your phone. Your phone data is pooled together with others' data in a single place to learn, for example, how to better predict next words on the keyboard of your smartphone. Then, once a new predictive model is ready, this improved model is pushed back to your phone. Inherently, the assumption is made either that the data pulled together in a central data lake is not too sensitive or that you are okay with sharing your data with the central entity. Obviously, this is not the case with health data, so the centralized model does not work as well in healthcare. With the decentralized model, the difference is that instead of bringing the data to the model, the model is delivered to the data, so the data does not travel anymore—it remains at rest.

In the decentralized approach, we send models to each of the locations where the data lives. It can be a mobile phone or larger data lakes owned by institutions. For example, if data is owned by different clinical institutions, a unique learning model can be developed at each of these institutions; they will basically each train their own model. Then, the key to machine learning is to combine the knowledge that has been learned at each of these institutions (or sites or devices) into a single new joint model. So, in the future, you will not need to consider how to gather data into a central location for storage and access; you will instead deploy a machine learning model to the network and receive back derived data.

So, why is this important? For starters, if it's my personal data we are considering, a lot can happen with my data once it's copied and whisked off out of my control. If it's at rest within my system, or within my phone, I have more control. That peace-of-mind aspect is important to the consumer and the general public when you consider the constant stream of data breaches that show no sign of abating. Further, by leaving the data where it is, you suppress copies and introduce digital scarcity. Combined with blockchain, that's all you need to create a decentralized marketplace. If data threats could be significantly decreased with a decentralized system that is still able to deliver the value of advanced knowledge that can only come from the extensive data analytics of many data sets, health and healthcare as we know it will be transformed.

An additional benefit of combining blockchain with machine learning, even in centralized machine learning models, involves sourcing and training data to have the cryptographically verified provenance of every data element that is ultimately included in a training set. That can go a long way toward resolving explainability problems and other long-standing issues with being able to source training data, understand where it came from, and determine whether the data itself was corrupted. Decentralizing the learning function and decentralizing the sourcing of training data is low-hanging fruit and represents a huge incremental benefit when conducting learning on decentralized data. Therefore, the convergence of blockchain infrastructures with decentralized machine learning approaches is absolutely necessary.

This may be news, but the ability to conduct decentralized machine learning has existed for quite some time. However, it has yet to be embraced by the healthcare industry because it has lacked the appropriate incentives. By integrating blockchain with these decentralized AI tactics for training models, we are able to connect incentives and to know conclusively exactly what permissions are granted, by whom, to do exactly what, for how long, etc. The combination of these technologies will be transformative for advancing healthcare.

Privacy in Depth

"Any sufficiently advanced technology is indistinguishable from magic."

—Arthur C. Clarke's Third Law

How do we ensure privacy and security? It's the question on everyone's mind when we are considering health data. It turns out that there is a family of advanced cryptographic privacy-preserving techniques that are being utilized in new ways that will have a profound impact on personal health information and regulatory compliance in healthcare and life sciences. A prime example of this is **zero-knowledge proofs** (ZKPs). It would take multiple chapters of another book to go over ZKPs and these other privacy-in-depth techniques in detail. So, from a high level, here is a brief look at ZKPs and how they are substantially different from standard legacy cryptographic models or methods that are generally used today.

ZKP cryptography has been around for thirty years, but it is getting extra traction in recent years, especially as it relates to blockchain. What ZKPs do is allow you to prove that a statement is correct and true without revealing the statement that is at the heart of the confirmation. Its value is to prove that you know something that you want to keep secret, and to convince another party or the rest of the network that you do actually know the secret, but without actually revealing the secret.

As a real-world example, think about your birthdate as a data element and all the times you have to enter your birthdate in order to demonstrate your age, for whatever reason. In a world where ZKP cryptography was brought to global industrial scale, the data elements of your birthday would almost never need to be transferred. Instead, a cryptographic proof that your birthday was higher than or lower than or within the decade of the birthday requirement—yes or no—would be all that the other system would store. The month, day, and year of your birthday would remain at rest. That is just one simple example. If you imagine all the data that is involved in clinical, scientific, and business workflows in our industry, ZKP cryptography, along with the rest of the family of privacy-in-depth cryptography, has endless applications.

Why and how are these advanced cryptographic privacy-preserving techniques used in the context of this whole stack we are describing? First, they add more authenticity to the shared derived data. For example, imagine that a patient, Alice, must use a remote private inference service that screens patients prior to scheduling a consultation with a very busy specialist named Bob. Bob's policy implies that the secure inference service returns a prediction with a probability greater than 80 percent in order to book an appointment with him. When Alice gets the prediction back, it's been encrypted such that she's the only person who can decrypt it. Now Alice wants to present her diagnosis to Bob to request an appointment. How can Bob be certain that the prediction Alice is presenting has indeed been obtained from the secure inference prediction service? There is no way to do that *unless* Alice can provide a cryptographic proof that the prediction value actually came from the specified inference service. In ZKP terms, this means proving that the plaintext prediction sent by Alice to Bob corresponds to the encrypted content she received from the service. Not only does Alice send the prediction to Bob, but she also adds a ZKP of the correct decryption alongside the prediction number. Note that the whole process never revealed Alice's input healthcare data in plaintext to the prediction service or to Bob.

Along with privacy-in-depth, there's one other important aspect, and that's the notion of secure inference. Inference is the function of a machine learning model making a prediction. After a model has been trained and is doing what it's meant to do, it is theoretically making a prediction that might guide clinical decision making. It might guide patient behavior. It might guide access to care. It might guide anything where these technologies are implemented in our industry. It is critical that the resulting data can not be reverse engineered or inappropriately used to derive information about the data's origin or source. Only the intended inference is produced by the model.

For those who wish to research these three technologies further, consider the following:

- **Blockchain**

    - Decentralized Apps ("DApps") – *Web3 User Experience*

    - Optional Tokenization – *Creating Digital Scarcity*

    - Smart Contracts – *Secure Automation Across Organizational Boundaries*

    - Blockchain Networks – *Public, Private, and Hybrid*

- **Decentralized AI**

    - Federated learning in blockchain networks

    - New paradigms in training data provenance, incentivization, and secure inference

    - Intelligent agent-based simulation and automation

- **Privacy-in-Depth**

    - Zero-Knowledge Proof Cryptography (ZKPs)

    - Trusted Execution Environments (TEEs)

    - Secure Encrypted Virtualization (SEV)

    - Verifiable Computation

    - Secure Multi-Party Computation

    - Blind Computation

    - Differential Privacy

    - Homomorphic Encryption

    - Quantum-Resistant Encryption

Source and Derived Health Data

Now that we've had a high-level discussion of these three game-changing technologies, let's consider a paradigm shift in value creation—moving copies of data is no longer the *only* way to create value from data.

In health, source data is enterprise data that lives behind firewalls, or the patient's self-sovereign data, the volume of which has been exploding in scale. Source data in health has been expanding exponentially for the last fifteen years, and this will continue with the widespread availability of 5G wireless connectivity, the internet of medical things, and the growing understanding of social determinant data *as health data*. Currently, most of our strategies have to do with copying and moving source data from place to place: trying to centralize larger and larger bodies of source data.

Let's define **source data**:

1. **Enterprise** data is behind firewalls – *at rest,* not *in motion*

2. **Patient** self-sovereign data – *within cloud storage infrastructures or at the edge on devices*

Source data has been **expanding exponentially** for the last fifteen years. As **data** grows, we are reaching the logistic extremes of data lakes and other centralization strategies. The statistics demonstrate the magnitude:

- 1100 Terabytes (TB) per lifetime of exogenous data (behavior, socioeconomic, environmental, etc.) representing roughly 60 percent of the determinants of an individual's health

- 6 TB per lifetime of genomics/epigenomics data representing roughly 30 percent of the determinants of an individual's health

- 0.4 TB per lifetime of clinical data representing roughly 10 percent of the determinants of an individual's health

Another consideration is associated metadata, which are descriptions of the source data. Finally, there is the product of the attempts to create value out of source data, which we call derived data, composed of analytical findings and insights. As such, the current centralized system is a sunsetting paradigm. It is slow, labor intensive, error prone, and untrusted. Decentralization with a blockchain framework is the emerging paradigm. It will be rapid, automated, quality controlled, and trusted.

Today, we have to copy and move data everywhere. Analysis can only be performed on that of which we can secure custody. Often, we make compromises by de-identifying data, which introduces a huge spectrum of new challenges and risks. In this emerging paradigm source, data will be able to remain at rest in enterprise infrastructures or in patient self-sovereign infrastructures. Most of the time, it will become the exception instead of the rule that the data has to be exchanged for a workflow to occur. Analysis will frequently be performed in federated analytics models across network participants and the source data. Further, source data will be able to remain fully identified and clinically actionable without ever exposing it, sharing it, or transferring ownership.

In this new paradigm, normalization and analysis will change substantially. Normalization will occur by distributing rule sets and automating that normalization: operating on the data where it resides at its source. The analysis will be also performed where it resides at its source, and only that derived data will be shared. The aggregated findings will be shareable and, importantly, also cryptographically verified.

The new paradigm is a shift to a new person-centered health data architecture as part of this healthcare industry transformation. This includes five architectural components, all of which are interdependent and necessary:

1. The individual's self-sovereign identity

2.   The individual's verifiable credentials

3.   The diametric workflows that connect the individual represented
to the physical person it represents

4.   A self-sovereign data lake where all of an individual's data can be
brought together—and where N equals one, for that individual
alone, so that it is not a giant target for hackers.

5.   Finally, the ability to transact with a tokenized value, to earn, to
trade, and to hold all forms of a tokenized value

All of this will require privacy-preserving technologies, primarily for health-focused, decentralized machine learning. This is what we call **federated learning**.

Federated Learning

What does it look like to combine federated or decentralized machine learning with a blockchain infrastructure and privacy-in-depth? What is the heart of the value proposition for doing that technically? The synergy between blockchain and decentralized AI comes into play as we implement access control and content management of data, including data sharing. This is merely the low-hanging fruit for initial implementation.

If we just manage consent and access on the blockchain, but still rely on the old primitives of moving data around, we come back to the paradigm of copying and creating multiple copies of data. And, therein lies the problem of not being able to create digital scarcity. As such, we are unable to increase the value of the data, but we do increase its vulnerability. For example, we become the victims of data breaches that are totally out of our control—even though we have recorded our access—and have been denied specific access to our own data.

If you could access data in a decentralized model—as opposed to our strategies today, where sourcing training data is the single greatest inhibitor to performing machine learning functions—greater use of the data would be possible. The reality is that it is very difficult for data scientists and machine learning practitioners to obtain the data they need to create models. In this decentralized approach, we can turn the scarcity and the behavioral economics of that dynamic completely upside-down and gain/allow access to vast datasets without ever having to centralize them. Could this make a difference in the amount of total data available and the degree to which we could trust that data and its provenance in this new blockchain-facilitated decentralized AI?

If you look at most of the studies that are being run on healthcare data, it is rare to reach very large scales in terms of data, unless we are speaking of very carefully crafted datasets, and that is a complex and costly endeavor to put into place. Whereas, if you flip the paradigm around, everyone is able to contribute their personal data, healthcare data, or data that is only secondarily related to their health. You could contribute data from, for example, smartphone applications that receive requests from a clinical trial project. In this example, the project would be just using your data and not transferring your data, or owning your data, or being aware of its content while it's being used. It is only giving the project/party permission to use it. That party cannot see it, doesn't know what it is, and is never going to know what it is. This will create an incentive to come back and request more data to be used—and only that which is needed—instead of accumulating and stashing all of the data somewhere on an infrastructure—maybe securely and maybe not—with the hope of potentially using it someday.

We are shifting away from the old logic, which goes something like this:

- You can rarely monetize your data.

- Monetizing your data requires that you literally sell your data once and for all.

- Use of your data involves creating a whole new copy.

So, what we are discussing here with all this decentralization business is switching from data selling to data lending/leasing, and only providing the key elements.

Along with privacy-in-depth, there's one other important aspect, and that's the notion of secure inference. Inference is the function of a machine learning model making a prediction. After a model has been trained and is doing what it's meant to do, it is theoretically making a prediction that might guide clinical decision making. It might guide patient behavior. It might guide access to care. It might guide anything where these technologies are implemented in our industry.

Conclusion

The combination of blockchain, decentralized AI, and privacy-in-depth is the data holy grail that has been missing from the fragmented, firewalled, and siloed systems that are currently in place in healthcare. We can free up more data for research and evidence-based medicine, get more expert eyes on all aspects of health, and allow more access to data without sharing and copying that data endlessly. This will allow more medical discovery and improved health outcomes without the exposure of people's personal data and the risk of massive hacks and data breaches. When you layer these three areas of emerging technology together, you now have the complete technology stack that is both necessary and sufficient for the needs of the healthcare industry.

CHAPTER 17

Formal Blockchain Research and Education

This chapter is based on an interview between Vikram Dhillon and Tory Cenaj, in which Tory talks about her journey toward creating a formal educational space to study blockchain when most of the work was still being done informally and disseminated largely through developer blogs. *Blockchain in Healthcare Today* is a prominent peer-reviewed journal today in the blockchain space, with an editorial board that has a very broad spectrum of experiences.

VD: *What was your inspiration for starting the journal? What pushed you to think about the need for rigorous scientific process to evaluate blockchain technology?*

TC: My entire career has focused on or included evidence-based research output, publication planning, medical publishing, research consulting, medical education, and disseminating research data. I headed a portfolio of international multispecialty journals and society peer-reviewed publications. For me, publishing and communications always presented a creative outlet for new and breakthrough innovations. Communicating with a trusted evidence-based journal elevates both research and dissemination of the work and/or discovery.

I learned about the crypto sector from a friend. He was launching an asset that rewarded the use of solar energy, and I began mining it. As I learned more about the technology, I thought about potential applications in healthcare.

At the time, the financial marketplace was a swirling cesspool wrought with nefarious actors more concerned with swindling the public and making a quick buck versus creating a safe environment where regulation and a new world market could be created.

Since my background was healthcare and focused on publishing, it made perfect sense to me to launch a new peer-reviewed journal creating a market for blockchain technology in healthcare.

357

© Vikram Dhillon, David Metcalf, and Max Hooper 2021
V. Dhillon et al., *Blockchain Enabled Applications*, https://doi.org/10.1007/978-1-4842-6534-5_17

As founder and publisher, I opted to launch a traditional scholarly peer-reviewed journal, anticipating the unfamiliar territory of the editorial mission. The healthcare sector, at large, had to build familiarity and confidence with the technology and understand its vast applications. *Blockchain in Healthcare Today* peer-reviewed journal provided the broadest, most rapid adoption to scale proficiency and agility with the technology for leadership, early adopters, and, ultimately, all stakeholders to fill in blanks and learn more.

My thought was [that] conforming with traditional scholarly outlets at the outset would engender acceptance for both journal and use of the technology faster. Those that understood and engaged with research understood this. Those that were new to the market struggled with communicating and writing acceptable papers. There were some arrogant skeptics, of course, but the journal has proven its value to and for the market in that it validated the technology for healthcare, gave it credibility with a peer-reviewed journal, and today it both shapes and reflects market growth and innovation. We are read in over seventy countries and just launched licensed editions of the journal in the Gulf Cooperation Council (GCC) and Egypt. I'm quite happy with the growth trajectory. To learn more about the journal's inaugural edition, you can always read my publisher's letter at https://doi.org/10.30953/bhty.v1.25.

VD: *What sort of resources did it take to start the journal? I know you've been involved with crypto-communities in the past; talk to us about your past experience and how that helped you with starting the journal.*

TC: From the get-go, I stayed away from crypto, wouldn't publish anything related to it, and only addressed it at conferences since there was such hoopla around it. I have always maintained unless it has real monetary value, it may as well, and usually is, used as a behavior modification tool in our market.

Every once in a while I will ask a physician what they think of blockchain technology. The answers I receive are related to investment opportunities, so I know a deep disconnect still exists. That's why we've developed a new medical education program for doctors and pharmacists (CME) and are looking for sponsors now.

VD: *You have managed to put together such a diverse group of editors/reviewers. What sort of expertise were you looking for when you put together this board? How did you figure out the right group of people to bring on?*

TC: The caliber of our board is stellar, and it is because all these individuals are extremely passionate about changing healthcare and legacy systems. They are curious virtuosos and experts that push the envelope, have no fear, and are comfortable taking risks. The editors on our board had their name attached to a journal (BHTY) that was still relatively unknown and they all risked their reputations with the affiliation. I am very cognizant of this. *BHTY* aims to lead the market as the premier and preeminent journal in the sector.

I have always believed that everyone brings a different perspective to the table. I look for the best, from all corners of the world, to bring new facets to the journal and our audience as *BHTY* matures in the marketplace. It is a volunteer position, and their time is a reflection of the quality of the journal. It is a team effort, and we are all proud of our collective efforts.

VD: *What kinds of studies are you most excited to receive for publication in the journal and why? How has building the journal for the past [little] while changed your mind about the direction that blockchain technology is headed?*

TC: We typically summarize trends we see in the market in our annual "Blockchain Predictions" article, inviting board members and conference speakers to participate to share their predictions for the technology [in the] short and long term. It is a popular article that receives a lot of media attention.

I am excited to see blockchain technology being adopted across every industry and not just healthcare. We have seen an uptick in US government initiatives and have published papers reflecting these initiatives. What I want to see is broad adoption, popular understanding of the technology in that it is an underlying and connective mechanism and platform to use to link disparate parts in a new era of tech, but am still waiting for realization of the cost efficiencies for the US market. We see this abroad. In addition, there is a general assumption [that] blockchain is expensive and difficult to implement due to coding. This must also be overcome as it is not true.

VD: *What are the new avenues (or verticals) in terms of content that you are exploring as a journal and for publication? Being tied to a cutting-edge technology like the blockchain allows for some room to experiment [in the] editorial process—any blockchain-based editorial activities planned in near future?*

TC: I can share we are the first health science journal to timestamp articles on the blockchain and provide a blockchain-based ledger of record for research in collaboration with ARTiFACTS, where we provide authors a custom dashboard to share and amplify work and ensure provenance and reproducibility in [the] scientific community. We tell authors to use repositories for work and are also working on a global initiative for research communities. We have launched a University Council, Ambassador chapters around the world, and are always on the lookout for new and reputable partners and collaborators to work with. Drop us a note.

CHAPTER 18

Blockchain Simulation

The University of Central Florida's Institute for Simulation and Training has been awarded by the ARO (Army Research Office) a DURIP (Defense University Research Instrumentation Program) award to build a blockchain and quantum defense simulator. This unique program allows for state-of-the-art technology to be built not only to serve the U.S. military but also to provide for research and experimentation throughout academia, industry, non-profits, and other partnerships. As America's Partnership University,™ UCF is creating critical infrastructure that will enable broader access to cutting-edge technologies in a research environment along with mentorship necessary to use new tech for extending blockchain-platforms. With the age of quantum computing at our doorstep, the cryptographic methods used and the security of the entire process, including the people, processes, and technology, could be susceptible to bad actors.

Scope

The purpose of the blockchain and quantum defense simulator is not only to set up quantum gateways and a multi-testnet blockchain array, but also to design scenarios that include humans in the loop processes that can surface many potential risks and threats, the least of which is social engineering—the human hacking that is often the most effective attack vector. While we anticipate significant cyber-defense projects and programs, our first project is in response to the 2020 COVID pandemic. Dr. Dexter Hadley is retooling his NIH Breast Cancer imaging predictive artificial intelligence (AI) platform to instead look at a large population of COVID lung imaging. The use of powerful AI combined with blockchain for validation and verification of medical records and the privacy and security of the research protocol and records may show promise as a response to the current health crisis. Covidimaging.com provides additional details and the current state of results in this novel program. In his recent book, *Blockchain for*

© Vikram Dhillon, David Metcalf, and Max Hooper 2021
V. Dhillon et al., *Blockchain Enabled Applications*, https://doi.org/10.1007/978-1-4842-6534-5_18

Medical Research, Dr. Sean Manion cites the need for technology like the blockchain to improve research quality, verification, and repeatability using common data sets (Manion et al., 2020).

While the initial use case and operations for the blockchain and quantum defense simulator will only leverage the blockchain mining array of over two petahash of processing capability, future iterations and other projects plan to leverage the quantum security features of this program and its capabilities. Best of all, students are able to access this through UCF's affiliation with Blockchain Innovation Village for further education on intersection of new technologies in emerging disciplines such as blockchain and quantum. Students may also access the quantum learning lab with its series of quantum gateway computers for access to IBM's Q Network and other quantum simulators via classical computer simulation. Our team welcomes the opportunity to discuss the potential—beyond cryptomining—for a blockchain and quantum simulation to advance scientific discovery and help society with its most pressing issues.

As we continue our mission for education, we will continue to train the next generation of leaders and technologists in these emerging fields and provide broad and open access to people from many different backgrounds and levels of technical capability. Improving the understanding of our faculty and student population around complex but important principles may lead to exponential outcomes and rapid testing of new capabilities and discoveries. We're excited about what the future may hold and invite this community to continue the dialogue in these important areas.

APPENDIX A

References

This appendix includes detailed references used to prepare each chapter.

Chapter 1

1. Nakamoto, Satoshi. "Bitcoin: A peer-to-peer electronic cash system." (2008): 28.

2. Nakamoto, Satoshi. "Re: Bitcoin P2P e-cash paper." The Cryptography Mailing List (2008).

3. Velde, François. "Bitcoin: A primer." Chicago Fed Letter Dec (2013).

Chapter 2

1. Böhme, Rainer, Nicolas Christin, Benjamin Edelman, and Tyler Moore. "Bitcoin: Economics, technology, and governance." *The Journal of Economic Perspectives* 29, no. 2 (2015): 213–238.

2. Bulkin, Aleksandr. "Explaining blockchain — how proof of work enables trustless consensus." *Keeping Stock*. May 3, 2016. `https://keepingstock.net/explaining-blockchain-how-proof-of-work-enables-trustless-consensus-2abed27f0845`.

3. Kroll, Joshua A., Ian C. Davey, and Edward W. Felten. "The economics of Bitcoin mining, or Bitcoin in the presence of adversaries." In Proceedings of WEIS, vol. 2013. 2013.

4. Nielsen, Michael. "How the Bitcoin protocol actually works." Data-driven Intelligence. December 6, 2003. `http://www.michaelnielsen.org/ddi/howthe-bitcoin-protocol-actually-works/`.

5. O'Dwyer, Karl J., and David Malone. "Bitcoin mining and its energy footprint." (2014): 280–285.

© Vikram Dhillon, David Metcalf, and Max Hooper 2021
V. Dhillon et al., *Blockchain Enabled Applications*, https://doi.org/10.1007/978-1-4842-6534-5

Chapter 3

1. "Bitcoin Developer Reference." https://bitcoin.org/en/developer-guide.

2. Becker, Georg. "Merkle signature schemes, merkle trees and their cryptanalysis." Ruhr-University Bochum, Tech. Rep. (2008).

3. Franco, Pedro. *Understanding Bitcoin: Cryptography, engineering and economics.* John Wiley & Sons, 2014.

Chapter 4

1. Buterin, Vitalik. "Ethereum: A next-generation smart contract and decentralized application platform." *GitHub.* https://github.com/ethereum/wiki/wiki/%5BEnglish%5D-White-Paper (2014).

2. Delmolino, Kevin, Mitchell Arnett, Ahmed Kosba, Andrew Miller, and Elaine Shi. "A programmer's guide to ethereum and serpent." https://mc2-umd.github.io/ethereumlab/docs/serpent_tutorial.pdf (2015).

3. Ethereum Community. "Ethereum Homestead Documentation." *Readthedocs.* March 1, 2017. https://media.readthedocs.org/pdf/ethereum-homestead/latest/ethereum-homestead.pdf.

4. Wood, Gavin. "Ethereum: A secure decentralised generalised transaction ledger." Ethereum Project Yellow Paper 151 (2014).

Chapter 5

1. Atzori, Marcella. "Blockchain technology and decentralized governance: Is the state still necessary?" (2015).

2. Cuende, Luis, and Jorge Izquierdo. "Aragon Network: A Decentralized Infrastructure For Value Exchange." *GitHub.* April 20, 2017. https://github.com/aragon/whitepaper/blob/master/Aragon%20Whitepaper.pdf.

3. Merkle, R., 2015. *DAOs, Democracy and Governance.*

Chapter 7

1. Bonomi, Flavio, Rodolfo Milito, Jiang Zhu, and Sateesh Addepalli. "Fog computing and its role in the internet of things." In Proceedings of the first edition of the MCC workshop on Mobile cloud computing, pp. 13–16. ACM, 2012.

2. Bylica, Paweł, L. Glen, Piotr Janiuk, A. Skrzypcaz, and A. Zawlocki. "A Probabilistic Nanopayment Scheme for Golem." (2015).

3. Dannen, Chris. "Smart Contracts and Tokens." In *Introducing Ethereum and Solidity*, 89–110. Apress, 2017.

4. IEx.ec Team. "Blueprint for a Blockchain-based Fully Distributed Cloud Infrastructure." iEx.ec project. March 18, 2017. `https://iex.ec/app/uploads/2017/04/iExec-WPv2.0-English.pdf`.

5. Merriam, Piper. "Ethereum Computation Market 0.1.0 documentation." 2016. `http://docs.ethereum-computation-market.com/en/latest/`.

6. SOMN Team. "Supercomputer organized by network mining." *SONM*. March 19, 2017. `https://sonm.io/SONM_TECHNICAL_WP.pdf`.

7. Teutsch, Jason, and Christian Reitwießner. "A scalable verification solution for blockchains." (2017).

Chapter 8

1. Aarts, A. A., J. E. Anderson, C. J. Anderson, P. R. Attridge, A. Attwood, and Anna Fedor. "Estimating the reproducibility of psychological science." *Science* 349, no. 6251 (2015): 1–8.

2. Baker, Monya. "1,500 scientists lift the lid on reproducibility." *Nature News* 533, no. 7604 (2016): 452.

3. Begley, C. Glenn, and John PA Ioannidis. "Reproducibility in science." *Circulation Research* 116, no. 1 (2015): 116–126.

4. Dreber, Anna, Thomas Pfeiffer, Johan Almenberg, Siri Isaksson, Brad Wilson, Yiling Chen, Brian A. Nosek, and Magnus Johannesson. "Using prediction markets to estimate the reproducibility of scientific research." *Proceedings of the National Academy of Sciences* 112, no. 50 (2015): 15343–15347.

5. Etz, Alexander, and Joachim Vandekerckhove. "A Bayesian perspective on the reproducibility project: Psychology." *PLoS One* 11, no. 2 (2016): e0149794.

6. Gezelter, J. Daniel. "Open source and open data should be standard practices." (2015): 1168–1169.

7. Open Science Collaboration. "Estimating the reproducibility of psychological science." *Science* 349, no. 6251 (2015): aac4716.

8. Pashler, Harold, and Eric-Jan Wagenmakers. "Editors' introduction to the special section on replicability in psychological science: A crisis of confidence?" *Perspectives on Psychological Science* 7, no. 6 (2012): 528–530.

9. Scannell, Jack W., and Jim Bosley. "When quality beats quantity: decision theory, drug discovery, and the reproducibility crisis." *PloS one* 11, no. 2 (2016): e0147215.

Chapter 9

1. Dubovitskaya, Alevtina, Zhigang Xu, Samuel Ryu, Michael Schumacher, and Fusheng Wang. "How Blockchain Could Empower eHealth: An Application for Radiation Oncology." In *VLDB Workshop on Data Management and Analytics for Medicine and Healthcare*, 3–6. Springer, Cham, 2017.

2. Emily Vaughn. "A Universal Library for Health Care: Health Data Meets Blockchain Technology." *Gem HQ* blog. June 20, 2016. https://blog.gem.co/blockchain-health-data-library-e53f930dbe93.

3. Ekblaw, Ariel, Asaph Azaria, John D. Halamka, and Andrew Lippman. "A Case Study for Blockchain in Healthcare: 'MedRec' prototype for electronic health records and medical research data." In Proceedings of IEEE Open & Big Data Conference. 2016.

4. Mettler, Matthias. "Blockchain technology in healthcare: The revolution starts here." In e-Health Networking, Applications and Services (Healthcom), 2016 IEEE 18th International Conference on, pp. 1–3. IEEE, 2016.

5. Kuo, T. T., C. N. Hsu, and L. Ohno-Machado. "ModelChain: Decentralized Privacy-Preserving Healthcare Predictive Modeling Framework on Private Blockchain Networks." In *ONC/NIST Blockchain in Healthcare and Research Workshop*, 26–27. 2016.

6. Yue, Xiao, Huiju Wang, Dawei Jin, Mingqiang Li, and Wei Jiang. "Healthcare data gateways: found healthcare intelligence on blockchain with novel privacy risk control." *Journal of Medical Systems* 40, no. 10 (2016): 218.

Chapter 10

1. Cachin, Christian. "Architecture of the Hyperledger blockchain fabric." In *Workshop on Distributed Cryptocurrencies and Consensus Ledgers*. 2016.

2. Chen, Lin, Lei Xu, Nolan Shah, Zhimin Gao, Yang Lu, and Weidong Shi. "On Security Analysis of Proof-of-Elapsed-Time (PoET)." In *International Symposium on Stabilization, Safety, and Security of Distributed Systems*, 282–297. Springer, Cham, 2017.

3. Manuel Garcia. "Introduction to Blockchain and the Hyperledger Project." *SlideShare*. May 6, 2016. https://www.slideshare.net/ManuelGarcia122/introduction-to-blockchain-and-the-hyperledger-project.

4. Morgen Peck. "Do You Need a Blockchain?" *IEEE Spectrum*. September 29, 207. https://spectrum.ieee.org/computing/networks/do-you-need-ablockchain.

5. Prisco, Giulio. "Intel develops 'Sawtooth Lake' distributed ledger technology for the Hyperledger project." *Bitcoin Magazine* (2016).

6.   Sankar, Lakshmi Siva, M. Sindhu, and M. Sethumadhavan.
     "Survey of consensus protocols on blockchain applications." In
     Advanced Computing and Communication Systems (ICACCS),
     2017 4th International Conference on, pp. 1–5. IEEE, 2017.

7.   Sebastien Meunier. "When do you need blockchain? Decision
     models." *Medium*. August 4, 2016. `https://medium.com/@`
     `sbmeunier/when-do-you-needblockchain-decision-models-`
     `a5c40e7c9ba1`.

8.   Tracy Kuhrt. "Oscon 2017: Contributing to Hyperledger."
     SlideShare. May 12, 2017. `https://www.slideshare.net/tkuhrt/`
     `oscon-2017-contributing-tohyperledger`.

9.   Underwood, Sarah. "Blockchain beyond bitcoin."
     Communications of the ACM 59, no. 11 (2016): 15–17.

10. Vukoli'c, Marko. "Rethinking Permissioned Blockchains." In
     *Proceedings of the ACM Workshop on Blockchain, Cryptocurrencies
     and Contracts*, 3–7. ACM, 2017.

11. Wüst, Karl, and Arthur Gervais. "Do you need a Blockchain?."
     IACR Cryptology ePrint Archive 2017 (2017): 375.

Chapter 11

1.   Bob Summerwill, and Shahan Khatchadourian. "Enterprise
     Ethereum Alliance Technical Roadmap." *Ethereum Enterprise
     Alliance*. February 28, 2017. `https://bobsummerwill.files.`
     `wordpress.com/2017/02/enterprise-ethereumtechnical-`
     `roadmap-slides-final.pdf`.

2.   Chain Team. "Chain Protocol Whitepaper." Chain Developer
     Documentation. 2017. `https://chain.com/docs/1.2/protocol/`
     `papers/whitepaper`.

3.   Chain Team. "The Ivy Language." Chain Developer
     Documentation. 2017. `https://chain.com/docs/1.2/ivy-`
     `playground/docs`.

4. Daniel Larimer. "EOS.IO Technical White Paper." *GitHub*. June 26, 2017. `https://github.com/EOSIO/Documentation/blob/master/TechnicalWhitePaper.md`.

5. David Voell. "Quorum Architecture." *GitHub*. October 16, 2017. `https://github.com/jpmorganchase/quorum-docs/blob/master/Quorum_Architecture_20171016.pdf`.

6. David Voell. "Quorum Whitepaper." *GitHub*. November 22, 2016. `https://github.com/jpmorganchase/quorum-docs/blob/master/Quorum%20Whitepaper%20v0.1.pdf`.

7. David Voell. "Quorum Blockchain: Presentation to Hyperledger Project." *GitHub*. November 21, 2016. `https://github.com/jpmorganchase/quorum-docs/blob/master/Blockchain_QuorumHyperledger_20160922.pdf`.

8. Ian Grigg. "EOS—An Introduction." *EOS*. July 5, 2017. `https://eos.io/documents/EOS_An_Introduction.pdf`.

Index

A

Access Control List (ACL), 75, 78
American International Group (AIG), 3
Application Binary Interface (ABI), 51
Application-Specific Integrated Circuits
    (ASICs), 15
Aragon, 74
  Agent, 106
  components, 77, 78
  functional unit, 75
  fundraising app
    core idea, 78
    council, 79
    council members, 79
    DAI, 79
    DAO members, 79
    fundraising, 78
    options, 78
    pre-sale, 79
    token holders, 79
    tokens, 79
  identity management use case
    components, 81, 82
    concept, 80
    features, 80
    Keybase, 81
    registry contract, 81
    two-way bridge, 81
    two-way verification scheme, 80
  kernel, 75
  Keybase, 80
  organs, 76
Aragon Network Jurors (ANJ), 78
Aragon Network Token (ANT), 74, 79
Artificial intelligence (AI), 128

B

before balances[], 122
Beacon chain, 62
  block proposers, 63, 64
  committees, 64
  function, 63
  managing validators, 63
  rewards/penalties, 64
Birch-Brown-Parulava model, 233, 234
Bitcoin blockchain, 249
Bitcoin protocol, 38, 40
Blockchain, 6, 346, 347
  clinical trials
    components, 185
    use cases, 183, 184
  decision models, 232
    database, 233
    disintermediation, 234
    no trust, 233
    transactional
      interdependence, 234
    writers, 233
  definition, 21
  emerging landscape, 177

371

Printed in the United States
by Baker & Taylor Publisher Services

Printed in the United States
By Bookmasters